ENCYCLOPEDIA OF

Urban Legends

ENCYCLOPEDIA OF

Urban Legends

Jan Harold Brunvand

Artwork by Randy Hickman

W. W. Norton & Company

New York   London

Copyright 2001 by Jan Harold Brunvand
First published as a Norton paperback 2002

Library of Congress Cataloging-in-Publication Data

Brunvand, Jan Harold.
  Encyclopedia of urban legends / Jan Harold Brunvand ; artwork by Randy Hickman.
      p. cm.
Includes bibliographical references and index.
  ISBN 1-57607-076-X (hard : alk. paper) — ISBN 1-57607-532-X (e-book)
  1. Urban folklore—United States—Encyclopedias.   2. Legends—United States—Encyclopedias.   I. Title.
  GR105.34 .B78 2001
  398.2'0973'091732—dc21

                                2001000883

ISBN 0-393-32358-7 pbk.

W. W. Norton & Company, Inc., 500 Fifth Avenue, New York, N.Y. 10110
www.wwnorton.com

W. W. Norton & Company Ltd., Castle House, 75/76 Wells Street, London W1T 3QT

1 2 3 4 5 6 7 8 9 0

CONTENTS

PREFACE

The *Encyclopedia of Urban Legends* is a comprehensive general reference work covering the oral narrative genre that is widely known to the general public as urban legends and often referred to by folklorists also as contemporary legends or modern legends (or modern urban legends). Whatever the terminology, these stories abound in contemporary culture, both in "folk" (oral-traditional) and in "popular" (commercial media-disseminated) versions. In fact, the Internet has become a major conduit for the spread of once-strictly-oral urban legends, as well as a useful source of information about them. Urban legends have interested journalists and academic folklorists for decades, and many of these stories eventually found their way into literature, film, television, and even popular music, often with creative artistic variations and sometimes involving gross misunderstanding of their status as "folklore." One might say that, like the legends themselves, the *term* "urban legend," has acquired a life of its own, separate from the original restricted usage coined by folklorists.

This *Encyclopedia* is designed to provide an introduction to the scholarly side of urban legend studies as well as to the popularization and commercialization of this modern folkloric genre.

The heart of this book, so to speak, consists of hundreds of entries devoted to individual legends cited by their conventional titles like "The Boyfriend's Death," "The Hook," "The Mouse in the Coke," and "The Runaway Grandmother." When variant titles exist, one of them was chosen as the standard (i.e., "The Hairy-Armed Hitchhiker" or "The Hare Dryer") and a cross reference was inserted for an alternate title (i.e., "The Hatchet in the Handbag" and "The Resurrected Rabbit"). Generally the legend plots are summarized, but a generous sampling of actual texts both from published sources and oral tradition is included. (A bonus is four examples of urban legends quoted in their original foreign-language versions under the entries for France, Germany, Holland, and Spain.) In all these entries for individual-legends the reader must be sure to turn to the general references cited to learn the titles of specific sources that discuss the variations, scholarly analysis, and media exploitation (if any) of that particular legend. It is also important to bear in mind that since variation is the hallmark of folklore, any individual urban legend as it is transmitted (whether orally or in print) may differ somewhat from the recognized "type."

Besides titles of specific legends, there are entries for typical legend topics like Atrocities, Babies, Companies, Contamination, Fast Food, Homosexuality, Hunting, Malls, Nudity, Revenge, Supernaturalism, Telephones, Theft, and Violence. Further, there are entries for the main subject categories into which urban legends are often sorted: Automobiles, Animals, Accidents, Horrors, Sex, Crime, Celebrities, Academe, and the like. Some common legend themes (e.g., Embarrassment, Human Nature, Jumping to Conclusions, Poetic Justice, Racism, Slapstick Comedy, Social Class, Technical Incompetence and Xenophobia) are also included.

Steps in studying urban legends are covered in such entries as those for Analysis and Interpretation, Classifying, Collecting, Context, Definition, Performance, and Style while some general folkloristic background topics are included in the entries for Child Ballads, Communal Recreation, Folklore, Folktale, Motif, Tale Type, and Variants and Versions. Theoretical terms applying particularly to urban legends include FOAF, The Goliath Effect, The Gremlin Effect, Legend-Tripping, Proto-legend, and Ostension. Entries focused on approaches to interpreting urban legends include Comparative, Fortean, Freudian, Historical, Linguistic, Memetic, Sociological, and Symbolic. The relationships of urban legends to popular culture are discussed in such entries as those for Comics, Film, Literature, Music, Radio, Tabloids, Talk Shows, and Television. There are even entries here for Parodies of Urban Legends and for True Urban Legends.

A few topics marginal to urban legends per se are included since they often overlap with legends. These include such written or printed examples as "The Communist Rules for Revolution," "The Daughter's Letter from College," "The Good Old Days," "Grandma's Washday," and "The Wordy Government Memo." See also entries concerning genres related to legends like Hoaxes, Jokes, Myth, Pranks, and Rumors.

Although most urban legends seem to be truly international in their distribution, in general only urban legends known to be told in the United States are covered comprehensively here. However, a few specific foreign legends that are discussed in English-language publications are also included; some examples of these are "The Day Trip" (British); "The Contaminated Comforter" (Dutch), "Miracle at Lourdes" (Irish), and Viper Release Stories (French and Italian). Although urban legends are surely found in virtually every modern nation, foreign countries only have individual entries if published examples are available for citation. (See the heading International Urban Legends for a complete list.)

Sources cited in the reference lists of individual entries are abbreviated (author, short title, pages) only if the full citation appears in the Selected Bibliography. The Bibliography is, indeed, "Selected," since there exist nowadays many thousands of published sources concerning urban legends, ranging from scholarly tomes and academic articles to popular books, newspaper and magazine articles, and Internet websites. While popular undocumented anthologies of urban legends using paraphrased or summarized texts are included in the bibliography, no individual legends from these works are cited in the entry references.

It is the nature of folklore—especially modern or contemporary folklore—that anything published about the subject, whether in printed, broadcast, or electronic form, will soon become outdated. Tradition marches on. Thus, while every effort was made to make this encyclopedia as up-to-date as possible at the beginning of the new millennium (that is 2001, not 2000), beyond that, it is the reader's task to keep abreast of developments in the field. Welcome to the (wonderful) world of urban legends!

Jan Harold Brunvand

INTRODUCTION

Any folklorist who saw the 1998 Columbia Pictures film *Urban Legend* will probably remember the library scene for its depiction of one aspect of folklore research. In this scene the beautiful student Natalie (played by Alicia Witt) suspects that recent campus mayhem was inspired by urban legends, the same kind of stories she is studying in a folklore class at New England's "Pendleton College." As one reviewer put it, the plot of *Urban Legend* includes "the requisite killer in gender-concealing costume (a hooded parka rather than a Halloween mask covering the face here), who is methodically wiping out far-too-pretty college-age actors in reverse order of billing. Sensing a folkloric pattern in the crimes, Natalie goes to the college library to consult the ultimate reference work on the subject, a hefty tome titled *Encyclopedia of Urban Legends*. There she finds the proof she is seeking—an illustrated description of the method used in the latest killing.

No such reference work existed at that time, of course, but the very one you are now reading had already been in preparation for about a year. This *Encyclopedia of Urban Legends* is the real-life counterpart to the made-up Hollywood volume.

The folklore class in *Urban Legend,* as taught by "Professor Wexler" is of interest to folklorists since it shows us Hollywood's idea of what a college class in the subject might be like. Unfortunately, it's a poor example, since Professor Wexler's approach is merely to tell a lot of scary stories, show some slides, and encourage students to try "urban legend experiments," like drinking a can of soda after eating Pop Rocks candies to test whether the combination will explode in the stomach. All of the best-looking students—the stars of the film, that is—sit in the front row and respond to all of the teacher's questions; there is no evidence that anyone in the class ever takes a test or writes a term paper. However, there was one press release issued for the film in the form of a fake term paper, complete with authentic references.

Although publicity hype described *Urban Legend* as "destined to be the hottest of hip horror movies" and claimed that its "chills, thrills and a huge hook [have] universal appeal . . . that sets it apart from the other horror movies out there," most film critics trashed the film, as being, for example, "a schlocky rip-off of *Scream* with more blood and fewer brains." Another reviewer pointed out that *Urban Legend* was "actually a clone of last year's depressingly popular *I Know What You Did Last Summer,* from the same producer" (Neal H. Moritz). In what one reviewer termed "a nod to previous horror films," the part of Professor Wexler was played by Robert Englund who portrayed Freddy Krueger in *Nightmare on Elm Street.* Talk about your tough profs!

Still, *Urban Legend,* though merely a typical campus-slasher film loaded with Hollywood cliches, is noteworthy in the context of introducing the present reference work. This is true not because the film breaks any new cinematic ground (except for adding actual murders to legends that only contain threats of violence), but because it illustrates how modern folklore scholarship sometimes overlaps with popular culture. The film had pretensions of research underlying it, so we should take some account here of *Urban Legend* as well as the other popular-culture treatments of urban legends that now proliferate. After all, this encyclopedia is intended both for folklorists and for urban legend buffs.

No folklorists were directly responsible for the film's treatment of academic folklore study, but in a press release the script writers revealed that "We even went through all the books on urban legends." Another hint in PR materials of the producers' awareness of academic folklore came in their mention of a course taught at the University of California at Los Angeles by Peter Tokovsky and a bibliography of writings by folklorists Norine Dresser, Patricia Turner, and—yes—also the author of this *Encyclopedia.* How the filmmakers located their sources and used the background material they gathered was strictly their own decision.

Back to the character Natalie, whom curiosity nearly killed: she seems to be the only student in Professor Wexler's folklore class to recognize the urban legend clues, or even to know her way to the library. Natalie's research consists of edging her way through the spooky nearly deserted college library, while a menacing janitor lurks in the background; she finds the GR section of the Dewey-Decimal classified books, and consults that fictional *Encyclopedia*. You know when she's located the correct part of the library stacks, because right next to the urban legend encyclopedia on the shelf is a copy of my own 1986 book *The Mexican Pet*. (You can also spot a copy of my 1981 *The Vanishing Hitchhiker* among the books that Professor Wexler brings to class.)

It is a good indication of the awareness that the general public had of urban legends by 1998 that just a few clues and details were all it took to establish the folkloric genre that the film would exploit in such gory detail. In *Urban Legend*'s last violent scene Natalie is tied down and being threatened by a scalpel wielded by her fellow student Brenda; then all the assailant needs to say is that she is enacting her "favorite urban legend, 'The Kidney Heist'." Viewers of the film surely had heard that well-known urban legend of the early 1990s, or had read it in an e-mail. In common with many urban legends lately, "The Kidney Heist" had quickly moved from "folk" culture and word-of-mouth circulation to popular culture and the Internet.

Urban legends, once almost solely the folklorists' concern, had reached the public consciousness at least a decade before the filming of *Urban Legend*. In 1981, in a lecture delivered to the Folklore Society in London, the pioneer contemporary-legend scholar Stewart F. Sanderson had declared: "The modern legend constitutes one of the most, may indeed even constitute *the* most widespread, popular, and vital folklore form of the present day, and what strikes me as perhaps its most outstanding feature is the creativity, imagination, and virtuosity brought to its performance by all kinds of people . . ."[1]

I agreed with Sanderson's assessment, and in 1989 I quoted that passage as the epigraph to *Curses! Broiled Again!*, my fourth book about urban legends. But by 2001, some twenty years after Sanderson's lecture and eleven years after my book, the urban legend had much less vitality as an oral-narrative genre. Instead, urban legends had started to vanish (like the ghostly hitchhiker) from the realm of oral tradition and had mostly migrated from *folk*lore into *popular* culture where they became stereotyped, standardized, exploited, commodified, and repackaged in a number of ways. The most common medium for the circulation of urban legends now is the Internet, and thus their "performance" tends to be shaped more by this remote electronic medium than by the face-to-face processes of word-of-mouth transmission.

An article widely circulated in the press in 2000 put it well: "Urban legends can travel by word of mouth or print, but the Internet has become the prime vehicle for their dissemination."[2]

One headline for this article was "Hoax-busting Web site created by CDC"; another was "Health hoaxes, rampant on the Internet, have people scared to death"; yet another read, "Urban legends have created bizarre scares, lately through e-mail." All of the emphasis was on electronic, not oral, transmission of urban legends.

Reviewing in my latest book how recent needle-attack bogus warnings were spreading and being debunked, I concluded, "Maybe this is the true future of urban legends: rapid Internet circulation of doubtful stories, followed by rapid Internet denials."[3] I was partly joking, or maybe not.

I must explain at this point that what I mean by urban legends are all those bizarre, whimsical, 99 percent apocryphal, yet believable stories that are "too good to be true." They are too odd, too coincidental, and too neatly plotted to be accepted as literal truth in every place where they are told. Such stories deal with familiar everyday matters like travel, shopping, pets, babysitting, crime, accidents, sex, business, government and so forth. Although the stories are phrased as if factual and are often attached to a particular locality, urban legends are actually migratory, and, like all folklore, they exist in variant versions. Typically, urban legends are attributed to a friend-of-a-friend, and often their narrative structure sets up some kind of puzzling situation that is resolved by a sudden plot twist, at which point the story ends abruptly. I emphasize *story* throughout this informal definition; I am not including plotless rumors, gossip, bits of misinformation, etc., which share some of these features, as being technically the same as urban legends.

Put simply, urban legends are the modern narratives that folklorists have collected and studied under well-known titles like "The Runaway Grandmother," "Alligators in the Sewers," "The Killer in the Backseat," "The Microwaved Poodle," and "AIDS Mary."

Except that folklorists *don't* collect them as much any more from oral tradition. In what might be called the glory days of urban legends as a prime contemporary folklore genre—roughly the 1960s through the 1980s—everyone was telling them. As Sanderson observed in 1981 (continuing his previous quotation), they were told by "old and young, well read and barely literate, educationally privileged and educationally deprived."

The legend-related articles in folklore journals of that time were replete with texts, or at least summaries of collected texts; no sooner did folklorists pin down "The Dead Cat in the Package," "The Solid-Cement Cadillac," or "The Choking Doberman," than along came a new story sweeping the country, or indeed the world, like "The Elevator Incident," (starting about 1981), "The Mexican Pet" (1983) "Death on the Tanning Bed" [i.e., "Curses! Broiled Again!] (1987), or "The Resurrected Rabbit" (1988). The latest new urban legends that I noted that were really being *told* much were "The Kidney Heist" (starting about 1991) and "The Brain Drain" (or "Biscuit Bullet" story, in 1995); within a few months, both stories were circulating mainly on the Internet or being alluded to in popular culture as obvious fictions.

When American folklorists first started collecting and studying "urban belief tales" in the 1940s and 1950s the tradition was perceived as being mostly oral in its dissemination. Many of the first collectors were college professors and their students who noted the legends circulating on campus. Important early work in the area was done by folklorists Ernest Baughman, Richard K. Beardsley, B. A. Botkin, Richard M. Dorson, Rosalie Hankey, William Hugh Jansen, and J. Russell Reaver. Popular writers like Bennet Cerf and Alexander Woollcott, plus several newspaper columnists of the time, also played an early part in recording and publicizing the genre. (For references to typical early studies, see such entries as "The Corpse in the Car," "The Fatal Initiation," "The Phantom Coachman," "The Poison Dress," and "The Vanishing Hitchhiker.") Woollcott had the prescience to dub "The Vanishing Lady" story, which he had attempted to trace back through a succession of journalists, as "a fair specimen of folklore in the making." Eventually folklorists followed the leads of Botkin, Dorson, and others in recognizing that a good many of the oral traditional urban legends had a lively circulation in print as well as by word-of-mouth.

Jerome Beatty, who wrote "Trade Winds" in the *Saturday Review* for many years, published in his July 4, 1964 column a version of "The Nude Housewife" urban legend without realizing that it was a widespread story. He confessed his error and described how he became enlightened as to the nature of folklore in an article titled "Funny Stories" in the November 1970 issue of *Esquire:*

> . . . someone I know in Homewood, Illinois, told me about something that had happened to her friend, a housewife. The girl had gone into the basement to do some laundry, and while the wash was going, she threw in the clothes she was wearing. While waiting, she decided to brush a cobweb off the cellar window, and picked up a broom for that purpose. Then to protect her hair, she put on a football helmet that was nearby. Just then there was a knock and a call, "meter man!" She grabbed a raccoon coat that was stored there and quickly put it on. The meter man came down the stairs without waiting for an answer, shined his flashlight at the meter, and wrote

down the reading, all without saying a word. As he left, he glanced at the housewife, trying to hide in a corner and said,

"Hope your team wins, lady."

When I repeated this tale on one occasion, authenticating it by saying it had happened to "the friend of a friend of mine in Illinois," I was told that it had been in a national magazine. I couldn't believe it, but my informant eventually sent me a clipping dated March, 1961, locating the event in East Hampton, Connecticut. When I had a chance, I queried the Homewood, Illinois, source who said that the girl was a good friend and she had *said* it had happened to her, and no one was going to call her a liar. The question with this incident, as it is with the others, is: Did it ever happen at all? But this is a question that few people ask.[4]

In a letter to me dated October 26, 1983, Beatty added the information that the clipping came from *Reader's Digest* (see the "Nude Housewife" entry for the actual text), and he also admitted, "I was glad to see Ann Landers fall for it years later."

My own epiphany concerning the nature of urban legends came in May 1959 when, as a graduate student at Indiana University working under Professor Dorson, I was helping to proofread and index his book *American Folklore* to be published later that year. In the last chapter, "Modern Folklore," Dorson discussed "a ubiquitous department store legend 'The Dead Cat in the Package,'" among other examples. The very week when we worked on his book a version of that same story appeared in the local newspaper, the Bloomington, Indiana, *Daily Herald-Telephone,* credited as the true experience of a friend of the journalist in Indianapolis. I clipped the story, and it became the first item in what eventually grew to be my large archive of urban legend texts from myriad sources.

Indiana University became the center of urban legend collecting and studies in the late 1960s through the efforts of Professor Linda Dégh and her students who began publishing their findings in the journal *Indiana Folklore* in 1968. Interest in urban legends spread among other American and international folklorists in the following decades, a history best learned by reading the entries for individual legends and countries. Landmark events in urban legend research would surely include William Hugh Jansen's study of "The Surpriser Surprised" published in 1973, my own *The Vanishing Hitchhiker* of 1981, the first international conference on contemporary legends in 1982, the founding of the International Society for Contemporary Legend Research (ISCLR) in 1988, and the publication of Bennett and Smith's *Contemporary Legend: A Folklore Bibliography* (with 1,116 entries) in 1993. One hopes, as well, that the publication of this encyclopedia will constitute another landmark event.

As is evident from titles of some works already mentioned, not all folklorists use the term "urban legends" for the genre. Indeed, the ISCLR consistently puts the phrase in parentheses in its mission statements and conference announcements; the inside cover of *Contemporary Legend* (the journal) refers to "so-called 'modern urban legends'." A recent attack on the term was published by the English folklorist Jacqueline Simpson in that very journal; she stated flatly, "As a term of definition for the genre as a whole . . . *urban* is not a good choice."[5] More pragmatically, in his entry "Legend, Urban" for *Folklore: An Encyclopedia*, American folklorist Bill Ellis defined the phrase simply as "A popular term for a narrative concerning some aspect of modern life that is believed by its teller but is actually untrue"[6] The term that many folklorists prefer—*contemporary legend*—has its problems as well, but (as pointed out by folklorist Sandy Hobbs) it does have one claim to legitimacy in that F. Scott Fitzgerald used it more-or-less in the same way as modern folklorists do in his 1925 masterpiece *The Great Gatsby*.

> Gatsby's notoriety, spread about by the hundreds who had accepted his hospitality and so became authorities on his past, had increased all summer until he fell just short of being news. Contemporary legends, such as the "underground pipe-line to Canada" attached themselves to him and there was one persistent story that he didn't live in a house at all, but in a boat that looked like a house and was moved secretly up and down the Long Island shore.[7]

Contemporary legend (both the term and the concept) has an even longer history in France. Jean-Bruno Renard pointed out that the French magazine *Mélusine* (1877–1900) had a regular column titled *Légendes contemporaines* while *Revue des Traditions Populaires* had an article in 1886 asking the question "Don't cities have a folklore like that in the country?" Among the examples of contemporary legends discussed in these French journals were recent political stories, a variant of "The Devil in the Dancehall," and stories about child mutilation. Renard concluded his survey by asserting that "it is still useful for today's scholar to examine old folklore journals, since many analogs to contemporary legends can be found within them."[8]

Modern folk (but *non*folklorists) who have popularized and exploited urban legends include writers of children's books, compilers of popular anthologies of amusing stories for adult readers, professional storytellers, advertising and television writers, and (as already shown) filmmakers.

In recent years, members of the media have also enthusiastically embraced the general idea of urban legends, applying the term—or several variants like urban *myth,* urban *folktale, hoax,* etc.—to all kinds of phenomena. Hundreds of examples from previous years might be cited, but here are some from just late 2000 alone of the public's urban-legend awareness: An article (19 September) about Rick Lazio, New York State Republican Senate candidate, described an anecdote about school discipline problems that he included in his standard stump speech as being "the equivalent of an urban legend." A piece (28 September) on the Sydney Summer Olympic games opened "It has become an urban legend at these Games . . . [that] security guards are supposedly confiscating bottles of Pepsi-Cola from visitors at the gates of the Olympic Park." A news item (23 November) about whether penguins "topple over like dominos as they stare up at aircraft" quoted a scientist saying "I'm afraid it's an urban myth." A page from the Holiday 2000 L. L. Bean travel catalog recommended clothing styles to wear in Paris as being "Urbane Legends . . cool looks for the city of lights." An animated TV Christmas special, "Olive the Other Reindeer," described the story of Rudolph as being just "one of those urban legends." Clearly the folklorists' term *urban legend* has been widely accepted but drastically redefined in its media usage, coming to refer to such forms as doubtful anecdotes, rumors, misinformation, advertising hype, and jokes.

It is both thrilling and slightly discouraging for a folklorist to see the great contemporary scientist and writer Stephen Jay Gould adopt the term in one of his popular columns for *Natural History.* Gould eloquently opened his essay thus:

> An odd principle of human psychology, well known and exploited by the full panoply of prevaricators, from charming barkers like Barnum to evil demagogues like Goebbels, holds that even the silliest of lies can win credibility by constant repetition. In current American parlance, these proclamations of "truth" by xeroxing—if sufficiently benign to do little harm, yet embraced with all the force of a dictum running "from God's mouth to your ear"—fall into the fascinating domain of "urban legends." [9]

A folklorist might object that the tellers of urban legends are not usually deliberate liars, but rather are simply passing on what they assume is a bit of truth. However we may praise Gould for noting xeroxing as one common form of legend transmission, and I certainly agree that urban

legends are "fascinating." (Thank goodness, he didn't say "urban myths.")
A problem with Gould's essay, however, is that the example he has in
mind—the notion that "Scientists say that we use just 10 percent of our
brains"—has no narrative element and is thus more like a rumor than a
legend. Actually, it probably fits best under the rubric of simple "misinformation" (or "trivia," if it had happened to be true, which it isn't).

An instance of proper folkloristic use of the term *urban legend* in the
popular media is in *Overdrive: The Magazine for the American Trucker.*[10]
It should be noted that as sources the author lists yours truly along with a
comic book, one of several recent popular undocumented anthologies,
and three urban legend websites—a perfect mix of folk and popular
sources for the twenty-first-century understanding of urban legends.

Without detailing any further examples—whether good ones or bad—
I want to make it clear that the popularization and remaking of folklore
is nothing new; in fact, it's probably inevitable. It happened to European
fairy tales from the Grimm brothers down to Walt Disney. It happened
to folksongs, which most modern people know only from professional
performers and recordings. It happened to Halloween and several other
former "folk" holidays. It happened to traditional log construction, ranging from simple folk-built cabins to the huge multimillion-dollar designer log vacation homes that dot the landscape surrounding luxury ski
resorts like Utah's Deer Valley and Idaho's Sun Valley.

It's also true that the vanishing (or at least the decline) of oral-traditional urban legends does not mean that folklorists have nothing left to
study in the way of contemporary traditional narratives. There is a vast
amount of legend data in folklore collections and archives awaiting analysis and interpretation. The very processes and products of commercialization and the popularization of urban legends deserve folklorists' attention. The Internet circulation of rumors and legends has opened up
another new field of research. And with numerous warnings still flying
around—one way or another—about such things as needle and perfume
attacks, e-mail taxes, sabotaged ATMs and pay phone coin slots, road rage
incidents, danger at gas pumps from cell phone sparks, experiences with
camera-armed speedtraps, pranks with disposable cameras at weddings,
etc., etc., etc. Who knows what may come next in urban legend tradition?

NOTES

1. Stewart F. Sanderson, "The Modern Urban Legend." Katharine Briggs Lecture, No. 1. London: The Folklore Society, 1982. p. 14.
2. By Kirk Kicklighter, distributed by Cox News Service.

3. *The Truth Never Stands in the Way of a Good Story* . Champaign: University of Illinois Press, 2000. p. 208.

4. Pp. 48, 50.

5. "Are the Terms 'Modern' and 'Contemporary' Synonymous?," *Contemporary Legend,* New Series, 1 (1998), 134–148, quotation on p. 135.

6. Bill Ellis, "Legend, Urban" in Thomas A. Green, ed. *Folklore: An Encyclopedia of Beliefs, Customs, Tales, Music, and Art.* Santa Barbara, California: ABC-CLIO, 1997. p. 495.

7. "'Contemporary Legends,' 1924," *FOAFTale News,* No. 15 (September, 1989), p. 2.

8. "Old Contemporary Legends: 19th-Century French Folklore Studies Revisited," *FOAFTale News,* No. 32 (February, 1994), pp. 1–4.

9. "The Paradox of the Visibly Irrelevant," *Natural History* (December 1997/January 1998), pp. 12–18, 60–66.

10. Jill Dunn, "This Ain't No Lie! Truckers Become Heroes, Villains and Victims in Urban Legends," *Overdrive* (October, 2000), pp. 56–57.

Abductions

See "The Attempted Abduction"; Needle-Attack Legends; "The Phantom Clowns"

Academe, Legends of

College and university campuses, despite being centers of research, learning, and sophistication, are also fertile grounds for the growth of legends and other folklore. As Barre Toelken points out, students "can be seen as members of a distinct folk group, the members of which are separately literate but communally aliterate." That is, while campus folk are undeniably literate, much of their shared lore of campus life and traditions is transmitted not in print but by means of customary example and word of mouth. What is true of students in this regard is equally so of faculty and staff.

The legends of academe (ignoring here all the other folkloric forms found on campus) typically concern either eccentric faculty members ("The Acrobatic Professor," "The Trained Professor," etc.) or crises among students ("The Roommate's Death," "The Gay Roommate," etc.). Legends about examinations and term papers abound on campuses, including stories of "Resubmitted Term Papers," of a one-word exam question ("Why?"), of clever solutions to "The Barometer Problem," of a "Tricky Answer" to a question for which the student is unprepared, and especially of students' imaginative ways of beating the system using "The Second Blue Book." Two of the most popular examination legends describe a student's witty one-upping of an officious professor; these are "The Bird-Foot Exam" and "Do You Know Who I Am?"

Some campus legends influence behavior since they are accepted as official regulations, even though their circulation is merely traditional. These legends include the supposed "rule" that a student will receive straight-A grades if his or her roommate commits suicide, the conventional notion that students must wait in the classroom a specific number of minutes for a late professor (depending on his or her academic rank), and the widely held belief that sitting in the front row, maintaining eye contact with the professor, and smiling will guarantee a high grade.

The campus itself is the subject of legends in the stories about libraries supposedly sinking into the ground because the architect forgot to calculate the weight of books into the design, or the stories about supposed mix-ups that caused buildings to be erected on the wrong campus or facing in the wrong direction.

One of the rare urban legends to have been traced to its apparent source is the academic story of "The Unsolvable Math Problem." Legendary themes that have gone the other way—from being mere stories to becoming actual incidents—include the academic legends concerning student pranks (such as leaving an arm behind in a toll booth or stealing garden ornaments and sending them on "vacation").

Besides stories dealing directly with campus life, the larger themes of urban legends circulate freely among academics, especially now that computers with Internet access have become common on campus. In e-mail and on computer bulletin boards, websites, and in listserv exchanges, the latest stories are enthusiastically transmitted and discussed by students and professors alike. A surprising number of these "separately literate" folk seem to give some credence to wild tales that have no more support other than someone somewhere has set the story racing along the Information Superhighway.

See also "Roaming Gnomes"; Scotland

References: Simon J. Bronner, *Piled Higher and Deeper: The Folklore of Campus Life* (1990); Charles Greg Kelley, "Joseph E. Brown Hall: A Case Study of One University Legend," *Contemporary Legend* 2 (1992), 137–153; Kimberly J. Lau, "On the Rhetorical Use of Legend: U.C. Berkeley Campus Lore as a Strategy for Coded Protest," *Contemporary Legend,* New Series 1 (1998), 1-20; Barre Toelken, "The Folklore of Academe," in Brunvand, *Study of American Folklore* (1st–3rd eds., 1968, 1978, 1986).

"The Accidental Cannibals"

Just after World War II, in a food package sent by relatives in the United States, a family in Europe (often Eastern Europe) finds a jar of powder without a label or any note of explanation. Assuming it to be some kind of American instant drink, the family stirs spoonfuls of the powder into hot water and drinks it. In other versions the powder is used as a cooking spice or thought to be dried coconut, bread flour, or a cake mix. A letter arrives later, explaining that the jar contained the cremains of a relative who had immigrated to the States years ago, died during the war, and had wanted  to be buried in his or her native country. Sometimes the explanatory letter is in the same package, but it is written in English and nobody is available to translate it until after the cremains have been eaten.

A recent version of the legend describes the cremains of a relative shipped home from Australia to England and mixed there into the Christmas pudding. Half the pudding has been consumed by the time the letter of explanation arrives.

See also "The Corpse in the Cask"; Romania

References: *Baby Train,* 75–79; *Choking Doberman,* 114–115; *Too Good,* 198–199; *Vanishing Hitchhiker,* 117.

"The Accidental Stickup"

This legend is based on the familiar unwitting-theft theme in which an innocent person is mistaken for a thief and is robbed in retaliation by his or her supposed victim. The assumed "victim" in this case is a person who sets out shopping with just a single bill ($5, $10, $20, or $50). The shopper suddenly realizes that his or her money is gone, believes that a passer-by has stolen it, and fiercely demands—and receives—the money back. Returning home, the "victim" discovers that the money had been left behind. In England this story is known as "The Five-Pound Note." A related story, told both in the United States and abroad, describe the supposed theft of an entire billfold or of a pocket watch. Often the scene of this legend is a crowded bus or streetcar, or in some versions a car in which the "victim" has picked up a suspicious-looking hitchhiker.

See also "The Stolen Wallet"

References: Katherine M. Briggs and Ruth L. Tongue, eds., *Folktales of England* (Chicago: University of Chicago Press 1965), 101–102; *Choking Doberman,* 190–191.

Accidents

Accident legends represent a major category of urban legends that in cludes stories about perilous mishaps that are either gruesome or hilarious (sometimes both); almost always they are bizarre. Excluding the stories about automobile accidents discussed under that heading, there are about 30 well-known urban legends that focus specifically on interesting and dangerous things that supposedly happened by accident.

The gruesome-accident legends include stories about contact lenses "welded" to the cornea, butane lighters detonating in a shirt pocket, Pop Rocks candy exploding in the stomach, and fingers being slashed off when a power lawnmower is misused. Another lost-finger story describes an industrial accident in which a worker gestures to demonstrate how he lost a finger in a factory machine—thereby cutting off another finger in a repeat of the accident.

Hilarious-accident stories often describe equally gruesome situations—but with a laughable angle. For example, a husband is blown off an "exploding toilet," surely a painful experience. But the situation causes the rescuing paramedics to laugh so hard that they drop the stretcher he's being carried on. In another comical-accident story a woman has a painful skiing accident while her pants are pulled down (see "The Ski Accident" for details), which leads a ski instructor to have his own accident and eventually to confront the embarrassed woman with an account of his funny-but-painful experience.

The bizarre quality of most accident legends is well illustrated in the gruesome story of "The Scuba Diver in the Tree." The extremely unlikely means by which the victim ended up in such a situation are beyond belief, although many people retold the story as the gospel truth. Perhaps the most bizarre of all accident legends is "The Failed Suicide," in which multiple attempted methods of death cancel each other out in rapid succession and the would-be victim remains alive.

See also Automobiles; "The Barrel of Bricks"; Bogus Warnings; and "The Last Kiss"

"The Acrobatic Professor"

A professor promises his class that he will not give a surprise quiz in the course until "the day you see me come into the classroom through the transom." Then one day, after the class has arrived, their professor comes climbing through the transom with a gleeful grin on his face and a stack of quizzes clutched in one hand. It turns out that he had earlier worked as a circus acrobat. Variations on the story describe the quiz-toting professor entering through a second-story window or climbing out of a grand piano.

This story is told about a surprising number of American professors who are often named and given their correct academic specialties in these accounts, although none of these stories has yet been positively verified. Best known of the group was Guy Y. "Guy Wire" Williams (1881–1968), a chemistry professor at the University of Oklahoma (from 1906 until his death), who was described in one source as "a skilled gymnast and acrobat." However, even Williams's biographical sources do not specifically include the transom trick.

References: *Mexican Pet,* 192–195; *Too Good,* 436–437.

"AIDS Harry"

The title refers to the male equivalent of "AIDS Mary" (about a woman deliberately spreading AIDS to men, leaving behind a taunting message written on a wall or mirror). The victim of the male AIDS carrier is often a young woman vacationing in the Caribbean or another tropical site. In many versions she is a college student from the East or Midwest. She meets a handsome stranger and spends several days and nights with him. When taking her to the airport for her return home, the man gives her a package, instructing her to open it later. She opens it on the plane and finds a small coffin with a note inside reading, "Welcome to the world of AIDS."

The "Mary" versions of this legend spread internationally starting about 1986, but the "Harry" versions had mostly taken over by mid-1990. Details about the size, color, and fittings of the tiny coffin vary widely, and in some versions the coffin is replaced by a package of *coffee* or a coffee *maker*. Although this change is easily explained as a mere misunderstanding of the words, it achieves a certain logic in the plot when legend-tellers improvise the explanation that the woman thought her companion may have been trying to smuggle drugs into the United States, masking their smell with coffee. Alternatively, the man's explanation is sometimes said to be that she will need some coffee "for all the lonely nights you'll be facing."

References: *Baby Train*, 237; *Too Good*, 133–134.

"AIDS Mary"

A man traveling on business or attending a conference meets a beautiful woman in a bar or nightclub and accepts the invitation to spend the night with her. The next morning he awakens to find that the woman has gone; she left behind only a message written on the bathroom wall (or mirror) in lipstick reading, "Welcome to the [wonderful] world of AIDS." He reports this encounter to the police and learns that authorities have sought this woman for some time. She is an embittered AIDS victim who has vowed to give the disease to every man she can seduce.

This legend began sweeping the country in 1986 and was dubbed "AIDS Mary" (reminiscent of "Typhoid Mary") that year by Dan Sheridan writing in the *Chicago Sun-Times*. Simultaneously the story was rampant internationally, especially in Europe, where the sinister message sometimes read, "Welcome to the AIDS club." The barroom seduction of the victim is a motif also found in "The Kidney Heist," while the handwriting on the wall was earlier associated with "The Licked Hand"

and other horror legends; later this motif entered the "Kidney Heist" tradition. Prototypes of the modern legend in the nineteenth century described a vengeful woman spreading a venereal disease among her country's enemy forces. By 1990 the female form of the legend had largely been replaced by "AIDS Harry," a version in which a male AIDS carrier spreads the disease.

AIDS researchers are unanimous in asserting that this specific event never occurred, although certainly some people have tried to give the AIDS virus to others. In this country, so far, AIDS has spread mostly among homosexuals or via contaminated needles shared by drug addicts, although promiscuous heterosexual contacts do pose definite dangers as well. Certainly the legends of "AIDS Mary" and "AIDS Harry" warn against this latter possibility.

See also Poland

References: *Curses!*, 195–202; *Too Good*, 133–134

"The Air-Freighted Pet"

In this legend, airline baggage handlers are horrified to find a dead dog inside a pet-shipping container. They decide to take up a collection and send one worker out to buy a look-alike dog as a replacement. When the owner comes to claim the container she opens it for a look at her pet, and the new dog jumps out and licks her face. The woman faints, because she had been shipping her dead dog home for burial. Often the scene takes place at a foreign airport, with the owner returning from a trip to the United States during which her dog died.

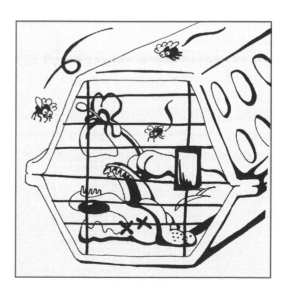

This legend circulated among airline employees in the 1950s and 1960s but reached a wider audience in the 1980s via publications and broadcasts, which then fed into oral tradition. Paul Harvey repeated a version from a Dallas listener on the air in 1987, and a report of speeches by Marine Lieutenant-Colonel Oliver North of the Iran-Contra scandal revealed that he told the story during a lecture tour in 1988. Earlier legends sharing at least one motif with this legend were "The Dead Cat in the Package" and one about a stolen dog corpse; "The Air-Freighted Pet" is itself the likely ancestor of "The Hare Dryer" (or "Resurrected Rabbit") legend that emerged strongly in 1988.

References: *Curses!,* 156–158; *Too Good,* 43–44.

"All That Glitters Is Not Gold"

A woman riding a Manhattan subway feels her gold neck chain being snapped loose just as the train slows down at a station. Reacting automatically, she reaches over and snaps off the chain that's around her attacker's neck, and he runs out the door and up the stairs. Later, a jeweler tells her that the chain she grabbed was pure gold. Her own chain was an inexpensive fake.

This story was heard by a New York City journalist in 1980 but could not be verified. It was included in a collection of urban legends because of its familiar unwitting-theft theme.

References: *Baby Train,* 125.

"Alligators in the Sewers"

Baby pet alligators are brought back from Florida (or sometimes purchased at Coney Island or at carnivals) by New York City children. When the gators grow too large for comfort, many are disposed of in the toilets by parents. Hundreds of tiny flushed amphibians have grown, mated, and reproduced in the sewer system, and eventually many of them turn white from the lack of sunshine. The existence of sewergators is officially denied by New York City authorities, but information about them occasionally leaks out.

Dismissed as "one of the sillier folktales of the late 1960s" in a book by herpetologists, this sewer legend continues to be mentioned in, among many other places, a serious novel of 1963 (Thomas Pynchon's *V*), a chil-

dren's book of 1974 (Peter Lippman's *The Great Escape*), a horror film of 1980 (*Alligator*), and a modern-art installation of 1993 (done by Anne Veraldi in a New York subway station as part of a city's Creative Stations program). Queries about sewergator rumors regularly arrive at the offices of the New Your City Bureau of Sewers and are routinely denied. Yet the Bureau sells T-shirts and sweatshirts alluding to the legend. Numerous cartoons, columns, and other popular-culture sources have alluded to "Alligators in the Sewers" as one of the best-known of all American urban legends, although, curiously, it is generally associated only with one city.

Robert Daley's 1959 book *The World Beneath the City* included an interview with a man claiming to have been sewer commissioner in the 1930s when a campaign was mounted to clean all the gators out of the sewer system, but spokespersons after the death of this informant revealed that he had never been commissioner and, in fact, had delighted in spinning outrageous yarns.

In 1935 a *New York Times* article described a full-grown alligator that had actually been dragged out of a city sewer. Names and specific places were identified, but there was no mention of flushed baby pets as a possible source. Although the origin of the American legend is still uncertain, it seems likely that there was some influence from a similar English legend of the nineteenth century as discussed in Thomas Boyle's 1989 book *Black Swine in the Sewers of Hampstead.*

References: Sherman A. Minton Jr. and Madge Rutherford Minton, *Giant Reptiles* (Scribner's: New York, 1973); *Vanishing Hitchhiker,* 90–98; *Too Good,* 182–185.

Amusement Park Dangers

Rumors and stories about crimes and serious accidents supposedly taking place at amusement parks have plagued these sites for decades, although their safety records are good and their crime rates are no higher than elsewhere. This folklore seems to suggest that behind the facade of innocent family fun and entertainment lurk hidden dangers that the press refuses to report. (In this respect, amusement park stories are similar to those concerning shopping mall crimes.) Commonly these legends name a specific nearby park and make the claim that someone—often a child—was injured or killed recently without any notice being released to the public.

Many such legends describe snakes, scorpions, spiders, or other venomous creatures lurking inside the rides and other attractions. There are accounts of water snakes in the Tunnel of Love and log-flume rides, rattlesnakes nesting in roller coasters or bumper-car rides, and other biting creatures infesting the merry-go-round horses. Usually, these intruders are said to have nested in the rides either during construction abroad (often India) or during winter storage; the creatures went undetected when the rides were set up in the spring.

In an updating of these stories, some "Playlands" of modern fast-food outlets are said to have poisonous serpents buried in the bins of plastic balls in which happy children jump and play. Nobody, of course, ever knows an actual child who was bitten, since the tragedy always occurs to a friend of a friend.

Another amusement park danger theme is that of electrocution when a person accidentally makes contact with a "hot" electrical wire in a fun house, a ride, or some other carnival attraction. One version of this theme claims that a boy was electrocuted when he sneaked out of a car and urinated on the electric rail of a ride.

A major fear of many parents is represented in legends about kidnappings that supposedly took place at amusement parks. Children are said to have been snatched from their parents—or else nabbed while they lag behind the rest of the group—and tossed over the fence of the park to a waiting accomplice. The kidnapper escaped, and the child was never found again, although sometimes it is said that he or she was recognized in a kiddie-porn film. No such actual crime has ever been documented, and these stories migrate from park to park and region to region.

See also "Snakes in Playland"; "Snakes in the Tunnel of Love"

References: *Curses!*, 37–39; *Too Good*, 348–349; *Vanishing Hitchhiker*, 182–184.

Analysis and Interpretation

In researching urban legends folklorists scrutinize the history, the variations, the distributions, and the structures of individual legends. Studies also focus on the motifs and themes common to several legends and legend-cycles, as well as on the styles and settings in which urban legends are communicated, whether by word of mouth or in written, printed, broadcast, or electronic media. Another avenue of research is evaluating the use of traditional urban-legend plots in literature as well as in films, television, cartoons, songs, advertising, and other pop-culture sources. Basic to all such studies is the fundamental question of definition: What *is* a legend, as opposed to, say, a rumor, proto-legend, joke, anecdote, or hoax? Also, what distinguishes an *urban* (or *contemporary* or *modern*) legend from the older traditional legends?

The basic requirements for good studies of urban legends are the same as for most other folklore research. Texts must be recorded accurately, and full documentation must be secured as to who has told the stories and to what audience, for what purpose, and with what response. Texts from published sources must be identified as to publication and date; when possible, it is useful to query the author of the work as to his or her sources for the legends.

Historical and comparative analysis of urban legends is facilitated by a classification of individual legends, such as the system included in *The Baby Train* (1993). Further published examples of urban legends and legend studies are referenced in collections such as *The Vanishing Hitchhiker* (1981) and in the bibliography *Contemporary Legend* (1993) compiled by Gillian Bennett and Paul Smith. Stith Thompson's *The Motif-Index of Folk Literature* (1955–1958) is an essential reference for tracing themes common in wider folk tradition, both internationally and in the past.

Although many people wonder about the origins of specific legends, few definitive answers are possible. Two legends (out of hundreds!) that were actually traced to their likely sources both enjoyed a considerable boost from the mass media and were followed back to their starting points largely via comparing these media sources. (See "The Heel in the Grate" and "The Unsolvable Math Problem.") Several other legends, including "The Choking Doberman" and "The Robber Who Was Hurt," clearly derive from older traditional legends. But for the vast majority of urban legends, the question of origin can best be explained by "communal re-creation"—the process by which each teller of a story re-creates the plot from a partly remembered set of details. The teller then unwittingly varies the story by adding, dropping, or changing certain details. Thus each storyteller helps to keep the dynamic story alive, whatever the ultimate origin of the plot may have been.

The meanings or messages of urban legends are often clear, concrete, and obvious; sometimes these meanings are even stated directly, as when a teller of "The Attempted Abduction" warns you never to let your child out of sight in a shopping mall or department store. Other urban legends advise more subtly, for example, that one should check the backseat of his or her car, distrust large corporations, and be suspicious of an anonymous gift (see, e.g., "The Killer in the Backseat," "The Procter & Gamble Trademark," and "The Double Theft"). It is safe to assume that every urban legend bears some kind of stated or implied message, whether or not it is directly intended by the individual teller.

While some people claim that most urban legends are told merely for entertainment—with the exception of stories with a clear stated moral—folklorists may point to elements of the stories that have powerful symbolic suggestions. "The Hook," for example, is a scary story sometimes told without any strong belief in the truth of the plot by adolescents at slumber parties or around campfires. On another level, however, it seems obvious that the story serves to warn teenagers against the dangers of "parking" in dark, secluded spots. Possibly the warning on the car radio of the escaped hookman represents the parents' typical warning, "Now be careful, and don't stay out too late!" Folklorist Alan Dundes has suggested that the hook itself may represent a phallic object that is symbolically torn off by the car's rapid departure, reflecting the fact that the boyfriend in the car hoped to "get his hooks into the girl" before his efforts were interrupted by the warning.

See also Comparative Approach; Context; Definition of "Legend"; Fortean Approach; Freudian Approach; Historical Approach; Linguistic Approach; Motif; Performance of Urban Legends; Sociological Approach; Structural Approach; Symbolic Approach

References: Hand, *American Folk Legend* (1971); Brunvand, *The Study of American Folklore* (1998), chap. 9, "Legends and Anecdotes," 196–228; *Vanishing Hitchhiker,* "Glossary" and "Appendix," 193–202.

Animals in Urban Legends

One whole section of a classification of urban legends (some 60 stories) concerns legends about animals; animals appear in the legends of several other sections as well. Gillian Bennett and Paul Smith's 1993 bibliography *Contemporary Legend* contains about 150 entries and several cross-references under "Animals," including species ranging from frogs, newts, slugs, and toads to elephants, cattle, monkeys, and wolves. Some of the classic urban legends are animal stories, such as "The Choking Doberman," "The Mexican Pet," "Alligators in the Sewers," and "The Dead Cat in the Package." Along with cars, crime, sex, and horrors, animals are among the most prominent themes in modern urban legends.

A high proportion of animals described in urban legends are pets, and, as often as not, these beasts come to some sad end, as when a dead rabbit is disinterred ("The Hare Dryer"), a gerbil is crushed ("The Bump in the Rug"), a poodle is cooked ("The Microwaved Pet" and "The Dog's Dinner"), or a hunting dog is detonated ("The Loaded Dog"). However, in other animal legends a pet or a creature from the wild may get its revenge, as when a cat's death leads its owners to have their stomachs pumped ("The Poisoned Pussycat at the Party"), a stunned deer trashes a person's car ("The Hunter's Nightmare"), a kangaroo makes off with someone's coat and its pocket contents ("The Kangaroo Thief"), or (as in most versions of "The Loaded Dog") when the unfortunate animal victim takes the hunters' new truck or camper with it.

Many animals in urban legends are depicted as infesting or contaminating either food (e.g., "The Mouse in the Coke," "The Kentucky Fried Rat," and "The Rat in the Rye Bread"), or even a human body (e.g., earwig stories, "Spiders in the Hairdo," and "The Bosom Serpent"). Other animal contamination stories that usually are classified under different headings are "The Bedbug Letter" and "The Spider Bite." Animals fill other roles in complicating humans' lives in legends like "The Cat (or Dog) and the Nude Man," "The Elephant that Sat on the VW," "The Elevator Incident," "The Flying Cow," "The Pig on the Road," "The Stuck Diver," and "The Turkey Neck."

See also "The Air-Freighted Pet"; Big Cats Running Wild; "The Colo-Rectal Mouse"; "The Crushed Dog"; "Fifi Spills the Paint"; "The Giant Catfish"; Hunting; "The Missionaries and the Cat"; Snakes; Spiders; "The Wildcat in the Suitcase"; and "The Zoo Section"

"The Animal's Revenge"

This is the generic title for a series of stories in which a sadistic person or persons attach an explosive to an animal, light the fuse, and release the animal. The intended animal victim, however, takes refuge in, near, or under some valuable property, blowing it to pieces. The animal thus wired, in various versions of the story, includes a coyote, a dog, a rat, a rabbit, a raccoon, a possum, a hawk, and even a shark. The property destroyed may be a truck or other vehicle, a boat, a tent, a chimney, a porch, or a whole building. In some versions the tormentor of the animal himself becomes the victim of its revenge.

A passage in the Bible (Judges 15:4–5) and an Aesopian fable called "The Burner Burnt" are prototypes for "The Animal's Revenge"; in these an animal is set afire and released into fields of ripe grain. In older versions of "The Animal's Revenge" the animal is wired with explosives in an attempt to injure another person or his property, but in more recent versions the cruel perpetrators are often hunters whose dog, a retriever, inadvertently picks up the explosive.

See also "The Deer Departed"; "The Kangaroo Thief"; "The Loaded Dog"; "The Plant's Revenge"; "South Africa"

References: *Baby Train*, 235; *Choking Doberman*, 67–68; *Mexican Pet*, 36–40; *Too Good*, 71–73.

Ankle Slashers

See "The Slasher Under the Car"

Ants or Termites Invade the Body

These burrowing insects are said to have entered either under a person's plaster cast or into someone's sinus cavities. In the former cases, a maddening itch under the cast is explained after it is removed and the infestation is discovered. In the latter cases, a child may scream uncontrollably and scratch at its head, finally jabbing the tines of a fork between its own eyes. Dozens of ants pour from the wound.

See also "The Bosom Serpent"; Earwig Stories; Octopus Eggs Impregnate Swimmer; "The Spider Bite"; "The Spider in the Hairdo"

References: *Vanishing Hitchhiker,* 80.

Architects' Blunders

Although architects are highly trained professionals whose designs must pass strict standards set by building codes and safety requirements, their work is often characterized in rumors and legends as being flawed, incomplete, unusable, and even dangerous. Sometimes these alleged problems are said to be flaws in the original designs—as when an architect fails to allow for the weight of the books to be stored in a new library. Other problems may be attributed to features of the building site, such as steep ground angles, swampy surroundings, or a forgotten tunnel. In other cases the architect's plans are satisfactory, but the builders either inadvertently switch plans with another project being built elsewhere or else they read the plans "backward" so the building ends up facing the wrong way.

Possibly some stories about architects' blunders result from the public's notion that designers are more interested in making an "artistic" statement or enhancing their own reputations than in designing comfortable settings for human habitation and work. Other stories may stem from people's sense that some buildings simply "look wrong" and therefore must have been designed or built "wrong" in the first place. Such stories are often told about the designs of the most famous and successful architects, particularly Frank Lloyd Wright, which is perhaps another illustration of the "Goliath effect."

Undeniably some architects and builders *have* blundered in some details of the countless buildings that are erected annually, but such mistakes are usually corrected within the terms of the building contracts before—or shortly after—the buildings are put into use. Nevertheless, the rumors and legends adhere to older buildings as well as to new ones, and virtually the same stories are told about buildings in many different places.

References: *Baby Train*, 299–304; *Curses!*, 253–258.

Argentina

In 1949 the Argentinian psychoanalyst Marie Langer collected several versions of "The Baby-Roast" that was circulating in Buenos Aires. Discussing the legend in her 1951 book *Maternidad y sexo,* she noted that it was rampant among servants, taxi drivers, and barbers; the story was also, as she put it, "accepted as truth by people generally capable of critical judgment." These early examples of the cooked-baby legend escaped the notice of most foreign folklorists until an English translation of the book *Folklore and Psychoanalysis* by the Argentinian folklorist Paulo de Carvalho-Neto was published in 1968 by the University of Miami Press. Here Langer's summary of "the most complete version of this strange story that was making the rounds" was provided:

> A young married couple hires a servant since the wife is pregnant and almost due. The baby is born. A few weeks later the husband and wife go to the movies one evening, leaving the baby in the servant's care. Until that time she has always been reliable. According to one version, on their return she receives them ceremoniously dressed in the wife's bridal gown and tells them she has prepared quite a surprise for them. She bids them come into the dining room to serve them a special meal. They enter and find a horrifying spectacle. In the middle of the table, placed there with great care, they see their son on a large platter, roasted and garnished with potatoes. The poor mother goes insane at once. She loses her speech and no one has heard her utter a single word since then. The father, according to several versions, is a military man. He pulls out a revolver and shoots the servant. Then he runs away and is never heard from again.

The details of this Argentinian version closely match the international tradition of "The Baby-Roast": The new parents go out for an evening of pleasure, leaving the baby with a caregiver who turns out to be mentally unsound, and she cooks the baby and serves it as food. The ending here—woman goes insane, man leaves town—is reminiscent of the usual conclusion of "The Nude Surprise Party." The two references in the summary to other versions of the story, as well as the lack of any factual background, further establish the story as legendary. If this urban legend was being told so long ago in Argentina, then surely other such rumors and stories must have been circulating there as well. Eventually, they came to light.

The legend of "The Baby Roast," first told in Argentina during the late 1940s, emerged again as a popular story in the 1960s. In the 1980s journalist Jorge Halperin (then-editor of the op-ed section of the leading Argentinian newspaper *Clarin*) noted this and many other such rumors and stories circulating in his country and started collecting and studying them. In 1993 Halperin lectured on Argentinian urban legends at the America Society in New York, and his book on the subject, *Mentiras verdaderas* (True Lies), was published in 2000.

Halperin's book—its title (but not its subject) inspired by the Arnold Schwarzenegger film—is based on about 100 urban legends told in Argentina with comparisons to the worldwide tradition of these same stories, particularly in Spain and Latin America, and including material from the Internet. The author finds numerous echoes of urban-legend themes in mythology, literature, fine arts, film, and other popular culture. Although not primarily a collection of legend texts, *Mentiras verdaderas* reveals numerous parallels of Argentinian legends to international modern-legend tradition, including local versions of such examples as "The Kidney Heist," Chinese restaurant stories, "The Gay Roommate," "The Accidental Cannibals," and many stories of contamination and other horrors. In one chapter Halperin traces 23 links in a chain of narrators repeating "The Mexican Pet," showing how mistakes in telling the story and the insertion of "bad information" contributed to variations of the basic plot.

These "true lies" of Argentina had barely been published as this encyclopedia was going to press, so it is not possible to describe its reception by readers in Argentina or elsewhere. However, if the success of similar books elsewhere is any guide, Halperin will find himself overwhelmed by responses, including many "new" urban legends or variations of the stories he included.

References: Brunvand, *The Truth*, 49–51 (Langer's and Carvalho-Neto's discussion); Marie Langer, "Le 'Mythe de l'enfant rôti,'" *Revue Française de Psychoanalyse* 16 (1952): 509–517 (French translation of the relevant chapter from *Maternidad y sexo*).

"The Arrest"

A driver who is weaving about the highway is pulled over by a state trooper and given the Breathalyzer test. Failing the test, the man is told he is under arrest, but just then a bad accident occurs on the other side of the highway, and the policeman orders the man to wait while he goes over to investigate the crash.

The drunk decides to escape; he jumps behind the wheel of the car and drives home, parking in the garage and telling his wife to say he had been home all night if the police should inquire. When the police manage to locate him, they ask to see his car and are taken to the garage where they find their own cruiser parked, the motor still running and the dome lights still flashing.

"The Arrest" surfaced in 1986 in numerous American states as well as in Australia and Great Britain, given a boost by several reports of the story published in newspapers or broadcast by Paul Harvey and others. Specific local details—highway numbers, make and model of car, and so on—made the story seem credible, but it has never been verified, and some law enforcement personnel say that the story had been told for many years but never witnessed firsthand.

References: *Curses!,* 101–103; *Too Good,* 109–110.

"The Assailant in the Backseat"

See "The Killer in the Backseat"

Atrocities

Legends of atrocities typically circulate during wartime and periods of rule by repressive regimes or arise in the context of foreign travel, especially in countries torn by racial, ethnic, political, or religious strife. Of course, actual atrocities do commonly occur in such situations, but certain bizarre stories with an ironic twist that circulate anonymously and without specific verification may be regarded as legendary (or perhaps, in some instances, as propaganda) until proven authentic.

One common theme in legends of atrocities is that the victim, despite having suffered horrible disfigurement or mutilation, manages to communicate his or her situation to family members via a hidden or coded message in a telephone call, photograph, or letter. In other stories the victim may not be able to communicate, but an acquaintance recognizes him or her—despite the disfigurement—in an exploitive film or a carnival freak show.

Fear and suspicion of outsiders are revealed in legends of abductions, torture, and even killings by foreign agents; the Japanese legend of "The Mutilated Bride" who is later recognized in the Philippines is a typical example of this theme. Similarly, the legends of Western tourists being kidnapped and mutilated or killed commonly refer to travel in places like the Middle East, Africa, and the Orient. Such modern stories recall the past accounts of missionaries being eaten by cannibals or forced to become the concubines of native leaders.

See also "The Message Under the Stamp"; Military Legends; "The Mutilated Boy"; Tourist Horror Stories

"Atrocity Stories"

See Legal Horror Stories

"The Attempted Abduction"

In this legend a small child is missing after his or her parents are momentarily distracted while at a shopping mall, department store, or amusement park. When the store or park authorities are notified, they seal off every exit except one and advise the parents to watch all departing persons, looking especially at the shoes of small children being taken out. It is explained that although would-be abductors may alter the child's appearance or change his or her clothes, they often forget to change the child's shoes. Sure enough, the parents recognize their own child—who has been sedated and disguised and is being carried out by a stranger—when they spot his or her favorite pair of tennis shoes with a distinctive logo. Sometimes the would-be abductor is caught in the act of cutting and dying the child's hair in a restroom.

Virtually the same legend with minor variations has been told about specific businesses since at least the mid-1970s, and it continues to be told, frequently about newly opened malls, stores, and parks. Often it is asserted that the abductors intend to force the children into making kiddie-porn films, and sometimes the abduction is said to be successful and the child is recognized later by someone viewing such a film. Often the legend concludes with the rumor that local police are familiar with the case but have suppressed the facts in order not to hurt business at the named company. This supposedly explains why local news media have failed to report these attempted abductions. Actually, many local media sources *have* done reports on these stories, but invariably the purpose was to debunk the rumors and legends of attempted abductions.

"The Mutilated Boy" is an older and more horrible form of the same story.

See also "The Mutilated Boy"

References: *Choking Doberman,* 78–82; Joann Conrad, "Stranger Danger: Defending Innocence, Denying Responsibility," *Contemporary Legend,* New Series 1 (1998), 55–96; *Curses!,* 207–208; *Mexican Pet,* 148–156; *Too Good,* 315–317.

Australia

The pioneering Aussie folklorist Bill Scott in 1969 took early notice of urban legends in his country when he discussed local versions of "The Ready-Mix Concrete Driver" (i.e., "The Solid Cement Cadillac") in a short article titled "Current Folk Tales" published in the magazine *Australian Tradition.* This led an American folklorist, the late Richard A. Reuss, to respond with an essay in the same magazine that identified this story and several others as international urban legends. Scott was intrigued by this revelation, and in his many following books and articles he continued to collect and publish Australian urban legends, as well as more traditional folklore from Down Under. He reprinted the original 1969 essays in his *Complete Book of Australian Folk Lore* (1976, pp. 359–363) and also included a chapter devoted to "Urban Folktales" in his 1985 book *The Long and the Short and the Tall* (pp. 223–251). The final story in the latter compilation, titled "Not Worth Going Back to Sleep," is a version of "The Baby Train" given a distinctive Australian style.

Bill Scott's most recent published contribution to the study of Australian urban legends is his 1996 book *Pelicans and Chihuahuas and Other Urban Legends.* The title refers to the local version of the "Pet Nabber" story in which a small domestic animal is carried off by a large wild bird. Two books by other collectors are titled (or subtitled) similarly, with reference to a favorite Australian story. Journalist Amanda Bishop in 1988 published *The Gucci Kangaroo and Other Australian Urban Legends,* and folklorist Graham Seal in 1995 published *Great Australian Urban Myths: Granny on the Roofrack and Other Tales of Modern Horror.*

Most urban legends told in Australia appear to be localized versions of modern stories that are known around the world. Legends such as "The Vanishing Hitchhiker," "The Choking Doberman," "The Hare Dryer," and many others circulate Down Under in texts that might have been told in England or the United States, except for the overlay of Australian place-names and slang. Other legends—including "The Elevator Incident" and "The Kidney Heist"—are told about Australians traveling abroad, often to the United States, but the essentials of their plots are consistent with versions told elsewhere. As in other countries, newspapers in Australia often publish scraps of bizarre stories that seem to be nothing more than urban legends then making the rounds.

Two international urban legends have deep roots in Australian tradition, as evidenced by references to them in literary sources of the late nineteenth century. James Brunton Stephens (known as "the Queensland poet") incorporated the old story of the eaten pet (a dog, in this instance) in his poem from about 1888 titled "My Other Chinese Cook"; in about 1899, Henry Lawson wrote "The Loaded Dog," based on the legend ("The Animal's Revenge") of the dog wired with explosives that turns on its tormentors. A recent example of Australian writing incorporating an urban legend is Peter Carey's 1981 novel *Bliss* (made into a film in 1985), which describes a circus elephant sitting on a small red car.

Gwenda Beed Davey, in her entry on "Modern Legends" in *The Oxford Companion to Australian Folklore* (1993, edited by Davey and Graham Seal) declares that "it is hard to identify a specifically Australian contemporary legend," and, in fact, she demonstrates that no collector has nominated any "uniquely Australian" modern legends. Even stories like "The Kangaroo Thief," concerning a unique Australian animal, are widely told elsewhere, both in the Australian setting or adapted to other locations; it is unlikely that the kangaroo versions are any older than those that feature, say, a North American deer, elk, or bear as the wild animal, which is presumed dead, then recovers and makes off with a person's property (coat, passport, rifle, camera, etc.).

A few modern legends from Australia do seem to have a distinctly Down Under flavor and are not known to be told elsewhere. Amanda

Bishop, for example, tells the story of "The Clever Dog," a stockman's dog that is sent back to camp for help after its owner is thrown from a horse and breaks his leg. The stockman sticks a note asking for help in his hatband and ties the hat to the dog's collar. But the dog, instead of seeking help, simply jumps on the stockman's bunk back at camp and goes to sleep. The man is rescued only when his mates follow the loose horse's tracks back to the scene of the accident.

Other candidates for Australian originality in urban legends are certainly the stories dealing with local celebrities, not well known abroad; chief among these are the businessmen Sir Frank Packer, Kerry Packer, and Reg Ansett. Other distinctly Australian legends are told about local politicians and entertainers. Another story that Graham Seal believes has a distinctly Aussie flavor is "The Airline Steward's Revenge." After being snubbed by a snooty first-class passenger, the steward is asked by her husband, "My wife was wondering about the situation with domestic help in Australia." Demonstrating the "rapier-sharp wit of the Aussie bloke," as Seal puts it, the steward replies, "I'm sure madam will have no trouble at all finding a job."

See also "The Runaway Grandmother"; "The Wife Left Behind"; Xeroxlore

References: *Baby Train,* 170, 231–236; *Curses!,* 250–251, 305–307; *Mexican Pet,* 65–66, 102–103.

Automobiles

Many apocryphal stories concern the automobile, which Richard M. Dorson in his 1959 survey of American urban legends called "the chief symbol of modern America." The mobility and convenience provided by the family car, the hazards of driving, the allure of cars to young and old alike, the mystiques of different models and makes of cars, the costs of car ownership, the technical aspects of cars and driving, and the relationships with other drivers all figure in the voluminous legendary lore of automobiles.

The legends range from the supernatural plot of "The Vanishing Hitchhiker" to the believable everyday situation depicted in "Revenge of the Rich" (in which the driver of a luxury car deliberately crashes into a poorer driver's car after losing the race to a parking spot). As automotive technology advanced and sophisticated options became standard, new legends emerged, yielding stories about such things as automatic transmissions, cruise control, and air bags. Sometimes when dramatic events make the news, an updated car legend soon follows. For example, shortly after the 1980 eruption of Mount Saint Helens, new versions of "The Vanishing Hitchhiker" circulated in the Northwest claiming that a mysterious woman in white had been encountered hitching on Interstate 5 and warning motorists of a second eruption to come. Similarly, after the 1989 Bay Area earthquake, a legend emerged about a car thief who was flattened by the collapse of a freeway section while he was driving a BMW stolen from the World Series parking lot at Candlestick Park.

Some automobile legends concern simple mishaps, such as changing a flat tire ("The Nut and the Tire Nuts") or forgetting someone ("The Wife Left Behind" and "The Baby on the Roof.") Others deal with accidents ("The Body on the Car"), often specifically accidental amputations ("The Hook"). Car-related crime is a popular theme represented in such legends as "The Killer in the Backseat," "The Slasher Under the Car," and "The Double Theft."

The automobile is merely in the background of legends focusing on sex humor such as "The Solid Cement Cadillac" and "The Unzipped Mechanic." The car is in the foreground in stories that focus on technical incompetence like "Push-Starting the Car" and "'R' Is for Race," although the first of these also has a gender-related theme whereas the latter is often told as a racist story.

Among the most popular automobile urban legends are those that represent fantasies concerning inexpensive and highly desirable cars. Some people (always friends of friends) are said to have discovered mint-condition vintage vehicles hidden away and available for a song; friends of friends are also described as discovering a $50 Porsche being sold by the disgruntled wife of a man who left her for another woman.

One of the longest-lived and most popular American urban legends about automobiles is "The Death Car." It combines a cheap-car fantasy with the almost supernatural motif of the ineradicable smell of death; as the legend has been told and retold over many decades; the makes and models of smelly cars have changed, the manner of the owner's death has varied, and the price of the bargain car has increased to match inflation. Today's $500 Corvette with the bad smell permeating the fiberglass body was yesterday's $50 Buick with odiferous upholstery.

See also "The Economical Car"; "The Elephant That Sat on the VW"; Rolls-Royce Legends

References: Dorson, *American Folklore*, 249; Stewart F. Sanderson, "The Folklore of the Motor-car," *Folklore* 80 (1969): 241–52; *Too Good*, 89–118.

"The Avon Flasher"

With a "ding-dong" at the door, the Avon Lady comes to call. After delivering a mediocre sales pitch, the tall, husky traveling saleslady asks if she can use the bathroom. A short time later she calls out from the bathroom that there is no more toilet paper. Since the woman of the house had just hung a fresh roll that morning, she becomes suspicious and calls the police. The cops arrive and find a naked man lurking in her bathroom.

Like "The Hairy-Armed Hitchhiker," this legend describes a man dressed as a woman who preys on women but is foiled. Variations of this story—popular in the mid-1980s—describe a washer repairman trying to lure the woman to the basement where he awaits her naked. Sometimes there is no repairman, but the woman simply hears her washer starting up and, suspicious, calls the police.

The Avon Lady version is known in Australia and, perhaps also, as Aussie folklorist Graham Seal speculates, "wherever else in the world that Avon calls."

References: *Mexican Pet*, 121.

Babies

As innocent victims of neglect or violence, babies are killed or seriously injured in most of the urban legends in which they appear. The four entries that follow, plus other legends discussed in this book, describe babies being abandoned, abducted, killed by a rampaging animal, lost, misplaced, mutilated, neglected, roasted, slain for their organs, and otherwise poorly or cruelly treated by those responsible for their care. The guilt of the caregivers extends to parents, siblings, and baby-sitters alike, although in some instances the neglect is inadvertent and accidental rather than deliberate.

In a rare example of a legend baby *surviving* a threat, an infant in its car seat, forgotten on the car roof by a distracted parent, is spotted by an alert bystander and rescued before suffering injury. In the most horrible and cynical example of a dead-baby legend, the corpse of an infant is said to have been hollowed out in order to smuggle drugs into the United States in the arms of a supposed parent on an international flight.

See also Children; Organ Thefts; "The Snake in the Strawberry Patch"; "The Stuffed Baby"

"The Baby-Roast"

The consistent feature of this legend, also called "The Cooked Baby" or "The Hippy Baby-sitter," is that a baby is roasted alive, either in a conventional or a microwave oven. Often the unfortunate infant is described as having been stuffed and garnished in the manner of a roast pig or other delicacy.

The horrible deed is done either by a family member (usually a sibling) or by a person hired to tend the baby in the parents' absence. In American versions, told since the 1970s, usually a teenage baby-sitter cooks the infant while under the influence of alcohol or drugs, sometimes reporting to the parents, "I've cooked the turkey for you." International versions of the legend may describe a naive maid from abroad or from a provincial village who is told to "keep the baby warm" but who misunderstands the command as "cook the baby." Occasionally the mother herself is the baby-roaster as a result of mental illness related to her unwanted pregnancy; this variation has been collected in Sweden, Turkey, South America, and Australia, among other places. Even farther afield, traditional stories collected in the South Pacific area of Micronesia describe children left in charge of their younger sibling who cook the baby, either out of spite for having to do the parents' work or because of a misunderstanding of orders given for the tot's care. The international folk-narrative motif represented here is J2460.1 (*Disastrous following of misunderstood instructions*).

Possibly the American legends of cooked pets from the 1950s gave rise to later stories of cooked babies, although there were rumors reported as early as the 1920s of nannies using a whiff of stove gas to tranquilize babies before bedtime. The widespread distribution of similar stories and motifs outlined above has not yet been resolved into a complete history of the baby-roast story, which is one of the most widely known and varied of all urban legends.

"The Baby-Roast" seems to confirm the worst fears of young parents—that their child will not be safe outside of their own loving care. The story may also reflect feelings of guilt about modern child-care practices—especially when both parents work outside the home—which relegate children for much of their early upbringing to day-care centers or live-in nannies; it is important to note that the parents are often said to be enjoying themselves—dining out, at a party, or attending a concert or movie—while the baby is roasted alive at home. Sibling rivalry is an obvious theme in many other versions of the story. The possibility of the oven as a symbol of the womb might be supported by one common slang term for pregnancy—"to have one [a bun] in the oven."

See also Argentina; "The Clever Baby-sitter"; "The Microwaved Pet"; Motif

> **References:** "The Baby-Roast Story As a 'New American Urban Legend,'" in 3rd ed. of Brunvand, *Study of American Folklore* (1986), updated and republished in *The Truth*, 38–61.

"The Baby Train"

The extraordinarily high birthrate of a particular town, suburb, neighborhood, apartment building, or other dwelling area is explained by the daily passage of an early-morning train whose loud whistle awakens couples. Since it is too early to get up for work or school and too late to go back to sleep, the couples make love—and produce more "whistle babies." Some couples fail to follow the local trend because they get used to the whistle (or are hard of hearing) and stay asleep.

The baby-train legend is popular as an American college story, told about married-student apartments all across the country, but it is also known, with adaptations to local cultures, in rural America, as well as in Europe, South Africa, Australia, and probably elsewhere. The story has been traced to early Industrial Revolution lore in England when trains were just developing into major transportation devices. The same supposed universal trait of human nature is reflected in the folklore concerning allegedly high birthrates just nine months after natural disasters such as earthquakes and hurricanes have knocked out power for lengthy periods.

> **References:** *Baby Train*, 33–37; *Too Good*, 325–326.

"Baby's Stuck at Home Alone"

A couple departs for an overseas vacation, leaving their baby strapped in its highchair, the caregiver (nanny, neighbor, grandmother, etc.) having just telephoned to say that she is on her way to their home. The couple cannot wait because their flight is imminent. However, the caregiver suffers a fatal accident on the way to the home, and the baby starves to death while stuck in its chair.

This legend circulated in Norway and Sweden in the early 1970s, then migrated to England, the United States, and probably elsewhere by the 1980s. In some versions the family's pet dog is also trapped in the house, and it kills and eats the baby.

Although this nightmarish situation may seem plausible to parents concerned about dangers to their infants, the plot is unlikely at best, since the caregiver would surely have told somebody about the long-term child-care job, and after her death someone certainly would have rescued the baby. A Norwegian newspaper attempting to verify versions of the story circulating in 1972 concluded that they were merely *ryktene* (rumors).

References: *Too Good,* 222–223.

"The Baby-sitter and the Man Upstairs"

A baby-sitter receives repeated telephone calls from a man who asks in a menacing manner, "Have you checked the children?" Sometimes he says that he has killed the children and soon he will kill her, too. The sitter, too terrified to check the children in their upstairs bedroom, calls the police, who advise her to keep the man on the line when he next phones so they can trace the call. After another threatening call, the police telephone her and warn her, "Get out of the house right away!" A policeman waiting outside explains that the calls were traced to the upstairs extension phone where the caller is found, having already murdered the children and poised to attack the baby-sitter.

Widely told since the early 1970s and especially popular among teens who baby-sit, this legend was developed into the 1979 horror film *When a Stranger Calls.* Like "The Killer in the Backseat" and "The Choking Doberman," this baby-sitting legend tells of an intruder hiding on the premises; the warning against him, as in the Doberman legend, comes via the telephone and commands the intended victim to "get out of the house!"

Folklorists have suggested that the death of children in the baby-sitter's care represents her ultimate failure as a future homemaker and mother; the killer's positioning upstairs—*above* the female sitter—may signify the traditional dominant role of men in sexual and power relationships.

References: *Choking Doberman,* 214–215; *Too Good,* 220–222; *Vanishing Hitchhiker,* 53–57.

Backward Buildings and Statues

In these legends a building is built backward on its site (switched front to back) because the architect's plans were read the wrong way. It is rumored that the architect committed suicide when he saw what had happened. A public statue faces the "wrong way," either as an error of placement or perhaps to make a statement about the person depicted.

Well-known backward-building legends include the Kelvingrove Art Gallery and Museum in Glasgow, the Town Hall of Liverpool, the Taj Mahal Hotel in Bombay, and the Tripler Hospital in Honolulu. In Copenhagen it is claimed that the distinctive exterior staircase on the steeple of *Vor Frelser's* (Our Saviour's) Church actually spirals the "wrong way" (counterclockwise) and that the eighteenth century archi tect, in despair, climbed to the top and jumped to his death. Backward buildings and other architectural blunders are common themes in American college folklore.

Backward-facing statues are often said to have been deliberately misaligned so as to insult one institution and call attention to another. For example, the statue of Scottish poet Robert Burns in the Octagon (a plaza in central Dunedin, New Zealand) is pointed out to have its back to St. Paul's Anglican Cathedral and its face looking toward the commercial section of the city. Similarly, the statue of Brigham Young, early leader of the Mormon Church (Latter-Day Saints) was positioned in downtown Salt Lake City with its back to the Mormon Temple and with one hand extended toward Zion's First National Bank. The statue has since been moved back from its original location in the middle of the intersection of two main streets, so the odd placement is no longer quite as obvious; however, local people continue to quote the traditional explanatory rhyme: "There stands Brigham, like a bird on a perch./His hand to the bank, and his back to the church."

See also Architects' Blunders; Sinking Libraries; Switched Campus Buildings

References: *Curses!*, 255–258.

"The Bargain Sports Car"

In this cheap-car fantasy, a mother finally decides to sell the old car that her son, who was killed in action, had left in her garage when he was sent to Vietnam with the military. She advertises the 1965 Chevrolet for $200 since it is ten years old and small ("It only holds two people.") Sometimes she calls a dealer to ask what a car of that age and size would be worth. A buyer who can only afford a cheap used car arrives to find that she has a classic Corvette set up on blocks and in perfect condition. He whips out his checkbook and buys it for the advertised price. Sometimes the man arrives just a few minutes too late, and he sees the Corvette being driven out of the garage by another buyer.

See also "The Death Car"; Mint Condition Vintage Vehicles; "The Philanderer's Porsche"

References: *Curses!*, 123–125; *Too Good*, 117–118.

"The Barometer Problem"

A physics professor asks students on an examination to describe how they could determine the height of a building by using a barometer. One clever student ignores the obvious suggestion of using a formula involving the different air pressure at the top and bottom of the building; instead, he answers, "Tie a long string to the barometer and lower it from the roof of the building; then measure the string plus the length of the barometer."

When the professor rules that this is an unacceptable solution, the student is given another chance and comes up with several different approaches involving such things as timing the fall of the barometer from the roof to the ground, measuring the shadows of the building and the barometer, or simply measuring up the side of the building in units of "one barometer." The professor rejects all of these solutions as well, so the student suggests that one could then trade the barometer to the building supervisor for the needed information.

References: *Baby Train,* 294–295; *Too Good,* 440–441.

"The Barrel of Bricks"

This is a hilarious-accident story told in the form of a written report, sometimes accompanying an insurance claim, by a worker describing the cause of his job-related injuries. Faced with the problem of moving a heavy load of bricks or roof tiles alone from the roof of a building to the ground, the man decided to lower them in a barrel using a rope and a pulley. But when he untied the rope he failed to let go quickly enough and was pulled to the rooftop by the weight of the bricks. When the barrel burst as it hit the ground, the man fell back down and landed on the bricks. He was further in-

jured by hitting the barrel (both going up and down), jamming his fingers in the pulley, landing on the bricks, and having the broken barrel land on him.

The worker's report describes all of this in a flat, unemotional style, concluding, "I respectively request sick leave." The same basic scenario has been adapted to several different building and manufacturing trades, and the worker is sometimes described as a nonnative speaker of English or an uneducated man, thus explaining his inappropriately placid style of describing a slapstick situation.

"The Barrel of Bricks" circulates in numerous anonymous typescripts, and it has appeared many times in print. It was used as a comic monologue on the radio and stage from at least the 1930s, and it has been rendered as a song usually titled "Dear Boss" or "Why Paddy's Not at Work Today." A cowboy poet created a version involving moving a whiskey barrel full of horseshoes.

An Irish-dialect version appeared in print in 1918. The claim that the story originated with a Revolutionary War corporal in General George Washington's army is highly unlikely, but the modern story may be related to Tale Type 32, which incorporates Motif K651 (*Wolf descends into well in one bucket and rescues fox in the other*).

References: *Curses!*, 180–188; *Too Good*, 166–168.

"Bart Simpson Acid"

See "Blue Star Acid"

"The Bedbug Letter"

A businessman traveling by train on a sleeper car finds his berth infested with bedbugs. He writes to the railroad company to complain and receives a letter from the president of the company that is full of abject apologies and promises to fire the workers responsible and to clean and disinfect the sleeping cars. The letter assures him that such a thing has not happened previously and will never happen again. Still attached to this polite reply, however, is a routing slip that reads, "Send this son of a bitch the bedbug letter." Sometimes, along with the apology, the original letter is returned with the "bedbug letter" directive rubber-stamped on it.

This story is always told about the old days of railroad travel, usually the 1940s, although some people claim (without verification) that it goes back to the turn of the century when George M. Pullman still presided over the sleeping-car company that gave his name to the cars themselves. The story does not seem to have become attached to modern Amtrak sleepers.

References: *Baby Train*, 158–162; *Too Good*, 255–257.

Belgium

Professor Stefaan Top and his students at Leuven University began collecting Belgian modern legends in 1982; in the first six years of the project they accumulated more than 500 texts of about 50 different story types. Urban legend–telling in Belgium seemed most popular among young people between 16 and 18 years old, but similar stories were also found printed in newspapers and discussed on the radio.

About a dozen well-known international legend types were collected, including local variants of "The Runaway Grandmother," "The Spider in the Cactus," "The Choking Doberman," "The Double Theft," and "The Hippy Baby-sitter." A story that seemed to be more specifically Belgian was "The Stolen Cobblestones," in which a man is loading some cobblestones from a city street-repair project into his car when he is caught by a policeman. The man claims he was dumping some extra cobblestones, and the policeman orders him to put them back into his car and leave. However, a similar story is told in Holland about stealing sand and in the United States about stealing bricks.

"The Stolen Cobblestones" and a few other stories demonstrate the occasional sense of humor found in Belgian modern legends. In general, professor Top found that "contemporary Belgian legends have only three shades of meaning: bad—worse—worst"; their incidents, he suggested, typically include the gradations "bad luck—accident—catastrophe." He illustrated this with the story of a farmer who accidentally kills his children who have hidden inside the combine harvester. The farmer sends his wife to the field without telling her what has happened, and while she is gone—discovering the tragedy—he shoots himself.

Professor Top concludes from his preliminary survey of Belgian urban legends that such stories "are to be considered as a kind of mirror of daily life in the present day . . . [and] may also function as an alarm signal for what is going wrong in our society."

References: *Baby Train*, 237–239; Stefaan Top, "Modern Legends in the Belgian Oral Tradition: A Report," *Fabula* 31 (1990): 272–278.

Belief Legend

After distinguishing folktales from legends on the basis of the strong element of folk belief in the latter, early folklorists also spoke and wrote of "belief legends" as a specific genre of traditional narrative. These *Glaubensagen,* as the Germans termed them, were distinguished from *Wissensagen,* or "knowlege legends" (what we call in English "historical legends"). In the early days of collecting modern legends in the United States such stories were also called "urban belief *tales,*" thus further confusing the terminology.

Eventually the term "belief legend" fell into disuse because, as Hungarian-American folklorist Linda Dégh wrote, "The peculiarly pivotal position of belief in legend makes *all* legends belief legends." Dégh opposes "the current legend name-giving inflation," and she concludes that "the term 'legend' serves our purpose fine." However, the English folklorist Gillian Bennett suggests that another once-used term, "belief *story*," should be revived to refer to "a type of informal conversational narrative that is at present badly served by existing terms." Bennett refers to a "private, personal repertoire" of stories (as opposed to well-recognized traditional stories) that some people tell when they engage in discussions of matters of belief with others.

References: Gillian Bennett, "Belief Stories: The Forgotten Genre," *Western Folklore* 48 (1989): 289–311; Linda Dégh, "What Is a Belief Legend?" *Folklore* 107 (1996): 33–46, followed by Gillian Bennett, "Reply": 47–48.

Big Cats Running Wild

Rumors of big cats—often identified as black panthers—running wild near urban or suburban areas sometimes develop into local legends with detailed accounts of the beasts' tracks, sightings, depredations upon domestic animals, supposed origins, and the like. Yet the big cats themselves are never captured, and the legendary accounts have a consistency of motif and structure that betrays a migratory story rather than an actual displaced feline predator.

Often the stories recur for several years in the same district. For example, there were panther sightings claimed in an

area of southeastern Michigan in 1984, 1985, 1989, and 1992. All were investigated by the Michigan Department of Natural Resources and by the local press without any panthers being found. The *Flint (Michigan) Journal* reported similar sightings in 1995, but again authorities were unable to locate any big cats. Similar searches for roaming cougars were reported near Moline, Illinois, in 1992, near Bethesda, Maryland, in 1994, and near Philadelphia in 1995.

"Phantom panther" sightings have been a staple of rumor outbreaks since the nineteenth century, both in the United States and abroad. Most of the stories can probably be explained as faulty observation of other animals native to the region. Sightings are influenced by the pop-culture images of slinking, ebony-colored big cats with bloodthirsty appetites—a far cry from the appearance and actual shy habits of most mountain lions. Since large black cats are native only to South America (jaguars) and Africa (leopards), any such creatures running wild in the rest of the world would have to be escapees from zoos or circuses, unlikely to be roaming long before they were reported missing.

The displaced–big cat theme is international. In Italy, for example, *felini misteriosi* were supposedly sighted in 1989–1990 in the suburbs of Rome. In England big-cat sightings have occurred repeatedly and have been dubbed in the media with such terms as "The Surrey Puma" or "The Exmoor Beast."

References: *Baby Train,* 217–218, 267–268.

"Bikers Versus Smokers"

A man smoking in the nonsmoking area of a café is asked by another diner wearing a motorcycle helmet and leather jacket to put out his cigarette. The smoker refuses, and when he leaves the café he defiantly kicks over a Harley Davidson motorcycle parked in front after putting a note on it reading, "This will teach you to mess with a smoker's rights."

But it was the wrong Harley, and its owner, a large, menacing man with a beard, roughs up the smoker and then turns him over to the police. The other diner's Harley was parked on the other side of the building.

One version of this story was published as a first-person account in the newsletter of a Mensa chapter, presumably to illustrate that even people with unusually high IQs may drive motorcycles.

See also "Truckers and Bikers"

References: *Baby Train*, 212–214.

"The Bird-Foot Exam"

The entire final examination in a college ornithology class consists of identifying a number of birds by their feet. The students are given either a page of drawings of bird feet or are shown a row of stuffed birds with bags covering all but their feet.

The students are outraged, and all except one apply themselves to the problem as best they can. The dissenter marches to the front of the room, slams his exam paper onto the professor's desk, and declares that "this is the stupidest test I've ever seen!" The professor glances at the blank examination paper and asks, "What's your name?" The student hitches up his pants leg, extends his foot, and says, "You tell me, Prof!" and stomps out of the classroom.

The themes of unreasonable testing procedures and of instructors in large colleges failing to know their individual students are both found in other academic legends.

See also "Define 'Courage'"; "Do You Know Who I Am?"; "The One-Word Exam Question"; "The Second Blue Book"; "Which Tire?"

References: *Curses!*, 275–277; *Too Good*, 442–443.

"The Blind Date"

There are two versions of this story, both of which refer to possible embarrassment when buying or using sex-related items. In the first, a young man buying condoms brags to the pharmacist that he has a blind date with a beautiful girl that evening and he hopes to "get lucky" with her. When he calls for the girl, he discovers that she is the daughter of the pharmacist.

The second version describes a young woman who must go to a hospital emergency room to have a "stuck tampon" removed from her body. That evening she discovers that the young doctor or intern who had done the procedure is her blind date for that night.

The condom story, known since the 1940s, is outdated now that these items are displayed openly in many stores, but a version still managed to get published as a true story in a 1994 Ann Landers column. The tampon story alludes to women's anxieties about the onset of menstruation and to embarrassment at being treated by a male medical practitioner. Both stories reveal the blind-date situation itself to be one of uncertainty and discomfort.

See also "Buying Tampax"

References: *Choking Doberman*, 138; *Mexican Pet*, 126; *Too Good*, 153–155.

"The Blind Man"

A woman has just undressed to take a shower when her doorbell rings. She calls out—"Who is it?"—and hears the reply, "Blind man." Assuming that a blind man would not know she is naked, she grabs a couple of dollars to make a donation (or to buy pencils or whatever he is selling) and opens the door. She thrusts the money at the man, who takes it with a surprised look and then asks, "Now where do you want me to hang these blinds?"

This story has been widely repeated for decades, both in folk tradition and by professional writers and comedians. Older versions mention Venetian blinds, as these window coverings were once called. Ann Landers published a version in 1986, commenting, "It's a funny story, whether it's true or not." She published it again in her October 13, 1998, column.

References: *Curses!*, 213–215; *Too Good*, 424.

"The Blood Libel"

As summarized by Alan Dundes, "According to this legend, which goes back to at least the twelfth century in Europe, Jews murder an innocent Christian infant or child for the ritual purpose of mixing the victim's blood with their matzo around Easter time" (p. vii). This grotesque and completely false story was told about (among many others, in scores of different countries) an English child called "Hugh of Lincoln" who was allegedly murdered by Jews in 1255. The legend was repeated in the traditional British ballad "Sir Hugh, or, the Jew's Daughter" (Child Number 155) and reworked by Geoffrey Chaucer in "The Prioress's Tale." When the ballad migrated to the United States, references to Jews were usually replaced by such phrases as "a jeweler's daughter," "a duke's daughter," or "a gypsy lady," although anti-Semitism is certainly well known in other areas of American folklore.

The traditional anti-Semitic legend, stripped of its religious prejudice, seems to underlie the modern urban legend "The Mutilated Boy" in which a child is castrated or has his penis cut off and is left bleeding to death in a shopping mall's restroom or other public place. Rather than Jewish murderers, the killers are often said to be members of some urban ethnic minority group or else homosexuals. The ritual aspect of the ancient legend is retained in versions that claim the crime was an initiation into gang membership.

In an ironic twist, as folklorist Bill Ellis has shown, anti-Christian versions of "The Blood Libel" circulated as an urban legend in ancient Rome. Ellis suggested that "we should not speak of modern legends, only modern texts."

References: *Choking Doberman,* 78–92; Alan Dundes, *The Blood Libel Legend: A Casebook in Anti-Semitic Folklore* (Madison: University of Wisconsin Press, 1991).

"Blue Star Acid"

Here, bogus warnings circulating in typescript, photocopied, and printed form warn that "a form of tattoo called Blue Star is being sold [or given] to school children [and] each star is soaked with LSD." The warning fliers claim that LSD can be absorbed simply by handling the tattoos and that some of them are "laced with strychnine." The designs on the sheets are said to be "the size of a pencil eraser" and may include images of blue stars, butterflies, Superman, Mickey Mouse, Bart Simpson, or other characters and designs. Symptoms of exposure to these tattoos are said to include "severe vomiting, uncontrolled laughter, and mood changes."

Presumably, the greatest danger comes when children use the printed designs as "lick and stick" tattoos. Readers of the warnings are urged to post and distribute copies of the flier since "young lives have already been taken." Sometimes the warnings are reproduced on the letterheads of schools, companies, churches, day-care centers, and the like, and there are often allusions to a supposed authority issuing the fliers (e.g., "We have been informed . . .") or even the name of a hospital and its spokesperson who allegedly issued the warnings. The excessive use of capital letters, exclamation marks, boldface, and other typographical devices marks the fliers as amateur and unofficial publications.

Such warning fliers have been distributed in the United States since the early 1980s, and they have spread internationally with much the same wording, having been directly translated into other languages. The warnings are sometimes printed in publications issued by well-meaning institutions who have failed to verify the information. Police and journalists investigating the claims have consistently debunked them. However, it is possible that the "Blue Star Acid" warnings originated from a misunderstanding of an actual police bulletin cautioning that children *may* mistake printed paper LSD "tabs" for tattoos.

Blue Star Acid is a nonexistent threat. Although "blotter acid" certainly does exist in the form of LSD-impregnated absorbent paper printed with cartoons and other designs (seldom blue stars or Mickey Mouse!)—none of it is in tattoo form or laced with strychnine; LSD is not absorbed through the skin, and nobody is giving or selling it to children in any large-scale way. If these claims *were* true, it would constitute a national drug emergency that would soon gain massive publicity. Although LSD, a popular illegal recreational drug of the 1960s, has made something of a comeback since the 1980s, it is not considered to be a problem of epidemic proportions compared to such products as methamphetamine and crack cocaine.

See also Bogus Warnings

References: *Choking Doberman*, 162–169; *Curses!*, 55–64; *Too Good*, 390–392.

"The Body in the Bed"

A couple checking into a Las Vegas hotel—often said to be the Excalibur or the Mirage—notice a bad smell in the room. They search unsuccessfully for the source and request a different room. But the hotel is full, and they are forced to endure the situation all night.

The next morning the smell is even worse, and they repeat their complaint to the front desk. That night when they return to their room they find a police guard at the door, and they are directed to another room where all their clothes and luggage have been moved. The chambermaid, while cleaning the room, had found a decomposing corpse inside the bed's base (or hidden in the box spring, or under the bed). Sometimes the victim is identified as a dead prostitute or a Mafia hit victim.

Versions of the legend in which the hotel management rewards the couple with lifetime free rooms for their trauma (or silence) recall "The Death Car," in which a buyer pays a bargain price for a car contaminated with the smell of a dead body left inside for some time. As in "Death Car" versions that describe an expensive automobile or a vintage sports car, "The Body in the Bed" concerns a luxury hotel in a posh vacation setting.

"The Body in the Bed" became a very popular legend beginning in 1991 and 1992, and actual instances of bodies found in hotel rooms were reported in the news in 1988 and 1989 and twice in 1994 and in 1996. However, none of the documented cases matches exactly the legend version, and they occurred in hotels in New Jersey and Florida. The modern legend seems to have a life of its own, although perhaps influenced somewhat by reports of similar incidents in real life.

References: *Baby Train,* 131–133; Barbara Mikkleson, "The Body in the Bed," *FOAFtale News* 43 (1988), 15–16; *Too Good,* 266–268.

"The Body on the Car"

A man drives home dead drunk in the wee hours of the morning. Despite his condition, he manages to park in the driveway and stumble into his house, where he immediately falls asleep. A few hours later he is awakened by his wife's screaming. She had gone out for the morning newspaper and found the body of a young girl embedded on the front grill of the car.

When this story was printed in a 1986 Ann Landers column it unleashed a flood of letters, both to the advice columnist and to folklorists, from people in the United States, Canada, and Europe who had heard the same story with differing details in their own hometowns. "The Body on the Car" is sometimes told as a cautionary tale at meetings of Mothers Against Drunk Driving and Students Against Drunk Driving, although neither group, when queried, could furnish an exact reference to when and where the incident occurred.

Prototypes for the anonymous story have circulated since the 1950s, and similar well-documented incidents can be found in news reports from as early as the 1930s. The modern legend would seem to combine elements of truth (actual hit-and-run accidents) with fantasy (the dramatic way in which the tragedy is revealed).

A similar legend is told about ships: An ocean liner, navy ship, or freighter supposedly struck a small sailboat without anyone on the larger ship noticing until the huge vessel has come into port and the smaller boat was found stuck to the front.

References: *Baby Train*, 22–23; *Curses!*, 92–95; *Too Good*, 110–111.

Bogus Warnings

Anonymous fliers—handwritten, typed, photocopied, and sometimes even professionally printed—sometimes warn in a sensational, alarmist style of some kind of danger, threat, conspiracy, or little-known opportunity. These bogus warnings are handed from person to person, posted on bulletin boards, sent out as company memos, and circulated in the mail; often they find their way into print, and nowadays they also spread on the Internet. Some well-meaning organizations that have sent out bogus warnings are churches, schools, scout troops, lodges, companies, and even military units.

Typical subjects of bogus warnings are crimes (especially drug crimes), computer viruses, and dishonest dealings by companies or government. What makes these warnings "bogus" is the lack of specific verifiable information either about the nature of the supposed danger or the source of the warning notice. Although there may be a hint of an official source (e.g., "We have been informed . . ." or "Authorities have noted . . ."), more detailed information is lacking. When, occasionally, a specific name or address is given, it invariably either turns out to be equally bogus or else the source given denies having issued the warning. When references are made to "proof" having been broadcast on a TV program such as *Oprah, 20/20,* or *60 Minutes,* a check with these sources proves otherwise; no such exposé was ever aired.

The style and format of bogus warnings certainly do not suggest that of an official source, such as the police or other government agency. The fliers are characterized by lavish use of capital letters and exclamation points, as well as numerous errors of spelling and punctuation. Often people recirculating a bogus warning will add a handwritten comment such as "PLEASE CIRCULATE!!!" or 'THIS IS NOT A JOKE!!!" Some bogus warning fliers include a suggested action on the part of readers—to boycott products, sign a petition, submit a claim, and so on.

Although most bogus warnings do not qualify technically as legends, since they are not orally transmitted and do not have a strong narrative element, they are similar to urban legends in being anonymous, stereotyped, bizarre or frightening, and subject to some variation.

See also "Blue Star Acid"; "The Good Times Virus"; "The Kidney Heist"; "Lights Out!"; "The Madalyn Murray O'Hair Petition"; Needle-Attack Legends; "The Procter & Gamble Trademark"; "The Stuffed Baby"; "The Veterans' Insurance Dividend"; "The Welded Contacts"; Xeroxlore

References: *Too Good*, 385–410.

"The Bosom Serpent"

Nathaniel Hawthorne used this phrase in a short story published in 1843 ("Egotism, or, the Bosom Serpent") referring to traditional legends in which a snake gets inside a person's body, usually through the mouth. Modern folklorists have adopted the term not only for snake-ingestion stories but also as a generalized reference to other legends in which living creatures enter the human body.

In the older European bosom-serpent legends especially well known in Ireland, a snake or snake eggs were either swallowed when a person drank from a stream or pond, or else the snake crept into the open mouth of a sleeping person. Often the creature was lured out by having the victim starve himself, then lie down with his mouth open near a bowl of milk. Milk was thought to attract snakes, although snakes in reality are carnivores with no particular fondness for milk.

"The Snake in the Strawberry Patch" is the clearest modern descendant of bosom-serpent legends. Other stories of body invasion focus on such creatures as ants, earwigs, frogs, and spiders. In urban legends on these topics, usually the creatures have to be removed surgically, but sometimes they depart on their own or even burst from the skin in the manner of the creature in the sci-fi horror film series *Alien*. (The Pop Rocks legend, al-

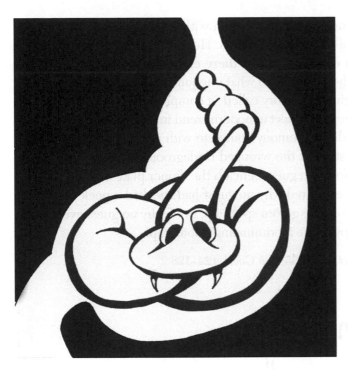

though about chemicals and not creatures, also features this bursting motif.)

Some analysts have suggested that bosom-serpent legends may represent pregnancy fears or fantasies, and, indeed, there is an urban legend about a female swimmer swallowing male sperm in a swimming pool and becoming pregnant.

See also Ants or Termites Invade the Body; Earwig Stories; Octopus Eggs Impregnate Swimmer; "Sperm in the Swimming Pool"; "The Spider Bite"; Tapeworms in Diet Pills

References: Daniel R. Barnes, "The Bosom Serpent: A Legend in American Literature and Culture," *Journal of American Folklore* 85 (1972): 111–122; *Choking Doberman,* 106–112; Richard C. Poulsen, "Bosom Serpentry Among the Puritans and Mormons," *Journal of the Folklore Institute* 16 (1979): 176–189.

"The Bothered Bride"

At a large, beautiful, and expensive society wedding, just before the final vows are taken, the bride turns to face her guests and makes a speech thanking everyone—her parents, her guests, her attendants, and so on. Then she turns to the groom and says that she wants to thank him "for sleeping with my maid-of-honor last night." She shoves her bouquet into the face of one of the traitors and departs the church.

In the late 1980s this story was widely reported from all across the United States and attributed to a variety of groups (Italian, Polish, Irish, Jewish, etc.). Anecdotal accounts appeared in print, and elaborated versions were published in tabloids. But no eyewitnesses came forward to verify the incident; neither could investigative journalists discover a source.

A "Grumbling Groom" variation of the legend appeared in the early 1990s. At the reception following his wedding, a bridegroom stands and announces that he is going on the honeymoon without his wife and that the wedding will be annulled when he returns. He tells the guests to look under their plates for an explanation, and there each one finds a photograph of the bride with the best man in what one journalist trying unsuccessfully to track the origin of the story called "a compromising position."

Both of these stories seem to reflect a modern trend for couples to compose a personalized wedding ceremony complete with original speeches by the participants. The story of the wronged bridegroom alludes to the custom of hiding a favor for each guest beneath the dinner plate at the reception. (No explanation is offered why no guest had sneaked a peek beneath his or her plate before the groom spoke up, or of why no guest ever seems to have saved a copy of the incriminating photograph.)

References: *Mexican Pet,* 134–135; *Too Good,* 124–128.

"The Boy Who Played Superman"

After viewing a Superman movie or TV program, a young boy ties a towel or curtain around his neck as a cape and jumps from a high place, believing he can fly like his hero Superman. Other such "Flights of Fancy" stories are told about children trying to fly like Mary Poppins or to demonstrate tremendous strength like Popeye.

Told by some people to demonstrate that comic books may lead to harm for suggestible children, such stories cannot usually be verified. Often the tales turn out to be merely a parent's guess about why a child dropped from a high place, or else they are misremembered news stories that do not quite match the legend.

References: *Baby Train,* 65–67.

"The Boyfriend's Death"

A young couple on a date are parked in a dark, lonely lovers' lane. When they are ready to drive home, the car will not start. The boy says he will walk back to the main highway to seek help, and his girlfriend should lock the door and wait inside the car. When her boyfriend does not return for a long time, the girl panics. She sees strange shadows moving across the windshield and hears a scratching noise on the roof. She cowers in the car all night while the frightening sights and sounds continue.

At dawn she hears someone coming and looks out to see a state police trooper who beckons her to leave the car and then starts to lead her away, cautioning her not to look back. But she *does* look back, and there is her boyfriend's lifeless body hanging upside down from a tree branch over the car, his fingernails scratching on the roof and his blood running down the windshield. Sometimes it is said that her hair turned white from the shock.

This classic teenage horror story was first collected in the United States in the early 1960s. Some versions emphasize the girl's passive role by mentioning that she could not walk with her boyfriend because her high-heeled shoes were unsuitable. Sometimes the radio-warning motif characteristic of "The Hook" may be included, or the killer may be described as "the hookman." A version collected from Navajo children suggests that the killer may have been a skinwalker, one of the traditional monsters of their folklore.

Tellers of "The Boyfriend's Death" often localize the setting and then embellish the tale with details of the scary sounds of scraping, scratching, knocking, and dripping as well as the sights of ghostly shadows, reflections, and the like. It is a favorite legend to tell at campfires, slumber parties, and similar social scenes. The legend migrated to Europe, where a characteristic detail is that the killer has decapitated the boyfriend and is sitting on top of the car bouncing the head on the roof.

Like Lot's wife in the Biblical story of Sodom and Gomorrah, or like Orpheus leaving the underworld in the Greek myth, when told not to look back the girlfriend disobeys. Invariably in folk narratives of all kinds, taboos are broken.

See also Freudian Approach

References: *Too Good*, 103–104; *Vanishing Hitchhiker*, 5–10.

"Bozo the Clown's Blooper"

The blooper in this story is an obscenity, or another impolite expression, blurted out during a live broadcast of the *Bozo the Clown* children's TV program. Usually it is said that a child from the audience participating in some kind of game or contest of skill bungles the task and then swears. When the clown tells the child that what he said was a "Bozo no-no," the child snaps, "Cram it, clown!" or some other rude comeback.

A less common version of the story has either the clown or one of the program's other adult figures caught by a live microphone at the end of the program saying something like, "That ought to hold the little bastards for another day."

These two blooper legends in several variations have been attributed to most of the many *Bozo* shows produced all across the United States, as well as to several other children's TV series. Some people claim to have witnessed the incident themselves, but all persons involved in creating and airing such programs—especially the Bozo players themselves—have denied that the incident occurred. Nobody has yet produced a videotape to prove otherwise.

The "little bastards" version of the blooper story clearly derives from a story about "Uncle Don," the longtime host of a children's radio program, but this version, too, has been stoutly denied and never proven authentic. Both expressions—"Ram it [Cram it], clown" and "That ought to hold the little bastards"—circulate apart from the legends as catch phrases that people sometimes apply, proverb-like, to specific situations in their own lives.

See also "Uncle Don's Blooper"

References: *Mexican Pet*, 184–185; *Too Good*, 328–329; *The Truth*, 84–94.

"The Brain Drain"

On a very hot day, on her way into a supermarket from the parking lot, a woman notices another woman bent over the steering wheel of her car holding one hand up to the back of her head. Vaguely upset by the sight, she checks that car again on her way out with her groceries and sees that the woman is still in the same posture. So she taps on the window and asks if she needs help.

The woman in the car—still bent forward, still with one hand on the back of her head—gasps, "Call 911! I've been shot in the head and my brains are coming out!" Sure enough, a gray, viscous substance is oozing out between her fingers. The other woman rushes back into the store to summon help and to call 911.

While the police, store manager, and paramedics crowd around the car, one of the emergency workers opens the door and very carefully pries the woman's fingers apart. Then he looks up and laughs: A can of Pillsbury Poppin' Fresh biscuit dough in the woman's grocery bag on the backseat of her car has exploded in the heat. The can's lid and the top biscuit in the can had struck her on the back of the head.

In some versions the rescuers check the woman's grocery receipt and discover that she had sat in the hot car for half an hour awaiting help. Sometimes the manager gives her a new can of biscuit dough. Other variants describe the "shooting" as taking place while the woman is driving home, and she pulls over to the roadside in panic where she is helped by a passing motorist.

"The Brain Drain" (or "Biscuit Bullet") legend was known in the winter of 1994, but it emerged as an extremely popular American urban legend only in the early summer of 1995, which proved to be a record-breaking hot season. By late fall the story had faded away except for a "joke" version that circulated on the Internet for a few months longer. In its heyday "The Brain Drain" was written up by numerous newspaper columnists, and it was adopted and retold as a supposed true family story by the comedian Brett Butler.

Despite the modern references and suggestions of the legend, such as fear of random urban crime, a well-known commercial product, and even the hot weather of 1995, "The Brain Drain" has some traditional folkloric prototypes. Two general motifs of older tales are obvious: Motif J1820 (*Inappropriate action from misunderstanding*) and Motif X1630 (*Lies about hot weather*). More specifically, there is a tall tale about popcorn exploding in a hot field, making a nearby mule think it is snowing, so it freezes to death.

Among European folktales is an animal tale—Tale Type 4—in which a fox puts some dough on its head and fools the wolf into thinking his brains are coming out. More likely to be a direct ancestor of "The Brain Drain," however, is a cycle of Anglo-American stories about a person stealing butter by concealing it under his hat. When the butter melts, it runs out and incriminates the thief. Mark Twain used this story in *Adventures of Huckleberry Finn* (1885) when he described Huck trying the trick. Aunt Sally jumps to the wrong conclusion, saying, "For the land's sake what is the matter with the child!—he's got the brain fever as shore as you're born, and they're oozing out!"

Americans telling the contemporary legend, however, have none of this folkloric background consciously in mind. Instead, their tellings reflect fear of urban crime that is allayed by comic relief when the real reason for the situation is revealed. Also there is a definite sense of domestic failure on the part of the stricken woman who not only foolishly jumps to the wrong conclusion but is clearly unable to bake "real" biscuits and must rely on a prepared mix. This last theme is especially strong in versions collected in the South, where "biscuits from scratch" are a strong regional tradition. Southern humorist Lewis Grizzard wrote about what he called "whomp biscuits" from a can: As he put it, "Whomp! Another poor man is being denied homemade biscuits. No wonder the divorce rate is so high."

References: *Too Good,* 28–29; *The Truth,* 23–37.

Bubble Yum

See "Spider Eggs in Bubble Yum"

"A Bug in the Ear"

See Earwig Stories

"The Bug Under the Rug"

An American couple traveling in the communist Soviet Union check into a hotel in Moscow. Although the hour is late, they search the room for listening devices, wary of Russian security and the possibility of being spied upon. Spotting a lump in the middle of the floor, they roll back the carpet and find a metal plate screwed to the floor. They remove the screws, replace the rug, and retire for the night.

The next morning as they are checking out, the desk clerk asks if they slept well. "Yes," they tell him, "Just fine."

"I am happy to hear this," says the clerk, "because the couple in the room just below yours complained of having a terrible night."

"What was the problem?" asks the American couple.

"The chandelier fell on them late last night."

This is sometimes told about an American diplomat or other official assigned to Moscow. Before this glasnost-era version of the story circulated in 1989–1990, the same incident was told in 1972 about Canadian professional hockey players touring in the Soviet Union, and before that "The Bug Under the Rug" was told in the United States as a story about a honeymoon couple fearful that their friends may have bugged their hotel room.

References: *Choking Doberman*, 94–95; *Too Good*, 45–46.

"The Bullet Baby"

A 1982 letter published in the "Dear Abby" advice column stated the following:

> It seems that during the Civil War (May 12, 1863, to be exact), a young Virginia farm girl was standing on her front porch while a battle was raging nearby. A stray bullet first passed through the scrotum of a young Union cavalryman, then lodged in the reproductive tract of the young woman, who thus became pregnant by a man she had not been within 100 feet of! And nine months later she gave birth to a healthy baby!

The person who sent the above virgin-birth account to "Dear Abby" cited a 1971 article in the "very reliable" magazine *American Heritage*. Indeed, "The Bullet Baby" did appear there, but it was merely the latest of a long series of retellings and variations of a hoax story that was first published in an 1874 medical journal.

The original source—allegedly a firsthand account—was written by a field surgeon who set the incident in Mississippi (not Virginia) and said that it happened to a Rebel (not a Union) soldier. He also claimed that the minié ball that had carried the man's sperm and caused the pregnancy was later found lodged in the scrotum of the baby boy, and that when the truth about the pregnancy was thus discovered the young woman married the soldier who had inadvertently fathered her first child.

This story gained wide circulation after appearing in an 1896 book, *Anomalies and Curiosities of Medicine,* even though the compilers of this peculiar volume had footnoted "The Bullet Baby" as "a curious example from the realms of imagination in medicine." Writers continued to credit the story, and it was repeated by those who read it until it finally received a scholarly debunking in 1981.

Actually, it had been clear almost from the start that "The Bullet Baby" was a hoax. Two weeks after its original publication in 1874, the editor of the medical journal admitted in a brief published note that the story had been sent to him anonymously as a joke. But recognizing the handwriting of the hoaxer, he turned the tables on the doctor who had sent it by publishing the story verbatim just as he had received it.

References: James O. Breeden, "'The Case of the Miraculous Bullet' Revisited," *Military Affairs*, vol. 45, no. 1 (February 1981): 23–26; *Choking Doberman*, 134–138; *Too Good*, 469–472.

"The Bump in the Rug"

A carpet-layer has just finished installing wall-to-wall carpeting in a home, but as he is standing back admiring the job and patting his pockets looking for his packet of cigarettes, he notices a lump in the middle of the floor. He does not find the cigarettes in his pocket, so he concludes that he must have dropped them while he was working and rolled the new carpet right over them.

He is not about to remove the new carpet just for a packet of cigarettes, so he takes a hammer from his tool box and pounds down the lump, neatly flattening it. As he puts his tools into his truck, he notices his cigarettes lying there on the dashboard. Just then the lady of the house comes out and asks, "Did you by any chance see my parakeet while you were working? It got out of its cage again."

Sometimes the missing pet is a hamster or gerbil. This story has been told among American carpet-layers and home decorators since at least the 1950s. A version appeared in *Reader's Digest* in 1964 and in *People* in 1990. "The Bump in the Rug" is also told in England, and probably in other countries as well.

References: *Choking Doberman*, 93–94; *Too Good*, 357–358.

"The Bungled Rescue of the Cat"

During a British firemen's strike in 1978, when the army took over fire-fighting duties, an elderly London woman requested help to get her cat out of a tree. An army unit responded and rescued the cat, using a ladder truck. The grateful pet owner invited the men in for a cup of tea, but driving off afterward in their truck they ran over the cat and killed it.

A firemen's strike did occur that year, and the bungled rescue was reported as a true incident, although never with any further identifications than "an elderly London woman" and "an army unit." Variations of the story continue to be told and published both in Great Britain and the United States; sometimes the bungling rescuers are members of the regular fire department. Thus this story has joined the ranks of dead-cat urban legends, whether its original source was a real occurrence or not. A similar accident is described in the legend about a mother rushing to take an injured child to the emergency room who backs her car over a second child playing in the driveway.

References: *Curses!*, 163–165; *Too Good*, 361–362.

Bungling Brides

A husband sees his new wife cutting a roast or a ham in half—or removing the drumsticks from a turkey—before roasting. He asks her why she does this and is told that this is how her mother always prepared such meats for roasting. Curious, the husband asks his mother-in-law about this; she explains that she simply never owned a pan large enough to accommodate a whole roast, ham, or large turkey. Variations on the theme include the bride misunderstanding the direction "leave room to rise" in a biscuit recipe or attaching small cotton balls to her screen door to repel flies (her mother had used cotton from pill bottles to plug holes in her screen door).

Although the helpless or naive bride is an outdated and sexist stereotype, such stories continue to be told, sometimes as an example of either the power of habit or of the need to question all traditions in order to learn their true sources and meanings.

References: *Curses!*, 191–192; *Too Good*, 146–147.

"Buried Saint Sells Property"

If a small plastic statue of Saint Joseph, patron saint of families and households, is buried in the yard, a home or other real estate offered for sale will soon attract a buyer. People disagree whether the statue should be buried right side up or upside down, which way the statue should be facing, whether in the front yard or back, whether close to or far from the "For Sale" sign, and whether the saint's statue should be dug up after the property is sold. (Some insist that the statue should be disinterred, cleaned, and displayed prominently in the sellers' new home.)

Starting in 1990, descriptions of this practice have circulated among property owners and real-estate agents and are also reflected in the steady sales of small, inexpensive St. Joseph statues in religious supply stores or through catalogs of home and garden products. Some people claim an ancient European origin for the practice, but this has not been verified. Catholic Church spokespersons consistently deny that there is any official church dogma resembling this practice.

References: *Baby Train,* 181–184; *Too Good,* 246–247.

Business Legends

Companies and corporations are frequent targets of rumors and legends—generally negative ones—that are sometimes also called "mercantile legends." These false claims tend to gravitate toward the largest firms or those with the major market share for their products. Thus the "Goliath effect," as Gary Alan Fine has labeled it, leads to most soft-drink stories focusing on Coca-Cola, to much pizza-company lore mentioning Domino's Pizza, to many computer virus rumors naming Microsoft, and so forth.

Claims of contamination are perhaps the most common theme in business-related urban legends, particularly regarding fast-food franchises. For example, McDonald's hamburgers were whispered to contain worms or kangaroo meat; Kentucky Fried Chicken suffered from the story that someone had been served a batter-fried rat; Church's fried chicken was said to have been laced with a chemical that rendered black males sterile; Bubble Yum supposedly contained spider eggs, to mention but a few such stories. Possibly the oldest such contamination story to plague a major company is the mouse-in-the-Coke legend that has been traced back to 1914 as an actual similar case; however, oral versions of the story with stereotyped plots and invented details became common only in the 1970s.

Other negative lore about businesses includes stories of a company charging an outrageous price for a "secret recipe," rumors of anticonsumer decisions at the corporate level, and tales of companies mistreating or deceiving their own employees. It must be admitted that many of the negative themes in business legends have some basis in fact throughout the history of commerce, but often the specific details of such shocking accounts cannot be proven and seem obviously to have been exaggerated or expanded via traditional folkloric patterns and motifs.

It is no mystery why there are few urban legends about the *positive* contributions of business to society. Clearly, there would be little suspense or humor in a story about a company's generous contributions to charity or its research and development programs producing some useful new products. Even when modern rumors and legends touch on such topics, there are inevitable apocryphal negative elements, such as the claim that a groundbreaking new product, like an amazing gas-miser automobile, was suppressed by powerful corporations (in this case, oil companies) that would stand to lose sales from the innovation.

A few legends do claim that a certain company will provide some valuable benefit or prize in return for a particular kind of wrapper or other packaging, or simply for registering with the company; such claims have circulated about Tootsie Pops candies and Gerber's baby food, among other products. The idea of collecting tabs from aluminum cans in order to redeem them for free time on a kidney dialysis machine is a similar concept.

See also "The Bedbug Letter"; Contamination; "Don't Mess with Texas"; "The Economical Car"; "Find the Hat"; "The Jewish Secret Tax"; Mercantile Legends; "The Mrs. Fields Cookie Recipe"; "Neiman Marcus Cookies"; "The Procter & Gamble Trademark"; "Red Velvet Cake"; Rolls-Royce Legends; "The Wife on the Flight"

> **References:** Fine, *Manufacturing Tales;* Koenig, *Rumor in the Marketplace; Too Good,* 251–268.

"The Butcher's Prank"

A fun-loving butcher arranges a wiener, a sausage, or a cow's udder inside his pants so that about two inches protrudes through his unzipped fly. When a customer discreetly calls attention to the supposed dangling appendage, the butcher says, "Oh, is that darn thing hanging out again?"

and then slices it off with a meat cleaver. The customer faints, sometimes even dying from the fall or from a heart attack.

Several older Americans remember this as an actual prank dating from about 1915 up to the 1930s, and it was reported in much the same detail in a 1931 book about life in France. Another European version occurs in a Czech film from the 1960s, *Closely Watched Trains*. Although pranks and hoaxes themselves are a form of folklore, "The Butcher's Prank" entered legend tradition when people elaborated upon the incident in retelling it. A claim that the story once appeared in *Reader's Digest* has not been verified, and this may also be part of a folk tradition. This story (obviously) and others reflect castration anxiety.

References: *Baby Train*, 47–49.

"Buying Tampax"

A woman checking out at a supermarket has a large box of Tampax tampons among her purchases, but there is no price sticker on the box. The clerk asks over the store loudspeaker for "a price check on super-size Tampax on aisle four." The customer is embarrassed enough at this attention directed at her, but then a stock clerk asks, again on the loudspeaker, "Do you want the kind you push in with your finger or the kind you pound in with a hammer?" The checkout clerk and other customers start laughing, and the woman runs from the store without paying for or taking her groceries. A few minutes later the stock clerk's voice again comes over the loudspeaker, "What happened to that price check you wanted on thumbtacks?"

Often repeated as a legend and sometimes enacted in stores, possibly as a prank by clerks, this story is sometimes told during training sessions for new employees. Despite the virtual replacement of price tags in supermarkets with printed product codes and automated checkout, the Tampax/thumbtacks story continues to circulate, evidence of the uneasiness some people feel about bodily functions associated with gender.

References: *Choking Doberman,* 138; *Too Good,* 155–156.

"The Cabbage Patch Tragedy"

When a child's Cabbage Patch Kids doll is damaged (chewed on by a dog, left out in a storm, run through the washer, etc.) the parents send it back to the factory for repair. Instead of repairing or replacing the doll, the manufacturer sends something like a death certificate, a bill for the funeral, or a citation for child abuse.

This short-lived legend was encouraged by the fact that the hottest toys of the 1983 and 1984 Christmas seasons were soft dolls that came complete with adoption papers from "BabyLand General Hospital." The logical extension of this sales ploy was that if a doll had documentation of its "birth" then similar papers should be produced for its "death." Although no death-related items really existed, according to news stories of 1985, there were actually summer camps

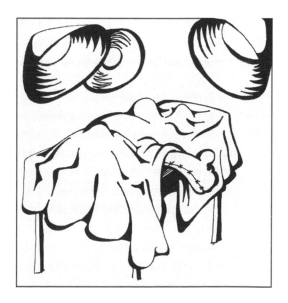

for Cabbage Patch Kids as well as a Canadian dentist offering to fix their (nonexistent) teeth. Neither activity was endorsed by the doll's manufacturers, Coleco Industries.

References: *Mexican Pet,* 74–75; *Too Good,* 268.

Cadavers

The need to dissect human corpses in order for medical students to learn anatomy has led to hoaxes, pranks, jokes, and legends common among doctors-in-training. Many of these items involve the amputation of a limb, or even of a penis, and prankish use of this appendage. The most developed cadaver narrative tells of a medical student discovering that the body assigned to him or her for dissection is that of a recently deceased relative.

See also "The Relative's Cadaver"; Toll-Booth Pranks.

Campus Rumor Scares

Repeatedly at American universities rumors have spread that a psychic predicted that a mass murderer will strike on campus soon or at a particular date, often Halloween. Allegedly, the warning came during a popular TV talk show, often *Geraldo, Donahue,* or especially *Oprah.* Talk-show spokespersons insist that no such prediction was ever made on their programs, and university officials, although cautioning student alertness, regard the rumors as hoaxes. Newspaper investigations consistently fail to find any evidence either of such predictions or of the rumors proving true.

Campus scare rumors are usually quite specific, but their details often fit more than one university. For example, the murders are claimed to be predicted for a dormitory that is built at the highest—or *lowest*—spot on campus; the site may also be described as "very, very flat," or near a river, a pond, a graveyard, or a hill. The building is often described as shaped like a letter—*L, T, X,* or *U,* for example—rather common designs of campus housing. The actual floor of the dormitory where the murders would occur is also mentioned, but usually it is a low number (two to four) that could probably include about 90 percent of resident halls on American college campuses.

When the murders are predicted for Halloween night, usually the disguise of the killer is included in the story. The most common such detail is that the crimes will be committed by someone dressed as Little Bo Peep. The name of the targeted institution may be hinted at by reference to a certain letter that supposedly begins its name. When five people were shot to death at the University of Iowa on November 1, 1991, some people remembered a prediction that murders would occur on a campus in a state that began and ended with a vowel, but actually no such stories had circulated concerning Iowa.

Students hearing and spreading such rumors tend to remember any instances of actual campus crimes, straining to fit them into the pattern of the stories they've heard, and they tend to forget that the vast majority of such predictions are failures. Commenting on this typical rationalization, folklorist Edward D. Ives of the University of Maine said in 1991, "That's about like predicting that California will fall into the sea tomorrow and then pointing out after the fact that there had been a bad rockslide near Big Sur that day."

Autumn 1991 was a peak year for campus rumor scares in the Northeast, and a similar series of stories circulated widely at schools in the South and Midwest in 1988. But in virtually every year during the 1980s and 1990s, and even in some years earlier, such stories have run rampant at American institutions of higher learning. One further example: A news item in the *Detroit Free Press* published on October 30, 1998, was headlined "Halloween massacre story haunts MSU, U-M" (referring to Michigan State University and the University of Michigan).

References: *Baby Train*, 116–119.

"The Can of Snakes"

Two fishermen walking along a stream pass a little boy who is fishing with a pole, hook, line, and bobber; he has a tin can of worms next to him. The men ask, "How are they biting?" and the boy replies, "The fish aren't biting so well, but my worms sure are." The men chuckle at this odd answer, but returning later in the day they find the boy dead on the river bank. His worm can turns out to be full of baby rattlesnakes (copperheads, water moccasins, etc.), which had bitten him to death.

Although more of a rural than an urban legend in its setting, "The Can of Snakes" continues to be told in contemporary contexts. The story is related to other "bed of snakes" lore circulated especially in the South and Midwest and often involving swimmers and water skiers rather than fishermen.

See also "The Hapless Water-skier"

References: *Mexican Pet,* 28.

Canada

Canada has a long history of rich collections and analysis of diverse forms of folklore from native peoples, Canadiens (French Canadians), Anglo Canadians, and many ethnic minorities. But urban legends were relatively late to be recognized by Canadian folklorists, and the amount of material accumulated so far is relatively small considering the size and the academic interest there.

The first folklorist to call attention to Canadian urban legends was Edith Fowke of York University, Toronto, who published a few such stories collected in 1973 by her student Susan Smith in *Folklore of Canada* (1976). Smith's texts came from teenagers in Toronto and its suburbs and included familiar legends such as "The Hook," "The Boyfriend's Death," and "The Baby-sitter and the Man Upstairs." Besides Smith's version of "The Vanishing Hitchhiker," Fowke included another Toronto example collected in 1985 in her *Tales Told in Canada* (1986). Beyond Ontario where Fowke worked, Kay Stone at the University of Winnipeg, Manitoba, encouraged her students to collect urban legends; some texts collected by Judy Wagner appeared in Stone's *Prairie Folklore* (1976).

The predominance of horror stories in these collections led Fowke to describe urban legends in her 1988 survey *Canadian Folklore* as "rather gruesome accounts of misadventures or strange happenings . . . usually told as true [and] said to have happened to someone in the vicinity." Fowke conceded that most of these legends were "known all over North America and some in other parts of the world as well." Indeed, it is hard to find any particularly "Canadian" aspects of most of these texts, beyond the occasional mention of a local place-name or institution. For example, the hookman is said to lurk "at Lover's Lane near Midland, Ontario," and the baby-sitter's near-murder occurred to a girl who was "in Montreal baby-sitting for three children in a big house." More typically, a Toronto version of "The Vanishing Hitchhiker" is said to have happened merely to "one of my girlfriend's best friends and her father."

However, there are a few contemporary legends that seem to have distinctive Canadian roots, or at least branches. The "Not My Dog" story, for example, now well known in North America and even England, was first published by Lucy Maud Montgomery (author of *Anne of Green Gables*) in her 1924 children's book *Emily Climbs*. It's likely that Montgomery was repeating a story told on her native Prince Edward Island in eastern Canada. A story from Alberta in western Canada, "The Lost Wreck," as reported in a 1985 newspaper article seems to be derived from a nineteenth-century Norwegian legend that may have been carried to Canada by immigrants. Although a Canadian version of "The Arrest" seems identical to versions collected in the United States, the horrendous "Drug-Smuggling Legend" includes specific details about a border-crossing near Fargo, North Dakota. (Similarly, some Canadian versions of "The Runaway Grandmother" set the scene at the Canada-U.S. border.)

Modern mercantile legends seem to spread in Canada as well as the United States, although the evidence is slim. Writer John Robert Colombo heard a version of "The Wife on the Flight" in 1970 from a Toronto businessman who had heard it on a business trip to the United States. Later Colombo heard the story repeated on Canadian radio programs. Similarly, "The Bedbug Letter" was told on a Canadian Broadcasting Corporation program heard in western New York in November 1991. Perhaps the most distinctively Canadian urban legend collected so far is "Stopping the Detroit Car," as reported in *Curses! Broiled Again!* (pp. 112–113). When Royal Canadian Mounted Police near Windsor, Ontario, stop a large luxury car with a Michigan license plate to warn of a minor infraction (such as a burned-out headlight), the occupants, four large men in dark suits, immediately get out, lean over the hood of the car, and spread their legs for the expected search. The story emphasizes the Canadians' image of organized criminals from the United States.

In recent years, the international study of urban legends has become centered in Canada, specifically at Memorial University of Newfoundland (MUN), in St. Johns. Paul Smith, founder of the "Perspectives on Contemporary Legend" conferences that began at the University of Sheffield, England, in 1982, joined the faculty of the MUN Department of Folklore in 1990. The legend conferences had spawned the International Society for Contemporary Legend Research (ISCLR) in 1988 with Smith as its first president, and Smith began editing *Contemporary Legend,* the ISCLR yearbook, with the first volume appearing in 1991.

A colleague at MUN, Philip Hiscock, became editor of the ISCLR newsletter, *FOAFtale News,* in 1994. The seventeenth international conference on contemporary legends convened at MUN in St. Johns in May 1999.

A unique, detailed analysis of Canadian contemporary legends is under way by MUN's Diane E. Goldstein. In a preliminary report published in 1992, she discussed how the Newfoundland welcome-to-the-world-of-AIDS legends reveal "the complex culture of Newfoundlanders . . . a world of trust in home and trust in your own . . . a world that alters foreign messages that don't make sense and that creates local ones which do." Meanwhile at the University of Western Ontario, London, Michael P. Carroll has done a series of Freudian analyses of urban legends, including "The Hook" and "Alligators in the Sewers," but most of his materials are not drawn specifically from Canadian tradition.

References: Michael P. Carroll, "Alligators in the Sewer, Dragons in the Well, and Freud in the Toilet," *Sociological Review* 32 (1984): 57–74; Diane E. Goldstein, "Welcome to the Mainland, Welcome to the World of AIDS: Cultural Viability, Localization, and Contemporary Legend," *Contemporary Legend* 2 (1992): 23–40.

"Car Stolen During Earthquake"

As told in a letter from San Francisco:

A couple, supposedly friends of my friend's boss, drove to the World Series game on October 17th [1989] in their brand new white BMW. The car had "500 miles on it, max." They parked in the Candlestick Park lot—in an out-of-the-way spot so their new car would not get scratched. They took their seats for the game, the earthquake hit, the game was cancelled and everybody cleared out of Candlestick Park fast—except these people. They figured that with all the commotion and panic, it would be safer for their car if they waited until everybody else had left and then drove away in peace and safety. When they finally straggled out to the lot, their car was gone!

They made a report to the police, filled in all the insurance forms, etc. They were surprised not to hear anything further about their car. It wasn't

found; it wasn't seen; they heard nothing at all from the police. Weeks later, finally, they got a call. Their car had been found—under the collapsed Nimitz Freeway, with someone inside, crushed beyond recognition.
Whew!

In another version, the car was a new Porsche and the owners found out what had happened when a policeman showed up at their front door holding their license plate.

This account, sent to me in January 1990 by Barbara Bernstein of San Francisco, is typical of the car-theft stories circulated in Northern California following the disastrous earthquake of October 17, 1989. In its style this written version echoes the oral tradition, complete with a reference to variation. Others telling the story mentioned different makes and models of luxury cars, different locations of the smashed car, or else specified that the thief was supposedly a member of a racial minority. Journalists in the region investigated possible sources for the incident and concluded that "Urban Pancake" (as one writer dubbed the tale) was fictional.

References: *Baby Train*, 146–148; *Too Good*, 85–86.

"Career Decisions"

A country boy, down on his luck in a big city, is refused a job as bookkeeper in a brothel when it is learned that he is illiterate. Feeling sorry for him, the house's madam gives him two red apples. The boy places them on top of a trash can while tying his shoe, and a stranger comes by and buys them. The boy buys more apples, sells them, and eventually parlays his sales into ownership of a grocery store, then of a whole chain of stores. Late in life, a rich man, he is honored as businessman of the year; then a journalist discovers that the man is still illiterate. "Sir," he asks, "what do you think you might have become if you could read and write?" The man answers, "I guess I would have been a bookkeeper in a whorehouse."

Readers of W. Somerset Maugham will recognize this as a variation of the plot of Maugham's 1929 short story "The Verger" (the title referring to the British term for a church caretaker). In Maugham's version, the protagonist is fired by the vicar of his church when it is discovered that he is illiterate. After a series of lucky breaks he becomes owner of a string of fashionable shops in London, and he tells a reporter that had he been able to read and write "I'd be verger of St. Peter's, Neville Square."

Confronted with a similar plot in another work, Maugham explained that the story was "a well known bit of Jewish folklore," and indeed, Sigmund Freud told yet another traditional version in which an illiterate Jewish man becomes an oil magnate, whereas had he been able to read and write he might have become "schammes in Rzezow."

Different "Career Decision" stories are told about other professions. For example, a football coach is said to recruit players by touring the countryside and asking farm boys whom he sees plowing behind a horse which way to the university. If the boy lifts the plow to point, the coach signs him up for an athletic scholarship. Although this story was told about Bronko Nagurski among other American football greats, the basic plot goes back to European stories dealing with recruiting soldiers for the czar's, king's, or emperor's army.

All such stories appeal to people because of the often accidental nature of their own real-life career decisions or their college majors, job changes, and the like. A related category of personal anecdote is "How I Met My Partner or Spouse," a sure-fire conversation-starter in any group of couples.

References: *Baby Train*, 155–157; Elliott Oring, *The Jokes of Sigmund Freud: A Study in Humor and Jewish Identity* (Philadelphia: University of Pennsylvania Press, 1984), 55.

"The Castrated Boy"

See "The Mutilated Boy"

"The Cat (or Dog) and the Nude Man"

One way or another, a man who happens to be naked has an encounter with the family's pet dog or cat that startles him, causing a painful "hilarious accident." Sometimes the man is taking a shower when his wife screams to him that the water heater (or kitchen sink) has suddenly sprung a huge leak.

Without stopping to get dressed, the man comes running and gets down on his hands and knees trying to shut off the water. His dog cold-noses him in the rear end (or his cat paws his testicles), causing the man to jump up and bang his head hard enough to knock himself out. Paramedics are summoned, and when they hear how the man was injured they laugh so hard they drop the stretcher on which they are carrying him.

Often this story begins with a reference to an outdoor plant or a living Christmas tree being brought inside a home. When a snake crawls out of the flowerpot or the root ball, the wife screams so loudly that the man comes running from the shower. He gets down on his hands and knees to search for the snake under the kitchen sink, behind the sofa, or the like. Sometimes the wife spots the snake a second time and screams again, just in time to startle the paramedics who, of course, drop the stretcher. Alternatively, the paramedics themselves are startled by the snake.

Both themes—nudity and laughing or careless paramedics—as well as dogs, cats, and snakes are found in several other urban legends.

References: *Choking Doberman*, 220–221; *Mexican Pet*, 114–116; *Too Good*, 364–365.

"The Cat in the Package"

See "The Dead Cat in the Package"

Celebrities

Not to be confused with deliberate promotion and gossip about celebrities—often concocted by publicists and typically circulated in the media—genuine "folk" rumors and legends about celebrities are anonymous in origin, informal in circulation, and usually variable in content. Although not a large category of modern folklore, some apocryphal stories about celebrities are surprisingly persistent.

"The Elevator Incident," for example, is a legend that has circulated since 1981 attached to various black athletes and entertainers ranging from Reggie Jackson to Eddie Murphy. In every version the unrecognized man's innocent comment is mistaken by a white passenger in the same elevator as a threat. This somewhat racist story of mistaken identification has nonracial prototypes in much earlier traditions involving other kinds of verbal misunderstanding.

Even older is the story of "Bozo the Clown's Blooper," a story attributed to nearly every children's show broadcaster—but true of none. No solid evidence has yet been produced to prove that either the host or a young guest on such a TV broadcast cursed on camera. Instead, the tradition can be traced back to the earliest days of radio as an account of every broadcaster's nightmare.

Some typical themes of other celebrity lore include the untrue report of a person's demise (e.g., "Paul is Dead"), the supposed secret of a celebrity's health and good looks (e.g., "The Dolly Parton Diet"), negative lore about attractive celebrities (e.g., "Gerbiling"), and chance encounters with a celebrity (e.g., "The Ice-Cream Cone Caper").

There are probably more *anecdotes* about celebrities, past and present, than actual legends, the distinction being that anecdotes are generally short (a single episode), are at least partly true, and often incorporate a witty remark or comeback. Legends, in contrast, have longer, and more diverse plots and they stray much farther from any actual facts. The story of a jazz musician replying to the question "What is jazz?" is essentially an anecdote by this definition, whereas the story about another jazzman sitting on a small dog ("The Crushed Dog") is clearly a legend.

Celebrities themselves have mixed reactions to these stories. The few rumors and legends that are truly vicious and damaging, of course, are firmly denied, although it might perhaps be better simply to ignore such tales, allowing them to fade on their own. Sometimes celebrities seem amused by the unlikely stories that are told about them and even vie with each other to claim an apocryphal story as part of their own cult of personality.

See also Generation Gap Legends; Mistaken Identifications; Talk Shows and Urban Legends; "The Youngest Fan"

References: *Mexican Pet,* 178–190.

"The Celebrity's Car Breakdown"

In this legend, a driver stops to help another motorist stranded beside his or her disabled car. Often the setting is at night and/or on a busy freeway. The helper changes a tire, provides a tow, transports the other driver to a service station and back, and so on. Although the stranded motorist does not identify himself or herself at the time, later the Good Samaritan receives an expensive new car or some other lavish gift and learns that the person he had helped was a celebrity or the wife of a celebrity.

This story has been told since the 1950s on musicians including Perry Como, Louis Armstrong, and Nat King Cole, and also on the wife of boxer Leon Spinks. Note that three out of four of these people are black and that a singer-celebrity who did occasionally give new Cadillacs to strangers was Elvis Presley, who styled many of his early hits after the manner of black performers.

References: *Curses!*, 114–116.

"The Celebrity's Telephone (or Phone Card) Number"

Burt Reynolds was on *The Tonight Show* about 1981 when he told Johnny Carson that he had recently won a big settlement against the telephone company and would have free calls for a specified time (or on a specific date). He announced his telephone credit-card number on the air and invited viewers to make all the free calls they wished on the same number.

Similar stories were told at about the same time concerning Robert Redford releasing his own credit-card number, and in earlier decades about Steve McQueen and Paul Newman asking their fans to help them use up a large credit they had acquired when the telephone company refused to pay back a deposit on long-distance calls they never made.

In 1984 another celebrity phone rumor circulated: It was claimed that the ten-digit product code number on Michael Jackson's *Thriller* album was actually the singer's private telephone number. Supposedly this information was revealed on an MTV broadcast. Large numbers of calls were made for a short time to a beauty salon in Bellevue, Washington, whose telephone number happened to coincide with the product number on Jackson's album.

References: *Choking Doberman*, 203–208; *Curses!*, 234–235; *Mexican Pet*, 181–182.

"The Cement-Truck Driver"

See "The Solid Cement Cadillac"

"The Chicken in the Hat"

See "The Shoplifter and the Frozen Food"

Child Ballad

This refers to any of the 305 traditional British ballads collected and published by Harvard professor Francis James Child (1825–1896) in his monumental work *The English and Scottish Popular Ballads* (1882–1898). A *ballad* is a narrative folksong—a traditional song that tells a story. Although gathered by Child primarily from manuscript and early published sources, the "Child Ballads," as they continue to be called, have also had wide circulation in oral tradition, both in Britain and the United States. Folklorists invariably refer to them by their number and title in the Child collection (e.g., Child 155, "Sir Hugh, or, the Jew's Daughter," is related to the ancient blood-libel legend and is thus part of the background of the urban legend "The Mutilated Boy"). The term "Child Ballad" has nothing whatever to do with children, either as the subjects or singers of traditional ballads.

Children

A glance at the index of any collection of urban legends under the general heading "Children" shows that from tots to teens they are depicted as victims, often of horrible crimes and abuse. The index subheadings include abduction of children, accidents, castration and castration threats, dog attacks, drug soliciting among children, misplaced and missing children, murder, mutilation, pornography involving children, satanic ritual child abuse, sexual initiation of children, and threats against children. The sad truth is that all of these things do occur in the real world, but the comforting second thought is that most of the specific details of widespread urban legends about children are completely fictional.

For example, children are sometimes abducted by strangers, but not by "Phantom Clowns" roaming cities in vans or by shopping mall predators who color a young girl's hair and change her clothing in a restroom in order to smuggle her out; at least this attempted-abduction legend has a happy ending, since the girl is recognized by her shoes, which the villain neglected to change. A worse version of this story claims that a young boy was castrated by gang members in a shopping mall restroom; "The Mutilated Boy" in this legend usually bleeds to death.

The natural concern that parents and other adults have for the safety and health of children encourages well-meaning circulation of bogus warnings that describe threats to children. But neither "Blue Star Acid" (or "Mickey Mouse Acid") nor Halloween sadists represent an actual crime scenario, although there are perennial outbursts of fliers and public statements cautioning against these imagined dangers.

Similarly, automobile accidents take many children's lives, but the scenario described in legends like "The Body on the Car" and "The Baby on the Roof" represent folklore, not reality.

According to other legends, children may be no safer at home than away: in "The Mother's Threat Carried Out," for example, a mother's rash, threatening words uttered in anger and frustration are fulfilled by another of her children with fatal results. Even playing alone, a child may fall into danger, as another youngster does in the story of "The Boy Who Played Superman."

Despite this dismal array of urban legends depicting dangers to children, we should recognize that stories about happy, healthy children with no crises in their lives would not make very memorable stories. Narratives of all kinds require some degree of conflict and uncertainty; thus, the modern stories about children at risk merely exaggerate some typical plot situations partly drawn from real life.

In one instance an actual child suffering a medical crisis has become the focus of international concern and donations that still continue, long after the child has recovered. The "Postcards for Little Buddy" legend provided the background for this case, and it eventually evolved into "The Craig Shergold Legend."

See also Babies; Satanic Panic

Chinese Restaurants

Although ethnic restaurants in general are the subjects of numerous food-contamination legends, Chinese restaurants in particular seem to attract the bulk of the rumors and stories. Slanderous claims about foreign matter in the food of Chinese restaurants are especially common in Great Britain, Scandinavia, and Germany, but they also circulate in the United States. To some degree it appears that "Chinese" in such stories is merely a convenient shorthand term for "foreign," since similar stories circulate to a lesser degree about Greek, Yugoslavian, East Indian, Vietnamese, and many other ethnic eateries. (In the United States, often Mexican restaurants are as much maligned as those of any other ethnicity.) All of these legends reflect a distrust of immigrants and dislike or misunderstanding of the eating habits of other peoples.

The simplest Chinese-restaurant allegations are simply that someone found a rat bone, a finger, or some other foreign matter in the food. Sometimes the claim is made more specific—a finger was found in a restaurant's chop suey (even though chop suey is not an authentic Chinese dish and is certainly not served in restaurants). The severed finger may be said to have come from a cook who has leprosy and whose digits are gradually dropping off.

In a narrative development of these themes, a scientist of some kind is dining in a Chinese restaurant when he finds a tough, stringy bit of meat in his food. He quietly pockets the item, takes it back to his lab for inspection, and discovers that it is a finger. (Alternatively, the diner may forget about the finger in his pocket, but it is reported to the police when he takes his jacket in for dry cleaning.) A variation of this story describes a diner getting a bone stuck in his throat; after it is removed, an emergency medical worker identifies it as a cat bone.

Another group of Chinese-restaurant stories focuses on inspections of kitchens, either formal checks by health authorities or accidental discoveries by workers removing the refuse containers. Skins and heads of cats and dogs are said to have been found in the garbage. The notion that Orientals eat cats and dogs as a regular part of their diets leads to further stories about people's pets being nabbed to satisfy the perverse culinary taste of foreigners.

Local outbreaks of Chinese-restaurant stories frequently focus on a particular business, and the word-of-mouth hysteria may lead to a loss of business for the place or even to its forced closure.

See also "The Dog's Dinner"; "The Eaten Pets"; South Africa

References: *Choking Doberman,* 121–122; *Mexican Pet,* 103; *Vanishing Hitchhiker,* 83.

"The Choking Doberman"

A woman comes home from shopping and finds her Doberman pinscher lying in the entry of her home gagging and choking. She immediately drops her purchases, puts the dog in her car, and rushes to the veterinarian. The vet says that he will have to operate to remove the obstruction, and he advises her to return home and wait for his call.

Back home, as the woman is opening her door she hears the telephone ringing, and she hurries to answer it. The vet is calling, and he urgently commands her to hang up the phone immediately and run outside; he has already called the police, who will explain.

The woman does as he says, and the police soon arrive. They tell her that the vet found two fingers stuck in the Doberman's throat. They search the house and find a burglar hiding in a closet; he is in shock and has two fingers bitten off one hand.

Variations of this legend mention different breeds of dog, different hiding places of the intruder, and sometimes other numbers of fingers, often specified as "black fingers" or "Mexican fingers." Sometimes the intruder is not found, but police identify him when he shows up—minus two fingers—at a local emergency room for treatment. Alternatively, fingerprints may be the incriminating evidence. Occasionally the vet simply takes the dog to the operating room while the owner waits, then returns with the fingers on a tray and summons the police to escort her home.

The story, in whatever variation, reflects people's fear of crime, especially from the hands of racial and ethnic minorities, and their trust in the police for protection. The intended victim is nearly always a woman, often one living alone, who has a Doberman—or some other breed of dog thought to be especially fierce—as her protection. The danger to her is not apparent as the mystery unfolds but becomes shockingly clear at the climactic ending of the story. Reference to the guard dog, the vet, the telephone, and the police all give the story the air of authenticity and timeliness.

"The Choking Doberman" began to circulate in the United States in 1981 and quickly spread coast to coast and even abroad. However, far from a true recent incident, it is actually a story that stems from much earlier foreign sources. The Welsh legend about Prince Llewelyn and his dog Gelert tells of the prince returning home to find his infant's cradle overturned and empty while the dog lies with a bloody mouth in the hallway. The prince kills the dog, thinking it has killed the child, only to discover that his faithful hound had actually defended the baby from a wolf. The dead wolf and the safe baby are found inside the house.

Although it is popularly believed in Wales that "Llewelyn and Gelert" tells the story of an actual thirteenth-century incident, the plot stems from Middle East folklore where various fables tell about a household pet's behavior being misunderstood leading to the animal being unjustly slain. As the Welsh legend spread to the New World the wolf was transformed to a burglar and the slaying of the faithful dog was altered to become a hasty trip to the vet's office.

The motif of a warning by telephone ("Get out of the house right away!") also occurs in "The Baby-sitter and the Man Upstairs," while the general idea of a threatening person hiding on the premises occurs both in the baby-sitter legend and "The Killer in the Backseat." It is also notable that a veterinarian is the person to resolve the mystery, just as in "The Mexican Pet." Severed fingers and hands figure in a number of other legends, including "The Hook," and the racist theme is similar to that in "The Elevator Incident." Thus "The Choking Doberman" seems to be a central and typical "new" urban legend of the 1980s.

References: *Choking Doberman,* 3–49; Adrienne Mayor, "Ambiguous Guardians: The 'Omen of the Wolves' (A.D. 402) and the 'Choking Doberman' (1980s). *Journal of Folklore Research* 29 (1992), 253–268; *Mexican Pet,* 41–47; *Too Good,* 51–52.

Church's Chicken Rumors

The rumor, as summarized by folklorist Patricia A. Turner, is that "the KKK, who allegedly owns Church's Fried Chicken, has tainted the chicken recipe so that black male eaters are sterilized after consuming it." Similar rumors about Klan ownership of companies, or other dangerous additives to products that are marketed to blacks, have circulated among African Americans concerning other companies, including TROOP athletic wear and Tropical Fantasy soft drinks. Although the ru-

mors are completely untrue, the companies named in them have suffered various degrees of damage to their images or to their sales.

Church's Fried Chicken began as a single stand run by San Antonio
businessman George Church in 1952. As the company expanded in
Texas and beyond, George Church Jr. took over, and the company went
public in 1965. In 1989 Church's was taken over by Popeyes Famous
Fried Chicken and Biscuits, and eventually the rumors waned.

Patricia Turner's analysis suggests that the name "Church's" may have
been confused by some with the Ku Klux Klan's support base among
southern white-supremacist churches and that the southern roots of the
company as well as its southern-flavored menu may have contributed to
the spread of the rumor. Neither the product nor the rumors about it are
well known to white Americans, although, of course, other contamination rumors and fast-food legends abound.

References: Patricia A. Turner, *I Heard It Through the Grapevine* (1993),
82–92, 105–107, 139–144.

Cigar Insurance ("Cigarson")

A man buys a full case of expensive cigars and insures them against fire.
After he has smoked them all, he files a claim with the insurance company saying that they were destroyed "in a series of small fires." The
company pays him—then has the man arrested for arson; he is convicted
and sentenced to one year for each count. This story arose and faded on
the Internet in 1996, although it is still circulated there occasionally.

The "Cigarson" story, despite being untrue, is sometimes referred to
in discussions of supposed outrages in the American legal system and
the need for tort reform.

References: For details, see www.snopes2.com/business/genius/cigarson.
htm.

Classifying Urban Legends

All collected folklore data must be arranged in some sort of classification system in order to facilitate archiving, comparisons, and analysis

of the texts. Folk narratives as a group are often divided into three major subheadings: Myths (accounts of ancient times, often involving deities), Legends (oral narratives about the historical past that are regarded as true), and Folktales (fictional stories, ranging from fairy tales to jokes).

In general, legends themselves are often subdivided into the categories Religious, Supernatural, Historical, Personal, and Local. Urban legends would seem to fit somewhere between supernatural and local in this system, since they are accounts of bizarre, if not exactly impossible, occurrences that are said to have happened at specific locations.

Even the titling of urban legends by scholars implies some kind of classification system that allows us to speak of, say, "The Vanishing Hitchhiker" or "The Boyfriend's Death" as a distinct story type. This would be an imperfect system for good research, however, since titles are seldom adequate to describe all variations of a given story; for example, "The Hairy-Armed Hitchhiker" character may be recognized by his chin stubble rather than by his arms, or perhaps not spotted at all until the police find "The Hatchet in the Handbag" (an alternate title for the same legend) after the disguised man has escaped.

Although there is no complete acceptance of a single classification system for all urban legends, most folklorists seem to favor an organization based on content, that is, on subject matter. Thus collected rumors and stories are grouped according to their main actions or characters, such as automobiles, pets, crime, business, and government. One such system based mostly on American urban legends was published as "A Type Index of Urban Legends" in *The Baby Train* (1993). Here are the major categories and subheadings from that source:

1. Legends about Automobiles
   Ghost Stories
   Travel Mishaps
   Accident Stories
   Automobile Horror Stories
   Cheap-Car Fantasies
   Dalliance or Nudity Involving Automobiles
   Technical Incompetence
   Automobile Sabotage or Crime

2. Legends about Animals
   Animal Disasters
   Animal Infestations or Contaminations
   Trusty Watchdogs

3. Horror Legends
   Baby-sitter Stories
   Medical Horrors
   Other Horrors

4. Accident Legends
   Gruesome Accidents
   Hilarious Accidents

5. Sex and Scandal Legends
   Aphrodisiac Stories
   Contraception Stories
   Sex-Education Stories
   Sex Scandals
   Other Sex Stories

6. Crime Legends
   Theft Stories
   Atrocities and Kidnappings
   Drug Crimes

7. Business and Professional Legends
   Companies and Businesses
   Telephones
   Other Technology
   Computer Folklore
   Professions and Trades

8. Legends about Governments
   Inefficiency
   Conspiracy
   Science Versus Religion
   Military and Wartime Legends
   Miscellaneous Government

9. Celebrity Rumors and Legends
   Celebrities
   Musicians

10. Academic Legends
    Faculty and Research
    Students
    Blue Book and other Examination Legends

There are further subdivisions of many of these categories. For example, the "Sex Scandals" section includes subgroups of stories about people being "Caught in the Nude" or "Caught in the Act"; "Theft Stories" includes some stories about "Unwitting Thefts" and others about "Thefts of Food," as well as general stories about stealing.

As with almost every attempt to classify data of any kind, some categories overlap. If, for instance, a story involves a car, a crime, *and* sex, it would be necessary to select one place in the system to file it while inserting cross-references at the other topics. Sometimes the placement of a particular legend is arbitrary: "The Choking Doberman" is certainly a crime story, but it was categorized in the above system under "Trusty Watchdogs" adjacent to "The Licked Hand," another dog/horror story. Both of these legends were then cross-referenced under other topics.

The possibility of classifying urban legends according to themes, meanings, functions, or other features has been explored but not developed into a complete system. In *Too Good to Be True* (1999), for example, stories are grouped by such themes as "Jumping to Conclusions," "Just Deserts," "Losing Face," and "Baffled by Technology." Other categories could be devised to index urban legends by their countries of circulation, their periods of popularity, their plot structures, their styles, or other aspects.

Beyond the question of creating large-scale classification systems for the whole genre of urban legends, there is also the task of classifying versions and variants of a specific legend under study. Thus texts of "The Mexican Pet" might be subdivided by the species of animal involved, the place where it was "adopted," the means of discovering its true identity, or the cultural "messages" in the different versions. As with the content categories, these, too, may overlap.

See also Motif; Myth

References: *Baby Train*, 325–347.

"The Clever Baby-sitter"

Also known as "The Harried Baby-sitter," this story tells of someone on a bus or subway who overhears two young women comparing notes on how they put infants to sleep when they are baby-sitting: "I just turn on the gas and hold their head over the stove burner or in the oven until they fall asleep."

Popular in the United States since the 1920s, when gas stoves and ovens still had to be lit with a match, "The Clever Baby-sitter" continues to be told (sometimes as an account of a past event) even in modern times when gas appliances are self-lighting. Older versions are reported from England where two nannies are overheard chatting in Hyde park: "I just hold the gas ring over her dear little face and give her a whiff."

References: *Choking Doberman,* 77–78; *Mexican Pet,* 69–70; *Too Good,* 216–217.

"The Climax of Horrors"

A traditional European folk story (Tale Type 2040) in which a servant greets his long-absent returning master by declaring that there is "no news" to report except that the dog died. But, when questioned, the servant describes a series of catastrophes that had occurred—leading up to the death of the master's wife—and only incidentally involving the death of the dog.

The story is sometimes called "No News" or "The Dog Died" and was circulated in old schoolbooks and other printed sources as well as orally either in the form of a tale or a recitation. "The Climax of Horrors" is still occasionally told by urban storytellers somewhat in the style of a contemporary legend.

References: *Baby Train,* 92–94.

Cokelore

Traditions about the supposed corrosive and other chemical properties (some dangerous, some useful) of Coca-Cola. The nickname "Coke" is a registered trademark but also used as a folk generic for other cola drinks; yet specifically Coca-Cola is said to be effective in such applications as reviving dead batteries, cleaning windshields, removing rust, or opening clogged drains. Taken properly, Coke is thought by some people to be an effective contraceptive douche or a good hangover cure; however, Cokelore also claims that the misuse of Coke may lead to a Coke addiction, make you drunk, dissolve your teeth, or eat away at your tongue or stomach lining.

Most Cokelore is transmitted in the form of simple statements with minimal anecdotal evidence, often attributed to a friend of a friend. The most developed narrative about Coca-Cola is the urban legend "The Mouse in the Coke."

References: L. Michael Bell, "Cokelore," *Western Folklore* 35 (1976): 59–64; reprinted in Brunvand, *Readings in American Folklore* (1979), 99–105.

"The Colander Copier Caper"

Police in a small department are interrogating a suspect whom they strongly believe is guilty of the crime under investigation, but the man refuses to confess. The police rig up a colander on the man's head and attach it with wires to a copier machine, telling him that it is a lie detector. They have placed a sheet of paper printed with "He's lying!" under the copier's lid, and every time the suspect replies to a question, they push the "Copy" button and a sheet emerges reading "He's lying!" The suspect soon confesses to the crime.

Remembered by some informants from earlier in the 1070s, this story was first reported in 1977 by *Philadelphia Inquirer* columnist Clark DeLeon, who said the confession came before Judge Isaac Garb, who had suppressed that evidence in the court action. Variations of the story have been widely repeated and reprinted, often attributed to Radnor, Pennsylvania, in Delaware County, where law enforcement authorities consistently and firmly deny that it happened there. However, in 1993, Judge Garb asserted that the incident did indeed come before his Court of Com-

mon Appeals in Bucks County, Doylestown, Pennsylvania. The judge did not, however, provide a date or any details of the crime involved.

"The Colander Copier Caper" is a story well known to both police authorities and trial lawyers all across the United States, many of whom have heard it from others in the profession but none of whom ever claim to have been present when the trick was used. It has been repeatedly published (in variant versions) as true by writers willing to believe that if an earlier publication *says* that police resorted to such a trick, then it *must* have happened. The caper has also been dramatized for use on at least two TV cop shows.

This prank story, familiar to insiders, has reached the general public by several different paths and, in at least one instance, seems to have actually made its way to a court of law. Journalist Chuck Shepherd, compiler of the syndicated "News of the Weird" column, insisted in 1996 that the story might be true, citing an undated and unidentified news clipping mentioning Radnor, which he had not verified and declined to share with folklorists. His belief was sustained by the idea that "nearly every cop you talk to has in fact arrested not one but many people he would concede are stupid enough to fall for something like that." In other words, Shepherd held that if the incident *could* have happened then it *might* have happened, so it cannot be considered a legend. Whatever the possible "truth" of one or more occurrences of the incident, however, the stories themselves may be regarded as urban legends in traditional circulation.

See also "The Homemade Lie Detector"

> **References:** *Baby Train,* 139–145; *FOAFtale News* no. 38 (December 1995): 12 [a 1986 version] and no. 39 (June 1996): 9 [Shepherd's claim]; *Too Good,* 303–305.

Collagens in Cosmetics

See "The Secret Ingredient"

Collecting Urban Legends

Although journalists—especially columnists—had for a long time recorded and written about all kinds of odd stories that circulated orally—including what we now call "urban legends"—the systematic collection of such stories began only in the 1940s and 1950s with the work of academic folklorists and their students. Even today, journalists, professors, and students remain the major collectors of urban legends.

"Systematic" is an overstatement, since even most of the scholarly collections of urban legends have been rather random, and they were seldom, if ever, made according to the professed standards for good recording of folklore data. As folklorist Bill Ellis has written, "While the *ideal* of verbatim transcription is widely espoused, the *practice* shows considerable confusion about just what ought to be preserved in the printed record of a legend in performance." Ellis demonstrated one method for recording a true verbatim text of "The Hook" in his 1987 essay, but the result is thick with detail and somewhat difficult to read.

The earliest published texts from the collecting work of American folklorists and their students appeared as scattered notes on individual stories, usually in regional folklore journals. By the 1960s several large campus folklore archives had developed, containing a high percentage of materials popular among the undergraduates who were enrolled in folklore courses. Typical items included anecdotes, jokes, and urban legends. As these archives were drawn upon for research, larger collections of variants of urban-legend texts began to appear in journals and eventually in books.

Besides texts of orally transmitted legends, published collections began to draw heavily on examples from literature, broadcasting, and especially the print media and the Internet, thus demonstrating the pervasiveness of urban legends in our culture. Roughly the same pattern occurred—from journalism, to academic collections, to media and electronic sources—as urban-legend studies spread beyond the United States. In collecting stories from print and broadcasting, it is essential to keep track of the date and source of each item, information that is easily lost if the reader/listener is inattentive.

Whether consistently followed in practice or not, the *ideal* of collecting verbatim texts with close attention to context, function, and performance ought to guide the efforts of anyone making a collection of urban legends. This means not only writing down, recording, or filming the exact words of the storytellers but also noting the complete surrounding atmosphere and style of the telling. Who tells these stories; to whom are they told; and in what situations?

Another aspect to be aware of is whether the story is in fact "told" by a single individual or is instead produced by the interaction of several people, each of whom contributes to a conversational dialogue about that particular legend. Accordingly, folklorists and others collecting urban legends need to develop strategies for overhearing, eliciting, and discussing urban legends in realistic performance situations.

Possibly questionnaires or field experiments will be used more in future collections, and the great popularity of urban legends on the Internet lately raises a whole new set of questions about the best methods for collecting urban legends.

References: Bill Ellis, "Why Are Verbatim Transcripts of Legends Necessary?" in Bennett, Smith, and Widdowson, *Perspectives on Contemporary Legend II* (1987), 31–60; John Niles, "The Berkeley Contemporary Legend Files," in Bennett and Smith, *The Questing Beast* (1989), 105–111; *Vanishing Hitchhiker,* 197–202.

"The Colo-Rectal Mouse"

A friend of a friend knows someone working at a local hospital who supposedly was present when a homosexual man came into the emergency room to have a live mouse or other small creature removed from his rectum. He had used a greased plastic tube to insert the mouse, having heard that this would give him the ultimate sexual thrill. The string he had tied to the mouse broke when the man tried to pull it out. Sometimes a mouse skeleton is stuck inside the man, or the creature is a small lizard whose tail broke off when the man tried to pull it back out.

This story appeared in 1984 and quickly spread across the United States. The animal came to be referred to consistently as a gerbil in subsequent years when this legend was applied specifically to several male media figures who were thought by the public to be homosexual.

See also Gerbiling

References: *Mexican Pet,* 78–79.

"Come and Get It!"

Unexpected guests arrive at a couple's home while either the husband or wife is in the shower. The showering spouse, unaware, emerges naked and calls out, "Come and get it while it's clean!" Alternately, the male guest is invited to take a shower after doing some yard work and before dinner. The wife, thinking her husband is in the shower, reaches through the shower curtain, pulls on the guest's penis, and says, "Ding-dong, dinner bell!"

Versions of "The Stranger in the Shower" are documented since the 1940s, and the story is known in England with the punch line "Ding-dong, dinner bell!" (or "tea time"). The situation is similar to that in "The Unzipped Plumber or Mechanic."

References: *Too Good,* 149–150; *Vanishing Hitchhiker,* 146–47.

Comics and Urban Legends

Because of their simple plots, bizarre situations, stereotyped characters, and often sensational or slapstick action, urban legends have long appealed to comic artists. In the popular media, there have been innumerable cartoon allusions to and retellings of such stories as "Alligators in the Sewers," "The Hook," "The Dead Cat in the Package," "The Microwaved Pet," and "The Killer in the Backseat." The publications using such illustrations have ranged from *The New Yorker* to freebie local-events papers.

Sometimes an entire comic book centers on a legend, as in the artist Stan Lee's 1976 "Red Sonja: She-Devil with a Sword" feature and his 1987 "Daredevil: The Man Without Fear!" feature, both of which were issues of Marvel Comics based on the alligator legend. An entire urban legend comic book, *Urban Legends No. 1,* was published by Dark Horse Comics in 1993. Among the legends included here were "The Kentucky Fried Rat," "The Vanishing Hitchhiker," and "Baby in the Microwave."

Among the many serial comics and cartoon features that have drawn on urban legends are "The Born Loser," "Captain Easy," "Garfield," "Mother Goose and Grimm," "Sherman's Lagoon," "Tumbleweeds," "Zippy," and several from Gary Larson's "The Far Side" series. Apart from the mainstream comics, urban legends often provide plots for comic strips appearing in the alternative, or underground, comics, as in Gilbert Shelton's use of "The Blind Date" story in a 1972 episode of his "Fabulous Furry Freak Brothers" strip.

Almost without exception, books of urban legends around the world have used cartoon-style drawings as illustrations. Carrying this to its logical extreme, *The Big Book of Urban Legends* (1994) presented fully 200 urban legends, all rendered as comic strips, and each one drawn by a different artist. The *Big Book* contains an impressive display of the varying styles of modern comic art.

In some instances urban legends themselves have borrowed from the comics. "Mickey Mouse Acid" is an obvious example, with the cartoon character in these bogus warnings eventually switching to Bart Simpson. In "The Boy Who Played Superman," a child imitates a comic-book hero with disastrous results; the same basic theme is enacted by an adult character in "Superhero Hijinks."

Communal Re-creation

When an urban legend is transmitted through a community (i.e., any group) each teller *re-creates* the story, rather than repeating it verbatim. In other words, people remember the general outline and some details of the story, but they invariably retell it with some items dropped, added, or changed. By way of this process, variant versions are introduced that the community may accept or ignore depending upon how well the new variants confirm the group's notion of a good legend. The re-creation of the legend is thus said to be *communal*.

If an individual's change in a story is illogical or puzzling, listeners may either drop that version or else try to make sense of it in their own tellings. For instance, when the "Welcome to the World of AIDS" note was said by someone to have been concealed in a can of *coffee* instead of the usual tiny *coffin*, the few people who repeated that detail suggested that perhaps the coffee was used to mask the smell of drugs hidden in the package for smuggling into the United States.

Communal re-creation was a theory advanced in studies of traditional ballads (narrative folksongs), but it applies equally well to the analysis of changes in the telling of oral narratives, including urban legends.

References: *Baby Train*, 88; *Vanishing Hitchhiker*, 14–15, 193.

"The Communist Rules for Revolution"

This refers to a numbered list of rules, usually ten of them, distributed in printed or written form and claimed to be copies of a master plan for a communist takeover of the West that was "captured in Dusseldorf,

Germany, in 1919 by the Allied Forces." Sometimes titled "Rules for Bringing about a Revolution," the items refer to decline of religion, increased interest in sex, holding of strikes by labor unions, registration of firearms, government extravagance, and other subjects dear to the hearts of ultra–right wing zealots. A typical "rule" reads, "Destroy the people's faith in their natural leaders by holding the latter up to contempt, ridicule, and obloquy."

Far from being a document from 1919, the "Communist Rules" originated in a British publication of 1946. They have been repeatedly debunked by leading conservative spokespersons and in many publications. (Three well-documented sources are listed below.) At least three times members of Congress have been quoted denying the authenticity of the "Communist Rules" on the pages of the *Congressional Record.*

Still, even in the 1990s, and despite the breakdown of communism worldwide, radical-right publications continue to reprint the "Communist Rules," and warnings about them sometimes appear in letters to editors of daily newspapers. A letter writer from Provo, Utah, for example, in 1990 quoted five of the rules, adding such comments as, "Innocent people who are fighting for gun control, unknowingly are helping the communist goal."

References: Paul F. Bolloer Jr. and John George, *They Never Said It* (New York: Oxford University Press, 1989), 114–116; *Choking Doberman,* 184; John George and Laird Wilcox, *Nazis, Communists, Klansmen, and Others on the Fringe* (Buffalo, N.Y.: Prometheus, 1992), 445–447; Morris Kominsky, *The Hoaxers* (Boston: Branden Press, 1970), 600–611; *Mexican Pet,* 108–109.

Companies

Urban legends about business often focus on specific companies, usually the largest ones and those with the major market share. In alphabetical order, companies and products that have been the targets of urban legends include Bubble Yum, Burger King, Church's Fried Chicken, Coca-Cola, Corona beer, Domino's Pizza, Gerber's baby foods, Ikea furniture stores, Kmart stores, Kentucky Fried Chicken, McDonald's hamburgers, Mrs. Fields cookies, the Neiman Marcus department store, Pop Rocks candy, Procter & Gamble, Reebok sports gear, Rolls-Royce, and the Waldorf-Astoria hotel.

Of course, there are many rumors and legends about smaller companies and local businesses as well, and sometimes the stories focus on an individual who represents the company in the public mind (like Bill Gates or Donald Trump) rather than the company itself and its products or services.

See also Business Legends; Mercantile Legends

Comparative Approach

Texts of a particular urban legend are compared with each other, or with similar legends, in order to identify consistent elements versus varying details. Stories are classified into types and subtypes and, within the categories, by their dates and localities. This *comparative approach* is usually carried out somewhat informally in urban-legend studies, but it derives from the rigorous historic-geographic method followed since the turn of the century by international folktale scholars.

Formal comparative studies of ancient and rather complex folktales sought to establish an "archetype," or hypothetical original form, of the story, as well as a likely date and place of origin. Comparisons in urban-legend studies are unlikely to seek origins as much as simply to account for the migrations and variations of the plot.

Some comparisons are inevitable in any legend study (indeed, in most studies of any kind of folklore); however, some analyses are more systematic about their comparisons than others. Virtually every general book or article about urban legends uses comparisons to illustrate theme and variation, but a brief review of three examples of longer comparative analyses can illustrate their typical techniques and findings.

William Hugh Jansen's classic study of "The Nude Surprise Party" reviewed 28 texts collected over a span of 45 years. He concluded that the tradition comprised three major story types. Jansen found that each version, however altered by individual storytellers, made some reference to an *attitude* toward the shocking situation, an *occasion* for the party, and for an *aftermath* when the nude couple is discovered. Whereas the occasions varied widely (birthday, wedding shower, housewarming, blind date, etc.), the aftermath was quite consistent (the boy left town and the girl lost her mind).

Gordon McCulloch's study of "The Tale of the Turkey Neck" compared versions in three separate "transmission chains" of a legend about a practical joke collected in Scotland in 1982 over a period of ten days. As a prelude to close analysis of the performances and styles of a dozen texts of the story, McCulloch compared the persons involved, the details of the prank, and the resulting injury to the victim's wife. Essentially in all stories some "edible material" (like a turkey neck) is placed in the open fly of a sleeping man; when his wife sees an animal (a cat or dog) nibbling at the protruding object, she faints and is injured (breaking her ankle or her wrist).

Using questionnaires, William S. Fox collected and compared information on "The Suicide Rule" from 232 students in sociology classes at one private college and one state college in New York in the spring of 1985. His comparisons of the data yielded four tables illustrating knowledge and sources of the belief among students in each institution and among those living on-campus versus off-campus. Variations of the belief included certain conditions that supposedly had to be met for the "perfect" grade to be awarded and the claimed reasons for the (nonexistent) policy.

References: Fox, "The Roommate's Suicide and the 4.0," in Bennett and Smith, *A Nest of Vipers* (1990), 69–76; Jansen, "The Surpriser Surprised: A Modern Legend," in Brunvand, *Readings in American Folklore* (1979), 64–90; McCulloch, "'The Tale of the Turkey Neck': A Legend Case-Study," in Smith, *Perspectives on Contemporary Legend* (1984), 147–166.

Computers

As the subject of urban legends, as conduits for circulating urban legends, and as aids in studying urban legends, computers have come to fill a central role in the world of contemporary-legend tradition and research. Computer folklore, however, extends far beyond legends, encompassing jokes, chain letters, "folk" games and graphics, heroic accounts of brilliant programmers and technicians, industry-insider anecdotes, "hacker" jargon, and more, little of which has been systematically collected or studied.

Many of the computer-related legends—apocryphal stories presumed true by their tellers—hinge on things that may go wrong, such as program glitches, bugs, or viruses. Although such errors and acts of deliberate sabotage do exist, the stories tend to stereotype, dramatize, and exaggerate reality. Such legends are often repeated as groups of stories about

"mystery glitches" or "famous bugs" without distinguishing the actual examples from the unverifiable.

The imaginative style characteristic of certain computer viruses (or *virus legends*) is expressed in such names as "Cookie Monster," "Friday the 13th," "Michelangelo," and "Good Times"; when a programming glitch was anticipated to occur at the turn of the millennium, it soon acquired the nickname "Y2K" (Year 2000). Accounts of what might happen on January 1, 2000, ranged from realistic fears about dated programs failing to recognize the new century numbers to irrational concerns that cars would not start, digital watches would freeze up, and power and telephone service would stop.

A popular genre of computer legends centers on the naive or frustrated user struggling to get assistance from the manuals that came with his (or, more commonly, *her*) computer or from a company's helpline. Usually it turns out that the user has done something extremely foolish such as fail to plug in or turn on the machine, or to attach a cable to the printer, or to understand the instruction "strike any key." The response of the helpline worker may be that the user should box up the whole system and return it to the store, "Because you're too stupid to own one." Alternatively, the user finally gets help nearby, usually from a youngster in the family or neighborhood who was raised in the digital age.

Computer newsgroups, bulletin boards, chatrooms, and e-mail have increasingly become major channels for the transmission of urban legends and, indeed, of all kinds of folklore. Crime and horror stories, humorous legends, celebrity rumors, and bogus warnings in particular flourish on the Internet, alongside debunkings and discussions of urban legends both by professional folklorists and others. Although computerized communication spreads such material globally and extremely quickly, most texts are simply forwarded at the click of a button without variation and with minimal comment. Such "cyberlore" lacks the performance features and style of oral storytelling, but it develops its own flavor in parodies of urban legends that circulate on the Internet.

Computers offer interesting possibilities for research on urban legends. Scholars may use online databases to search for themes and topics in both the academic and popular press, or they may easily query other users about emerging rumors and legends. Several Internet sites are devoted to urban legends. E-mail provides a quick, easy, and inexpensive method to coordinate research with other scholars, to plan conferences, and to work on joint publications. Computerized archives of legends have not yet been created, but surely that is just a matter of time.

For college students and even schoolchildren writing papers, the Internet has useful resources on urban legends and many other topics, besides providing a way to contact authors directly to ask about their publications and projects. Whether the authors will respond in a useful way to e-mail queries is another matter, as some may feel that what they have to say about the topic is already easily available in print.

See also "The Good Times Virus"; Internet Resources; "The Modem Tax"; Naive Computer User Stories

References: Erik Brunvand, "The Heroic Hacker: Legends of the Computer Age," in Brunvand, *The Truth* (1999), 170–198; Karla Jennings, *The Devouring Fungus: Tales of the Computer Age* (New York: Norton, 1990); Michael J. Preston, "Computer Folklore," in Brunvand, *American Folklore: An Encyclopedia* (1996), 154–155; Paul Wallich, "Cyber View: This Is Not a Hoax!" *Scientific American* (November 1998), 54.

Conspiracies

Published articles, rumors, and occasionally oral legends circulate suggesting that certain groups have conspired in secret to take over the reins of power or otherwise to subvert our social and political institutions. The perpetrators may be claimed to be Jews, racial minorities, communists, international corporations, so-called secret societies (like the Masonic orders, Jesuits, or the Roman Catholic Church), and especially governments, including our own (often via the CIA or the FBI). Sometimes the conspirators are simply alleged to be members of vaguely conceived organizations like "One Worlders," "Secular Humanists," or promoters of "The New World Order."

Minority groups may fear conspiracies from larger entities. For example, Patricia A. Turner in her 1993 book *I Heard It Through the Grapevine* devoted two chapters to rumors that either the Ku Klux Klan, international corporations, or the United States government had conspired in plots against African Americans.

Alleged government conspiracies are often described as "cover-ups" to shield the public from the truth about such phenomena as the Kennedy assassination, UFOs, cattle mutilations, and the mystery of the Bermuda Triangle. Reasonable explanations of such occurrences backed by scientific evidence and observation fail to convince the "true disbelievers," as Eric Eliason has dubbed them; he described them as forming "subcultures of intellectual dissent from official, mainstream cultural analysis."

Perhaps the most developed strains of the conspiracy virus in American oral-narrative tradition concern either the hysteria about satanic ritual abuse or the persistent stories about landed Martians whose presence has supposedly been kept secret by the government for decades.

See also "The Blood Libel"; "The Communist Rules for Revolution"; "The Jewish Secret Tax"; Satanic Panic

References: Eric Eliason, "Conspiracy Theories," in Brunvand, *American Folklore: An Encyclopedia* (1996), 157–158; Bill Ellis, "Cattle Mutilation: Contemporary Legends and Contemporary Mythologies," *Contemporary Legend* 1 (1991): 39–80.

"The Contaminated Comforter"

Het Wandelende Dekbed is a Dutch urban legend reported by writer Peter Burger of Leiden, The Netherlands, in 1990:

My brother told me last year about a woman who buys an eiderdown [down-filled comforter] for a suspiciously low price. She is very pleased with it and puts it on her bed. When she enters the bedroom again, it has slipped to the floor, so she replaces it. The first time she sleeps under the new eiderdown she wakes up in the middle of the night because the thing has slipped from the bed once more. Finally she opens the cover to have a look at the quilting, and she discovers that it is full of maggots. Flies have laid eggs in the blood that was sticking to the chicken feathers which, rather than real eiderdown, were used for the filling.

This legend may be known elsewhere in Europe, but it has not been reported in the United States, where down-filled comforters are less common. However, the story contains two themes familiar in modern American legends: contamination (see the next entry) and a poor value in low-priced goods. Also, maggots are an international sign of gross uncleanliness in many stories.

References: *Baby Train*, 237–238.

Contamination

The introduction of foreign matter—usually deliberately—into food and water is a major theme of modern urban rumors and legends. Usually the alleged guilty companies are named or clearly identified, though few, if any, of these stories have even the slightest basis in fact. Large fast-food franchises and packaged-food manufacturers are typical targets in the United States, with the products including canned goods, soft drinks, candy, cereal, hamburgers, fried chicken, pizza, and Mexican foods. Typical contaminants named include insects, pets, mice, rats, snakes, worms, dog food, human parts, semen, and saliva.

The supposed motivation for contaminating foods is often said to be disgruntlement of employees over salaries, working conditions, or mistreatment because of gender or sexual orientation. For example, one series of stories told nationwide claims that a worker, bitter because he was infected with AIDS and being fired, had masturbated onto a large company's pizzas, sometimes calling customers to inform them of it only *after* they had eaten the pizza.

The contamination of municipal water supplies is usually attributed to a corpse found in the main water tank—but with no explanation of why someone had left it there. Older traditional legends about contaminated village wells, however, specified that the water was poisoned for some military or political reason. Similarly, a European rumor of 1978 claimed that oranges from Israel had been contaminated with mercury in order to sabotage the economy and hence the peace process in the Middle East.

Related to contamination is the theme of infestation of the body and of homes or merchandise with hordes of living creatures, including spiders, insects, maggots, snakes, rats, and the like. New York City's "Alligators in the Sewers" is a prime example of an infestation legend, as are the stories of snakes infesting imported blankets, spiders or scorpions infesting potted cacti, and earwigs eating their way into a person's brain. Stories about computer viruses and "backward masking" of satanic messages on music recordings are examples of a more abstract tradition of infestation described in modern rumors and legends.

Contamination legends reflect distrust of products that are imported, ethnic, or manufactured and that are distributed by large corporations. The stories may also derive partly from people's guilt for relying too much on packaged and fast foods instead of preparing more nutritious meals at home from fresh ingredients. Concern about hygiene in places where food is packaged, stored, and prepared is already somewhat shaken by news reports of unclean conditions revealed in official inspections; the contamination legends focus on, exaggerate, and stereotype the findings.

See also Chinese Restaurants; Church's Chicken Rumors; "The Corpse in the Cask"; "The Finger in the Pickle Jar"; Halloween Sadists; "The Kentucky Fried Rat"; Masturbating into Food; McDonald's Rumors; "The Mouse in the Coke"; "The Secret Ingredient"; Tapeworms in Diet Pills; "Wormburgers"

References: *Choking Doberman,* 103–130; Susan Domowitz, "Foreign Matter in Food: A Legend Type," *Indiana Folklore* 12 (1979): 86–95; Robert M. MacGregor, "Québec's Killer Beer: a Dark T(ale)," *Contemporary Legend* 5 (1995), 101–114; *Mexican Pet,* 83–109; *Too Good,* 173–200; *Vanishing Hitchhiker,* 75–101

Contemporary Legend

"Contemporary legend" is the term preferred by some folklorists instead of "urban legend," "modern legend," or the combined term "modern urban legend." All of these terms as well as others ("urban myth," "belief legend," "rumor legend," etc.) are sometimes used synonymously, especially in the popular press, but some scholars insist upon the superior logic of one particular term over others. "Contemporary legend" obviously has strong academic adherents, since it was chosen for the name of the scholarly organization devoted to the study of the genre (the International Society for Contemporary Legend Research, or ISCLR), as well as to that group's annual journal.

Definitions and terminology were debated at the first Conference on Contemporary Legend held in Sheffield, England, in 1982 that spawned the founding of the ISCLR in 1988. The "problem of contemporaneity" continued to engage scholars in this area, and when the ISCLR was founded the term was agreed to refer "not only to so-called 'modern urban legends' but also to any legend in active circulation in a given community."

The question of what is contemporary in a legend tradition that has some roots in ancient folklore cannot be answered definitely except in terms of case studies of individual legends and their histories.

See also *Contemporary Legend* (Journal); Definition of "Legend"; International Society for Contemporary Legend Research

> **References:** Noel Williams, "Problems in Defining Contemporary Legend," in Paul Smith, *Perspectives on Contemporary Legend,* vol. 1 (1984), 216–228; Jacqueline Simpson, "Are the Terms 'Modern' and 'Contemporary' Synonymous?" *Contemporary Legend,* New Series 1 (1998), 134–148.

Contemporary Legend (Journal)

This is the title of the annual journal of the International Society for Contemporary Legend Research (ISCLR). The first volume appeared in 1991 under the editorship of professor Paul Smith of the Department of Folklore, Memorial University of Newfoundland, Canada. *Contemporary Legend* (CL) "aims to promote and encourage research, and to provide a forum for those working on this vibrant area of traditional narrative scholarship." Typical issues contain research findings, case studies, theoretical articles, bibliographic essays, book reviews, and the like. *CL* has an international editorial board that reviews contributions. The journal is sent to all ISCLR members and is subscribed to by many libraries. From 1984 to 1990 five volumes of the *Perspectives on Contemporary Legend* series published some of the papers presented at ISCLR meetings; this series was ended with the introduction of *Contemporary Legend.* Instructions to contributors and information about ISCLR membership and *CL* subscriptions appear on the inside back cover of each issue. In 1998 after some years of delays in publication of the first five volumes (1991-1995), *Contemporary Legend* New Series was launched with volume 1.

See also *FOAFtale News;* International Society for Contemporary Legend Research

Context

The immediate setting for passing along an item of folklore, plus the larger social and cultural features of the community in which the item circulates, constitute the *context* that surrounds the *text.* For a full understanding of any folk narrative, its literal text must be collected and analyzed along with a full description of the actual context (or contexts) of its transmission.

But, as author Mark Glazer has pointed out, "There is no structured context for the narration of contemporary legends. . . . There is no possible way a folklorist can know where and when the performance of a contemporary legend will take place." Instead, as Glazer shows, the typical settings in which they are told are merely "casual and spontaneous."

Urban legends may be told in such common social situations as parties, dormitory bull sessions, sleepovers (or slumber parties), camping trips, commuting and other travel, work breaks, and in domestic settings. But they are also transmitted by telephone, radio, and TV talk shows as well as via the Internet; sometimes they are published in newspapers and other print media. Each different context has its own conventions of pattern, style, and performance that influence the nature and the reception of the text.

Other contextual features that affect urban legends and their meanings include the attitude of the storyteller and audience, their familiarity with details of the story, and whether any other versions of the story are known to the teller or audience. Thus repeating an urban legend about a shopping mall crime may have one kind of response if the story's setting is localized, if the teller regards it as true, and if nobody hearing the story has heard it before. But if the setting is vague, and if the teller (or listener) expresses doubt, and if people are aware of other such tales, then it becomes—as they say—just another story.

The ages, degree of sophistication, and educational levels of storytellers and audiences clearly influence which urban legends are told and how they are regarded. Nowadays, most everyone has heard old horror stories like "The Hook" and "The Roommate's Death," but to an adolescent made wary by crime reporting, and hearing such legends for the first time from a wide-eyed peer, even these hoary yarns may be fresh, shocking, *and* believable.

Age and gender affect urban-legend repertoires and performance style. It makes a difference whether a story is told among peers of the same gender or, say, by parents to children (or vice versa), or by persons of the same or the opposite sex. Similarly, the reputation of the legend-teller for accuracy or for having "inside information" helps determine how the story is received. For example, printed or e-mailed bogus warnings about supposed crime waves are effective in spurring hysterical responses when they come from the top in an organization and when they are reproduced on the letterhead or in the memo format of the company.

The culture of the larger community influences folk narratives via such factors as the predominant religion, the political system, racial and ethnic makeup, and the community's economic base and range of affluence. In a study that goes "beyond textual studies," Eric L. Montenyohl describes how (in Lafayette, Louisiana) "contemporary legends and rumor [concerning supposed incidents of Satanism] became dangerous because the original and relatively short-lived oral tradition eventually entered the community's official (institutionalized) view of itself, and this provided a charter for authorities to act."

Contexts for collecting legends may be natural—that is, if the folklorist is skilled as well as lucky. A natural-*seeming* context may be subtly induced by a collector, or a completely artificial context may be forced, as when thrusting a microphone into someone's face and simply asking for a good story. The collector of legends is also part of the context, and any approach, however unnatural, may yield interesting texts for analysis. As Dan Ben Amos reminds us, "The performance of folklore forms can be within their culturally defined events or outside their boundaries, but they can never be out of context."

See also Collecting Urban Legends; Performance of Urban Legends

References: Dan Ben-Amos, "Contextual Approach," in Brunvand, *American Folklore: An Encyclopedia* (1996), 158–160; Mark Glazer, "The Contexts of the Contemporary Legend: 'The Vanishing Hitchhiker' and 'Gravity Hill,'" in Bennett and Smith, *A Nest of Vipers* (1990): 77–87; Sylvia Grider, "Dormitory Legend-Telling in Progress: Fall 1971–Winter 1972," *Indiana Folklore* 6 (1973): 1–32; Eric L. Montenyohl, "Beliefs in Satanism and Their Impact on a Community: Moving Beyond Textual

"The Cooked Pet or Baby"

See "The Baby-Roast"; "The Microwaved Pet"

"The Corpse in the Car"

In a European legend of World War II, a hitchhiker predicts the death of Hitler or the end of the war on a particular date and that the person(s) who picked him up will find a corpse in the car by the end of the day. The second prediction comes true, but the first does not. Usually the corpse is that of a person whom the driver stops to help after an automobile accident; the injured person dies in the car en route to the hospital.

This "myth" was the subject of a famous psychoanalytic study by Princess Marie Bonaparte of Greece, who first heard it in September 1938 with the prediction that "Hitler will be dead in six months." The story persisted in various versions throughout the war years and was occasionally incorporated into "The Vanishing Hitchhiker." Double predictions are found in earlier traditional legends as well.

Bonaparte collected several variations of the legend, and her analysis suggested that the story demonstrated a "regression" caused by anxieties concerning the war that "must have reactivated the need to offer a human victim in propitiation to fate."

Two psychologists, Sandy Hobbs and David Cornwell, reviewed the available data and noted the "comparative neglect" of this legend by folklorists. Their study demonstrated how scholars' own comments on "The Corpse in the Car" have contributed to confusion about the definition, classification, and analysis of contemporary legends.

References: Marie Bonaparte, *Myths of War,* trans. by John Rodker (London: Imago Publishing, 1947), chap. 1, "The Myth of the Corpse in the Car"; Sandy Hobbs and David Cornwell, "A Behavior Analysis Model of Contemporary Legend," *Contemporary Legend* 1 (1991): 93–106; *Vanishing Hitchhiker,* 30.

"The Corpse in the Cask"

In this legend, an English family discovers a barrelful of rum stored in the basement of an old house they recently purchased. Over the course of a year or two they consume the rum in drinks and cooking; then they cut the barrel in half to use it as a planter. Inside they find the body of a man who had been shipped home from the colonies long ago, preserved in spirits.

Corpses of fallen military officers and other officials were, in fact, sometimes returned to England inside barrels of wine or other spirits. Even Lord Nelson's body was preserved in a barrel of brandy after he fell at the Battle of Trafalgar in 1805 and in that container was sent back to England for burial. One tradition claims that sailors drilled into the barrel and sipped out some of the brandy with straws, giving rise to the expression "tapping the admiral."

"The Corpse in the Cask" is similar to American legends about bodies found in city water tanks, and it is also reminiscent of various legends about accidental cannibalism.

References: *Choking Doberman*, 114–118; *Too Good*, 197–198

CPR Annie Legend

This legend is summarized in *The Choking Doberman* (1984, p. 98):

> A beautiful young girl named Annie died for lack of anyone properly trained in CPR (cardio-pulmonary resuscitation) techniques to save her life. So her wealthy father financed the development of a lifelike practice dummy for CPR training, stipulating that the face on the model should be that of his beloved daughter and that all the future dummies made on this design should be known as "Annies" in her honor.

This is a generic retelling of a story repeated in many first-aid publications and by most CPR instructors when the practice dummy is introduced. The age of the alleged victim varies from that of a toddler up to the midteens, and the claimed accident was either a drowning or an automobile crash. Some people date the incident as far back as the 1930s while others say it occurred in the 1950s or 1960s. The incident may be located in Chicago or another American city or abroad.

Each CPR training mannequin manufactured by Laerdal Medical Corporation, a Norway-based company, does indeed wear a tag bearing the name "Resusci Anne," and the name is pronounced "Annie" by everyone involved in CPR instruction. The lifelike dummy that resembles a teenage girl was introduced in 1957 after two Norwegians, businessman Asmund S. Laerdal and a doctor from Stavanger, collaborated with Peter Safar, a Baltimore doctor, to create the training aid.

In 1987, on the thirtieth anniversary of the development of Resusci Anne, the Norwegian company held a celebration honoring her. In July 1988 David Hacker, a *Detroit Free Press* writer, interviewed a Michigan representative of Laerdal Medical Corporation and published an article telling her true story.

None of the people involved in developing Resusci Anne had lost a daughter in an accident; neither did they model the mannequin's face on anyone whom they knew personally. The face was actually based on a death mask made from the body of an unidentified young woman found early this century floating in the Seine River in Paris. Her case became a popular European story, and the image of her face was well known. The name "Anne" was adapted from a baby doll named "Anna" that was at one time manufactured by Laerdal.

From the rather prosaic facts about the origin of Resusci Anne, people have created more dramatic legends. Some of the stories include garbled fragments of the actual story, such as references to "Dr. Asman Leauridal" and to his daughter supposedly falling into "one of the canals of Norway" or drowning while swimming in "a fjord at Stavanger, Norway."

The Craig Shergold Legend

Craig Shergold, a seven-year-old boy in Carshalton, Surrey, England, is dying of a brain tumor. His last wish is to appear in the *Guinness Book of World Records* as the collector of more business cards than anyone else in history. Please send him your card at the address shown below and circulate this letter to ten other people or companies. [Address deleted to protect Craig.]

Countless numbers of this appeal, in printed, faxed, and e-mail formats, have circulated since 1989 when Craig Shergold, then seven years old, did indeed set out to break the *Guinness Book*'s record for postcards that had been established by Mario Morby, a young English cancer patient who had collected 1,000,265 postcards. The idea for the collection seems to have come from an appeal started in 1982 for a nonexistent Scottish boy, "Little Buddy," who supposedly wanted to set such a record.

Buddy and Mario soon faded from the world's attention, but Craig Shergold's long-abandoned appeal lives on in the chain letters, faxes, and e-mails, even though Craig was brought to the United States in 1991 and operated on successfully to remove a benign brain tumor. Craig has recovered, grown up, and lived normally ever since, except for the endless stream of letters and packages still arriving at his home bringing cards of all kinds for his collection.

Typical of a folk tradition, there are countless variations circulating of the spelling of Craig's name, the details of his address, and the nature of his collection (postcards? get-well cards? business cards?) Craig's age is often given as seven or eight years; by 1998, however, he had turned 16. The Shergold family made numerous appeals for the mail to stop, and the Guinness company discontinued the card-collecting record after Craig's astonishing 33 million pieces in 1990. The true story was given wide publicity, but cards of all kinds continue to arrive.

See also "Postcards for Little Buddy"

References: Anna Kearney Guigné, "The 'Dying Child's Wish' Complex: The Case of the Craig Shergold Appeal," *Contemporary Legend.* New Series 1 (1998), 116–133; Charisse Jones, "A Dream Comes True and Comes True . . . ," *New York Times* (September 1, 1993); John Pekkanen, "The Boy and the Billionaire," *Reader's Digest* (March 1991); *Too Good,* 461–465.

Crime

Numerous stories of thefts, frauds, scams, assaults, murders, kidnappings, and drug violations reveal crime as a major theme in urban legends. Indeed, crimes are involved in many stories of other categories as well—particularly automobiles, sex, and government—suggesting almost an obsession with the topic among contemporary legend-tellers. Moreover, most of the urban legends about crime are told internationally.

Balancing this prevalence of crime as a legend topic, many of the crimes described are actually rather minor. Thefts, for example, typically involve things like cookies, car parts, a restaurant meal, or a frozen chicken. Furthermore, many of the attempted crimes are thwarted, and even the successful criminals described in legends usually are said to be caught eventually.

Sometimes when a person has committed a theft, worse harm comes to the criminal than to the victim, illustrating poetic justice. Thus a thief steals a package but gets only a dead cat or a urine sample; he steals a car but also gets a dead grandmother who was tied on the roof rack; or perhaps the car thief is crushed to death in an earthquake while driving away. A would-be gas thief gets a mouthful from the RV's sewage-holding tank rather than the gasoline he intended to siphon. In "The Robber Who Was Hurt" the intruder never makes it inside the home and is badly burned in the attempt; similarly, in "The Choking Doberman" the robber does gain entry but loses two fingers in the process and is captured later.

Several urban legends describe the threat of a crime rather than the criminal action itself. This is true especially of automobile legends: In "The Hook," "The Killer in the Backseat," and "The Hairy-Armed Hitchhiker" earlier assaults and murders are implied, but none takes place in the story as it is told. In contrast, "The Boyfriend's Death" contains a vivid description of a grisly slaying.

Of course, there are plenty of actual atrocities and killings to be found in urban legends. Although the criminal in "The Attempted Abduction" is thwarted, there is no such luck in "The Castrated Boy." In "The Kidney Heist" not only does the victim actually lose an organ (sometimes even two); the perpetrators are not identified beyond their general characterization as someone involved in a transplant scam. The killer responsible for "The Body in the Bed" is never said to have been caught, although those who tried to smuggle drugs inside a dead baby *are* nabbed at the border.

Some supposed insight into the criminal mind is offered in a number of legends. In "The Unstealable Car," for example, the well-protected car is proven not to be safe after all, and the crook leaves a mocking note for the owner. In "The Toothbrush Photo" thieves leave gross photographic evidence of their crime, while in some stories about contaminated fast foods the guilty parties are said to telephone the victims to confess their actions. One holdup man foils the plan of another in "The Two Hitchhikers," and housebreakers work a clever scam in "The Double Theft." But even members of organized crime rings can be foiled, as shown in "The Helpful Mafia Neighbor."

See also Bogus Warnings; "The Colander Copier Caper"; Halloween Sadists; Police; "The Rape Trial"; Satanic Panic

References: *Baby Train,* 113–154; Michael Goss, "The Halifax Slasher and Other 'Urban Maniac' Tales," in Bennett and Smith, eds., *A Nest of Vipers* (1990), 89–111; *Mexican Pet,* 137–159; *Too Good,* 299–320; Eleanor Wachs, *Crime Victim Stories: New York's Urban Folklore* (Bloomington: Indiana University Press, 1988).

"Cruise Control"

Someone buys a new camper-van equipped with every convenience and option, including cruise control. After being briefed by the salesman on the operation of the vehicle, the buyer drives out and heads home. Once up to highway speed, he sets the cruise and steps into the back of the van to make himself a cup of coffee.

This story of technical incompetence dates from the early days of cruise control (mid-1970s) and is reminiscent of similar legends about push-button gear shifts and automatic transmissions. In common with these other car legends, "Cruise Control" does not usually go on to describe the resulting crash.

The buyer in various versions may be described as a foreigner (often an Arab), a member of a racial minority, a senior citizen, a youngster with more money than brains, or a woman; thus, the legend variously displays xenophobia, racism, sexism, or ageism—a version for every narrow-minded teller, who presumably would never confuse cruise control with automatic pilot.

In a front-page article on humorous insurance claims, the *Wall Street Journal* (July 9, 1986) repeated a female version, claiming that an insurance company had actually paid for the damages. An inquiry to the newspaper's source revealed that it was simply a story in oral circulation among insurance claims managers.

See also "Push-Starting the Car"; "'R' Is for Race"

References: *Choking Doberman*, 63–65; *Too Good*, 295–296.

"The Crushed Dog"

A young man is a houseguest of a prominent family, usually people who are important to his own future. In his bedroom he accidentally spills an inkwell, spoiling a carpet or other furnishings. His attempts to clean up the mess fail, and he slips away in the night, too embarrassed to confront his hosts. Some time later he is forgiven and invited back, but this time he accidentally sits on a small dog concealed on an overstuffed chair in a dimly lit parlor. He hides the dog's body and flees again, this time never to return.

The two-episode structure of this story is unusual for urban legends. Indeed, much of the circulation of "The Crushed Dog" is in printed sources. But the story has an oral tradition as well, with variations on the reason for the overnight visit, the means by which ink was spilled, the breed of dog, where the body is hidden, and so on. Sometimes the episodes are reversed, and there are a few variations on the nondog portion of this farcical comedy.

"The Crushed Dog" illustrates the anxieties people may feel when trying to make a good impression, especially in an unsettling social situation. A few versions describe an American abroad who is intimidated and confused by foreign customs. The legend also reveals disdain for small breeds of essentially useless lapdogs that are preferred as pets by some wealthy folks.

See also "The Missionaries and the Cat"

References: *Curses!*, 135–137; *Too Good*, 58–60.

Culture-Clash Legends

Various stories of misunderstandings occurring when someone tries to behave appropriately in another culture. Several such anecdotes center on tea bags—well known in the United States but a puzzle to some foreigners. The unaware outsider may try to tear open the bag to get the tea leaves out; then, after having the use of the bags demonstrated, the outsider sweetens his tea with the unopened sugar packet. In a variation, Americans hoax a foreign delegation at an international conference by putting their tea bags into their own mouths and drinking hot water through the bag. The foreigners follow suit.

Doubtless there are similar stories about Western tourists misusing chopsticks. Another kind of revenge for such embarrassment comes in stories about Americans adopting some text in Chinese or Arabic script as a decorative device, not realizing that the text contains an off-color or otherwise embarrassing message. In one version a woman knits Chinese characters into a sweater, taking the pattern from a restaurant menu. Later someone translates the text on her sweater as, "This dish cheap but unmistakably good."

Culture-clash legends are often told in the context of discussing relations between countries in social, business, or political matters. Some of the stories are, in fact, true; a famous example is President John F. Kennedy's grammatical gaffe when he declared in a speech in Germany, *"Ich bin ein Berliner,"* literally meaning not "I am a citizen of Berlin" but "I am a sweet roll."

References: *Baby Train,* 223–225.

"Curses! Broiled Again!"

A young woman wants, or *needs,* to get a fast suntan. The tanning salons in her city all have a 20-minute per-day limit. So she visits every salon in town, tanning at each of them for the maximum period allowed over a period of several days. Besides acquiring a deep tan, she begins to suffer from a bad smell emanating from her body. No matter how often she bathes or how much cologne she pours on, the smell persists, and she also begins to feel weak and sick. Finally, visiting her doctor, the young woman confesses her behavior and is told that the tanning rays have cooked her insides and that she has only a few weeks to live.

The motivations for the dangerous tanning regime vary from being a bridesmaid to the young woman's honeymoon, tropical vacation, or cheerleading camp. The legend burst upon the American scene in the summer of 1987 and was particularly hot, so to speak, through the better part of the following year. Often people were very specific about the local tanning salons, clinics, hospitals, and doctors supposedly involved in the tragic case, but they never knew the name of the young woman herself, only her general description as a vain but foolish person.

"Curses! Broiled Again!" obviously confuses the effects of ultraviolet tanning rays with those of the microwaves emitted in an oven. Besides this technological naïveté, the story comments on youthful vanity and carelessness. But the story ignores the real dangers of overexposure to tanning rays—severe sunburn and skin cancer.

References: *Curses!*, 29–36; *Too Good*, 292–293.

"The Cut-off Finger"

A woman is shopping at a large mall while her husband or boyfriend waits outside for her. But when the mall is starting to close, she still has not appeared, so he asks security to search for her. The woman is found in a fitting room where someone, often thought to be a black assailant, has cut off one of her fingers in order to steal her diamond ring. She has lost blood and has fainted, so they rush her to an emergency room for treatment. The thief is never caught.

This American legend of the mid-1970s to early 1980s, like several others, takes place in a shopping mall (or a mall parking lot). Folklorist Eleanor Wachs has interpreted the story in terms of its themes of conspicuous consumption, racial tensions, and "fear of urban crime and physical attack."

The severed-fingers theme also appears in an automobile legend of that title as well as in "The Choking Doberman." The legend of "The Hook" is about an attacker's severed hand (really its hooked substitute). Severed fingers and hands also appear in the traditional folktale "The Robber Bridegroom," also called "Mr. Fox" (Tale Type 955). An urban legend in which the attacker himself suffers injury to his finger is "The Robber Who Was Hurt."

A separate legend ("The Rider with the Extra Hand") describes the finger- or hand-lopping criminal finally being caught, usually on a bus or subway, when the severed appendage in his pocket is dripping blood and he is found to have the stolen ring or rings there as well. This story is occasionally heard in the United States but is better known abroad, including in Sweden, Spain, and Colombia.

See also Denmark; "The Sawed-Off Fingers"

References: *Baby Train*, 122–124; Eleanor Wachs, "The Mutilated Shopper at the Mall: A Legend of Urban Violence," in Bennett and Smith, *A Nest of Vipers* (1990), 144–160.

"The Cut-out Pullman"

Back in the 1940s, a New York businessman was returning home from a conference in Chicago on an overnight New York Central train. Unable to fall asleep, he put on his bathrobe and slippers and walked to the club car for a nightcap. There he met a young woman, and after a few preliminaries the two of them went to her compartment to spend the rest of the night. The businessman woke up the next morning in a Pullman car parked in the railroad yards in Buffalo; the young woman was gone, and so was his billfold. Her Pullman car had been shunted off to Buffalo, and the man's clothes and luggage were in his own compartment in the car bound for New York City.

This is a legend of decades ago when most business travel was still by train. The rude-awakening tale was then known to many railroad personnel on various train lines. Possibly this story influenced "The Nude in the RV" story of a later period, for here, too, a man is left behind in a state of partial undress—but on a highway rather than in a railroad car.

References: *Vanishing Hitchhiker*, 136–138.

"The Daughter's Letter from College"

Parents receive a long-awaited letter from their daughter at college and are dismayed to find it a catalog of appalling disasters. However, the letter concludes by denying all of the problems and mentioning instead the fact of her low grades. She writes:

> There was no dormitory fire; I did not have a concussion or a skull fracture; I was not in the hospital; I am not pregnant; I am not engaged. I do not have syphilis. . . . However, I am getting a D in history and an F in science, and I wanted you to see these grades in the proper perspective.

This letter usually circulates in anonymous photocopies, sometimes titled "Perspective," and is occasionally reported as a prank by a college student wanting to alarm and amuse her parents. Some variations contain class-based, anti-Semitic, or racist elements, implying that the daughter is living with a partner who would be anathema to her conservative parents. From a parent's viewpoint, the letter exposes the supposed pernicious influence of modern, ultra-liberal college life; from a student's perspective, the letter suggests, perhaps, the desire to experi-

105

ment during the college years, finally free of the parents' immediate control.

References: *Baby Train,* 312–314; *Too Good,* 439–440.

"The Day Trip"

This is an English story about travel troubles whose flavor is best revealed in a direct quotation from a native source. It is summarized by Rodney Dale in *The Tumour in the Whale* (1978), with a few explanatory notes inserted:

> A party of Cambridge people on a gasworks outing [a factory workers' group vacation) to Yarmouth [a seaside resort town] had to help one of their number back to the coach [the tour bus] because he was helplessly drunk.
>
> On reaching Cambridge, they took him home and put him to bed to sleep it off. When he woke, he was astonished to find himself at home in Cambridge because he hadn't been a member of the coach party but was in the middle of a fortnight's [two weeks'] holiday in Yarmouth and had merely fallen in with the crowd of his workmates who happened to be on the works outing.
>
> Meanwhile, his wife [who was with him in Yarmouth] had reported him missing to the police. (p. 128)

In another version of the story the man is on his honeymoon when he meets with strangers in a pub and gets drunk. They identify him from his wallet contents and ship him home, leaving his bride in the honeymoon suite wondering what has become of her husband.

Both of these stories portray the dangerous possibilities of misbehaving while traveling, a lesson familiar from the much more widely known legend "AIDS Mary."

See also "The Mystery Trip"

References: *Baby Train,* 229–230.

"The Dead Cat in the Package"

A thief steals a package or plastic bag from a shopper but gets only the body of a dead cat that the other person had been intending to dispose.

Sometimes two packages are accidentally switched—the cat's corpse with a package of steaks, a ham, or the like.

This classic urban legend of poetic justice—the thief gaining only an undesirable item—is extremely widespread and varied. In the United States the story can be traced as far back as 1906, though it reached its peak popularity in the 1950s, and it has persisted ever since. "The Runaway Grandmother" tells much the same tale, with a different stolen corpse, and "Alligators in the Sewers" is another urban legend about the disposal of a dead pet.

Most older versions describe someone's pet cat dying; the owner, an apartment-dweller, wraps the dead pet with the intention of giving the package to a friend whom she will meet in a department store; the friend will bury the cat in her suburban yard. But the package is stolen by a little old lady who passes out in public when she peeks into the package.

Later versions describe a shopper accidentally running over a stray cat in a shopping mall parking lot. She puts the cat into a plastic bag with a store logo, leaves it on the top of her car, and it is stolen. Often these versions end with the unconscious thief being carried from the mall on a stretcher with the unopened plastic bag placed on her chest by a helpful bystander. The details of the cat's death, the mall, the store logo, and the thief's behavior are all made very specific and local in these versions.

When the story includes the accidental switching of two packages, usually the pet owner has wrapped the package, intending to dispose of it during the day. But each time he or she tries to abandon it, the package is returned by a "helpful" stranger. Back home that evening, the owner discovers the switcheroo.

"The Dead Cat in the Package" has inspired numerous cartoon illustrations, at least two songs, and a poem in mock Middle English. The Russian author Yevgeny Yevtushenko included a version in his novel *Wild Berries* (1981).

References: *Baby Train*, 20–22, 245–246; *Choking Doberman*, 216–219; *Mexican Pet*, 31–34; *Too Good*, 74–76; *Vanishing Hitchhiker*, 103–111.

"The Death Car"

A late-model car, often a luxury model, is offered for sale cheaply at a dealership because the original owner died in the car and the body was not discovered for a long time. The smell of death cannot be removed from the vehicle, despite heroic efforts.

This classic cheap-car fantasy has evolved from a $50 Buick in the 1940s to a $500 Porsche or Corvette in the 1990s. The death may be said to have occurred in a remote forest or in the desert. The local dealership is never positively identified, but the storyteller knows someone whose friend actually saw, and presumably *smelled,* the very car.

Other legends about remarkably inexpensive cars are "The 50-Dollar Porsche" (abandoned wife sells car) and "The Bargain Sports Car" (unaware mother sells dead son's car). "The Body in the Bed" is another legend about the smell of death permeating a location.

Despite the wide circulation of "The Death Car" in myriad variations, Richard M. Dorson believed that he had found the legend's origin in an actual incident involving an old Model-A Ford that occurred in a small Michigan town in 1938 about which people were still talking in the 1950s. His claim was disputed by English folklorist Stewart Sanderson and others who identified key differences between the Michigan event and the legend tradition, as well as the likely influence of the ancient motif "The Ineradicable Bloodstain" (Motif E422.1.11.5.1).

A genuine death-related luxury car—a low-mileage 1959 Cadillac held as evidence for years after the owner had been murdered in it—was reported in the July 1990 issue of *Automobile* magazine. Although the editors were reminded of the legend, they verified this instance as true, but significantly different, since the car did not smell. The legendary version of the story had been circulating for decades before the "Death Cadillac" was discovered, bought, and installed in a museum.

"The Death Car" can probably best be understood as a legend of wishful thinking (for a good, cheap car) that had its first popularity in the postwar years when new cars of any kind were scarce and expensive. The death motif would seem to be updated from older traditional legends about the lingering "proofs" of a murder or other tragic death remaining at the site of the incident.

See also Mint Condition Vintage Vehicles

References: *The Truth,* 15–21; *Choking Doberman,* 212–213; *Mexican Pet,* 12–13; *Too Good,* 236–237; *Vanishing Hitchhiker,* 20–22.

"The Death of Little Mikey"

This story was nicely summarized in a short item headlined "Rocks Redux," published in *Adweek* (Western Advertising News edition) on July 20, 1987:

Mikey lives. And, as a result, so does General Foods' Pop Rocks candy.

Because rumormongers had Life cereal's little spokesguy biting the dust after biting into one of the carbonated candies, Pop Rocks were pulled from the market in 1980.

Now that Mikey is back to Life—he appears on new cereal ads—so are the nonlethal Rocks. The sweet fizzies have been reintroduced to a rock-starved public in several Western markets.

"Mikey," played by actor John Gilchrist, actually never spoke in the Life cereal TV commercials introduced in 1971 when he was three years old. But he did eat the new cereal offered to him by his older brothers, leading them to exclaim, "Hey! He likes it!" Shortly after Pop Rocks—a hugely popular effervescent candy—was introduced in 1974, the rumor arose that Little Mikey had drunk soda after eating Pop Rocks and had died when his stomach exploded.

General Foods defended the safety of its product in full-page newspaper ads but never mentioning the Mikey rumor. Eventually, however, the product was withdrawn and the story died. Later both Mikey (as a teenager) and Pop Rocks reappeared, still never officially linked in any advertising or news releases issued by the companies involved.

Although this represents a textbook example of how corporations are best advised to handle negative rumors, the fact is that a product and possibly also an actor did suffer from the oral tradition.

References: *Choking Doberman,* 103–106; *Too Good,* 171–172; *Vanishing Hitchhiker,* 89.

Decapitated Riders and Drivers

A child or a dog has its head out the car window while riding on a busy highway. Another vehicle passes the car very closely and takes its head clean off. Sometimes the decapitation is so quick and neat that others in the car do not notice the incident for some time.

A motorcyclist is passing a large truck loaded with a stack of thin steel plates. One plate slips out sideways and takes the head clean off the cyclist. The headless body continues to ride past the truck, frightening the driver.

The former version is more common in the United States, the latter in England. A character in Charles Dickens's *Pickwick Papers* (1836) described the decapitation of a woman riding atop a stagecoach passing under a low arch; she had a sandwich in her hand but "no mouth to put it in." In some modern American versions of the dog story the pet is sitting on the lap of a child who keeps on petting the headless animal. In the motorcycle story sometimes when the truck driver sees the headless cyclist he has a heart attack, loses control of his huge vehicle, and plows into a group of people at the edge of the road.

References: *Mexican Pet,* 56–57; *Too Good,* 96–97.

"The Deer Departed"

A deer hunter has dropped a huge buck sporting a magnificent rack of antlers with a single shot. He decides to take a picture of himself with his prize, placing his new rifle across the deer's rack. But while the hunter is arranging his camera on a tripod, the deer—merely stunned from a flesh wound—gets up and walks into the woods, carrying the expensive rifle (scope, sling, etc.) away.

This story is one of several dumb-hunter stories repeated annually during the deer season. The theme of an animal's revenge is found in several other urban legends, including "The Kangaroo Thief" and one about tourists in Yellowstone Park posing their child for a photo on top of a bear. The bear, like the stunned deer (and the kangaroo), departs with its load.

See also "The Hunter's Nightmare"

References: *Mexican Pet,* 24–25; *Too Good,* 341–342.

"Define 'Courage'"

In this legend, a college student is faced with a single examination question: "Define 'Courage.'" She writes only, "This is courage," then hands in the otherwise blank sheet of paper. She receives an A on the examination. Sometimes the question is a crucial entrance requirement, or the only question on a final examination in a philosophy class, or the entire preliminary examination for a doctoral degree.

This is one of the most popular stories about tricky questions and answers on college examinations. It is known in England as well as the United States (a French version asks the students to define *l'audace*).

Usually, the professor's seemingly impossible demand is easily solved by a clever student, that is, the question is merely "Why?" and the winning answer is "Because" or "Why not?" In another case, however, the professor tests his students' excuse that they were delayed by a flat tire and missed his final exam; the first question on the makeup test is "Which tire?" and the students are placed in separate rooms to write their answers.

Reflecting an actual practice of some professors, a student is supposedly asked to write his own examination question and then answer it. One student asks himself, "Do you play the tuba?" then answers "No."

See also "The One-Word Exam Question"; "The Open-Book Exam"

References: *Too Good*, 444–447.

Definition of "Legend"

Folklorists have difficulties defining the individual genres of material that they study in a precise way, and, in fact, even in defining "folklore" in a manner that satisfies all scholars studying the subject. Still, there is general, tacit agreement on both the dimensions of the entire field and on the individual categories of material to be studied.

"Legends" are generally assigned to the folkloric category of Oral Narratives and are distinguished from the related forms of Folktale and Myth. Complications arise when we consider that transmission of all of these stories nowadays may occur via print, broadcast, or electronic media as well as oral tradition and that "narrative" itself is not easy to define.

Still, the term "oral narrative" is widely accepted as useful for anonymous stories passed on in variants, mostly by word of mouth. Within this general category, "myths" are defined as once-believed ancient accounts of deities and the creation of the world; "legends" as believed accounts of incidents in the historical past; and "folktales" as stories with fictional plots (fairy tales, jokes, tall tales, etc.) not to be believed literally.

Although the legend criteria—narrative, belief, set in the historical past—seem clear enough, each criterion has numerous exceptions when applied to actual examples. This frustrating situation led folklorist Robert Georges to declare in a 1971 essay that "a legend is a story or narrative that may not be a story or narrative at all; it is set in a recent or historical past that may be conceived to be remote or antihistorical or not really past at all; it is believed to be true by some, false by others, and both or neither by most."

One solution to the definitional problem as proposed by Timothy R. Tangherlini was to survey a large body of possible definitions and examples of legends in folklorists' own writings and extract the common traits. The short form of the definition that emerged from this approach was stated thus: "A 'legend' is a monoepisodic, localized, and historicized traditional narrative told as believable in a conversational mode. . . . Psychologically [it is] a symbolic representation of folk belief [that] reflects the collective experiences and values of the group to whose tradition it belongs."

Older traditional legends are often religious, supernatural, or historical in subject matter and are frequently attached to specific persons, places, and events. Reflecting each legend's individual emphases, the stories could be subclassified in categories such as Hero Legends, Ghost Stories, Place-name Legends, and many others.

Besides abstract explanations of legends' characteristic forms, definitions also need to take into account the contexts in which legends are told and the manner of their telling (i.e., their "performance"). Further, we need to distinguish the migratory legends' fixed and variable content features as they are localized to different settings. Defining "legend" is, indeed, no easy task.

Defining "urban legends" more specifically as a subtype of legends is also difficult, and it is certainly not merely a matter of calling them just modern or contemporary manifestations of traditional legends (whatever *they* may be). Further complicating this aspect of legend definition is deciding what constitutes "urban," "contemporary," and "modern" subject matter and, again, how to define "narrative" and to distinguish the various means of legend transmission. One attempt at a concise definition states that an urban legend is "an apocryphal contemporary story, told as true but incorporating traditional motifs, and usually attributed to a friend of a friend" (Brunvand 1996, p. 730).

Evidence of a continuing effort to define legend genres consistently is found in the 1997 reference work *Folklore: An Encyclopedia* (edited by Thomas A. Green) wherein three prominent folklorists offer three individual statements as basic definitions of related genres. For "legend," Linda Dégh began, "Short, oral prose narrative based in the reality of performers and audiences." Defining "contemporary legend," Paul Smith offered, "A short traditional narrative, or *digest* of a narrative, that has no definitive text, formulaic openings and closings, or artistically developed form. . . . Contemporary legends are primarily nonsupernatural, secular narratives that are set in the real world." And for "urban legend," Bill Ellis wrote, "A popular term for a narrative concerning some aspect of modern life that is believed by its teller but is actually untrue."

To encourage further discussion of definitional problems, and as a guide for reviewing the matter, Paul Smith has drawn up a list of more than five dozen "persistently recurring definitional characteristics" of contemporary legends, grouping them as Primary Characteristics (legends described as what they are or are not) versus Secondary Characteristics (legends described in terms of what they may or may not be). These characteristics fall into 13 main categories, most of them having several subsections. The main groupings Smith uses are Narrative Status, Form, Structure, Style, Dissemination, "Narrators," Context of Narration, Content, Truth, Belief, Selection, Meaning, and Function. The illustrate the usefulness of this outline, taking the crucial matter of "truth" in contemporary legends, here is Smith's clear and sensible statement:

> A contemporary legend may or may not, in whole or part, be true. This may not necessarily be *literal* truth, but perhaps truth which comes from typifying life in the twentieth century.

On the specific question of the contemporaneity of modern legends, Smith published another useful statement in the journal *Folklore* (no. 106, 1995: 98–100). Here he refers to a "contemporary legend" as "a 'body' to be 'clothed' in performance . . . in order to provide a vehicle for the discussion of relevant contemporary issues." Despite the mixed metaphor, this observation along with the rest of the short article help to clarify the senses in which any legend is or is not "contemporary."

See also Classifying Urban Legends; Contemporary Legend; Folklore; Folktale; Joke; Linguistic Approach; Myth; Proto-Legend; Rumor; Scary Stories; Supernaturalism in Urban Legends; Urban Belief Tale; Urban Myth

References: Brunvand, "Legends and Anecdotes," chap. 9 in *The Study of American Folklore* (1998), 196–228; Hand, *American Folk Legend* (1971); "Legend: Definition," in Bennett and Smith, *The Questing Beast*

(1989), 27–101 [four essays by different scholars]; Paul Smith, "Definitional Characteristics of the Contemporary Legend," *FOAFtale News* no. 44 (May 1999), 5–8; Timothy R. Tangherlini, "Legend," in Brunvand, *American Folklore: An Encyclopedia* (1996), 437–439.

Denmark

Contemporary Danish folklorists have collected a number of urban legends from their country, publishing them mostly in their own language. An exception is a short discussion of "The Unzipped Fly" that included a text from Copenhagen in an English translation sent by Carsten Bergenhøj to *FOAFtale News* (no. 24, 1991). Other modern migratory legends (*vandrehistorier*) reported in Danish include "The Runaway Grandmother" and the one about immigrants stealing people's pets and eating them, in one variant of which the dog has been shaved for butchering before it is rescued.

Surely some folklorist in Denmark will eventually compile a collection of urban legends to rival those from elsewhere in Europe. In the meantime, there are a few further examples available in Reimund Kvideland and Henning K. Sehmnsdorf's book *Scandinavian Folk Belief and Legend,* including this version of "The Severed Finger" as told by Danish folklorist Bengt Holbek while visiting a Swedish archive:

> I heard this story from the wife of a lawyer. She had heard the story from an acquaintance who worked at the police station in Hørsholm.
>
> A woman was driving on Hørsholm Road (now Helsingør Road), on her way home from Copenhagen. When she got to an area where there are not many houses, a gang of motorcyclists drove up behind her. Her car was small and not very fast. The motorcyclists passed her and tried to push her to the side of the road. They were trying to get her to stop, and she knew they would probably rape her. Just to scare her, one of them drove right up to her slowing car and struck the windshield with a chain, knocking a hole in it. Of course, she was terrified, but she pushed the gas pedal to the floor and drove away from the motorcyclists. To her surprise they did not follow her. She drove to the nearest police station to report what had happened. There she realized that the chain was tangled in the windshield, and two of the motorcyclist's fingers were stuck to one end of it.

See also Norway; Sweden

References: Reimund Kvideland and Henning K. Sehmsdorf, eds., *Scandinavian Folk Belief and Legend* (Minneapolis: University of Minnesota Press, 1988), 381–382; *Too Good,* 142–143 ("The Unzipped Fly").

Dental Death

When a patient dies in the chair, supposedly the dentist will carry the corpse to the restroom, leaving him to be discovered. This happens sometimes when a dentist has two treatment rooms and tries to work on patients in both chairs at once. One time a dentist had his "corpse" come walking back in, since the trip downstairs to the restroom had revived the patient, who was only deeply sedated.

Such stories stem from people's dread of dental work and distrust of dentists, but they are completely impossible, not only because of medical ethics but also because a dental assistant, receptionist, or another patient would surely observe the crime or a relative would know where the person was going that day. Besides, if such were a general practice, sooner or later a guilty dentist would be caught, leading to massive publicity.

References: *Curses!,* 68–69; *Too Good,* 207.

Department Store Snakes

See "The Snake in the Store"

"The Devil in the Dance Hall"

A handsome stranger, often dressed all in black, enters a dance hall and sweeps all the young women off their feet. He dances on and on with partner after partner, until late into the night. Then one of the women notices that he has chicken feet (or cloven hoofs, or a tail, etc.). She screams "The Devil!" and the stranger rushes out in a cloud of sulfurous smoke and gallops away on his fiery black stallion. He may leave burn marks on the floor or even on his last dancing partner.

This is an old and widely distributed supernatural legend with prototypes in European folklore. In the New World it is especially popular among French Canadians, French-speaking Louisianans, and particularly Mexican Americans. Modernizations of the story have the devil appear at a bar or discotheque or even a casino (particularly at one run by Native Americans).

Modern versions of the story retain some ancient devil lore, such as how the devil is recognized, but an equally typical older legend, "The Devil at the Card Party," has not turned into an urban legend. It is possible, however, that the card-party legend had some role in the development of the dance-hall story, since both may describe the devil's cloven hoof as a recognition motif.

References: William A. Owens, "Trailing the Devil in Louisiana," *Southwest Review* 42 (1957): 144–148; *Too Good,* 247–250; *Vanishing Hitchhiker,* 180–181.

"Dial 911 for Help"

The emergency telephone number should be publicized as "nine-one-one," not "nine-eleven," because one time someone was unable to place a 911 call because he or she could not find the 11 button on the telephone. It's an easy mistake to make under the pressure of a life-or-death situation.

This notion has circulated as a serious warning as well as a joke and shows up periodically in newspaper advice columns and on radio talk shows. Some tellers include a detailed account of exactly what the emergency supposedly was and the dire consequences that ensued because of the misunderstanding.

Not only has the 911 problem never been authenticated as an actual incident, but there was a "Little Moron" joke of the 1940s that centered on the same mistake. When nine-eleven was chosen for the emergency dialing code, perhaps it was inevitable that the old joke would spawn a new urban legend.

References: *Baby Train,* 42–43; *Choking Doberman,* 208–209; *Too Good,* 333–334.

"Ding-Dong, Dinner Bell"

See "Come and Get It!"

"The Dishonest Note"

A driver returns to his parked car to find it damaged from a collision with another car leaving the lot. A note placed under the windshield wiper reads, "The people watching me think I am leaving my name and address, but I am not."

"The Dishonest Note" has been repeated as a story since the 1960s both orally and in newspaper columns, but it has also actually happened a number of times, as attested by both victims and perpetrators who have come forward. Some tellers expand on the details, describing a crowd of people watching the guilty party write the note; but nobody ever seems to have taken down his license-plate number.

References: *Curses!,* 118–120; *Too Good,* 330–331.

Dissertation Legends

The importance of a doctoral dissertation in an academic career and the stresses involved in writing an acceptable dissertation have given rise to a number of legends. They are based on such very real possibilities as plagiarism, inadvertently duplicating work done by others, lost or corrupted data needed for the dissertation, whimsical objections to the dissertation by the approval committee, and (most common of all) loss of the final copy of the dissertation itself.

What distinguishes legend from reality here is that the apocryphal stories have anonymous generic characters (e.g., a graduate student in a California college) and the crisis in the legends always occurs after many years of hard work and cannot by any means be overcome. Another legendary trait, of course, is that variations of the same stories are told in many different parts of the country and, indeed, around the world.

Plagiarism stories usually involve a graduate student stealing from an obscure source, only to have one of his committee members happen to be acquainted with the same work. Lost-data stories are typical of scientific topics where carefully designed experiments may go awry because of something as simple as a power outage or someone opening the wrong door or window, exposing the controlled laboratory atmosphere to outside air or light.

The single existing complete copies of dissertations were supposedly lost, in earlier legends, as a result of fires, floods, thefts, or even by such simple means as blowing page by page off the backseat of the student's convertible as he drove to campus to deliver the work to his adviser. Although such disasters are certainly possible, the stories fail to identify the supposed victims, and they ignore the institutional requirements for multiple copies as well as the prudent student's understanding of the necessity of making backups.

Recent versions of dissertation legends describe the demoralizing loss as the result of a computer crash, naturally (ignoring standard computer procedure) without a backup of any kind. Although outlines, proposals, drafts, chapters, or subsections of works are truly lost when computers fail or, more often, when users make irreversible errors, the possibility of someone risking an entire dissertation in a single computer copy seems unlikely. The implications of the legends, perhaps, are that anyone this foolish probably does not deserve a doctorate anyway, and also that qualifying for an advanced degree is no guarantee of common sense.

References: *Baby Train*, 322–324.

"Do You Know Who I Am?"

A college student writes for a few minutes after time is called on an essay examination for a large class and is told by an officious proctor or by the instructor that his blue book will not be accepted. He will fail the course. "Do you know who I am?" the student asks. The class is large, and the reply is, "No, and I don't care." The student says "Good!" and shoves his own examination booklet into the middle of the large pile of blue books on the desk. (Sometimes he knocks the pile to the floor before adding his own booklet to the mass.)

This is another academic legend about examinations, similar to "Define Courage," "The One-Word Exam Question," and "The Second Blue Book" in that the clever student outwits the demanding instructor. In some versions the instructor accuses the student of cheating on the test but still does not know that student's name. The theme of the unknown student also appears in "The Bird-Foot Exam," while the general Do you know me? theme occurs in stories with nonacademic settings.

References: *Curses!*, 275–276; *Mexican Pet*, 198–199; *Too Good*, 443-444.

"The Dog in the High-rise"

A man comes to pick up his date, who lives in an apartment in a high-rise. While she is getting ready in another room, he tosses a ball for her dog to fetch. On the third throw the ball bounces out the open door, onto the balcony, and over the railing into the street far below. The dog jumps after the ball.

Writer Truman Capote told this story frequently as a true story about a model, her blind date, and her Great Dane, but other versions, usually about smaller breeds of dogs, also circulate. Similar to "The Crushed Dog," this legend describes a pet's unfortunate death as a result of a nervous visitor's faux pas. The plot has been used in at least two TV productions, one a sitcom episode and the other a beer commercial.

References: *Choking Doberman*, 96–97; *Too Good*, 60-61.

"Dog's Corpse Is Stolen"

A large dog—the pet of a woman living in a New York City apartment—dies. A call to the humane society or other agency reveals that she must deliver the body to them for burial, so she puts her dead dog into a large suitcase or trunk and heads for the nearest subway station. A stranger offers to help her boost the heavy case over the turnstile, but when she gets inside and turns to receive the load, the man keeps the case and runs up the stairs to the street.

This incident was reported, tongue in cheek, with varying details in 1987 and 1988 by columnists for two New York newspapers who attributed it only to hearsay. One version said the dog was a Great Dane, the other a German shepherd. The initial problem in the story of dead-pet disposal, followed by the unwitting theft of the corpse, mark this as a likely transformation of the much older "The Dead Cat in the Package."

References: *Mexican Pet*, 32–33; *Too Good*, 63-65.

"The Dog's Dinner"

A couple traveling in the Far East with their toy poodle are dining in a Chinese restaurant where nobody speaks English. They want to get a meal for their pet, so they use sign language—pointing to the dog, then to their mouths. The waiter nods, smiles, and scoops up the little dog and carries it off to the kitchen. Later they are served from a large covered dish, inside of which they find their pet dog roasted and garnished with pepper sauce and bamboo shoots.

This story circulated as a news item about a Swiss couple in Hong Kong in 1971 and was widely reprinted. Oral versions have circulated internationally since the late 1930s, sometimes with the dog identified as a Chihuahua and the waiter explaining, "Your dog was dish number eight." "The Dog's Dinner" is sometimes told as a story about deaf travelers trying to make themselves understood in an ethnic restaurant by means of sign language.

"The Dog's Dinner" reveals both uneasiness about travel in a country where one cannot speak the language, as well as the common idea that Orientals prefer dog meat as a regular part of their cuisine. Among the discrepancies in the story is the fact that most countries require a quarantine period before pets may be brought in, so that casual vacation travel with one's pet is an unlikely situation.

See also "The Eaten Pets"

References: *Choking Doberman,* 95–96; *Too Good,* 53-54.

"The Dolly Parton Diet"

In 1981 the story spread orally and by means of photocopies that Dolly Parton had lost weight following a strict diet that consisted of essentially all you wanted to eat of one food each day, plus servings of "T. J.'s Miracle Soup." Numerous people, mainly in the Midwest, followed the diet, some claimed with great success. None reported any enlargement of bust size, a stated hope of some women who had tried the diet.

Some copies of this diet were titled "The Hollywood Diet" or claimed that it had been developed by "Sacred Heart Hospital–Spokane." A parody called "The Stress Diet" was circulating at about the same time; this one began each day with a light breakfast, then progressed through the day with more and more cookies, pizza, beer, and snacks. The parody also included a list of "Diet Tips" such as, "If no one sees you eat it, it has no calories" and "snacks consumed in a movie don't count."

Ricki Fulman's investigative article on this story in the *New York News* is a case study in debunking an oral tradition by means of following up on each person's stated source. Fulman's search found no verification for the story, only a chain of friends of friends, and she concluded that "after interrogating close to 50 persons about this, enough is enough."

References: *Mexican Pet,* 186–190.

"Don't Mess with Texas"

In 1987 the State Highway Department of Texas began an antilittering campaign that was promoted by the slogan "Don't Mess with Texas" used in advertisements, bumper stickers, T-shirts, refrigerator magnets, and the like. Supposedly, when a Texas businessman sought backing for a new venture from a New York City bank, he was turned down. Asking why, the Texan was shown "Don't Mess with Texas" stickers posted in the bank's offices, a reference to falling oil prices that had hurt the Texas economy.

Unable to verify the story, *Texas Monthly* magazine suggested, "Perhaps it's just the latest urban legend."

References: *Mexican Pet*, 265–266.

"The Dormitory Surprise"

Here's how I summarized this campus story, sometimes called simply "The Surprise," as I remembered it from Michigan State University in the mid-1950s:

> Forgetting that it was visitor's day, one resident of a men's dorm went down the hall to the shower leaving his two roommates chatting in the room. Coming back, wearing only a towel, the freshly showered man heard voices coming from the room and assumed it was his roommates still chatting.
>
> He decided to make a dramatic entrance. He whipped the towel off, held his penis in one hand, kicked the door open, and jumped in yelling "Bang bang, you're all dead!"
>
> The voices he'd heard, however, were those of his mother, father, and hometown girlfriend who had just arrived to visit him. (*Baby Train,* p. 305)

Widely told, but never by eyewitnesses, on countless American college campuses from the 1950s to the present, this is a typical caught-in-the-nude legend. The campus setting is appropriate because for many students it is their first experience at living away from the restraints of home and family for any extended period. Both parents' and students' concerns about dormitory living are reflected in the legend. Another theme is students' propensities to sometimes play crude pranks.

Variations of the story involving a young woman returning from the shower wearing only a towel may describe her wrapping the towel around her head so that nobody can recognize her. A male counterpart version with this detail has the young man wrap the towel around his head like a turban before making his grand entry, penis in hand and shouting in a faked foreign accent.

All stories of nudity in campus housing seem to have been more common *before* the days of coed dormitories, despite the fact that such confrontations would seem more likely in the present. Perhaps students have become more liberal or are simply jaded by the constant presence of the opposite sex in the same living unit.

References: *Baby Train*, 305–307; *Mexican Pet*, 201; *Too Good*, 430-431.

"The Double Theft"

A thief steals one item as a preliminary to stealing further and more valuable items. There are two typical scenarios:

The first is that woman's purse is stolen by someone reaching under the partition between stalls in the restroom of a large department store. The woman reports the theft to the store management and goes home. Later she receives a telephone call from someone saying that the store has found her purse. But when she returns, nobody at the store has made such a call, and she finds that her home was burglarized in her absence by someone using the keys taken from her purse to gain entry.

The second describes someone's car being stolen, but it is returned the next day with a note of thanks saying that the thief needed transportation for an emergency. Two tickets to a popular show are enclosed. When the car owners return from the theater, they find that their home was burglarized while they were out.

Both versions of "The Double Theft" have had wide international distribution (from Scandinavia to Australia) at least since the early 1970s. In each country the story is localized with names of specific department stores and of particular theaters or performances. In the United States often it is just the car's battery that is stolen, or even something as minor as a barbecue grill. The tickets sent to the victims may be for ballet or opera performances at one end of the cultural scale or for hockey games or rock concerts at the other end.

Although criminals may actually sometimes use similar ploys to gain access to a home or to assure the owners' absence, the schemes outlined in "The Double Theft" are more elaborate and risky than necessary. There are simpler ways to burglarize a home safely without securing expensive tickets or setting up tricky scams.

See also "The Robber Who Was Hurt"

References: *Choking Doberman*, 193–194; *Too Good*, 308–309.

"The Dream Warning"

See "The Phantom Coachman"; "Room for One More"

Drug Horror Stories

Rumors and stories grossly exaggerate the dangerous effects of drugs, particularly LSD and PCP (known on the street as "angel dust"). The most common "mythic tale," as one investigator has labeled them, is that a group of college students in the 1960s, high on LSD, stared directly into the sun until they lost their eyesight. A similar story claims that people high on PCP have plucked out their own eyes. Other violent self-destructive behavior supposedly typical of crazed drug users includes jumping off roofs and extracting their own teeth; some addicts allegedly gained enough strength when high on drugs to tear themselves free from locked handcuffs. Stories of users cooking babies or of smugglers using an infant's hollowed-out corpse to smuggle drugs are also part of the drug horror story tradition.

As bad as drug addiction and drug crimes are in today's world, none of the above stories is literally true. Still, they are sometimes repeated by antidrug groups and even by police authorities as dire warnings against the evils of drug use.

See also "The Baby-Roast"; "The Stuffed Baby"

References: *Baby Train,* 109–112.

A Drug-Smuggling Legend

See "The Stuffed Baby"

"Drugged and Seduced"

Here is a composite summary of the legend from the 1973 article cited below:

A young college girl, usually a freshman, goes on a blind date with a fraternity boy to a party at his fraternity house. In the course of the evening, the boy slips a drug into the girl's drink, which causes her to lose consciousness. He begins to molest her, but she wakes up just in time. In some versions, however, the girl does not regain consciousness until the next morning, and can only realize what happened at that time. A variant form of this legend ends with the girl's drinking punch to which LSD had been secretly added. In this case, she is either raped while drugged or else experiences various unpleasant effects from the drug.

"Drugged and Seduced" was a common story circulated on college campuses in the 1960s and 1970s, especially near the beginning of the academic year as a warning to new students. The tellers, however, had neither experienced the incident nor knew anyone personally who had. In the 1990s, however, with the appearance of Rohypnol, the so-called rape drug, the legend became reality, to some degree, as a number of actual cases of date rape facilitated by the drug occurred. A similar story describes a dentist taking advantage of female patients while they are under anesthesia for treatment.

See also "The Gay Roommate"

References: *Choking Doberman,* 133; Andrea Greenberg, "Drugged and Seduced: A Contemporary Legend," *New York Folklore Quarterly* 29 (1973), 131–158.

Dutch Urban Legends

See Holland

Earthquake Stories

Rumors, legends, personal experience stories, jokes, and other oral lore are often triggered by earthquakes; these items circulate among the direct victims and witnesses of seismic events as well as among outsiders who are fascinated and horrified by the damage and its human toll. Similar kinds of disaster folklore arise from other dangerous events, both natural (floods, hurricanes, blizzards, etc.) and those caused directly by humans (riots, wars, toxic spills, etc.).

Typical earthquake lore includes claims about supernatural predictions of quakes, conflicting reports of a quake's severity, talk of conspiracies to suppress the extent of quake damage, miraculous-rescue stories, rumors of unpaid insurance claims, and accounts of bizarre behavior during and following the event. The best example of an urban legend developing after a recent earthquake is the one about a car thief who was crushed while escaping during the Northern California earthquake of October 17, 1989.

See also "Car Stolen During Earthquake"

References: Gail Matthews-DeNatale and Doug DeNatale, "Disaster Folklore," in Brunvand, *American Folklore: An Encyclopedia* (1996), 202–203.

Earwig Stories

The earwig got its name from an ancient folk belief claiming that this insect likes to enter the human ear and then bore its way deep into the head. The idea was probably strengthened by the earwig's appearance, with a sharp, pincer-like appendage extending to the rear. However, earwigs are herbivores, and they are no more likely to enter an ear than are ants, bees, flies, or any other small insect. Even when earwigs do occasionally find their way into human ears, they cannot burrow through the skin and into the brain.

Modern urban legends about earwigs elaborate upon the theme of ear-burrowing with accounts of a doctor supposedly extracting an earwig from the opposite ear from its entry point and declaring it to be a female that must have laid eggs during its transit of the brain. A further elaboration of this notion is an anonymously photocopied "Earwig Alert" that pretends to be a medical bulletin advising patients infested with earwigs to take vitamins fortified with large amounts of iron and then have the "wiglets" (or "larvalettes") extracted with a strong electromagnet.

Earwig stories have entered popular culture in science-fiction plots involving small voracious creatures put into the ears of enemies. There is also a punk-rock song with the chorus "You got an earwig, crawling toward your brain."

References: *Curses!*, 40–43; *Too Good*, 187–191.

"The Eaten Pets"

The common folk idea in the West that some foreigners, especially Eastern Europeans and Orientals, eat cats and dogs as a regular part of their diets has given rise to numerous rumors and legends claiming that immigrants are stealing our cats and dogs for their dinner tables or to serve in ethnic restaurants. Such stories have a long history in Europe and Australia but have emerged more recently in the United States, especially with waves of new immigrants coming from Asia since the late 1960s.

Local police, health officials, and journalists have repeatedly investigated such stories, almost always concluding that they are untrue. Spokespersons for the targeted immigrant groups have explained that dogs and cats are seldom eaten in their home countries and that in the United States, with so many other kinds of meat readily available, there is no motivation for hunting down people's pets for food.

Besides the ethnic stereotyping evident in such stories, the actual disappearance of many pets seems to lend credibility to the claim. ("If those Asians are not eating our missing pets, then where *are* they disappearing!?") Often these eaten-pet rumors and legends, as well as news stories about them, imply that even though such practices have not been documented locally, they do exist in other states, California being a leading example to be cited.

A degree of skepticism about the stories is suggested by a sick joke that a new Vietnamese cookbook is titled *100 Ways to Wok Your Dog*.

See also Chinese Restaurants; "The Dog's Dinner"

References: *Baby Train*, 255–258; *Choking Doberman*, 122–127; *Mexican Pet*, 99–103; *100 Good*, 362–364.

"The Economical Car"

Someone's new car gets phenomenal gas mileage—sometimes as much as 1,000 miles per gallon. The driver is astounded and mentions it to the dealer from whom he bought the car. The dealer realizes that the customer has accidentally been sold an experimental model that the factory was desperately trying to locate and recall. The man is given a huge cash bonus for returning the car, or else is promised a new car annually for the rest of his life.

Variations of "The Economical Car" have circulated at least since the late 1940s when, supposedly, new cars would improve greatly by incorporating the technical advances pioneered in the recent war. The legend resurfaces periodically with different details, especially in times of oil crisis and high gasoline prices. The reason for the claimed miracle mileage is usually said to be a revolutionary carburetor that the oil companies, in a conspiracy with automobile manufacturers, are suppressing.

Despite the complete lack of any scientific or engineering support for such claims, the economical-car and miracle-carburetor rumors and stories continue to circulate, and some people always seem eager to purchase or invest in the phantom products, even in the face of fantastic claims, such as that the device will allow automobiles to be fueled by water.

References: *Vanishing Hitchhiker*, 175–178; *Mexican Pet*, 161–163.

"The Elephant That Sat on the VW"

An elephant in a circus parade, or one recently retired from a circus now giving rides in a zoo, spots a red Volkswagen. Apparently believing it to be the red stool on which it sat during its act, the elephant lumbers over to the VW and sits on it, crushing the front end. Driving home in the badly damaged car, the VW owner stops for a drink to calm his nerves, then is pulled over by the police who ask about the damage to the car. He explains that an elephant sat on his VW; the police breathalyze him, then cite him for driving under the influence.

Variations of this story have been around since the early 1960s, and it was debunked in the Volkswagen company's periodical *Small World* in 1970, but it persists. The legend is well known in England, Germany, Sweden, France, Canada, and even in Australia, where it was retold in Peter Carey's 1981 novel *Bliss* (involving a red Fiat) and depicted in the 1985 film based on the novel. American versions are invariably localized to a particular zoo, amusement park, or circus. Sometimes the story is told to explain an insurance claim for a badly dented small car.

References: *Choking Doberman*, 58–61; *Too Good*, 107–108.

Elevator Accidents

In the 1940s a legend circulated about a disturbing dream that warned someone away from a fatal elevator accident. In 1959 Richard Dorson wrote of "another macabre legend" about an elevator accident in a Detroit department store in which only the head of the victim rolls into the elevator car while the body falls down the shaft or is left outside in the hallway. The hair of the victim, and sometimes of the witnesses, turns white from the shock.

These legends apparently did not survive into the later twentieth century, perhaps because elevators have proven to be extremely safe and because nowadays stores and shopping malls primarily use escalators to move people between floors.

See also "Room for One More"

References: Dorson, *American Folklore*, 254.

"The Elevator Incident"

This is one of the most durable and popular urban legends of the late twentieth century. The modern form of the story emerged in the early 1980s, telling of a large black man with a dog on a leash entering an elevator that contained just two or three white middle-aged women. He says "Sit!" or "Sit, lady!" and the women, thinking him a mugger, sit on the floor. He laughingly explains that he was talking to his dog. Later they learn that the man was baseball star Reggie Jackson.

With innumerable variations in the setting, the command, the identity of the celebrity, and the aftermath, the legend continues to circulate nearly two decades later both at home and abroad, although foreign versions usually set the scene in the United States. Generally the incident is said to take place in a major resort city such as Las Vegas, Atlantic City, or

New York City. The victims are either vacationers or people from out of town on a business or shopping trip. Sometimes they are set up for their misunderstanding by repeated warnings to be careful in the big city.

The accidental supposed mugger in the legend has also been identified as Lionel Richie, Wilt Chamberlain, Arsenio Hall, Larry Holmes, Mike Tyson, O. J. Simpson, and many others, but especially in recent years Eddie Murphy. The command may be quoted as "Hit the floor!" or "Hit fo!" (i.e., hit the button for floor four). Following the incident, the black celebrity may send the victims a note, money, roses, or champagne, and/or pay their hotel bill, their restaurant bill, and so on.

The obvious racist themes in "The Elevator Incident" include the notion that whites cannot tell black people apart or understand their accents. Since the white victims expect the worst from the black man on the elevator (who is sometimes accompanied by his dog and/or bodyguards), they misinterpret the man's words in the worst possible way. Seemingly "excusing" this racism is the fact that the black man turns out to be good-humored and generous. The comic persona of Eddie Murphy in his popular films helps to fit the legend to him, although Murphy has strongly denied that any such thing ever occurred.

Older versions of an elevator-incident legend do not involve a black man but instead a person named Neil. When someone calls out the name, bystanders misunderstand it as the command to "Kneel!" and immediately obey. Victims in the Neil/kneel versions are usually intimidated by someone in a position of authority or who has a "commanding" appearance.

A scene evidently based on an "Elevator Incident" prototype appeared in the episode of "The Bob Newhart Show" first broadcast on December 1, 1973. A black client (not a celebrity) of Dr. Bob's has a large dog named "Whitey." When he commands the dog, "Sit, Whitey!" a white character in the scene hastily sits on the edge of a desk. Although the characters are not on an elevator, the doors of the office elevator are visible in the background. The pun on the name of the dog sounds like a scriptwriter's addition to what was probably at that time a traditional story beginning to take shape as an urban legend.

References: *Baby Train*, 15; *Choking Doberman*, 18–28; *Curses!*, 21–22; *Too Good*, 413–416.

Embarrassment

Numerous urban legends depict people suffering various degrees of embarrassment because of something foolish they have said or done. In telling or hearing such stories, people are reminded of their own past slipups and indiscretions. Perhaps people suffer vicariously, to some degree, the same embarrassed feelings; but the telling of these legends also allows us to laugh a little at our former embarrassments.

Simple ignorance is one cause of embarrassment described in urban legends: someone using a computer or following a recipe or responding to an order, for example, simply gets it wrong, usually in a particularly hilarious way. Another typical theme is mistaking the identity of another person with results that may be embarrassing to one or both of the parties. The social blunder (or faux pas) is a third common means of someone embarrassing himself or herself in legends. Specific examples of such legend types include "Bungling Brides," "Buying Tampax," "The Elevator Incident," and "The Crushed Dog," among many others.

Probably the greatest anxiety reflected in urban legends—and hence the major cause of embarrassment—is represented by the sexual theme. People are constantly chagrined and left red-faced in legends by such things as being caught in the nude, or caught in the sexual act, or caught otherwise straying from the straight and narrow path of virtue. In other words, when people act naturally and impulsively in legends they can expect to be observed and embarrassed.

It might be argued that virtually all urban legends about such themes as human nature, jumping to conclusions, poetic justice, revenge, scandal, and even some accident and horror stories involve a degree of embarrassment. Thus the examples mentioned above and listed below merely suggest the range of potentially embarrassing situations found in urban legends.

See also "The Accidental Stickup"; "The Blind Man"; "Bozo the Clown's Blooper"; Computers; "The Dormitory Surprise"; "The Exploding Bra"; "The Exploding Toilet"; "The Fart in the Dark"; "Not My Dog"; Nudity; "The Package of Cookies"; "The Pregnant Shoplifter"; "The Shocking Videotape"; "The Ski Accident"; "The Stolen Wallet"; "Superhero Hijinks"; "The Unlucky Contact Lenses"; "The Wife Left Behind"; "The Wrong Teeth"; Zipper Stories

References: *Too Good*, 135–156.

England

Stewart F. Sanderson, who at the time was director of the Institute of Dialect and Folk Life Studies at the University of Leeds, published the earliest extended study of urban legends in England: "Folklore of the

Motor Car," appearing in the journal *Folklore* in 1969. Then, in 1981, when the study of contemporary legends had finally become established among British scholars and writers, Sanderson chose as his topic for the first Katharine Briggs Lecture for the Folklore Society "The Modern Urban Legend." In that lecture (published in 1982 by the Folklore Society as a separate pamphlet) he included these encouraging words:

> The modern legend constitutes one of the most, may indeed even constitute *the* most widespread, popular, and vital folklore form of the present day; and what strikes me as perhaps its most outstanding feature is the creativity, imagination, and virtuosity brought to its performance by all kinds of people, old and young, well read and barely literate, educationally privileged and educationally deprived.

Sanderson also mentioned in his lecture that he had discussed the genre of modern legends at a 1963 conference in Portugal with his compatriot Katharine Briggs and with the American folklorist Richard Dorson, and that Briggs shortly after began to collect examples and to publish them first in 1965.

Scattered notes in various English folklore journals appeared in the 1970s on legends including Chinese-restaurant stories, "The Packet of Biscuits," and "The Double Theft." More substantial studies were Jacqueline Simpson's essays ("Rationalized Motifs in Urban Legends," *Folklore* 1981) concerning "The Robber Who Was Hurt" and Simpson's study of "Urban Legends in *The Pickwick Papers*" (*Journal of American Folklore* 1983).

A landmark work from outside the academy in England was Rodney Dale's *The Tumour in the Whale* (1978), a compilation of many stories that introduced the enduring term "FOAF" (friend of a friend). Dale's second collection *It's True . . . It Happened to a Friend* appeared in 1984. A similar popular collection published in 1992 by Phil Healey and Rick Glanvill was somewhat inaccurately titled *Urban Myths.* Yet another term was employed in two popular books compiled by Paul Smith, *The Book of Nasty Legends* (1983) and *The Book of Nastier Legends* (1986).

Smith, then attached to the Center for English Cultural Tradition and Language (CECTAL) at the University of Sheffield, organized the first international conference on contemporary legends, which was held at Sheffield in 1982. Papers from that conference were published by CECTAL in 1984, followed by four additional conferences and their resulting published papers. In 1988 the International Society for Contemporary

Legend Research (ISCLR) was founded, with Paul Smith as president; Smith himself moved to the Memorial University of Newfoundland, continuing his research on urban legends and his activities as a promoter and organizer of conferences and publications. The ISCLR returned to England for its annual conference in 1996, convening at the University of Bath.

Most of the urban legends circulating in England will be familiar to Americans; indeed, the English repertoire of such stories overlaps in large part with the contemporary legends of the rest of Britain and Europe as well as of Canada and Australia. It is often difficult, if not impossible, to identify the country of origin for a particular popular legend. Such localized legend titles as "The Surrey Puma" or "The Exmoor Beast," for example, merely refer to English examples of the international legend type that might be called "Big Cats Running Wild."

Distinctive English legends, however, have been identified and studied. To cite just three examples published in the *Perspectives* volumes of conference essays (contained in the Bibliography of this book), see Ervin Beck's study of "The Meat that Never Spoils" (1984), Gorgina Boyes's study of "The Curse of the Crying Boy" (1989), and Michael Goss's study of "The Halifax Slasher" (1990). Especially notable in the same series are the essays by Gillian Bennett, ranging from her study of "The Phantom Hitchhiker" in the 1984 volume to her anatomizing of a storytelling session in the 1989 volume. Works by other English students of contemporary legends (e.g., Marion Bowman, Brian McConnell, Venetia Newall, et al.) may be located using Smith and Bennett's invaluable compilation *Contemporary Legend: A Folklore Bibliography* (1993).

Contemporary Legend, the journal of the ISCLR, was published in England from 1991 to 1994, and the term "contemporary legend" remains the favorite designation for urban legends used in that country as well. England's best known legend subject is the card-collecting effort focusing on Craig Shergold. (See entries on these topics for details.)

See also "The Accidental Cannibals"; "The Accidental Stickup"; "The Bungled Rescue of the Cat"; "The Corpse in the Cask"; "The Day Trip"; "The Five-Pound Note"; "The Flying Cow"; "The Ghost in Search of Help"; International Society for Contemporary Legend Research; Ireland; "The Mother's Threat Carried Out"; "The Mystery Trip"; "Roaming Gnomes" ; Rolls-Royce Legends; Scotland; "The Spider in the Cactus"; "The Stolen Speedtrap"

The Escalating Medical Problems

Someone goes to a clinic or hospital for treatment of a minor ailment, but the rules and procedures require a full physical examination, which in turn reveals a potentially more serious condition. However, when treatment of this condition is botched, the patient is left worse off than before. After a long convalescence, when the person is finally ready for release, it is noted by the same intern who had admitted the patient that the original minor problem has still not been corrected.

Sometimes called "The Kafkaesque Hospital Visit," this story may begin and end simply with the patient's ill-fitted eyeglasses, with an inept proctoscopy leading to peritonitis or other complications in the middle (so to speak). Other medical horror stories, some with a basis in fact, tell of wrong organs being removed, flopped X-rays, fatal colonic explosions, and endless hospital and insurance paperwork that delays or even prevents proper medical care. Obviously, deep suspicions and fears about health-care providers underlie these stories.

References: *Too Good,* 206–207.

Exploding Animals

Birds that eat rice thrown at weddings followed by a drink of water supposedly swell and explode. Seagulls that eat Alka-Seltzer tablets thrown to them by sailors also blow up. Small pet birds treated by inept or student veterinarians burst into flame and disappear in a puff of smoke and feathers when an electric cautery is used after giving the bird ether. Bees sucked up in a vacuum sweeper blow up when the person trying to remove the pests from a kitchen directs oven gas into the sweeper and it ignites from a spark in the motor.

The exploding-animal theme becomes more detailed and specific in legends about pets or wild animals wired with explosives or put into a microwave oven.

See also "The Animal's Revenge"; "The Loaded Dog"; "The Microwaved Pet"

References: *Baby Train,* 254–255, 260–261; *Choking Doberman,* 107; *Mexican Pet,* 35.

"The Exploding Bra"

A woman (sometimes a flight attendant) is wearing an inflatable brassiere on an airplane trip. As the cabin pressure changes, her bra expands alarmingly. She rushes for the restroom, sometimes making it in time to deflate her bra discreetly, but in other versions the bra explodes en route. Alternately, the inflated bra may be stuck with a pin—either by the wearer trying to stop the extra expansion, or (in nonairplane versions) by a young man pinning a corsage onto his date's dress.

Inflatable bras do, of course, exist, but the stories of surprising expansion due to changing air pressure are highly doubtful and always told second- or thirdhand. Similar stories are sometimes told about silicon breast implants, although the claims for their further expansion are even more dubious with these products.

References: *Baby Train,* 80–82; *Too Good,* 375–376.

"The Exploding Butane Lighter"

This story was summarized in his column of December 21, 1979, by the legendary San Francisco columnist Herb Caen:

It came to me on official-looking U.S. Dept. of Transportation stationery, but it's a hoax. I mean the story that two Union Pacific welders were killed when a spark ignited their butane lighters, which exploded "with the force of three dynamite sticks." Sighs UP Flack Al Krieg: "That story swept the country the past month but we have no record of such an accident. It keeps popping up everywhere. Some myths die hard."

Photocopied fliers—bogus warnings—circulating in the late 1970s and early 1980s described this supposed accident involving welders, usually said to be Union Pacific workers. (Disposable butane lighters were introduced by the Bic Corporation in 1972.) The rating of the explosion as equal to three sticks of dynamite was a consistent detail, yet the entire story was fictional. However, in the mid-1980s dangerous problems with such lighters began to surface, and in 1986 the first case against a manufacturer of butane lighters went to trial and ended in a $3 million settlement against the company. However, neither this case nor others involving such lighters involved welding sparks or actual explosions; instead, the problems were caused by flare-ups of lighters that had failed to extinguish completely after use.

The folk legends evidently did preserve the general memories of such accidents, which had been settled out of court for years, while at the same time confusing and inventing some details. Another legend involving a welding accident describes contact lenses becoming fused to a person's corneas.

See also "The Fused Cornea and Contacts"

References: *Choking Doberman,* 155–157; Tamar Lewin, "Lawsuits, and Worry, Mount Over Bic Lighter," *New York Times,* April 10, 1987; *Mexican Pet,* 164–165.

"The Exploding Toilet"

Some kind of volatile substance—typically insecticide or hair spray—is put into a toilet, usually by a man's wife. She does not flush. When her husband uses the toilet while smoking a cigarette, he flips the butt under his butt and blows himself off the pot. Paramedics carrying him to an ambulance, hearing how he was injured, laugh so hard they drop the stretcher, causing him further harm.

There are endless variations of this story, sometimes linking several household accidents, and nearly always ending with the laughing-paramedics motif. For example, the wife may have caused an earlier acci-

dent that sends her husband to the hospital, and she paints the bathroom while he is gone. She disposes of paint thinner into the toilet, and the second and third accidents follow after her husband's return.

A popular recent variation of "The Exploding Toilet" describes the husband accidentally driving his new motorcycle through a plate-glass window or door into the house. While he is being treated for cuts and bruises, his wife cleans up the mess, pouring the mopped-up gasoline into the toilet, with predictable results.

In 1988 "The Exploding Toilet" was reported as a news item from Tel Aviv. Before the story was debunked as mere oral tradition a few days later, this account of "A Blast Heard 'round the World" had spread internationally and was widely reprinted.

"The Exploding Toilet" derives from a rural gag about a volatile substance (kerosene, naphtha, gasoline, etc.) poured into the pit under an outhouse. The Canadian poet Robert Service elaborated this traditional story in his poem "The Three Bares" published in 1949, but the anecdote surely circulated much earlier, and it was known at about the same period in Australia as well. Punch lines of the joke versions generally follow the formula, "It must have been something I et."

See also "Stuck on the Toilet"

References: *Mexican Pet,* 13–16; *Too Good,* 370–372; *The Truth,* 108–122; *Vanishing Hitchhiker,* 181.

"The Failed Suicide"

A desperate man tries to arrange multiple, simultaneous methods to bring about his own death, but they cancel out one another. For example, the man may stand on a high cliff above the sea with a noose around his neck tied to a tree, a loaded gun in one hand, and a vial of poison in the other. He drinks the poison, fires the gun toward his head, and jumps; but the shot severs the rope, he survives the fall, and the seawater that he swallows causes him to vomit up the poison. He swims to shore.

A less complicated version of the story describes a man leaping from a high window after having an argument with his wife in their apartment or being fired by his boss. The would-be suicide lands on top of his wife (or his boss, who has gone out for lunch after the unpleasant job of firing the man). The wife (or boss) dies, but the man lives.

Variations of these stories have circulated orally, in typescript, and on the Internet but are also published from time to time, sometimes to illustrate human behavior, the random nature of events, legal and moral aspects of suicide, and the like. One such printing by a British expert on forensic medicine described the multiple-means-of-death version as "a classic of its kind . . . not susceptible to confirmation."

References: *Baby Train,* 86–87.

"The Fallen Angel Cake"

This story was published in 1980 in a Sydney, Australia, newspaper and, in 1982, in a slightly different version in a small-town Canadian newspaper. Both reports described it as an actual incident well known to the local population, so probably it is a widespread apocryphal account, that is, a modern legend. Less likely—indeed barely possible—is that the same mishap occurred twice in far distant places.

A woman bakes an angel food cake for her church's bake sale, but when it comes out of the oven the center of the cake collapses. Lacking time to make a second cake, the woman uses a roll of toilet paper to build up the center of her cake, and she frosts over the whole thing. She rushes her cake to the church sale, then gives her daughter some money and instructs her to hurry to the sale, buy it back, and bring it directly home. But the daughter arrives too late; the cake has already been sold. The next day the cake-baker goes to her bridge club, and she finds that the hostess has bought her cake and is serving it for dessert. Before the woman can warn her, the hostess acknowledges a compliment on the beautiful cake, saying, "Thank you. I baked it myself."

References: *Too Good,* 70–71.

"The Fart in the Dark"

This is a story of the general "Surpriser Surprised" type (and "The Nude Surprise Party" subtype) in which a person is embarrassed by his or her shocking behavior in the presence of others who have been brought together to surprise the victim. The surprisers are themselves surprised, in this instance by the victim's indiscreet breaking of wind (expelling gas from the intestine). The story is told in the United States and England (and perhaps elsewhere) as both a legend and a joke, as well as being distributed in the form of a piece of Xeroxlore titled "The Gastronomical Bean Story."

A person has a great fondness for baked beans but has to give them up because of their effect—causing severe attacks of intestinal gas. Unluckily, the bean-lover indulges himself/herself in a large serving of beans on his or her birthday. The gas has built up alarmingly when the person's spouse (or girlfriend, boyfriend, roommate, etc.) announces a surprise. The bean-lover is left alone blindfolded in an empty room to await the surprise. Unable to hold it any longer, he or she breaks wind loudly and repeatedly. Then the party-planner returns and removes the blindfold, revealing a roomful of friends gathered to celebrate the birthday.

Another version of "The Fart in the Dark" describes a young woman's flatulence overheard by a double-dating couple seated in the rear of a car but unobserved by the victim when she is let into the front seat.

References: Paul Smith, *Nastier Legends* (1986), "The Bean Feast," 31–32; *Too Good,* 34–36; *Vanishing Hitchhiker,* 148–149.

Fast Food

Fast-food franchise restaurants selling mainly hamburgers, pizza, Mexican food, and related side dishes are often the targets of negative rumors and legends, particularly those that claim serious contamination of the foods. Likely there is some element of guilt involved in circulating such lore, as people realize that fast foods offer speed, low cost, and efficiency at the expense of a balanced diet and wholesome food prepared at home from fresh ingredients.

Some typical contaminants described as having invaded fast foods are worms, pet food, meats considered inedible for most humans (e.g., cats, dogs, horses, kangaroos), and body substances (semen, pus, blood, urine). Such stories are told about named companies, indeed, even about specific local franchises, and the stories tend to gravitate toward the largest companies (the so-called Goliath effect) and to switch from company to company. Actually, most fast-food restaurants are probably operated in a more consistent and hygienic manner than are many small individual eateries.

Besides contamination, fast-food stories may claim that companies are owned by unsavory conspirators or that a portion of their enormous profits are diverted to support evil ends.

See Also: See Church's Chicken Rumors; Contamination; The Goliath Effect; "Hold the Mayo"; "Hold the Mozzarella"; "The Kentucky Fried Rat"; Masturbating into Food; McDonald's Rumors; Satanic Panic; "Snakes in Playland"

"The Fatal Boot"

A legacy of the American frontier, this tall tale continues to have some currency as a modern legend. A man is struck by a rattlesnake whose fangs penetrate his boot and kill him. Unnoticed by anyone, one fang breaks off in the boot, and two successive generations of men in the family wear the same boot and are killed by dried venom remaining on the fang. Finally, someone inspects the boot closely and discovers what has happened. The boot in the story may be that of a cowboy, rancher, logger, hiker, hunter, and so on. In an updated version, a rattlesnake's fang is broken off in a rancher's truck tire, killing a mechanic who changes the tire.

Although thoroughly discredited by herpetologists, this rattler story (among others) has persisted since the late eighteenth century. In the 1960s a roadside tourist attraction in Florida displayed a shoe with the fatal-boot story attributed to it, and probably other such places have exploited the same tale.

See also "The Wrong Rattler"

References: *Curses!*, 76–78; *Too Good*, 347–348.

"The Fatal Golf Tee"

An avid golfer plays the game frequently and is in the habit of putting his tee into his mouth after his first shot and keeping it there during the whole game. Eventually he dies from pesticides that were transferred from the golf course's grass via the tees to his body.

Fairways and greens heavily treated with chemicals have, indeed, been the cause of illness and even occasionally death among golfers, particularly professionals who play often and long. But there are no verifiable reports of this contamination coming specifically from a tee carried in someone's mouth.

References: *Curses!*, 65–66; Nancy Lloyd, "Lethal Grass: The Perilous Pesticides on America's Lawns," *Washington Post* (September 16, 1991).

"The Fatal Initiation"

A legend of modern college life is based on the traditional narrative motif (N384) of someone's death resulting from severe fright. As part of his initiation into a fraternity, a young man is blindfolded, then made to believe that he has been cut and is bleeding or has been branded with a red-hot iron. (Actually, although he is shown a knife or the branding iron in advance, *after* he has been blindfolded, he is touched only with a piece of ice.) The initiate dies from the shock. In a variation, the fraternity pledge is led to a high cliff, blindfolded, then told he will be pushed over the edge. Although he is merely pushed over a drop of two feet, he dies from shock as he stumbles and falls.

The appeal of this horror legend in colleges during the 1940s diminished as some fraternity initiations actually did lead to deaths in later years, usually as a result of binge drinking.

See also "The Graveyard Wager"

> **References:** Ernest Baughman, "The Fatal Initiation," *Hoosier Folklore Bulletin* 4 (1945): 49–55; Dorson, *American Folklore*, 258–259.

FBI Stories

There may be a larger genre of legends about the major U.S. government law enforcement agency, but so far only two FBI stories have been noted by folklorists.

"The New Identity" claims that after the FBI furnished a Mafia informer with a completely new identity—name, invented background, plastic surgery, a new profession, and so on—no sooner had they moved him into his new home than the man received a fund-raising letter from the alumni association of his alma mater. It was addressed to his original name.

"Watch the Margins" claims that J. Edgar Hoover, the longtime director of the FBI, enforced strict guidelines for the length of memos and the widths of top and bottom margins. Once when an agent's report had margins that were too narrow, the director wrote on it, "Watch the borders!" Immediately a horde of extra agents was assigned to the American borders with Canada and Mexico.

> **References:** *Baby Train*, 128–129.

"The FCC Petition"

See "The Madalyn Murray O'Hair Petition"

"Fifi Spills the Paint"

Professional painters know this ploy—and some may actually have prac-ticed it—as a way to place the blame for a spillage on the cus-tomer' pet: A painter working in-side an expensive home happens to tip an open can of paint onto a valuable rug or a beautiful par-quet floor. He grabs the cus-tomer's yappy little toy poodle, sticks the dog's feet into the mess, and exclaims, "Fifi! Bad Dog! Look what you've done!"

A variation on this story has young boys or girls put the blame for eating some forbidden food onto the family pet.

See also "Kitty Takes the Rap"

References: *Curses!*, 132–134; *Too Good*, 61–63.

"The 50-Dollar Porsche"

See "The Philanderer's Porsche"

"Filmed in the Act"

Here is the story, as written in a letter to author Jan Brunvand dated March 27, 1991, by Brenda Sommer, then working as a bartender in Austin, Texas:

Dear Doc:

Springtime is upon us here in Texas. As I amble about my yard, sprinkling fertilizer hither and yon, my thoughts turn to another form of manure spreading, which prompts my letter to you.

The other day at the bar I hopped into the back kitchen to grab some more cold beer, and the two cooks were giggling over something, one proclaiming, "No way, man," and the other responding, "Swear to God, it's true."

Couldn't help myself; had to ask.

Seems that the cook's girlfriend's sister's neighbors in New Jersey had gone to a resort in Las Vegas. Couple No. 1 turned on the TV in their room and were tickled to find a crudely made, one-camera, soundless video of a couple making love.

Inspired by the topic, they proceeded to do likewise. They had a wonderful trip and recommended the resort to couple No. 2, who "six months later," took a holiday at the very same resort.

They, too, turned on the TV in their room, saw a poorly made porn video, and upon closer inspection, recognized Couple No. 1 as the unpaid actors. It seems that someone at the resort had been taping the guests.

Just thought you ought to be aware of this, and consider it when making travel arrangements.

In most versions of this widely known story the same couple visits the honeymoon resort twice, seeing themselves on the return visit as the stars in a sex video and then suing the management. In the eastern United States the most common resort area mentioned is the Pocono Mountains of northeastern Pennsylvania. Sometimes the couple sees a video of the husband cavorting with a woman other than his wife.

Some who believe in "Filmed in the Act" claim that certain honeymoon resorts can offer bargain prices because they reap huge profits from selling homemade porn tapes. These resorts may be said to have banned repeat visits, but one couple bypasses the rule by registering under a different name. Against all odds, they select the video of their own performance to show in their room.

Not surprisingly, not a shred of evidence exists (e.g., no peepholes, cameras, lawsuits, and certainly no films or videotapes) to substantiate this legend, and resort owners and police all across the country wherever it is told have firmly denied it. Still, "Filmed in the Act" continues to be circulated, including most recently on the Internet in versions containing even the supposed names of the victims ("Len and Beth wanted to get wild, so . . .").

See also "The Shocking Videotape"; "The Videotaped Theft"

References: *Choking Doberman*, 139–140; *Too Good*, 128–130.

Film and Urban Legends

Because of their uncomplicated, fast-moving plots, bizarre subject matter, widespread appeal, and—perhaps most of all—their anonymous free circulation in the public domain, urban legends have had a strong appeal to many filmmakers. Numerous examples of these modern folk narratives have found their way into the movies, either as the primary plot element of a feature film or as an episode or digression within a film. Seldom are urban legends merely told (rather than dramatized) in commercial films; a rare example is Bill Murray's telling of "The Hook" as a campfire story in *Meatballs* (1979).

Two films starring Doris Day were among the earliest major Hollywood productions to incorporate urban legends. In *The Glass Bottom Boat* (1966) the "Heel in the Grate" story was incorporated as a comic digression, and in *With Six You Get Eggroll* (1968) the "Nude in the RV" story appeared. Probably the first American feature film to be based entirely on an urban legend was *When a Stranger Calls* (1979), which developed its plot from "The Baby-sitter and the Man Upstairs." The next year (1980) saw the film *Alligator* borrow the central idea of "Alligators in the Sewers" and expand it to a complex science-fiction plot. (One reviewer called the film "a poor man's *Jaws.*")

Humorous legends have had an enduring appeal for filmmakers, and there are many examples of funny anecdotes from oral tradition showing up as staged incidents in popular movies. Examples include "The Runaway Grandmother" and "The Leashed Pet" in *National Lampoon's Vacation* (1983), "The Elephant that Sat on a VW" in *Bliss* (an Australian film of 1985), "The Baby on the Roof" in *Raising Arizona* (1987), "The Poisoned Pussycat at the Party" in *Her Alibi* (1989), and "Old Versus Young" in *Fried Green Tomatoes* (1991).

More serious treatment of a humorous urban legend was presented in two short films based on the "Package of Cookies" story. The first was *Boeuf Bourgignon*, a Dutch film of 1988, and the second (independently created with a wholly different setting and style) was *Lunch Date*, an American film of 1990.

The sinister nature of horror legends probably influenced the whole genre of so-called slasher films, especially the *Halloween* series of films with their allusions to rumors of Halloween sadists and the like. A campus setting was necessarily used for the horror film *Dead Man on Campus* (1998), which dealt with "The Suicide Rule," a legend of academe.

The 1992 film *Candyman* pioneered the merging of the horror film with the idea of actual urban legend research; in this moderately successful production a graduate student investigating folklore confronts a threatening character who may be summoned by a ritual reminiscent of "I Believe in Mary Worth" and who seems to personify the hookman of urban legends.

Thus far the most obvious reference to urban legends and their study in film (unfortunately a flawed attempt) was the 1998 film *Urban Legend*. The opening sequence of this campus-slasher movie dramatized "The Killer in the Backseat," and the plot went on to show "The Death of Little Mikey," "The Roommate's Death," "The Boyfriend's Death," and (almost!) "The Kidney Heist," among other stories. Students depicted in the film, which is set at a New England college, are shown taking a folklore class that seems to consist mostly of legend-telling and class discussion of the possible truth of these stories. When one student suspects that a string of campus deaths were really urban legend–inspired murders, she goes to the library and consults the *Encyclopedia of Urban Legends* (not the volume in your hands now but a Hollywood-invented predecessor).

Released in 2000 was a quasi sequel to *Urban Legend* titled *Urban Legends: Final Cut*. This time the premise was that a group of film students are vying for the "Hitchcock Award" in filmmaking and one student is doing an urban-legend horror film. Only the first of several murderous attacks in this dismal Hollywood slasher-flick is related to an actual urban legend. The cleverest sequence of the film turns out to be the final credits where the spirit of the old Hitchcock television series is humorously evoked.

Urbania is, finally, an artistic and gripping film inspired by urban legends. This independent low-budget film premiered at the 2000 Sundance Film Festival, received raves from film critics, and went into general release later in the year. Written and directed by Jon Shear, *Urbania* stars Dan Futterman as a gay man on a quest to avenge his murdered partner. From the opening line of dialogue— "Hear any good stories lately?"—the film includes several urban legends either told, alluded to, or enacted, each of them in some way relevant to the larger plot. Among the legend themes included are kidney thefts, needle attacks, microwaved pets, the baby left on the car roof, the unexpected inheritance story, the infamous toothbrush-photo legend, and "AIDS Mary." The cinematic qualities of *Urbania* are exceptional, and it would be a successful film with or without the legends.

In a few instances films themselves have inspired urban legends. For example, the persistent rumors of "snuff films" spring from the graphic simulation of killings in many films; there is no evidence that anyone was ever actually murdered on camera. Similarly, the rumors of a hanging supposedly depicted in *The Wizard of Oz* are false, and the supposed sexual images hidden on videotape boxes for Disney films are purely in the imaginations of the beholders.

Perhaps the best-known film-related urban legend is the one about a ghost image in the 1987 film *Three Men and a Baby,* although the "ghost" (really just a life-sized cardboard cutout of an actor seen out of focus in the background) was not noticed until the film was released in videotape format in 1990.

Documentary filmmaking by folklorists of urban legends has not been done (at least not for general release), with one notable exception: *Tales of the Supernatural* (1970), produced by Sharon R. Sherman, depicts a group of children telling several well-known horror legends and offers some scholarly analysis by a narrator.

References: Larry Danielson, "Film and Folklore," *Western Folklore* 38 (1979): 209–219; Sharon R. Sherman, "Film and Folklore," in Brunvand, *American Folklore: An Encyclopedia* (1996), 263–265; Scott Aaron Stine, "The Snuff Film, The Making of an Urban Legend, *Skeptical Inquirer* (May/June 1999), 29–33.

"Find the Hat"

Back in the days when men still wore hats, a traveling salesman or other businessman lost his hat on a windy day on a business trip to Chicago. When he filed his expense report, he asked for reimbursement from the accounting department, but he was refused. On his next trip the man padded several expenses to cover the cost of his lost hat, then attached a note challenging the accountants, **"Find the hat!"**

Much the same story is still told about lost raincoats and umbrellas, by women as well as men, in various different cities. All versions illustrate the business maxim, "If you have questionable expenses, pad the legitimate expenses to cover them."

References: *Curses!,* 259–260; *Too Good,* 261–262.

"The Finger in the Pickle Jar"

Very simply, someone finds a finger in a jar of pickles. Presumably, it was cut off from a worker's hand during the packing process. Somehow the jar had escaped the notice of plant inspectors, and somehow the incident escaped the attention of the news media, since it seems to be preserved, so to speak, only in oral tradition.

Of all the foods that may be said to have been contaminated by diverse ingredients, fingers and pickle jars occur together surprisingly often in urban rumors and legends. Perhaps it is because some pickles—or pickle sections—are about the size of fingers, and fingers would be the most likely appendage to be sliced off during packing operations. Also, the color and scent of the pickling fluid might suggest that a finger could become discolored enough in the jar to escape notice until the jar is opened. Possibly such an incident really happened, although the severing of a finger seems much more likely than its pickling, bottling, and shipping from the plant.

Unlike the stories of mice in soda bottles or batter-fried rats, the rumors of fingers in pickle jars seldom develop much of a narrative form or content.

References: *Choking Doberman,* 119.

Finland

Finnish urban legends have been collected by professor Leea Virtanen of the University of Helsinki. About 100 representative texts with notes and commentaries were published in her 1987 book *Varastettu Isoäiti* (The Stolen Grandmother). Although the language barrier poses a difficult challenge for non-Finnish folklorists, professor Virtanen discussed her material in English at an international conference in 1989 where she also distributed summaries of the stories in German. A brief report in English based on these sources has also been published.

Besides the obvious international character of the title story, the illustrations in Virtanen's book and her summaries reveal a high percentage of well-known urban legends circulating throughout Finland. These include "The Shoplifter and the Frozen Food," "The Relative's Cadaver," "The Vanishing Hitchhiker," "The Hairy-Armed Hitchhiker," "The Microwaved Pet," "The Boyfriend's Death," and many others. Sometimes even the Finnish title reveals an international legend; for example, the story *Tarantella jukkapalmussa* is obviously the legend known elsewhere in Europe as "The Tarantula in the Yucca Palm." The Finnish version of "AIDS Mary" even has its punch line in English: "Welcome to AIDS-club!"

The references in Virtanen's notes, as well as the book's bibliography, further reveal a close connection of the story repertoire to international legendry. To the question of whether there are any uniquely Finnish urban legends, Virtanen has suggested that one story in her collection without known parallels elsewhere may qualify: a boy suffers a frozen brain after disobeying his mother and not wearing a cap outdoors on a bitter-cold day. Although the idea of a parent advising a child to dress warmly is certainly common elsewhere, the specific consequences of a frozen brain have not been reported in legends from other countries.

In 1996 Virtanen published her second collection of Finnish urban legends, *Apua! Maksa ryömii: Nykyajan tarinoita ja huhuja* (Help! The Liver Is Crawling: Legends and Rumors of Today).

References: *Baby Train*, 240–241.

"The Five-Pound Note"

See "The Accidental Stickup"

"Fixing the Flue"

When a mason builds a chimney for a new house, if he has any concern about being paid promptly for the job, he will mortar in a pane of glass to block the flue. Then when the client calls to complain that his chimney smokes, the mason promises to fix it as soon as he is paid for the job. After payment, the mason simply drops a brick down the flue to break out the glass.

This has been told—and possibly practiced—by generations of masons and contractors. When Tracy Kidder heard the story repeatedly while researching his 1988 book *House,* he concluded that the incident "must lie mainly among the wishful thoughts of the building trades, like the retort you think of only after the argument."

See also "The Roughneck's Revenge"

References: *Curses!,* 260; *Too Good,* 277–278.

"Flights of Fancy"

See "The Boy Who Played Superman"

"The Flying Cow"

English folklorist Paul Smith in *The Book of Nasty Legends* (1983) tells the story of a motorist in Scotland surprised when a cow drops from above onto the "bonnet" (i.e., the hood) of his car. It turns out that a truck driver had struck the animal, sending it flying back along the road. Smith recalls another version of "The Flying Cow" he heard around 1965, and he asks "What is it about cars, cows, and Scotland?"

Another flying-cow story came out of Russia in the 1990s. In this instance, some soldiers had stolen two cows and were transporting them by military jet, but they were forced to push the animals from the plane when they became unruly during the flight. One cow landed on a Japanese fishing boat, leading to complicated and comic results. This story was probably inspired by a popular Russian film, and it has circulated largely in the press or via the Internet. A Reuter's article on the story's history released in 1997 suggested that "it bears all the hallmarks of an urban legend." A Russian newspaper put the story in the category of *baiki,* or "invented stories."

References: *Baby Train,* 273–275; *Too Good,* 346–347.

"The Flying Kitten"

A couple's new kitten climbs to the top of a small birch tree in their yard and stays there. In order to rescue it, the owners throw a rope across a high branch and pull the top of the tree down; but the rope slips or breaks, and the kitten is launched high into the air and over their fence. The couple are unable to find the kitten. A week or so later, one of the kitten's former owners is in a supermarket and meets a neighbor who is buying cat food. "I didn't know you had a cat," says the first shopper. "We didn't, until last week when the cutest little kitten just fell out of the air and into my husband's lap."

This story was reported in a 1987 *Washington Post* article as told by a woman who heard it as a "true story" by her hairdresser. Several other versions have been collected, both from published and oral sources. Cats, of course, are the subjects of numerous urban legends, and in many of these stories the felines suffer some kind of harm or trauma, though often landing on their feet and surviving.

References: *Curses!*, 162; *Too Good*, 359–360.

FOAF

The acronym "FOAF" was coined by English writer Rodney Dale in his 1978 book *The Tumour in the Whale* and means "friend of a friend," the oft-mentioned supposed original source of the incidents described in urban legends. "This really happened," a storyteller may say, "to a friend of my next-door neighbor"—in other words, to a FOAF. Dale preferred the lowercase "foaf" (rhymes with "loaf"), but in its adoption by folklorists the letters are typically capitalized.

In his second collection of urban legends, *It's True, It Happened to a Friend* (1984), Dale explained: "Foaf is a word I invented to stand for 'friend of a friend,' the person to whom so many of these dreadful things I am about to recount happens. I have omitted the word from this book as a gesture to neologophobes." However, international students of urban legends have accepted FOAF with enthusiasm as a convenient shorthand reference to the claimed source of stories, even titling the newsletter of the International Society for Contemporary Legend Research *FOAFtale News*.

FOAFtale News

FOAFtale News, the newsletter of the International Society for Contemporary Legend Research (ISCLR), has been published since 1985 at irregular intervals and is sent to members of ISCLR. It contains news and announcements pertaining to ISCLR and its annual meetings, short articles on urban legends, notes and queries, reports of legendary items circulating in the press and on the Internet, lists of recent publications, and the like. The issues of *FOAFtale News* are numbered sequentially, and number 47 appeared in October 2000 under the editorship of Mikel J. Koven of the University of Wales, Aberystwyth. E-mail messages to the editor should be addressed to foaftale-news@aber.ac.uk.

Folklore

Urban legends are part of folklore, and folklore study has been an established academic field since the late nineteenth century. (The American Folklore Society was founded in 1888 and has published its quarterly journal continuously to the present day.) The word "folklore," coined in England in 1846, originally referred to antiquated "peasant" traditions of language and custom, but its meaning was expanded to include "modern" traditions and "material culture" as well. Although contemporary folklorists differ in their exact definitions of the word, the following statement summarizes some points of general agreement:

Folklore may be defined as those materials in culture that circulate traditionally among members of any group in different versions, whether in oral form or by means of customary example, as well as the processes of traditional performance and communication. (Brunvand, *The Study of American Folklore,* 4th ed., 1998, p. 15)

To the degree that urban legends are anonymous stories transmitted orally from person to person and developing variant versions, they may be clearly identified as part of our modern folklore. The publication of urban legends in newspapers and other print media, as well as the incorporation of urban legends into film, radio, television, cartoons, and other pop-culture forms, stretch the definition of folklore considerably, as does the frequent transmission of urban legends via photocopies and the Internet. As a result, the collection and study of urban legends are carried out not only by folklorists but also by sociologists, pop-culture specialists, journalists, storytellers, and a host of interested amateurs (many of the latter and exchanging material via the Internet).

References: Jan Harold Brunvand, "Folklore," in Brunvand, *American Folklore: An Encyclopedia* (1996), 285–287; Brunvand, "The Field of Folklore," in *The Study of American Folklore,* 4th ed. (1998), 3–21; Thomas A. Green, ed., *Folklore: An Encyclopedia of Beliefs, Customs, Tales, Music, and Art,* 2 vols. (Santa Barbara, Calif.: ABC-CLIO, 1997).

Folktale

Technically, the word "folktale," as used by folklorists, refers to fictional oral narratives such as fairy tales, formula tales, tall tales, and jokes. However, in common usage—and sometimes even in professional writings—the word is employed generically for any traditional oral narrative—myths, legends, anecdotes, and other "true story" forms included.

See also Classifying Urban Legends

References: Stith Thompson, *The Folktale* (New York: Dryden Press, 1956; rpt. Berkeley: University of California Press, 1977).

"The Foreign Hotel"

See "The Vanishing Lady"

Fortean Approach

Modern followers of Charles Hoy Fort (1874–1932)—an eccentric American gentleman who devoted much of his life to documenting the "data that science has excluded"—call themselves "Forteans." For years, Fort scoured old and obscure publications in British and American libraries, compiling four volumes of reported anomalies of weather, zoology, everyday mysteries, and all manner of other unexplained phenomena. (Fort's books are still available in a Dover Books reprint published in 1974.) Fort himself, it is important to note, specifically omitted *folk* narratives from his collections, calling them "conventional stories" and characterizing them as having details such as "'clanking chains' in ghost stories and 'eyes the size of saucers' in sea serpent yarns." But some of the anomalies that fascinated Fort seem to have more than an accidental similarity to certain traditional motifs of folk stories.

Continuing Fort's collection of such data with fieldwork as well as library collections, and also attempting to find explanations for weird news items, modern Forteans have organized themselves into an international society. *Fortean Times: The Journal of Strange Phenomena* is published monthly in London and has a website at <www.fortean times.com>. The publishers of *Fortean Times* host an annual two-day "UnConvention" in London where urban legends are among the many topics presented for discussion.

Some typical subjects of Fortean investigation are animals sighted out of their natural range, monsters, haunted sites, and UFOs. Cryptozoology, the study of unknown animal species, is often regarded as a branch of Forteanism. The studies of the Forteans overlap with urban-legend studies especially in such areas as reports of alligators in sewers, big cats running wild, phantom clowns, and vanishing hitchhikers.

Loren Coleman, a prominent American Fortean, describes the viewpoint of his colleagues in the field thus: "An open-minded attitude to the many unexplained situations is the stock and trade of the Fortean." For himself, Coleman states, "I 'believe' in nothing and the possibility of everything."

References: Loren Coleman, *Mysterious America* (Boston: Faber and Faber, 1983) and *Curious Encounters* (Boston: Faber and Faber, 1985).

France

French folklore study became well established in the late nineteenth century and flourished until the beginning of World War I; an early promising focus on legend studies was provided by Arnold Van Gennep's 1910 book *La Formation des Légendes* (The Shaping of Legends). However, after folklore studies languished in France, the revival of interest in contemporary legendary material that occurred in the late twentieth century focused mostly on rumors; this study was, to a large extent, carried out by psychoanalysts, sociologists, and social psychologists. The very word "folklore" became something of an academic embarrassment.

A landmark work that followed a Freudian approach to examine aspects of the "Vanishing Hitchhiker" tradition in World War II–era Europe was Marie Bonaparte's book *Mythes de guerre* (1946), published in English the next year as *Myths of War*. A more typical French sociological approach to rumors was a book by Edgar Morin and others, *La rumeur d'Orléans* (1969), translated and published as *Rumour in Orleans* (1971). Morin and his colleagues reported extensive fieldwork and close analysis of a mass of completely unfounded stories circulating in the city of Orleans, claiming that young girls had been abducted from dress shops owned by Jews and forced into "white slavery" (i.e., prostitution).

In their 1990 bibliography of French rumor scholarship, Véronique Campion-Vincent and Jean-Bruno Renard listed nearly four dozen items, several of which were collections of studies, but very few of them had appeared in any language other than French. Fortunately, later that same year (1990) Jean-Noël Kapferer's important 1987 book *Rumeurs: Le plus vieux média du monde* (Rumors: The World's Oldest Media) was translated and published as *Rumors: Uses, Interpretations, and Images*. Kapferer, a professor of communications, discusses legends (traditional narratives) as well as rumors (unverified reports), but he consistently refers to examples such as "The Hook" and "The Stolen Grandmother" as "migratory rumor stories," "exemplary stories," or simply as "rumors." (Many folklorists would use the label "legend" for any such item with a clear narrative structure.) Kapferer's work is especially useful for demonstrating the French analytic approach to the creation, change, spread, and control of rumors; another good example of his work available in English is an article on the French versions of "Mickey Mouse Acid" published in *Contemporary Legend* volume 3 (1993). (Jean-Bruno Renard had traced the passage of LSD tattoo-transfer rumors from North America to France in an article published in *Folklore Forum* 24, 1991).

Campion-Vincent and Renard's book *Légendes urbaines* (1992) is the first full-length treatment in French of urban legends, although it, too, retains the term "rumor" in its subtitle (*Rumeurs d'aujourd'hui* [Rumors of Today]). Besides discussions of many well-known international urban legends ("Alligators in the Sewers," "The Choking Doberman," "The Hippie Baby-sitter," etc.), the authors discuss other stories that are more specifically Gallic, such as claims of the supposed satanic significance of the Louvre Pyramid monument constructed in 1988. Another series of legends that circulated in France from 1980 to 1985—viper-release stories—was discussed by Campion-Vincent in two 1990 articles in English, one (appropriately titled "A Nest of Vipers") published in the *Perspectives on Contemporary Legend* series, and the second in volume 31 of *Fabula*. The same author's major work on organ-theft legends was published in volume 56 of *Western Folklore* (1997), among other places.

A useful summary of French and international urban-legend collecting and research published in 1999 is Jean-Bruno Renard's small paperback *Rumeurs et légendes urbaines*. Renard surveys precursors of modern legend study, the emergence of this new field of research, subgenres of legends, methods of both internal and external analysis, and the themes and symbols found in such legends. His concise definition of "urban legends" translates as follows:

> A brief anonymous story, existing in multiple variants, with surprising or unusual content, but told as true and recent within a particular social milieu, and expressing something of that group's fears or hopes.

A characteristic narrative form sometimes compared to urban legends in France is referred to as *fait divers,* literally "diverse facts," but sometimes translated in English with the journalistic term "human-interest stories." *Fait divers,* Campion-Vincent has explained, are short published accounts of such events (or supposed events) as murders, catastrophes, bizarre accidents, and hilarious occurrences. A good example of such an item as published in a French newspaper in 1968 bore the dateline "Avignon" (a city in southern France).

Referring to the mistake of a 19-year-old brunette Spanish girl working for a French family in a place called Vaison-la-Romaine, this story contains the obvious motif (as found in some "Baby-Roast" and "Microwaved Pet" legends) of a misunderstood word, in this case the French *gâteau* (cake) thought to be the Spanish *gato* (cat). Even a non–French-speaking reader can probably understand what happens to the family's magnificent angora cat "Fonfon" when Carmen, the maid, is told to put the cake into the refrigerator and later to serve it for dinner. Here is the story, as William F. Buckley reprinted it (in the spirit of passing on a *fait divers*) without translation in his magazine *National Review* on March 26, 1968:

> Avignon. "Mettez le gâteau au réfrigérateur," avait dit à Carmen sa bonne, une brune Espagnole de dix-neuf ans, une habitante de Vaison-la-Romaine. Ne se trouvant en France que depuis deux mois et ne connaissant que des rudiments de la langue française, la jeune fille, si elle entendit bien le mot gâteau, le traduisit par "gato," ce qui, dans sa langue maternelle, signifie "chat." Obéissante, elle empoigna "Fonfon," le magnifique chat angora de sa patronne et l'enferma dans le réfrigérateur. Ses maîtres ne devaient revenir que le soir et c'est l'issue d'un dîner, qu'elle offrait à des amis, que la maîtresse de "Fonfon" mesura l'étendue du drame. Ayant demandé a Carmen d'apporter le gâteau, quelle ne fut pas sa stupeur et sa douleur de voir arriver sur un plateau le cadavre de "Fonfon," complètement frigorifié.

See also "The Corpse in the Car"; "The Kidney Heist"; Viper-Release Legends

References: *Baby Train,* 48–49, 250–251; Véronique Campion-Vincent and Jean-Bruno Renard, "French Scholarship; on Rumor: An Annotated Bibliography," *FOAFtale News* no. 18 (June 1990): 1–5; Jean-Bruno Renard, "Contemporary Legends about Parisian Monuments: The Eiffel Tower's Hydraulic Jacks and the Pyramid du Louvre's Satanic Significance," *FOAFtale News* no. 26 (June 1992): 1–3; Gerald Thomas, "Review Essay: The Contemporary Legend in France," *Contemporary Legend* 4 (1994): 158–164.

Freudian Approach

The application of the ideas of Sigmund Freud and his followers to urban legends (indeed, to any kind of folklore) involves, in general terms, seeking to identify in the texts and contexts symbolic references to the unconscious needs and desires of the people who invent, tell, and listen to the stories. Just as dreams, neurotic behavior, and memories of childhood are reviewed by psychoanalysts for their possible symbolic meanings—often sexual ones—it is assumed that folklore must reveal similar symbolic strategies.

Professor Alan Dundes of the University of California–Berkeley has long advocated Freudian interpretations of folklore, publishing his own studies in numerous articles and in such books as *Analytic Essays in Folklore* (1975), *Interpreting Folklore* (1980), and *Folklore Matters* (1989). Although Dundes usually investigates other forms of folklore—myths, fairy tales, proverbs, jokes, and the like—one of his earliest essays with a Freudian approach dealt with urban legends. His paper titled "On the Psychology of Legend," delivered at a 1969 symposium at UCLA, was published in the book *American Folk Legend* (1971), edited by Wayland D. Hand. Here Dundes challenged the propensity of most folklorists to collect and classify legends without delving into interpretations, and he put forth daring and unique readings of several popular modern legends.

The best known of Dundes's interpretations concerned "The Hook," which he characterized as a sexual fable about the fears of young women concerning the likely intentions of their dates. Dundes suggested that the hook itself symbolized "an erect aggressive phallus," which, after contact with the girl's "door" on her side of the car, is torn off when the car is suddenly started, thus symbolically castrating the threatening male. He concludes, "The girl in the story (and for that matter the girls who are telling and listening to the story) are not afraid of what a man lacks, but of what he has." In a similar fashion in the same essay Dundes offered psychological interpretations of the legends of toll-booth pranks, of "The Runaway Grandmother," and even of the story of George Washington and the cherry tree.

Although Dundes hoped to inspire academic interest by showing "the rich potential that legends have for folklorists willing to consider a psychological approach," he has seldom been followed in this kind of analysis and has, in fact, attracted strong critics. A typical negative reaction from an American folklorist is seen in Keith Cunningham's parody titled "Reflections and Regurgitations" published in *Folklore Forum* volume 5 (1972); it is a spoof of Freudian analysis as it might be applied to the legend about "Red Velvet Cake." However, Gary Alan Fine, in his essay "Evaluating Psychoanalytic Folklore: Are Freudians Ever Right?" concluded that such approaches have real merit, and he defended Dundes's interpretation of "The Hook" as internally consistent and plausible. Fine applied some psychological analysis of his own to the legends "The Promiscuous Cheerleader" and "AIDS Mary." All three of these essays were reprinted as chapters in Fine's book *Manufacturing Tales* (1992).

A useful survey of this whole interpretive approach to folklore appeared in 1993 in an issue of the journal *Psychoanalytic Study of Society* devoted to Alan Dundes. Included is a long essay introducing Dundes's work by Professor Michael P. Carroll of the University of Western Ontario, followed by Carroll's own study of "The Boyfriend's Death," in which he suggests that although females generally suffer more in real life than males do from teenage sexuality, "The Boyfriend's Death," which is most popular among young women, reverses the situation and punishes the boy instead. Since the boy cannot get pregnant, he is killed—significantly by being hanged and/or decapitated (i.e., punished at his neck for "necking")—and then suspended upside down over the car as the final reversal in the story.

Carroll is the most active and convincing Freudian folklorist besides Dundes himself, and his other publications include two articles in the English journal *Folklore* on "The Castrated Boy" (vol. 98, 1987) and "The Roommate's Death" (vol. 103, 1992).

See also "The Hairy-Amed Hitchhiker"; "I Believe in Mary Worth"; "The Ice-Cream Cone Caper"; "Red Velvet Cake"; "Spiders in the Hairdo"; "The Vanishing Hitchhiker"

References: Margaret Bruchez, "Psychoanalytic Interpretations of Folklore," in Thomas A. Green, ed., *Folklore: An Encyclopedia of Beliefs, Customs, Tales, Music, and Art*, vol. 2 (Santa Barbara, Calif.: ABC-CLIO, 1997), 668–670; Hasan El-Shamy, "Freudian Psychology," in Green, *Folklore: An Encyclopedia* (1997), 383–385; Jay Mechling, "Psychology and Folklore," in Brunvand, *American Folklore: An Encyclopedia* (1996), 601–602.

"The Frozen Brain"

See Finland

"The Fused Cornea and Contacts"

See "The Welded Contacts"

"The Gay Roommate"

A male college student reports to the campus medical center complaining of repeated and persistent headaches, especially in the morning, just as he is waking up. A complete physical reveals nothing that would cause headaches, but the examining physician finds evidence of rectal bleeding and warns the student not to engage in frequent homosexual activity. The student is aghast, since he is heterosexual. Suspicious, he searches his dormitory room while his roommate is out and finds a bottle of ether or chloroform and a sponge in the roommate's closet. The gay roommate has been sedating the student at night and having sex with him. In some versions of the story the victim wreaks cruel and violent punishment upon his roommate.

Various forms of this legend swept American college campuses from about 1989 to 1991, but the story goes back much farther. Accounts of a similar incident circulated among military units in several countries during World War II and probably earlier; an 1882 source mentioned a Middle East official abusing young foreign sailors after plying them with drinks.

Gay-rights activities and people's homophobia have certainly encouraged the spread of this modern campus legend, but concern among students about the possible truth of the story may also reflect some suppressed homosexual attraction between young college men. Like many

163

other urban legends, the versions of "The Gay Roommate" are often quite specific as to location and details of the assaults; yet not a single authenticated case of this kind has been proven.

See also "Drugged and Seduced"

References: *Baby Train*, 308–311; *Too Good*, 431–432.

Generation Gap Legends

Invented (or discovered?) in the 1960s, the so-called generation gap represents the supposed inability of older versus younger people to understand each other's lives and values. Oldsters, for example, claim to find the slang, music, and clothing fashions of youth largely incomprehensible, whereas youngsters cannot appreciate—or even understand—the history and accomplishments of their parents' generation. The perception of a gap was underscored by such slogans as "don't trust anyone over thirty" and "youth is wasted on the young."

A series of stories, supposedly true, describes young people who mix up or misunderstand events in history, including quite recent history (in adults' perception). The kids may confuse Neil Armstrong (the astronaut) with Neil Young (the pop musician), or even with Jack Armstrong or John Glenn. Another source of confusion is the original Beatles lineup versus performing groups organized by members of the quartet after their breakup.

See also "Old Versus Young"; "The Package of Cookies"; "The Youngest Fan"

References: *Baby Train*, 217–219.

The Gerber's Settlement Hoax

A baseless story that gained wide circulation in 1996 claimed that the Gerber's baby food company had lost a class-action lawsuit and was required to give every American child under the age of 12 a savings bond (ranging in value from $500 to $1,500). Parents were advised in these bogus announcements (circulated by hand, by fax, and over the Internet) to send their child's name and a copy of birth records or a Social Security card to a post-office box in Minneapolis.

The Gerber Products Company did not have a post-office box in that city, and on its website it debunked the story, calling it merely rumor and misinformation. A 1996 settlement involving pricing of infant formulas did not involve the Gerber company but may have led to confusion among customers seeking to file the hoax claims.

"The Gerbil- (or Snake-) Caused Accident"

This legend of slapstick comedy and jumping to conclusions has several variations, usually claimed as true, although localized to different times and places. An actual similar incident may well be the ultimate origin of the plot, of which the following is a typical summary:

A woman is driving to her son's school with his pet gerbil in a box to deliver it to him for a show-and-tell session. The gerbil gets out of the box and begins to creep up one leg of the woman's slacks. Unable to shake the creature free, she pulls over to the side of the highway, leaps from her car, and begins to jump up and down, shaking her pant leg.

A passing motorist thinks she is having a seizure. He stops his car, jumps out, runs to the woman and wraps his arms around her, trying to calm her.

A second motorist, seeing the man struggling with the woman, also stops and runs over. He punches the "attacker" in the face as hard as he can, knocking him out. The woman then explains the situation.

Variations in the story include transporting a snake or a lizard, sometimes to a veterinarian rather than a school. The creature may crawl into the woman's blouse or up her skirt, and the two "rescuers" may adopt somewhat different lines of action. Besides these inconsistencies in the story, what further suggests its legendary status is the neat three-part structure of the plot and the lack of closure to explain what happened next.

Such bizarre situations are sometimes invented or elaborated from actual cases for use in law-school examinations, posing the problem for students of identifying the various legal issues involved.

References: *Mexican Pet,* 60–62; *Too Good,* 368–369.

Gerbiling

The sketchy "Colo-Rectal Mouse" rumor of 1984 quickly evolved into a story packed with circumstantial details about an assumed gay male celebrity who supposedly gratified himself by inserting a live gerbil into his rectum. His behavior was allegedly discovered when he came to a hospital emergency room to have a stuck rodent removed. This homophobic (and sometimes AIDS-tinged) story was attached to a TV broadcaster in Philadelphia and to a major film star in Hollywood, among several other prominent men, but it is implied in all versions that "gerbiling" is a standard practice among many homosexual males.

Misinformation is rife in the accounts of gerbiling. Not only is there the usual vagueness about hospital treatment of the supposed perpetrators; some writers have implied that published medical records support the claim that gerbiling is an actual practice. Searches of medical databases have found no such reports. Other people point to the "proof" that gerbils cannot be found in Southern California pet shops, but the reason for this is not that homosexuals have cornered the gerbil market, or to protect the animals from perverted misuse, but simply to protect the state's ecology and agriculture; gerbils, which multiply rapidly, are illegal to keep or sell in that state. A recent account of a supposed gerbiling accident treated in a Salt Lake City hospital was completely fictional, even to the point of naming a nonexistent local health-care facility.

See also "The Colo-Rectal Mouse"

References: Norine Dresser, "The Case of the Missing Gerbil," *Western Folklore* 58 (1994): 229–242; Becky Vorpagel, "A Rodent by Any Other

Name: Implications of a Contemporary Legend," *International Folklore Review* 6 (1988): 53–57.

Germany

The earliest folklorists of Germany—where folk narratives have been assiduously collected and studied for generations—were deeply concerned with the definition, style, content, and meaning of legends. It is not surprising, then, that urban legends have captured the attention of modern German folklorists. German interest in traditional legends dates back to the second edition of Jacob Grimm's *Deutsche Mythologie* (1844), where the famous fairy-tale collector and editor compared the two genres. "As the fairy tale stands related to the legend, so does legend to history," he wrote, stressing the implied connection of legends to places, persons, and incidents of real life.

The long history of German scholars' work on traditional legends cannot be covered in this entry, but the reader may gain a sense of the subject from the translation and notes to *The German Legends of the Brothers Grimm* prepared by American scholar Donald Ward. The Grimms published their collection from 1816 to 1818, and Ward's two-volume translation was published in 1981 in Philadelphia by the Institute for the Study of Human Issues. Another important survey in English is W. F. H. Nicolaisen's essay "German *Sage* and English *Legend:* Terminology and Conceptual Problems" (Bennett and Smith, 1988, pp. 79–87) with a short "Clarification" published in 1992 (*Contemporary Legend* 2: 165–166). Nicolaisen points out that the word *sage* is often directly translated as "legend," but to German speakers it is always closely associated with the verb *sagen* (to say) and thus "implies formlessness or multiformity," whereas the English word "legend" has an "association with scripted story," that is, it relates specifically to narrative rather than spoken traditions in general. Although German collectors of urban legends have referred to them sometimes as *sagen aus der modernen welt* (legends of the modern world), one writer has suggested that a better term might be *aktuelle [volks-]erzählung* (topical [folk] narratives).

As early as 1974 Helmut Fischer was collecting contemporary-legend texts verbatim from oral tradition in the region of the Sieg River; his book *Erzählgut der Gegenwart* (The Story Repertoire of the Present Day) was published in Cologne in 1978 and contained numerous texts, although these could more accurately be termed "regional stories" rather than the widespread urban legends of the modern tradition. In later articles, and especially in his 1991 book *Der Rattenhund* (The Rat-Dog, i.e., "The Mexican Pet"), Fischer turned to what we may call "urban legends proper," treating them with the highly commendable approach of providing multiple variations and thorough annotations.

The first actual collection of modern urban legends published in the German language, however, was a translation from Swedish of Bengt af Klintberg's book *Rattan i Pizzan* (The Rat in the Pizza) first published in Stockholm in 1986. The German edition (*Die Ratte in der Pizza und Andere Modern Sagen und Großstadtmythen*) appeared in 1990. As Rainer Wehse pointed out in a brief review, "The translation from Swedish diminishes in no way its relevance to Germans because this kind of tradition is nearly 100 percent international." Wehse praised the book as "certainly one of the best of its kind." In the same review, however, Wehse was highly critical of the first collection by his compatriot Rolf Wilhelm Brednich, whose book *Die Spinne in der Yucca-Palme* (The Spider in the Yucca Palm) also appeared in 1990 (Munich: H. C. Beck Verlag); Brednich, he charged, printed only paraphrased versions of stories collected by his students with minimal notes or commentaries. Brednich's book, nevertheless, became popular in Germany and has been followed, so far, by three others, all from the same publisher: *Die Maus im Jumbo-Jet* (The Mouse in the Jumbo Jet, 1991), *Das Huhn mit dem Gipsbein* (The Chicken with the Peg Leg, 1993), and *Die Ratte am Strohhalm* (The Rat with the Straw Stalk, 1996). Brednich's latest collection contains an index to the four books, and all of them describe their contents in subtitles as *Sagenhafte Geschichten von Heute* (Legendary Stories of Today).

The close similarity of German urban legends with those circulating in many other countries may be easily appreciated by even the monolingual reader who reviews some of the story titles in Brednich's collections. Cognate words in German and English make it clear what the parallels are in such legend labels as *Der Elefant im Safari-Park, Die gestohlene Großmutter, Der Pudel in der Mikrowelle,* and *LSD-Bilder.* For the latter, often called "Mickey Mouse Acid" in English, Sigrid Schmidt provided a useful published discussion from a German newspaper with an English translation in *FOAFtale News* (no. 16, 1989: 1–4). Schmidt has discussed unique German modern legends in her essays about traditions concerning the direction faced by a sculpture atop Berlin's Brandenburg Gate (*FOAFtale News*, No. 18, 1990) and about tour guides' stories concerning the painted ceiling of a thirteenth-century church in Hildesheim (Bennett and Smith 1989, pp. 179–190). Although Schmidt concludes the latter essay with the question "To what extent may we call such stories 'legends'?" it seems clear that the varying versions of stories told in the present—even if by tour guides alone—are truly legendary.

As in the United States and other countries, in Germany the popular press often recycles urban legends as quasi–news stories. A short example of this phenomenon provides a German text that is easy to translate with just a few helpful hints. The following story appeared in the newspaper *Bild* on September 20, 1981, accompanied by a photograph of a house cat with the headline *Katze warf Junge—Familie ins Krankenhaus* (The Cat Has Kittens—the Family Goes to the Hospital). Although the story was datelined Freiburg, and specific first names and ages of participants were given, this article was clearly just a retelling of "The Poisoned Pussycat." In this instance the family had gathered mushrooms (*pilzen*) and tried some on their cat before making their own meal on the fungi. But no sooner had they finished the mushrooms when the cat suddenly began to act up—writhing and shrieking. They rushed to a hospital to have their stomachs pumped. Returning home, they found their "poisoned" cat with its *zwei Junge*—two new baby kittens! The original is provided below:

Der Kaufmann Werner F. (46) hatte mit seiner Frau und den beiden Kindern (12 und 15) Pilze gesammelt und davon eine Mahlzeit zubereitet. Aber ganz sicher waren sie sich nicht, ob unter den Pilzen nicht vielleicht doch auch ein giftiger sein könnte.

Deshalb gaben sie zuerst ihrer Katze zum Probieren. Katzen, wußte die Ehefrau, rühren niemals etwas an, was ungenießbar oder gar giftig ist.

Der Katze schien es auch geschmeckt zu haben. So machte sich die ganze Familie übers Pilzgericht her. Die Teller waren noch nicht leer, als sich das Tier plötzlich krümmte und jämmerlich miaute.

Entsetzt lief Werner F. zum Telefon. In Todesangst alarmierte er den Notarztwagen. Der raste mit der ganzen Familie in die Klinik; die Ärzte standen schon bereit. Allen Familienangehörigen wurde der Magen ausgepumpt.

"Es war eine scheußliche Sache," sagt der Kaufmann.

Als er, seine Frau und die Kinder bleich nach Hause kamen, sahen sie das Ergebnis der "Pilzvergiftung" ihrer Katze: Sie hatte zwei Junge bekommen.

See also "The Technology Contest"

References: Rainer Wehse, "Topical Narrative Research in German: Bengt af Klintberg and Rolf Wilhelm Brednich," *FOAFtale News* no. 22

(1991): 4–5; Rainer Wehse, "Concepts and Change of Concepts in Contemporary German Legends, Including a Proposition for a New Genre Terminology," *Contemporary Legend*, 5(1995) 132–153.

"The Ghost in Search of Help"

Late at night in his home during a raging blizzard, after a hard day's work, a doctor is summoned by a persistent knocking at his door. There he finds a young girl in threadbare clothing who begs him to accompany her to the bedside of her desperately sick mother. Although he is very tired, the doctor puts on his coat, takes his medical bag, and follows the girl out into the storm and into a shabby tenement apartment. There he finds the mother, seriously ill, and is able to treat her. When he mentions her daughter who had led him there—and who had disappeared at the entrance to the building—the woman is stunned. "My daughter died a month ago," she says, and points to the girl's clothes hanging in the closet. Among them is the same red cloak that she had been wearing, still damp from the storm.

This version of the ghost story is often attached to Dr. Silas Weir Mitchell (1829–1914), a well-known physician from Philadelphia. Evidence suggests that Dr. Mitchell himself sometimes spread the story, possibly as a deliberate hoax. Other "folk" versions refer to anonymous doctors in unspecified times, and the story has been repeatedly revised and reprinted in popular sources, including a book about angels by evangelist Billy Graham and a number of books of mystery stories for young readers. A subtype of the legend told in England and Russia describes a priest or a rector summoned by a ghost to the home of a dying person.

The connection of this old story to modern urban legends comes in the occasional appearance of the same "portrait identification" motif as is found in many "Vanishing Hitchhiker" versions. In these legends the doctor or priest, unaware of the ghostly messenger's true nature, returns to the home the next day, learns that the victim has died, sees a portrait of the messenger, and is told that this was the victim's child or mother who died years before.

References: Brunvand, "The Folklorists' Search for the Ghost in Search of Help for a Dying Person," in *The Truth*, 123–136; *Too Good*, 239–242; *Vanishing Hitchhiker*, 33–35.

"The Ghostly Videotape"

In 1990, when the 1987 film *Three Men and a Baby* was released on videotape, people began to notice for the first time a "ghost" image, apparently of a young boy, in the background of one scene. Stories developed explaining that the son of the owners of the New York apartment used for the film had committed suicide there and had returned as a ghostly presence that could be seen only in the film. Some viewers thought they could also see the rifle he had used to kill himself alongside the spirit; others claimed that the supposed ghost was merely a young relative of the film's director, Leonard Nimoy, who had been promised an appearance in it.

Debunking these stories, the film's producers explained that the New York "apartment" was really a soundstage in Toronto and that the image was an out-of-focus view of a cardboard cutout of actor Ted Danson, who stars in the film, used as part of the apartment decor. Rumors then began to circulate that the film's distributors themselves had started the stories in order to promote video rentals and to draw attention to their sequel *Three Men and a Little Lady* (1990). Unmentioned in most of the discussion of this short-lived legend was the fact that supposed spectral images of dead persons in photographs have long been a part of folk tradition. Most commonly, such images were claimed to be visible in photographs of groups of miners or other workers who had lost one or more companions in occupational accidents.

References: *Baby Train,* 89–91; Charles Greg Kelley, "Three Men, a Baby, and a Boy Behind the Curtain: A Tradition in the Making," *Midwestern Folklore* 17: 6–13; *Too Good,* 243–246.

"The Giant Catfish"

Divers who do maintenance work at the base of dams supposedly report giant catfish—as big as dogs, calves, even Volkswagens—lurking there. The huge fish may threaten the divers themselves (chewing on arms or legs), or they may be circling a sunken vehicle, lured by the decomposed bodies of accident victims trapped inside. In the murky water at those depths the catfish loom in and out of the shadows like ghostly blimps. The sight of these monsters, and their activities, are so horrible that some divers' hair turns white from the shock, and many vow never again to engage in that line of work.

Although some varieties of catfish do grow very large, at least by sportfishing standards, the legends obviously exaggerate their size as well as their voracity. The addition of the hair-turned-white motif to some versions of the story is another sure marker of fiction, not fact. Giant catfish stories are most common in the South, the Midwest, and in the vicinity of the large dams in the Southwest. Occasionally such stories are told about giant carp.

References: Jens Lund, "Catfish" in Brunvand, *American Folklore: An Encyclopedia* (1996), 130–132; *Mexican Pet*, 26–27; *Too Good*, 344–345.

"The Girl on the Gearshift Lever"

A boy slips some Spanish Fly (*Lytta vesicatoria,* or dried blister beetles, also known as cantharis, believed to be an aphrodisiac), into his date's drink while they are at a drive-in movie. But he has unwittingly overdosed her with twice the amount required for good results. When he returns to the car from buying popcorn, he discovers that in her sexual eagerness the girl has impaled herself on the gearshift lever, sometimes with fatal results.

This story, also called "Stick-Shift Frenzy," was well known in the 1950s when four-on-the-floor shifters and drive-in movies were more common. Other seduction stories have replaced it in recent years.

See also "Drugged and Seduced"; "The Gay Roommate"

References: *Choking Doberman*, 133–134; *Too Good*, 123–124.

"Give Me a High Three!"

See "The Sawed-Off Fingers"

"The Golf Bag"

A golfer, angry at his poor play after hitting several consecutive shots into a pond on the eighteenth hole, in full view of the clubhouse crowd, flings his golf bag into the pond and stalks off the course. A few minutes later, the same group notices him walking back to the pond. They watch as he uses a groundskeeper's rake to fish out the bag, extract his car keys from a zippered pocket, throw it back into the water, then head again for the parking lot.

This story is repeated as a true incident, both about local golfers and about certain short-fused celebrities, but never about golf professionals.

References: *Baby Train,* 203–204.

The Goliath Effect

As identified and named by Gary Alan Fine, the Goliath effect suggests that "a larger percentage of American legends than predicted by chance refer to the most dominant corporation or product in a particular market." The subclass of urban legends to which Fine applies his analysis includes those that "frequently feature businesses and corporations as central images and actors"; these he describes as "mercantile legends," and such legends are almost exclusively negative.

Legends exhibiting the Goliath effect reflect "Americans' fear of bigness," Fine asserts, pointing out that even legends that may begin with a smaller company often tend to switch to a larger one as they are repeated. Another factor tending to attract such traditions is prestige, with the most prestigious companies tending to be mentioned most often. Actual companies that have suffered from negative rumors and legends include Coca-Cola, Corona beer, Domino's Pizza, Kentucky Fried Chicken, McDonald's, and Procter & Gamble. Even regional companies, when they become dominant in an area, may become the target for Goliath-effect stories.

There seems to be no evidence that such negative modern folklore is started by rival companies; as Fine mentions, such stories do not appear to have any "lasting effect on corporate profits."

See also Mercantile Legends

References: Gary Alan Fine, "The Goliath Effect: Corporate Dominance and Mercantile Legends," *Journal of American Folklore* 98 (1985): 63–84; reprint, in Fine, *Manufacturing Tales*, 141–163.

"The Good Old Days"

Often circulated as Xeroxlore or in printed form, and frequently appearing in publications, are sets of strict rules for employees, supposedly deriving from a specific factory, business, or school during the 1850s, 1860s, or 1870s. Usually the "message" of these lists—either stated or implied—is "so you think you have it hard nowadays. . . ." Thus nostalgia for the good old days is tinged with horror at the actual harsh conditions that supposedly sometimes prevailed. Long hours, hard labor, and company interference with employee's private lives are the stated norm.

The lists are numbered (usually eight to 12 items), and there is a great deal of repetition and variation among versions. For example, one list may require employees to provide their own pens while others specify that employees must "whittle nibs" carefully for the office pens. Most versions of the list contain the requirement to attend church and contribute generously, and versions from Mormon Utah specify that employees should pay their tithing and attend fast meetings. The rules cover everything from working hours and office duties (including bringing coal for the company's stove) to personal dress and hygiene, and they often conclude with the statement that "every employee should lay aside from each pay a goodly sum of his earnings for his benefit during his declining years, so that he will not become a burden on society or his betters."

Similar lists of rules circulating by the same means purport to be strict regulations from the past for teachers or nurses, and yet another variation purports to be instructions to girls by a turn-of-the-century home-economics teacher on how to be good wives and mothers. A similar set of "school rules" for pupil behavior specifies the number of lashes (from one to ten) for a list of 30–40+ infractions ranging from quarreling and fighting to "playing Bandy" or "blotting your copy book."

Although work, school, home, and hospital conditions were certainly more harsh and demanding in the past than they are today, nobody has produced an authentic, dated copy of these rules from an actual employer or supervisor from the nineteenth century. All citations checked so far have gone no farther back than to published versions of the 1930s or later, and it seems likely that people composed and first circulated the lists long after the purported timeframe.

See also "Grandma's Washday"

References: *Curses!,* 240–242; Barry O'Neill, "The History of a Hoax," *New York Times Magazine* (March 6, 1994): 46–49; *Too Good,* 271–272.

"The Good Times Virus"

Perhaps the most widespread bogus computer-virus warning, and certainly the most thoroughly debunked and parodied, was the "Good Times" virus alert of the mid-1990s. Countless warnings were circulated via e-mail and in publications warning that a message with the subject line "Good Times" or its attached file contained a virus that could do irreparable harm to one's personal computer and its files. Computer experts unanimously branded the warnings a hoax, implying deliberate misinformation spread by a malicious individual or group. Another viewpoint might be that it was simply a joke, mistaken for a real warning by a public accustomed to receiving similar bogus warnings and never knowing whether to believe them or not. (The fact that real computer viruses can spread via e-mail attachments was proven in March 1999 with the appearance of the notorious and damaging "Melissa" virus.)

The most pointed parody of the "Good Times" warning—among many—described the "Bad Times" virus that would (among numerous other attacks) "scratch any CDs you try to play" and "give your ex-wife your new phone number."

References: Peter H. Lewis, "Who Should Be Afraid of Good Times Virus?" *New York Times* (February 27, 1996): B12; *Too Good,* 395–397.

Government Legends

Proving once again that folklore can coexist with mass communications, technology, and even bureaucracy, the oral and customary traditions of government service are abundant, although little collected and studied by folklorists. Typical genres include slang and jargon, jokes, personal anecdotes, and office rituals marking milestones and anniversaries. These items circulate both in face-to-face communication and on the electronic links between government agencies. The range of subjects goes all the way from institutionalized, though unofficial, traditions of the U.S. Supreme Court down to nicknames and pranks found at a local U.S. Post Office branch or recruiting center.

Urban rumors and legends among the American public concerning the government portray Washington agencies and the national military establishment as being bloated, inefficient, aloof, indifferent to citizens' needs, inclined to conspiracies, and often out of step with most people's values. According to the legends, in any conflict between science and religion, the government will downplay the latter; and following any potentially embarrassing government action, the authorities will organize a cover-up. Although far from painting a flattering picture, the whole genre of government legends is often tinged with humor, suggesting that a major function is to release part of the pressure caused by frustration at some government actions (or inactions). There is no reason to think that the government legends and their functions in other countries are not similar.

See also "The Communist Rules for Revolution"; Conspiracies; FBI Stories; "Grenadians Speak English"; "The Madalyn Murray O'Hair Petition"; Military Legends; "The Missing Day in Time"; "The Veterans' Insurance Dividend"; "The Wordy Government Memo"

References: *Choking Doberman*, 194–200.

"Grandma's Washday"

Here is a version of this piece of nostalgic lore from a printed placemat used at the Crane Orchards Cider Mill and Pie Pantry Restaurant in Fennville, Michigan:

Grandma's Washday Receet
1. Bilt fire in back yard to heet kettle of rain water.
2. Set tub so smoke want blow in eyes if wind is pert.
3. Shave one hole cake of lye soap in bilin' water
4. Sart things, make three piles—one pile white, one pile cullured, one pile wark-britches and rags.

5. Stir flour in cold water to smooth then thin down with bilin' water rub dirty spots on board, scrub hard and bile, rub cullured, don't bile, just rench in starch.
6. Spred tee towles on grass.
7. Hang old rags on fence.
8. Pour rench water in flower bed.
9. Scrub parch with hot soapy water.
10. Turn tubs upside down.
11. Go put on clean dress, smooth hair with side combs, brew cup of tee, set and rest and rock a spell and count blessings.

Numerous copies of this list—typewritten, printed, photocopied, and occasionally handwritten—with various different titles, numberings, and misspellings have been spotted all across the United States and even in a New Zealand mining museum. All of them claim to be authentic documents of a bygone era received from a local source, but so far none can be traced to a verifiable early date. Some variations among the lists suggest that the list has been passed, perhaps orally, from person to person; for example, "rub dirty sheets" also appears as "rub dirty spots," and some of the lists are better punctuated and spelled than others.

Although the description of washing clothes in pioneer times seems generally accurate, and some of the dialect is believable (e.g., "pert," "rench," and "bile"), such spellings as "tee," "heet," "hole," "cullured," and "spred" appear to be inserted for a "folksy" effect rather than reflecting any genuine spelling or pronunciation problem of a person capable of writing down such a list with numbered points and a neatly ironic punch line. Some versions of the list go so far as to spell "stir" as "stur" and render "soap" as "sope." In others the word "tea" is spelled both correctly and in dialect as "tee."

Unless proven otherwise, "Grandma's Washday" appears likely to be a relatively modern composition revealing more about how we imagine our ancestors living than how they may actually have lived.

See also "The Good Old Days"

References: *Curses!*, 243–246.

"The Graveyard Wager"

This traditional European folktale (Tale Type 1676B, "Clothing Caught in Graveyard") has survived as a New World story and occasionally surfaces in the form of a modern urban legend. The heart of the story is that a person accidentally pins himself/herself to the ground while proving his or her courage in entering a graveyard late at night. The challenge was to plunge a sword, knife, pitchfork, wooden stake, or the like into a certain grave to prove one's presence there. But the implement accidentally pierces the person's cape, coat, or other garment, and he or she believes that some ghoulish force is pulling downward. The victim is found dead the next day, apparently from a heart attack.

In the older forms of this story, some dating from the Middle Ages, the victim is often a soldier wearing a long cloak and wielding a sword. Similar variations continued to be told in many parts of the rural United States. The most recent versions, however, have cast the victim as a teenage girl at a slumber party where ghost stories are being told, or a South African medical student; the former unwittingly pushes a stake through the hem of her skirt, and the latter sticks a knife through the sleeve of his academic gown.

"The Graveyard Wager" has also entered popular culture as the basis of a *Twilight Zone* episode first aired in 1961.

References: John A. Burrison, "The Fork in the Grave," in *Storytellers: Folktales and Legends from the South* (Athens: University of Georgia Press, 1989), 215–216, note on 249; *Curses!*, 79–81.

"Green M&Ms"

A playful rumor of the 1980s—possibly believed by nobody—was that eating green M&M candies would enhance one's sex appeal. A popular expression of the idea was that "green M&Ms make you horny." Journalist Stephen G. Bloom reviewed the idea in a semiserious way in his article "Passion Power!" in the *Dallas Morning News* (May 22, 1984), and the tabloid *Weekly World News* treated it in a more sensational style ("Green M&M's—It's the Candy for Lovers," July 17, 1984). A Shoebox Greetings card of 1986 alluded to the notion by showing a dish full of the green candies with the caption, "I'm saving the green ones for you." As reported in the *Wall Street Journal* on January 21, 1997, Mars Inc., makers of M&M candies, made a direct reference to the rumor in their advertising aired during the Super Bowl that year.

Although it may appear that "Green M&Ms" has more life in the media than in oral tradition, the basis of these articles was modern folklore, and there developed some fairly consistent "folk" customs of offering the green candies to someone as a flirtatious gambit or even as a humorous sexual invitation.

References: *Mexican Pet,* 111–113.

"Green Stamps"

This is one of the rare urban legends that is sometimes told as a true first-person experience. It is difficult to accept it as an account of an actual experience, however, because several different people at varying times and places have claimed the same experience. The oddness and unlikelihood of the incident casts some doubt on all the claimants, yet most remain firm in their stories. In any case, the plot is well known in tradition and continues to grow and spread.

The basis of the story is that a woman during a vaginal examination is found by her gynecologist to have some S&H Green Stamps stuck to her person. She had been forced to use a public restroom before the exam and, finding the toilet paper dispenser empty, had used a tissue from her purse, evidently transferring some green stamps from the purse to her person. Both patients and doctors have repeated this as a true experience since about the early 1980s, setting the incident in the 1950s to 1970s when S&H trading stamps were offered by many merchants and were avidly saved by shoppers to paste into booklets and redeem for merchandise. A few variations mentioned other kinds of trading stamps, or even postage stamps, and an update to the story appearing in the 1990s describes a woman using what she thought was a spray can of "feminine hygiene deodorant" before her examination—but accidentally getting hold of a can of glitter-spray decoration instead.

Casting further doubt on nearly all such stories is the typical presence of a punch line (a feature of jokes, not legends) from the examining physician: "Gee, I didn't know you gave Green Stamps" or "Aren't we fancy today!" Whatever the truth of the stories, it is clear that their underlying theme is women's embarrassment and anxiety about such examinations, especially when performed by male doctors.

References: *Choking Doberman,* 139; *Mexican Pet,* 122–125; *Too Good,* 465–468.

The Gremlin Effect

The French phrase *l'effet gremlins* (the gremlin effect), coined in 1992 by Jean-Bruno Renard, refers to modern rumors and legends describing supposed dangers of new technologies, including such themes as "welded" contact lenses, people being "cooked" by tanning-salon lamps, power lawnmower accidents, and deaths or harm caused by microwave ovens. Renard borrowed the term from the 1984 American film *Gremlins,* which in turn had taken it from U.S. Air Force slang referring to imagined mischievous sprites that are said to be the causes of unexplained mechanical failures.

As Renard explained in his 1999 book *Rumeurs et légendes urbaines* (p. 101), the gremlin effect, typically, may take three different forms. Narratives may describe either misuse of an appliance (as when a microwaved poodle explodes); a defective appliance (as when stray microwaves from a home oven are said to cause sterility), or hidden injurious effects (as when microwave ovens are said to alter the structure of foods, rendering them poisonous).

Renard suggested that the gremlin effect appears not during the initial period of a technological innovation (when the product is little known and users are few), but rather during a period of "exponential growth" as the product becomes cheaper and users reach 50 percent of all potential consumers. Once the new product is well integrated into everyday life and most people feel comfortable using it, the stories that display this effect fade away.

"Grenadians Speak English"

During the 1983 invasion of Grenada by U.S. troops, the story was told that the government had selected Spanish-speaking soldiers for the assignment, not realizing that Grenadians speak English. Another story from this short military engagement was that a quick-witted soldier, trapped in a house and lacking radio contact with his unit, had used the home's telephone to call back to Fort Bragg and request fire support, charging the long-distance call to his own phone credit card.

Both stories are consistent with the typical image in urban legends of government being inefficient and often dead wrong.

"The Grocery Scam"

An elderly woman pushing a shopping cart full of groceries keeps staring at a young man shopping at the same supermarket. In the checkout line she tearfully explains that he looks just like her son who had been killed fighting in Vietnam, and she asks the young man if he will just call out "Goodbye, Mom!" to her when she waves at him as she leaves the store. He agrees to this. When he reaches the cashier with his few purchases, the total of his bill is enormous, and he is told that his "Mom" said that he would be paying for her groceries as well. His protests fall on deaf ears, since the checkout clerk had heard him say "Goodbye, Mom!"

Sometimes the scam takes place in a restaurant, and the victim may be a young woman (who supposedly resembles the older woman's late daughter). This story, known in Canada and Australia as well as the United States, may describe an actual scam with the two parties in cahoots in order to cheat the store or restaurant. There are also reports of impecunious actors or comedians using a similar trick to get free meals in restaurants. One person at a table leaves early, waves back at his friends, and tells the cashier, "The guy who's waving back at me is paying for my meal."

References: *Curses!*, 247–252; *Too Good*, 311–312.

"The Grumbling Groom"

This is the male version of "The Bothered Bride." Instead of the bride calling off the wedding midceremony and announcing the groom's infidelity, this time the groom enacts a similar revenge for the same cause. Usually he distributes compromising photographs of the bride at their wedding ceremony or reception.

See also "The Bothered Bride"

References: *Mexican Pet*, 135; *Too Good*, 125–128.

"The Gucci Kangaroo"

This is the Australian version of "The Kangaroo Thief" and the title of a collection of Australian urban legends.

See also Australia

References: *Baby Train,* 233–236.

"The Guilty Dieter"

A woman who is on a strict diet has bought only a cup of black coffee at a cafeteria. A nearby diner who has eaten one of the two sugared doughnuts on his plate leaves the other behind as he stands and then walks away from the table. The dieter—ravenous—gobbles down the abandoned doughnut but looks up just in time to see the other diner returning with a second cup of coffee. The embarrassed guilty dieter has powdered sugar spilled on her chin and chest.

This story, sometimes told at Weight Watchers and other diet-group meetings, is similar to "The Package of Cookies," another legend about unintended food theft in an eatery of some kind.

References: *Mexican Pet,* 141.

Hair Turned White

This is a traditional international folk narrative motif (F1041.7, *Hair turns gray from terror*) that surfaces in some modern horror legends. The dark hair of a terrified person is said to have turned snow-white immediately (or overnight) from the shock. The modern motif occurs especially in legends about elevator accidents, specifically in "The Boyfriend's Death" and "The Giant Catfish."

See also Motif

"The Hairdresser's Error"

A female hairdresser is prevailed upon to cut the hair of a man who shows up at her shop just at closing time. He explains that he is on a business trip, staying at a nearby hotel, and needs to look good for an important meeting the next morning. She fastens a sheet around his neck and reaches for her tools, then notices an up-and-down motion under the middle of the sheet—right in the man's lap. Jumping to the conclusion that he is masturbating, the hairdresser hits the man hard enough with a hair dryer to knock him out; then she dials 911 and asks for help.

183

The police arrive, remove the sheet, and discover that the man—who is just then regaining consciousness—had been cleaning his glasses under the sheet.

Sometimes the hairdresser hits the man with a bottle of shampoo or holds a straight razor to his throat while whipping off the sheet. In some versions she even pounds the center of the sheet with a hairbrush, whereupon the man swears to sue her. Whatever the hairdresser's reaction, and whether told in the United States, England, or New Zealand, where the story has circulated since about 1986, the man is always simply cleaning his glasses. Another twist places the scene on an airliner; a flight attendant sees the "action" occurring under a blanket and calls the captain, who confronts the man. He was merely trying to unjam a roll of film from his camera.

References: *Baby Train,* 44–46; *Too Good,* 36–37.

"The Hairy-Armed Hitchhiker"

The following is a newspaper report from England that contains the motif by which most subsequent versions of this legend continue to be known, despite the disappearance of the motif in many later variations:

> An extraordinary story is going the rounds in Leeds and the best efforts of experienced journalists have failed to establish its veracity—or otherwise.
>
> It is always told in the most circumstantial terms and the girl at its centre is often identified as working in a hospital or a bank.
>
> According to the story the girl was getting into her car during a power blackout when she was approached by an old woman who asked for a lift home as she could not find her way in the dark.
>
> The girl agreed and as the stranger was getting in "she" reached over to place a shopping bag on the back seat.
>
> The girl noticed that the hand holding the bag was large and hairy. . . .
>
> She thought quickly and asked the stranger to get out and check the car's rear lights because they had been faulty and she was concerned about the police.
>
> The stranger obliged. And the girl quickly drove off into the night.
>
> Later, it is said, the girl found that the bag on the back seat contained a hatchet.
>
> [From the *Yorkshire Evening Post,* November 11, 1977, quoted in Sanderson's 1983 case study of this legend, p. 163.)

The story of the disguised hitchhiker with the hairy arms, hands, or legs, or with extraordinarily large feet, or wearing men's shoes (etc.) who turns out to be a man evidently goes back to various disguised-robber legends known both in England and the United States since the early nineteenth century. The modern version of the legend, one of the best-known crime stories of the late twentieth century, developed in England during the "Yorkshire ripper" scares of 1977 and quickly spread and became localized elsewhere in England as well as in many countries abroad. Sometimes it is called "The Assailant in Disguise," "The Hatchet in the Handbag," or simply "The Sick Old Lady," and it is similar in several ways to "The Killer in the Backseat."

The original English circulation of this legend, as Sanderson and others demonstrated, reflected the public's extreme concern about a series of gruesome local crimes during a period of power blackouts. But the story soon spread to other regions and was even turned into a literary piece that was broadcast on the BBC. The clear warning of the story was that lone women drivers should never allow strangers, even innocent-appearing ones, into their cars.

In American versions of the legend, which began to circulate in the mid-1980s, the incident is often said to have happened in a shopping mall's parking lot. The intended victim—always a young woman—occasionally notices the person's hairy arms or hands, but more commonly she simply grows suspicious of the stranger's request for a ride home. She either invents an excuse to return to the mall, where she alerts a security guard, or else tricks the would-be assailant into getting out of the car, then locks the doors and drives off. Later she finds a knife, hatchet, meat cleaver, or the like inside the "old woman's" purse or bag. Some people telling the story emphasize that given the right strategy and with enough courage, a modern young woman may extricate herself from a dangerous situation rather than having to summon male assistance in the person of the mall security guard.

An updated version of the legend appearing in the 1990s described a man coming to a woman driver's aid when she finds that her car parked in a mall lot has a flat tire. The stranger changes her tire, then asks for a ride to his own car parked on the other side of the lot. The woman pretends to have other errands in the mall, declines to transport the man, locks her car, and returns to it only after staying in the mall for another hour. Later, in a bag left behind by the "helpful" stranger, she finds a rope, a knife, or other tools of the assailant's trade. She also discovers that her flat tire did not actually have a puncture. A moral for the story is sometimes attached: "Learn to change your own tires!"

"The Hairy-Armed Hitchhiker" is one of the most common and most fully analyzed of all contemporary legends. The story appeals to folklorists because of its long history, its numerous texts and variations, its similarity to some current crimes, and its thematic content. Among the significant aspects of the legend are the switched gender role of the assailant, the distrust of the driver directed against another woman (and a *sick* old woman at that), the presence or absence of an outside "rescuer," and the delayed revelation of the true intentions of the disguised person. Noting that this legend almost invariably involves an elderly woman packing an axe or hatchet, Michael Carroll speculates that the legend "is in some way concerned with a daughter's attitude toward her mother." Specifically, he suggests that the story represents "a projection of the infantile hostility which the daughter directs toward her phallic mother when she discovers that she lacks a penis." The latest versions, which lack the disguise motif, seem similar in their meaning to the other urban legends about threats to women from rapacious or murderous men.

References: Michael P. Carroll, "The Sick Old Lady Who Is a Man: A Contribution to the Psychoanalytic Study of Urban Legends," *Psychoanalytic Study of Society* 13 (1988): 133–148; *Choking Doberman,* 52–55; *Mexican Pet.* 157–159; Stewart Sanderson, "From Social Regulator to Art Form: Case Study of a Modern Urban Legend," in *Arv: Scandinavian Yearbook of Folklore, 1981* (Upsulala, Sweden, 1983), 161–166; Mary Seelhorst, "The Assailant in Disguise: Old and New Functions of Urban legends about Women Alone in Danger," *North Carolina Folklore Journal* 34 (1987): 29–37; *Too Good,* 100–103.

"The Halloween Party"

See "Sex in Disguise"

Halloween Sadists

The widely believed rumors that sadistic people frequently prey on children at Halloween by offering them poisoned candy or apples spiked with hidden razor blades or needles have been thoroughly debunked by folklorists, sociologists, and law enforcement officials. Despite broad dissemination of such findings in the academic and popular press, warnings against these so-called Halloween sadists still appear each October, and organized efforts to eliminate trick-or-treat or to submit children's Halloween treats to X-ray checks continue in many communities.

Sylvia Grider traced some of these anxieties to the 1974 murder of a Texas child by means of cyanide-laced candy put into the boy's Halloween bag of treats by his own father. Joel Best and Gerald Horiuchi surveyed references to Halloween sadists in four major American newspapers over a period of 27 years and found all such reports either to be unverifiable or else obvious hoaxes.

After years of X-raying Halloween bags of treats without finding any dangerous contaminants, and realizing that actual poisons would not be thus revealed anyway, some community leaders in recent years have dropped or scaled back such detection programs.

References: Joel Best, "The Myth of the Halloween Sadist," *Psychology Today* (November 1985): 14–16; Joel Best and Gerald T. Horiuchi, "The Razor Blade in the Apple: The Social Construction of Urban Legends," *Social Problems* 32 (1985): 488–499; *Curses!*, 51–54; Sylvia Grider, "The Razor Blades in the Apples Syndrome," in Smith, *Perspectives* (1984): 128–140.

Handwriting on the wall

This is a classic folk narrative motif (F1036, *Hand from heaven writes on wall*). It also appears in the Bible (Daniel 5:5). It may underlie the modern legend motif of a significant message found written on a wall or a mirror. In "AIDS Mary" the message informs a victim that he has contracted the dread sexually transmitted disease, and in "The Licked Hand" plus some versions of "The Roommate's Death" the mirror-message mocks survivors after the murder of their companions the night before. In these contemporary legends the message is usually written in lipstick or blood.

See also Motif

References: *Curses!*, 203–205.

"The Hapless Water-skier"

A water-skier in a southern reservoir gets too close to an area of sunken stumps and fences. He falls, and when the boat returns to pick him up the skier says he must have hit some barbed wire, as he can feel sharp punctures in his legs. When he is pulled from the water it turns out that he had fallen into a huge ball of water moccasins; shortly afterward he dies from the multiple snakebites.

Some form of this story is told about numerous lakes, especially in the South and Midwest. Water moccasins, also called cottonmouths, are quiet creatures, seldom seen, and not believed—at least by herpetologists—to live or travel in large groups. In fact, these snakes are not even known to exist in many of the lakes where hapless water-skiers are said to have perished.

See also "The Incautious Swimmer"

References: *Mexican Pet*, 29; *Too Good*, 343–344.

"The Hare Dryer"

Also known as "The Blow-Dried Bunny" and "The Resurrected Rabbit," this story swept the United States and then went international in 1988 and 1989. It was rampant in oral tradition, and everyone from local newspaper columnists to Johnny Carson was reprinting or retelling it. Some vestiges of this vigorous tradition lingered on for several more years. Here is a concise version as written out in 1995 by man in Virginia:

> I heard this "true" story recently. A woman in Fairfax owned a dog that was heartily disliked by her neighbors. One day while the

woman was doing her wash, the dog appeared with a neighbors beloved pet rabbit in its mouth. The rabbit was dead, and it was covered with dirt. So the dog owner, wanting to cover up her pet's crime, washed off the dirt, fluffed up the fur with a hair dryer, and carefully returned the rabbit to its cage.

Hours later, the dog owner heard piercing screams from the vicinity of the neighbor's yard. Assuming a look of innocence, she rushed to the scene and asked what had happened.

"Our rabbit died this morning, and we buried it," the shaken neighbor replied, "And now it's back in its cage!"

There are prototypes for the central plot element of this legend in an older story about a "dead" pet that seemingly revives when it is air-shipped home for burial. An even older rural tale describes someone putting a dead pig back in its sty, arranging it in a lifelike posture.

Cowboy poet and country musician Leo Eilts of Kansas City, Missouri, performs his versified version of the legend titled "Annie's Rabbit." A sample verse describes how the cowboys disposed of the dog-chewed body:

First we shampooed Fluffy's body of the dirt and gunk and grime.
Then we blew him dry and brushed him till his fur did fairly shine.
We took him to the garden, mumbled something holy.
And lay the little rodent near a stand of gladioli.

See also "The Air-Freighted Pet"

References: *Curses!,* 151–161; *Too Good,* 40–43.

"The Harried Baby-sitter"

See "The Clever Baby-sitter"

"The Hatchet in the Handbag"

See "The Hairy-Armed Hitchhiker"

"The Heel in the Grate"

This is one of the rare "true" urban legends, that is, a story that can be traced—despite its many variations—to a verifiable incident in a specific time and place. Here is a summary of how the story was quoted in *Reader's Digest* for January 1958 taken from a Lutheran periodical, which had in turn quoted it from a newspaper in Kitchener-Waterloo, Ontario, Canada:

> During the choir's recessional after a Sunday service in an Ontario church the last singer in the women's section got her spike heel caught in a heating grate in the aisle. She pulled her foot free, leaving her shoe stuck in the grate, and kept on walking and singing. The man behind her reached down to pick up the shoe, but the whole grate came up with it. "And then in tune and in time to the beat, the next man stepped into the open register."

Essentially the same story has been told and printed many times, sometimes describing the scene as a church wedding with the bride falling into the grate, other times saying the minister was the one who took the fall. In other versions the minister begins the benediction saying, "And now onto Him who will keep us from falling . . ." and the entire congregation collapses in laughter. The story took yet another twist when introduced into the plot of the 1966 film *The Glass Bottom Boat* with Doris Day portraying the woman who lost her heel in a space station's "clean room" grate and Dick Martin in the role of the man who fell into the open duct.

Signed testimonials from participants in the original incident—including from the actual choir member who fell into the opening—have established that it really happened in the spring of 1948 at the Presbyterian Church in Hanover, Indiana. Marj Heyduck, writing in the *Dayton Journal Herald,* described the incident in a 1957 column from which all subsequent variations seem to derive. Heyduck's version, expanded in speeches she gave, eventually added the "benediction" motif, which participants denied had been part of the incident.

Heyduck died in 1969; three participants furnished their testimonials in 1987. The case seemed to have been closed, but in 1993 a Denver woman came forward claiming to have been the soprano who got her shoe caught in a grate at the same Hanover Presbyterian Church—in

1943 or 1944! However, in this instance the "large and heavy" grate was only tipped, and the man who stepped on it fell to his knees but not actually into the heating duct. This account also claims that the minister *did* deliver the "keep us from falling" benediction.

Although the specific dating and details of the story are still difficult to sort out, it seems clear that all the later generic heel-in-the-grate legends did originate in some kind of incident that took place during the 1940s in a church in Hanover, Indiana.

References: *Curses!,* 167–172; *Too Good,* 457–461.

"The Helpful Mafia Neighbor"

Also known as "A Friend of the Family," this legend describes a couple who move to an expensive suburb and who find their home burglarized when they return from a weekend trip. When they ask their new neighbors if they had noticed any suspicious activity, the neighbors—soft spoken and well dressed—advise them not to report the crime to the police until they "make a few phone calls and see what can be done." Apparently the neighbors have good connections, because the next morning the burglary victims find all their possessions piled neatly on their front porch.

Although the suburban version is told in several large American cities as a recent occurrence, similar stories of stolen goods being returned after a discreet inquiry by a friend or acquaintance have circulated since the 1930s, sometimes said to have taken place in a foreign country. Older American versions imply that the helpful person had Stateside gangland connections, not necessarily Mafia-related.

References: *Mexican Pet,* 147; *Too Good* 305–306.

"The Heroic Hacker"

The computer hacker is often depicted in the popular press as a socially maladjusted teenager whose goal is to wreak malicious havoc on unsuspecting computer users. In the culture of the computer programmer, however, the hacker takes on a different aspect. The true hacker admired by these insiders is raised to heroic status in tales of amazing feats that are circulated through computer networks.

The best known and most widely disseminated of these accounts is "The Story of Mel: A Real Programmer," which began to circulate via computers in 1983. Although the author has been identified, the text is regarded as anonymous by many computer buffs, and it has several variations. Generally the story retains a sort of free-verse format, and it is always replete with highly technical jargon. "The Story of Mel" takes place at a time when "real programmers wrote in machine code," that is, directly in the strings of ones and zeroes that form the binary language that is actually "read" by computers.

Mel's incredible skills and defiant attitude toward "progress" amaze and inspire later generations of programmers "in this decadent era of lite beer, hand calculators, and 'user-friendly' software." The heroic story is alluded to in other hacker legends in which such a statement may appear as, "All I know is: Mel would have *loved* it!"

References: Erik Brunvand, "The Heroic Hacker: Legends of the Computer Age," in Jan Harold Brunvand, *The Truth*, 170–198.

Hilarious Reports

Lists of language boners, supposedly written by semiliterate or careless persons, are passed around in offices in written, typewritten, or photocopied form and more recently on the Internet. Often it is claimed that these errors originated in these same offices, but many have existed for many years in countless different places.

Among the forms these reports take are these (with a sample of each): "The Welfare Letter" ("In accordance to your instructions, I have given birth to twins in the enclosed envelope"); "The Accident Report" ("Coming home I drove into the wrong house and collided with a tree I don't have"); "Letters to the Army" ("I am glad to say that my husband who was reported missing is now dead."); "Parents' Excuses for Students" ("Please excuse Judy; she was in bed with gramps"); "That's What you Dictated, Doctor" ("The patient refused an autopsy"); and "From Actual Court Records" ("Was that the same nose you broke as a child?").

Other such hilarious boner lists purport to be quoted from signs posted in foreign hotels, announcements printed in church bulletins, and students' answers to examination questions. Some of the errors, of course, may really have been committed, but the long lists that have existed for many years, often with the same or very similar items, surely must contain mostly apocryphal items. "The Welfare Letter" has been documented longer than most such lists, with examples found as long ago as World War I.

References: *Curses!*, 236–239; *Too Good*, 280–283.

"The Hippy Baby-sitter"

See "The Baby-Roast"

Historical Approach

Although not an established "school" of interpretation with a rigorous methodology, the study of historical backgrounds of contemporary legends has long interested folklorists, especially those who practice the so-called historic-geographic (or comparative) method of analysis devised for the study of traditional folktales. In essence, this approach is *comparative* in the sense that varying versions from other times and places are examined as to their differences and similarities; the approach is *historical* in that versions of similar themes from the past are reviewed as possible prototypes for the modern tradition.

Often in such studies the historical connections are rather vague and may apply only to general similarities between old and modern legends. For example, a medieval exemplum (moral tale) tells of a spider infesting a vain woman's hairdo, but it cannot safely be concluded that this is the genuine ancestor of the contemporary legend on the same theme. Similarly the severed-fingers (or hand) motif is found in stories from the sixteenth century and the present, but it is difficult to prove a direct relationship between the larger narratives themselves. When an entire legend such as "The Choking Doberman" is linked to several older legends—even to the point of diagramming the suggested connections—the idea that this represents the true genealogy of the modern legend is merely conjectural.

Folklorists have more success in tracing the histories of modern legends with roots no deeper than the twentieth century, since then there are likely to be reliably dated and published texts. "The Heel in the Grate" and "The Unsolvable Math Problem" provide good examples of success with what might be called studies of the "modern history" of individual legends. For the distant past, Bill Ellis's study of "The Blood Libel" as it circulated as an anti-Christian story in ancient Rome stands as a rare example of a successful quest for the historical roots of a continuing tradition.

Another direction of the historical approach is to identify examples of interest in the legends of their own time on the parts of past writers. Among those who have been thus identified are Geoffrey Chaucer, Daniel Defoe, Charles Dickens, Nathaniel Hawthorne, and Jack London.

See also Comparative Approach; Literature and Urban Legends

References: Thomas E. Barden, "Early Virginia Analogues of Some Modern Legends," *Contemporary Legend* 2 (1992): 155–164; *Choking Doberman*, 34–37 (severed fingers); Bill Ellis, "*De Legendis Urbis:* Modern Legends in Ancient Rome," *Journal of American Folklore* 96 (1983): 200–208; Shirley Marchalonis, "Three Medieval Tales and Their Modern American Analogues," *Journal of the Folklore Institute* 13 (1976): 173–184, reprinted in Brunvand, *Readings in American Folklore* (1979), 267–278; *Mexican Pet,* 44–47 (choking Doberman diagram).

Hoaxes

Defined in Curtis MacDougall's classic book on the subject, a "hoax," strictly speaking, is "a deliberately concocted untruth made to masquerade as truth." Some writers use the term in reference to urban legends, particularly bogus warnings, but there is scant evidence of deliberate creation of untruth in the tradition of contemporary rumors and legends. Rather, these particular fictions can seldom be traced to a source, and they are passed along either in good faith by people who believe them, or else simply repeated as jokes. It would seem best, then, to reserve the term "hoax" for cases where there is a provable dishonest and conscious attempt to deceive, which is very seldom true for the circulation of urban legends.

It must be admitted that some of MacDougall's examples do overlap with urban rumors, legends, and other lore covered in this reference work. These include "The Graveyard Wager," "Hilarious Reports," "Redemption Rumors," and "The Vanishing Lady."

See also "The Bullet Baby"; Pranks; "The Stuck Couple"

References: Curtis D. MacDougall, *Hoaxes* (New York: Dover, 1940; rev. ed. 1958).

"Hold the Mayo"; "Hold the Mozzarella"

See Masturbating into Food

Holland

The recognition of urban legends as a modern folklore genre in Holland had an odd beginning with the 1978 publication of a collection titled *Broodje Aap: De Folklore van de Post-Industriele Samenleving* (Monkey Sandwiches: Folklore of the Post-Industrial Society) compiled by Ethel Portnoy, an American living in the Netherlands. Portnoy, as she explained in the preface, had heard the stories in the United States, France, and England, as well as in the Netherlands; even the title story, she admitted, was told to her in the Bronx, New York. According to this account, when trucks entering and leaving *een hot-dog fabriek* (a hot-dog factory) collided, it was discovered that the bodies of zoo animals—gorillas, monkeys, and bears—were being turned into hot dogs.

The American origin of her version of this contamination legend did not stop the Dutch from adopting the term *broodje aap* as a generic label for urban legends. Portnoy's book went into six printings before appearing in a revised and expanded edition in 1980, followed in 1992 by *Broodje Aap Met* (Monkey Sandwiches with Mayo). Portnoy's emphasis, as can be appreciated easily just from her books' illustrations, was on the gruesome and the sexy, with such familiar legends included as "Spiders in the Hairdo," "The Hook," "The Decapitated Cyclist," "The Nude Surprise Party," and "The Stuck Couple."

A broader selection of urban-legend themes was represented in the collection of *broodje aap* stories published in 1992 by the Dutch writer and publicist Peter Burger of Leiden. His title story in *De Wraak Van*

De Kangoeroe: Sagen uit het Moderne Leven (The Kangaroo's Revenge:
Legends from Modern Life) is easily recognized as a variation of "The
Kangaroo Thief," in this instance involving Dutch tourists in Australia.
Burger's book contained a good cross-section of urban stories told in
Holland and attributed to *een vriend van een vriend* (a friend of a
friend) along with sources, comparative notes, and a bibliography. Besides such international favorites as "The Microwaved Pet," "The Hook,"
and "Superhero Hijinks," the book contains some legends that seem
more specifically Dutch, or at least European, including *Het Wandelende Dekbed* (The Contaminated Comforter). Burger's concise text of
"Old Versus Young," titled *Parkeerproblemen* (Parking Problems), can
probably be understood—even when quoted in Dutch—if one knows
that the two quoted remarks are those of the drivers of a small versus a
large automobile following the usual crashing dispute over a parking
place:

> Op een volle Amsterdamse gracht glipt een Mini net voor een Rolls-Royce
> een parkeerplaats in. De bestuurder van de Mini stapt uit en zegt tegen de
> man in de Rolls: "Dat kun je doen als je een Mini hebt." Zonder een spier
> te vertrekken rijdt de bestuurder van de Rolls door en duwt de Mini de
> gracht in. "En deat kun je doen als je een Rolls-Royce hebt."

Peter Burger published a second collection of Dutch urban legends in
1995 titled *De Gebraden Baby* (The Roasted Baby).

Dutch Folklorists Theo Meder and Eric Venbrux submitted a distinctively Dutch modern legend to close scrutiny in their study "The False
Teeth in the Cod," first presented at the thirteenth annual conference of
the International Society for Contemporary Legend Research in San
Antonio, Texas, in 1995. (The paper was published in Dutch in 1996 and
in an English translation in *Contemporary Legend* volume 5 1995, pp.
115–131.) The researchers traced the multiple tellings and printings of a
story about a Dutch fisherman who in 1994 supposedly lost his false
teeth overboard during a fishing excursion on the North Sea. Three
months later it was said that another man caught a large cod that had the
missing teeth inside it. However, the folklorists remarked, "For those of
you who think there's something fishy about this 'False Teeth in the Cod'
story, let us assure you: there is!" It turned out that the story had been
circulating in Holland for some years previous to the alleged 1994 event,
and it was based on much older traditional motifs. Eventually an Amsterdam taxi driver admitted that he had planted the false teeth in the
cod and that the prank had been inspired by the existing folktale.

Meder and Venbrux have continued their study of the urban legends of the Netherlands as well as Flanders with a survey reported in the German journal *Volkskunde* (vol. 100, 1999: 73–95). Reporting on the results of a questionnaire that asked about stories "from guardian angels to concrete furniture" (quoting from their article's title), they found that many such legends were well known in rural as well as urban areas, among Catholics as well as Protestants, and among the elderly as well as the younger population. Among the best-known subjects of Dutch urban rumors and legends were those about contaminated food, burglary, hospitals, and automobile accidents; the favored themes seemed to be health, safety, good fortune, and salvation.

See also "The Contaminated Comforter"; "Old Versus Young"

References: *Baby Train,* 59–60, 237–239.

"The Holy Place"

Although members of a Catholic congregation always kneel and cross themselves at a certain point in one of the church aisles, nobody knows why. An older member of the congregation provides the explanation: Years before there had been an obstruction at that spot, and anyone walking by had to duck. Eventually this evolved into genuflecting, even after the obstruction was removed.

A similar military story also illustrates the power of tradition in maintaining a meaningless ritual. A soldier is always assigned to an artillery piece during firing to stand with one hand held straight out from his shoulder. Why? The job was left over from the days of horse-drawn cannons; the soldier's assignment then was to hold the horses so they would not bolt and run when the weapon was fired.

References: *Too Good,* 147.

"The Homemade Lie Detector"

This ancient international story about how a thief is tricked into revealing his guilt has many variations and occasionally surfaces in a modern setting (often in printed sources). The traditional motif is J1141.16 (*The thief is tricked into betraying himself in supposed ordeal*). Those credited with the trick include an Arab sheik, Argentinian gauchos, Native Americans, and European villagers, among others.

The essence of the trap is that a group of suspects, one of whom must be guilty, is told that a certain object, if touched, will magically identify the true thief. The guilty person is the only one *not* to touch the object, which usually has been smeared with some substance that shows up only on the hands of the innocent parties.

The "lie detector" may be an animal, such as cock or raven under a pot (black with soot), a donkey (its tail soaked in a mint solution), or a sheep (with soot-blackened fleece). Supposedly the animal would have made a noise when the thief touched it, but the real tip-off is the lack of soot or mint on the thief's hands. A Chinese version of the story has a bell smeared with India ink; a Japanese version has a dust-covered statue; and an American version from the Ozarks has a "poppet" (i.e., a doll) smeared with walnut juice. In most versions of the story, whatever the object used, the touching is done inside a tent, in the dark, or behind a curtain so that the thief thinks he cannot be detected in failing to touch the supposed truth-teller.

Although "The Homemade Lie Detector" seems to have no currency as an American oral legend, it has shown up in the twentieth century in a Jack London story, in comic strips, on an episode of TV's *M*A*S*H,* and in *Reader's Digest*.

See also "The Colander Copier Caper"; Motif

References: *Curses!*, 269–273.

Homosexuality

Male homosexuals—but so far not females—are the subjects of a few negative urban rumors and legends, just as they are targeted in countless denigrating jokes, rhymes, and quips found in modern tradition. Two well-known stories of the 1980s and 1990s constitute the major antihomosexual legends circulating; these are the accounts of "gerbiling," which describe a supposed cruel and exotic practice of gay men, and "The Gay Roommate," in which a gay man sexually assaults his heterosexual roommate in a college dormitory. A third urban legend involving homosexuality—"The Gay-Jesus Film Petition"—provoked international protests in the early 1980s before it was established that no such film project existed.

Gay men are sometimes blamed for crimes and other outrages in urban legends that otherwise have no essential homosexual content. For example, in "The Mutilated Child" story, those who perpetrate the atrocity may be described as homosexuals rather than the more common gangsters or members of a racial minority. Legends about disgruntled employees of a pizza-delivery company masturbating onto the food before it is delivered sometimes specify that the act was that of a homosexual employee who was being harassed or fired for his lifestyle. Male celebrities, especially young and handsome ones, are sometimes rumored to be homosexual and may become the targets of rumors and legends such as these. However, in legends about the AIDS epidemic, which does in reality involve many homosexuals, the focus is almost entirely on the possibilities of heterosexual transmission.

Besides these examples of urban lore directed against them, gay men themselves tell urban legends (as well as many jokes) that depict or comment on their lives. One example tells of an airline employee whose last name happens to be Gay; he is traveling on a company pass, using an empty seat on a flight. During loading it is found that his seat is actually needed for a paying passenger, so a flight attendant looks for the employee, asking a man, "Are you Gay?" But she has the wrong seat and the wrong man (it is not Mr. Gay) and also the right man (she picks a passenger who happens himself to be gay). Overhearing the flight attendant asking him to leave, the real Mr. Gay speaks up: "No, I'm Gay; I ll get off." Whereupon two other gay men in the airplane speak up, saying, "Well, *we're* gay too, and you can't throw us all off!"

References: Joseph P. Goodwin, *More Man Than You'll Ever Be: Gay Folklore and Acculturation in Middle America* (Bloomington: Indiana University Press, 1989).

"The Hook"

Most American teenagers, as well as many adults remembering their high school years and fears, will recognize a story that is summarized in a 1990 collection of urban legends from South Africa. The scene is the community of Bloemfontein on "that landlocked city's rather inaptly named central landmark" called Naval Hill, a favorite parking place for young couples on dates:

The car radio is playing romantic music. The night is warm with promise.

Suddenly a news flash interrupts the music. A lunatic has escaped from Groendakkies [a nearby mental hospital], and was last seen in the Naval Hill area. He can be recognised by the gruesome hook which he has in place of a hand.

The girl is nervous, but the boy is feeling amorous. He doesn't want to leave. She protests but he tries harder. She demands he remove his hands. He keeps them where they are. She reaches out and switches off the radio.

Next thing there's the sound of a scratch on the door. Terrified, the girl insists that they leave. The boy is furious and he pulls away with a squeal of tyres. At home, he goes round to the passenger door to open it for her and promptly passes out.

There, hanging from the door handle, is the bloody stump of the lunatic's hook. (From Arthur Goldstuck, *The Rabbit in the Thorn Tree*, p. 99)

Despite the numerous inconsistencies in the legend of "The Hook" (the maniac's being furnished a hook? trying to open the door with the hook hand? lurking outside the car just when the radio mentions him? the frustrated boy politely going around to open the door? and so on), the story has been told avidly and with considerable belief by American adolescents since the 1950s. The story has much older prototypes involving hands cut off when a robber threatens a mounted person; the modern version about an automobile has spread around the world and been localized in countless places. "The Hook" is also a favorite of folklore scholars; there are no less than 33 references to it in the standard bibliography of urban-legend studies published in 1993. The legend has also been incorporated into comic strips, films, and TV programs to such a degree that the very image of a hook dangling from a car-door handle is enough to suggest for most people the whole genre of urban legends. Although this image destroys the suspense necessary for the legend versions, it highlights the fact that "The Hook" is known even better nowadays as a simple scary story rather than a believed account of something that really happened. Parodies of urban legends almost inevitably allude to this story as well, making it in a sense the archetypal example of the genre.

With numerous texts to examine, a long history of the legend to review, and many specific and puzzling details to explain, folklorists have had a field day with interpretations. Best known of these claims is Alan Dundes's Freudian interpretation, which explains the hook itself as a phallic symbol and its amputation as a symbolic castration. Other scholars have been content to see the story more literally as a warning against parking, a dramatic example of the reason for parental concern for their children, an expression of fear of the handicapped, or a depiction of the danger possible from a rampaging antisocial person. The Swedish folklorist Bengt af Klintberg cites "The Hook" as an example of a story about "a conflict between representatives of normal people who follow the rules of society and those who are not normal, who deviate and threaten the normal group." Such a reading is encouraged by comparing "The Hook" to other urban legends in which fingers are lost when someone attempts to assault people who are in a moving car.

American folklorist Bill Ellis reminds us of the importance of securing verbatim texts of urban legends, using as an example a text of "The Hook" as told and discussed by three young women in Ohio in 1981. Although there is considerable phallic humor in this version, Ellis points out that the maniac may better be described as "a moral custodian" who breaks up the parking teens' amorous experiments. The hookman's handicap, in Ellis's view, is "his own lack of sexuality." He concludes that "the threat of the hookman [at least in this telling] is not the normal sex drive of teenagers but the abnormal drive of some adults to keep them apart."

See also Freudian Approach; Severed Fingers

References: Linda Dégh, "The Hook," *Indiana Folklore* 1 (1968): 92–100; Bill Ellis, "Why Are Verbatim Transcripts of Legends Necessary?" in Bennett, Smith, and Widdowson, *Perspectives on Contemporary Legend II* (1987), 31–60; Bengt af Klintberg, "Why Are There so Many Modern Legends about Revenge?" in Smith, *Perspectives* (1984), 141–146; *Too Good*, 94–95; *Vanishing Hitchhiker*, 48–52.

Horror Legends

Nearly every collection of urban legends, regardless of which country it originates from, has a separate chapter or section containing the most horrifying stories based on accidents, atrocities, contaminations, crimes, and the like. Because every category of urban legends in fact contains some horrors, it is somewhat arbitrary to classify some specifically as horror legends. The category was created mainly to highlight urban legends that seem to have horror as their major purpose or theme. Subsections of the category are Baby-sitter Stories, Medical Horrors, and Other Horrors.

Baby-sitters in urban legends may either be threatened by a killer who has slain the children and now threatens the sitter, or else the sitters themselves are guilty of horrible crimes against their charges. The children in these stories are sometimes gassed, microwaved, or left to starve.

Several medical horror stories play on peoples' fears of hospitals, operations, and even physical examinations, depicting the horrible ways these may go wrong. Other stories in this category deal with infections, cadavers, and cannibalism.

Other Horrors, always an ambiguous category, includes legends about gruesome deaths, unsanitary living conditions, terrifying experiences, and alleged satanic rituals.

Several modern horror legends are actually transformations of old folktales; conversely, some horror stories tend to be told more often nowadays as fictional scary stories than as believed legends.

See also "The Climax of Horrors"; Scary Stories

References: *Baby Train*, 65–112; *Choking Doberman*, 69–102; *Curses!*, 29–87; *Mexican Pet*, 69–82; *Vanishing Hitchhiker*, 47–73.

Human Nature

Although not a clear category based on particular stories' content or theme, human nature—our ideas of how we *think* people will normally react—is often illustrated in the behavior of characters described in urban legends. In the words of the source cited below, human nature in urban legends reveals peoples' tendencies to "jump to conclusions, seize at opportunities, miss the point, fudge the data, complain, criticize, rationalize, sympathize, brag, gloat, miss the boat, jump ship, blindly follow tradition yet yearn to be different." Part of the appeal of many urban legends is undoubtedly the sense that were we in the same situation we might well have reacted in the same way and have been similarly embarrassed or injured.

"The Baby Train" provides a good example of human nature supposedly at work: Given the opportunity, the story suggests, couples will "do what comes naturally," in this instance, have sex if accidentally awakened at an early hour. Other popular legends depict people telling "white lies" or committing minor crimes when they think that nobody will notice. Human nature can work both ways in a story; for example, in "Take My Tickets, Please!" a man leaves a pair of game tickets for a poorly performing local team in a conspicuous place in his unlocked car, knowing that someone will probably steal them. Instead, another disgruntled fan following the same psychology leaves his own two tickets beside the originals.

Even when a story illustrating human nature is proven false, as is the case with "Dial 911 for Help" (someone can't find the 11 button on the phone dial), the story continues to be repeated and believed because "that's just how dumb some people are!" Perhaps believing in urban legends is itself a good illustration of human nature.

See also "The Trained Professor"

References: *Too Good,* 321–334.

"The Hunter's Nightmare"

An unsuccessful hunter happens to hit a deer with his car while driving home. Although it is illegal to do so, he stops and puts the deer into the backseat of his car, affixing his state hunting tag to it. But the deer was only stunned; it revives and begins kicking and struggling to escape. The man swings at the deer with a tire iron but hits his hunting dog instead, and then the dog begins to attack him. The man stops the car, jumps out pursued by his dog, escapes into a telephone booth, and calls 911, telling the police that he is trapped in the booth and that a deer is destroying the inside of his car.

Numerous individuals and police departments have copies of what is said to be the original 911 audiotape recording the hunter's panicky call for help, which is often claimed to have happened between 1989 and 1992 in the local area. However, the only documented case of this kind occurred in Poughkeepsie, New York, in 1974, and not all of the tapes circulating have the same wording or details, although most are peppered with the same range of obscenities. Exaggerated claims are made for the number of copies of the tape in existence and for the interest in it on the part of U.S. government agencies. An older tradition of stunned-animal stories exists as well. It seems likely that dubbed and faked copies of the 1974 "stunned-deer/deer-stunt" tape have been passed around and that those who have heard it have assumed that the incident happened locally and recently. Attention to the story by newspaper columnists has encouraged this notion.

See also "The Deer Departed"

References: *Baby Train,* 270–272; *Too Good,* 381–383; *The Truth,* 76–83.

Hunting

Hunters in urban legends are routinely depicted as being unlucky, stupid, dishonest, or worse. "Dumb hunters" from out of state (Californians in Utah, Texans in Colorado, Chicagoans in Michigan, etc.) are said to have shot horses, cows, mules, or other domestic stock while deer hunting. But the local hunters are just as confused and ineffective in their own way, according to the stories. Hunting is an anachronism in modern life, and those who engage in the sport seem to be pictured in the folk stories as reverting to an earlier, more primitive way of life or mentality.

See also "The Deer Departed"; "The Hunter's Nightmare"; "The Loaded Dog"; "Shooting the Bull"

"I Believe in Mary Worth"

The title of this entry is the formula that is supposed to be chanted a set number of times (3, 10, 50, 100, etc.) while staring into a mirror in a darkened room (often the bathroom)—sometimes lit by candles—in order to summon out of the mirror the avenging spirit of a witch or ghoul. Who wants to do this? Usually groups of adolescent girls at parties or summer camps. The ritual is well known all over the United States, with only the name of the spirit changing. Variations include Mary Whales, Mary Worthington, Mary Johnson, Mary Lou, Mary Jane, Bloody Mary, and even Kathy. Sometimes the ritual demands that the speaker repeat "I *do* believe in [insert name]" or even "I *hate* [insert name]." In many places it is said that "Mary" will spring out of the mirror and scratch the face of the one calling on her, but why anyone would invite this attack is not explained. Nevertheless, many women rather nostalgically remember performing this scary ritual with friends during their adolescent years, although none ever claims to have seen the practice yield the rumored results.

The legend component of the ritual is sketchy, consisting usually of vague stories about some kind of tragedy suffered by the real Mary that disfigured her and made her determined to harm other young girls. Evidently the character has no relationship to the Mary Worth of the comic strip, but some folklorists have suggested that there may be a connection to the legend of La Llorona, the weeping woman of Mexican American folklore. Another traditional link must be to the mirror lore in fairy tales and folk beliefs.

Focusing on a group of versions from California college undergraduates that emphasize the "Bloody Mary" reference in a bathroom setting, Alan Dundes suggests that the ritual really concerns "the onset of the [young girl's] first menses . . . the dramatic change from girlhood to womanhood." After criticizing other folklorists for failing to interpret the ritual sufficiently, Dundes offers a cocktail of hypotheses, ranging from possible connections of the ritual to the Bloody Mary of English history and to the vodka-based drink (in its variant called a Virgin Mary) to speculation that the names "Mary Worth" and "Mary Whales" may refer to the "worth" of the adult female or to an emotional response of "wailing." Pursuing the bloody motif further, Dundes applies his method to "The Vanishing Hitchhiker," comparing the wet spot sometimes left on the car seat by the ghostly rider to the "telltale blood spots" of a menstruating young woman.

References: Alan Dundes, "Bloody Mary in the Mirror: A Ritual Reflection of Pre-Pubescent Anxiety," *Western Folklore* 57 (1998): 119–135; Janet Langlois, "'Mary Whales, I Believe in You': Myth and Ritual Subdued," *Indiana Folklore* 11 (1978): 5–33; *Mexican Pet,* 80–82.

"The Ice-Cream Car"

Illustrating how some periodicals borrow doubtful stories from one another and pass them on, is this version of "The Ice-Cream Car" from the June 1978 issue of *Traffic Safety:*

Automotive Engineering reports on an unusual complaint received by a Texas automobile dealer. A lady complained to the dealer that her car would not start whenever she bought pistachio ice cream. She explained that her family enjoyed ice cream, so on hot summer days she would stop at a local shop and pick up some to take home. Whenever she bought chocolate, vanilla, or strawberry ice cream she had no problem starting her car. But when she bought pistachio ice cream her car invariably stalled. The dealer at first thought the lady was crazy, but after making several ice-cream trips with the lady, he found that what she said was true. An engineering friend explained the problem to him. He observed that chocolate, vanilla, and strawberry were prepackaged flavors sold right out of the freezer, but take-home orders of pistachio had to be hand-packed. The extra time needed was just enough to allow the car to develop a vapor lock in the hot Texas sun.

What makes the story doubtful is the lack of specific names and places, the vagueness of the technical problem (sometimes described as "percolation" or simply stalling), the extreme unlikelihood of this problem occurring repeatedly, and especially the many other states of the union, models of cars, and flavors of ice cream that are mentioned in numerous variations of the story. Narrators also disagree whether the car's engine was stopped or left idling. The same basic car problem with the same lack of proof and inconsistencies was described as long ago as the 1940s when hand-packed ice cream was fairly common, and the story has shown up again in publications as recently as 1992.

References: *Curses!*, 121–122; *Too Good*, 296–298.

"The Ice-Cream Cone Caper"

Suddenly in the summer of 1986 film idols began showing up in ice-cream parlors across the nation, wowing their giddy fans (always women, according to the story) who completely overreacted (always in the same way). First it was Paul Newman or Jack Nicholson in a northeastern state, then Robert Redford in Santa Fe, New Mexico—just buying an ice cream cone and keeping cool. Enter the dazzled fan, who gets tongue-tied when she recognizes the star but manages to order her cone anyway. Back outside the store, however, the woman realizes that she has her change in her hand, but no ice-cream cone. Reenter the film idol, who leans close while licking his own cone, and says softly, "It's in your purse, right where you put it."

This story, with its possible Freudian overtones, was widely told and even more widely printed in publications ranging from serious news articles to gossip columns. Broadcaster Paul Harvey, among many others, repeated it on the air. When the story got back to the celebrities involved, Paul Newman was reported by *USA Today* to have said he would sue Nicholson and Redford "because the ice cream tale is *his* false story." Despite well-publicized denials and debunkings, the story has appeared again in print as recently as 1993, tending to be revived whenever one of the stars involved is making a new film.

References: *Curses!*, 173–176; *Too Good*, 422–424.

"The Improved Product"

As Henrik Lassen's survey documented, the "legend of a suppressed miraculous invention or, in more inclusive terms, a vastly 'improved product,' has made the rounds continuously in various contemporary disguises for almost two thousand years." The version of this theme told in classical times was a story about unbreakable or flexible glass; in contemporary legend, the best-known version is "The Economical Car." In both ancient and modern times the supposed new invention is said to have been kept off the market. In Lassen's summary of this basic tradition:

> A fabulous technological discovery has been made from which everyone, except certain powerful individuals, would profit immensely if it were made available to the general public, but these few people, in whose interest it is to keep the discovery away from everyone else, have enough power to suppress it indefinitely.

Among other improved products described in modern folklore are light bulbs that never burn out, tires that wear forever, nylon stockings that will not run, and razor blades that do not become dull. The powers that suppress the invention are usually said to be either the manufacturers of rival traditional products or the government. Occasionally a claimed improved product of doubtful utility will actually reach the market; recent examples are the "magic" washing balls or disks that are said to clean clothes in a washing machine without the use of a laundry detergent. We should also note that modern plastics have in most respects provided the world with unbreakable and somewhat flexible transparent products comparable to the ancient's imaginings of *vitrum flexile*.

References: Henrik R. Lassen, "'The Improved Product': A Philological Investigation of a Contemporary Legend," *Contemporary Legend* 5 (1995): 1–37.

"The Incautious Swimmer"

As in "The Hapless Water-skier," a swimmer dives straight into a nest of water moccasins (also known as cottonmouths) and is bitten to death.

These two closely related legends, like "The Can of Snakes," are part of the larger bed-of-snakes tradition of stories circulating throughout the Midwest and South.

A variation of "The Incautious Swimmer" appeared in Larry Mc-Murtry's 1985 book *Lonesome Dove* and in the TV production derived from the book.

References: *Mexican Pet,* 30.

"Indecent Exposure"

This legend of unknown origin first surfaced in 1991 and quickly spread internationally, being reported as recently as 1996. The story tells of a dastardly crime that is documented by the crooks themselves in a photograph, but—not surprisingly—nobody repeating the story has ever produced the photo.

A honeymoon couple in the Bahamas return to their hotel room to find it ransacked and everything stolen—everything, that is, except for their toothbrushes and their camera. They report the thefts to management and are given money to replace their goods and granted a free room for the remainder of their stay.

After enjoying the rest of their honeymoon without further incidents, they return home and take their film in to be developed. Viewing the prints a few days later, the couple are horrified to find a picture showing a close-up of someone's naked, hairy buttocks with their toothbrushes stuck into the rectum. Alternatively, in more discreetly told versions, the toothbrushes are spotted "in the one place in Jamaica where the sun doesn't shine."

"Indecent Exposure," also known as "The Toothbrush Photo," varies as to the location and the nature of the perpetrators; it often has a racist angle when the thieves are identified as blacks, Aborigines, or Rastafarians. Some versions, especially those told in Europe, claim that the outrage occurred during a family camping trip. Sometimes the offended couple is said to be showing their vacation slides to friends and family, unfortunately without first previewing the pictures.

References: *Baby Train,* 54–58; *Too Good,* 314–315.

"The Ineradicable Bloodstain"

This is a traditional international folk narrative motif (E422.1.11.5.1, *Ineradicable bloodstain after bloody tragedy*) that has been nominated as the prototype of the smell-of-death element in the contemporary legend known as "The Death Car." In older traditional legends the blood from a murder victim stains a floor or carpet and cannot be removed, despite years—even centuries—of scrubbing. In the modern urban legend the ineradicable feature is the smell of death.

References: William Kline and Marion Newell, "An Ineradicable Bloodstain," *Keystone Folklore Quarterly* 9 (1964): 30–31; *Vanishing Hitchhiker,* 20.

International Society for Contemporary Legend Research

The ISCLR was formed in 1988 to study "'modern' and 'urban' legends, and also any legend circulating actively." The organization grew out of a series of annual seminars at the University of Sheffield, England, beginning in 1982. After five volumes of *Perspectives on Contemporary Legend* series were published featuring papers drawn from these seminars (Sheffield Academic Press, 1984–1990), ISCLR in 1991 commenced publishing *Contemporary Legend,* a yearbook of legend studies. *FOAFtale News,* the ISCLR's occasional newsletter, reports on emerging legends, current bibliography, and the activities of legend scholars. An invaluable tool sponsored by ISCLR is *Contemporary Legend: A Folklore Bibliography,* compiled by Gillian Bennett and Paul Smith (New York: Garland, 1993); it contains 1,116 annotated items and a detailed general index. ISCLR holds an annual meeting, usually in the spring, in locations chosen from either the United State or abroad. Information about membership, publications, and conferences may be found at the ISCLR website: <www. panam.edu/faculty/mglazer/isclr/isclr.htm>.

International Urban Legends

A great many urban legends are told worldwide in one variation or another. Outstanding examples include "The Baby-Roast," "The Runaway Grandmother," "The Spider in the Cactus," and "The Vanishing Hitchhiker." Since the 1980s, collections of American urban legends have been translated into several other languages, often inspiring foreign readers to recollect their own national versions of the same stories. Foreign folklorists have produced a steady stream of urban-legend articles and books, documenting the truly international as well as local contemporary legends circulating in their countries. Without a doubt, some kind of contemporary oral narratives that we could accept as urban legends must exist in virtually every modern country.

This encyclopedia includes separate entries for several countries where substantial progress has been made to document and publish urban legends. The lack of an entry for a country in no way suggests that there are no contemporary legends told there; simply, nobody has yet to collect or study them (at least not to this author's knowledge).

Whenever possible, reference is made in the country entries to English language editions of foreign publications. However, both the language barrier and the difficulty of locating materials published abroad may limit American readers' access to these sources. Some of these works may be found via interlibrary loan from a university specializing in folklore research, or by searching databases via the Internet.

See also Argentina; Australia; Belgium; Canada; Denmark; England; Finland; France; Germany; Holland; Ireland; Israel; Italy; Japan; Mongolia; New Zealand; Norway; Poland; Romania; Russia; Scotland; South Africa; Spain; Sweden

Internet Resources

Excellent resources to promote and facilitate the collection, discussion, and study of urban legends exist in the form of Internet websites. Besides the two major sites devoted to general aspects of the subject, other sites are established from time to time either by companies affected by urban legends (e.g., Procter & Gamble, Gerber Products Company, and Neiman Marcus stores) or by individuals researching individual legends (e.g., expensive cookie-recipe stories and "Blue Star Acid"). A website is also maintained by the International Society for Contemporary Legend Research. People using the Internet to gather information on urban legends should use the search engines of their web browsers to locate other sites, including newly established ones, or to find recent articles on legends published in periodicals.

The older of the two comprehensive urban legend websites is that of the computer newsgroup alt.folklore.urban (AFU): www.urbanlegends. com. Popular for its wit and humor as well as its authoritative ratings of rumors and legends, AFU provides the novice with a good definition of the genre along with a file of frequently asked questions (so-called FAQs). The extensive Internet links, index, quotations, bibliography, and other information are credited to the founders and maintainers of AFU (Terry Chan, Peter van der Linden, and Sean Willard) and to the many regular visitors who contribute material and comments to this lively site. Stories in the AFU archive are categorized as True, Believed True, False, Mostly Untrue, and so on. The group even has posted online an official AFU poem—"Song of the Microwave." It begins:

> What can I say about ol' AFU,
> Read by the many
> Understood by the few?

The poem describes the frequent visitors to the AFU site thus:

> Lunkheads and eggheads
> Meet in delight
> To argue the trivia
> Far into the night.

An even larger and more ambitious urban-legend website is maintained by Barbara and David P. Mikkelson (the Urban Legends Reference Pages www.snopes2.com). This site has beautiful graphics and colors enhancing a wide range of features and topics. Users may search for themes, topics, and legends either randomly or with a specific interest in mind through a large archive of texts and discussions. The website includes special sections for legends about Disney, colleges, sex, horror, music, movies, radio, television, and a host of other subjects. Also included are listings of urban-legend books, the latest legends, "top-ten urban legends," and links to other Internet sites with related material. The Mikkelsons' impressive website has a chatroom and will send e-mail updates on current legends automatically to subscribers.

Besides the English-language websites, there are numerous sites concerning urban legends created in other languages by fans and researchers all around the world. These are too numerous to list here, but by way of example try entering the Italian word *"leggende"* in the search engine of your web browser and see what appears.

See also Hoaxes

Interpretation

See Analysis and Interpretation

Ireland

The rich traditional folklore of Ireland has been collected and studied for a long time, making it possible to trace some modern legend themes back to their older forms in that country. Many of the contemporary bosom-serpent stories, for example, have Irish prototypes, and "The Robber Who Was Hurt" has both older and modern examples in Ireland.

But the collection and study of urban legends in Ireland, after a promising start in the early 1980s, seems to have languished, although certainly there must be just as many such stories circulating in that country as elsewhere in Britain and beyond. The Irish folklorist Éilís Ní Dhuibhne reported on her collection of modern legends from Dublin at the first international Perspectives on Contemporary Legend conference held in Sheffield, England, in 1982. Only a short abstract was published in the conference proceedings (Smith, 1984, p. 230), but a full report appeared in *Béaloideas,* the journal of the Folklore of Ireland Society, in 1984. The article includes 23 samples of Irish urban-legend texts, one for each subcategory of a proposed list that comprises seven main categories. The collection also received publicity via an article ("Tales of the

Unexpected," *Irish Independent* (Dublin), December 1, 1982), in which the folklorist was quoted discussing the spread of legends:

> All folk stories have always been able to cross the water. In the past sailors or fishermen brought them home. Now they are spread by the media or holiday makers. Even international news agencies are responsible for disseminating them.

If there has been further progress on the collecting project since then, the rest of the world has not been informed of it.

The legends described in the *Béaloideas* article were categorized as either being ethnocentric or else concerning violence, theft, revenge, accidents, food, or the supernatural. Among the examples quoted were such familiar international legends as "The Runaway Grandmother," "The Dead Cat in the Package," and "The Vanishing Hitchhiker." The localization to Ireland of a widely known story is demonstrated in the following version of the legend about contaminated fast food as it was told by an Irish schoolgirl who had been chatting with the collector about the subject:

> There was supposed to be something like that in Portmarnock, in a van that sells chips and burgers and stuff. And the binman [i.e., garbage collector] was coming and he was collecting the bins, and he saw a lot of Kitikat [a cat food] cans, and he wondered where they were coming from. And the man was making burgers out of Kitikat. He was selling them to the people, and the people were eating them.

Lacking further texts and analysis, it is difficult to identify which modern legends may be distinctively Irish, or at least have a genuine Irish flavor; however, at least two stories that may qualify as typical, if not unique, are "The Kilkenny Widow" and "Miracle at Lourdes." However, the one legend mentioned by Dhuibhne as being "unknown outside Ireland" does, in fact, have a counterpart in the United States (and perhaps elsewhere), where it is usually applied not to a gasoline strike but simply to describe an instance of impolite behavior at the gas pumps and one driver's revenge. Here is the Irish version of "Revenge During Petrol Strike" from her *Béaloideas* article:

> During the petrol strike, a girl is about to join a petrol queue [line] outside a garage. She sees a gap in the queue quite near the garage and she slips into it. After a few minutes two men parked behind her come up to the car

window and complain that she is acting unfairly, since they have been queuing for hours and are now behind her in the queue. She ignores them, rolls up the window and begins to read the paper. When she gets to the pump she gets out and tries to take the cap off the petrol tank. She finds that it has been changed: her cap is gone and a new locked cap replaces it. So she can't get any petrol.

Although the beginning of a good documentation of Irish urban legends was made in the 1980s, so far the promise of that start has not been realized.

References: Éilís Ní Dhuibhne, "Dublin Modern Legends: An Intermediate Type List and Examples," *Béaloideas: The Journal of the Folklore of Ireland Society* 51 (1983): 55–70.

ISCLR

See International Society for Contemporary Legend Research

Israel

Folklore study in general has long been pursued by Israeli scholars, but interest in contemporary legends there is fairly recent, and it has been manifested so far mainly by researchers from Haifa. For example, Aliza Shenhar published a study of vanishing-hitchhiker legends from Israel in 1985 in the German folk narrative journal *Fabula* (vol. 26: 245–253). The texts and discussions are in German, under the title "Israelische Fassungen des Verschwundenen Anhalters (Mot. E332.3.3.1: The Vanishing Hitchhiker)." Shenhar discussed 37 texts of the legend collected by students at the University of Haifa from 1980 to 1983. Although the versions were highly localized to their Middle East setting, the basic motifs of the international legend tradition were well preserved.

Another of Shenhar's studies, "Legendary Rumors as Social Controls in the Israeli Kibbutz," was published in *Fabula* in 1989 (vol. 30: 63–82). Although the three examples of legendary rumors quoted here are not urban legends in the strict sense, their transmission, style, and functions certainly qualify them as contemporary *local* legends. Shenhar shows how these stories of sexual indiscretion, lapsed values, and wounded pride "reflect the process of change taking place in Israeli kibbutzim of the eighties." And like all oral folklore, the stories became "transformed in the process of transmission from one person to another." Another study of kibbutz narratives, this one by Haya Bar-Itzhak of the University of Haifa, appeared in *Contemporary Legend* (no. 5, 1995: 76–100).

Yet another University of Haifa scholar, psychologist Benjamin Beit-Hallahmi, studied "beliefs, myths, and literary expressions of men's fear of female genitals," publishing some of his findings in 1985 in the *British Journal of Medical Psychology* (vol. 58: 351–356). The primary urban legend of interest here is "The Stuck Couple," which Beit-Hallahmi was surprised to find well known even among medical professionals. He wrote:

> It is remarkable that this myth has attained a special popularity among medical personnel, physicians and nurses. Despite the fact that all authoritative sources on human sexual physiology doubt the possibility of the *penis captivus* phenomenon, such stories are still prevalent and can be heard on various occasions. (p. 354)

This researcher's data came about equally from Israeli and American sources.

A dramatic example of how a well-known urban legend repeated in Israel quickly became an international news item was the case of the exploding toilet in Tel Aviv, which appeared in a local newspaper in 1988 and was circulated worldwide by two news services and then printed in countless foreign newspapers before being debunked as a mere example of the popular modern legend. A full analysis of this case appears in Brunvand, *The Truth Never Stands in the Way of a Good Story* (2000, chap. 8, "A Blast Heard 'round the World").

Further evidence of an interest in contemporary legends in Haifa came at the seventeenth international conference of the ISCLR held in St. John's, Newfoundland, in May 1999. A paper by Larisa Fialkova and Maria N. Yelenevskaya was presented, titled "Ghosts in the Cyber World: Analysis of Folklore Sites on the Internet." Although the two authors were unable to attend the conference, their paper was read to the attendees. They had studied how "computer mediated communication," particularly on a website devoted to discussion of supernatural stories, revealed the existence of an "electronic culture" comparable to the workings of oral tradition circulating contemporary legends. They concluded that "when comparing ghost stories recorded in 1993 with recent postings, we can see a gradual decline of spontaneity which gives way to the development of literary features in texts and organizational rules in the practices of electronic folklore groups."

Italy

Interest in the urban legends told in Italy was stimulated by a 1980 newspaper article by the noted writer Italo Calvino, discussing an odd story he had heard that turned out to be well known internationally as "The Severed Fingers." In Calvino's version a young woman who is a *"conoscente di conoscenti di conoscenti"* (acquaintance of an acquaintance of an acquaintance), while driving home late one night, was terrorized by members of a motorcycle gang who threatened to break into her car. The woman locked her doors, and as she drove quickly away the gangsters swung heavy chains against the car. Back home, the woman found one piece of chain caught on her car; still attached to the other end of the chain was a torn-off hand.

In 1988 two foreign books on contemporary rumors and legends were published in Italian translations: French sociologist Jean-Noël Kapferer's 1987 book *Rumeurs* appeared as *Le Voci che Corrono;* and American folklorist Jan Harold Brunvand's 1986 book *The Mexican Pet* appeared as *Leggende Metropolitane*(also including a translation of the introduction of his 1981 book *The Vanishing Hitchhiker*). In 1990 Brunvand's *Curses! Broiled Again!* (1989) appeared in Italian as *Nuove Leggende Metropolitane,* and in the same year the translator of the Brunvand books, Maria Teresa Carbone, published her own intriguing little book titled *99 Leggende Urbane.* Carbone's work included short entries running from A to X (literally, from *Abbronzatura,* or "tanning tales," to Xeroxlore); it touched on such topics as alligators, baby-sitters, drugs, immigrants, nuns, sex, and supermarkets.

A landmark event for Italian urban-legend studies was announced in March 1991 in the first issue of the newsletter *Tutte Storie* (Nothing but Stories), marking the formation of the Centro per la Raccolta delle Voice e Leggende Contemporanee (Center for Collecting Contemporary Rumors and Legends). The center is directed by Paolo Toselli and its address is Casella Postale 53, 15100 Alessandria, Italy. The center has a website located at www.clab.it/cp/leggende. *Tutte Storie* has appeared on an irregular basis since then; it contains short articles and notices of legends circulating in Italy and reviews of current publications concerning them. Researchers at the center describe their subject matter as including people's accounts of doubtful veracity that are "told as true, or believed to be true" (*raccontate come vere or credute vere*). Many of these items are in the form of "improvised news items resulting from the process of communal re-creation" (i.e., rumors), whereas others are in the form of true legends with a distinct narrative content. The legends, of course, are passed from person to person as the supposed experience of a friend of a friend (*all'amico di un amico*). Both rumors and legends also appear frequently in the Italian mass media.

Although published in Italian, *Tutte Storie* provides concise summaries of each article in English or French for the benefit of foreign readers. (The English summaries also appear on the center's website.) Typical subjects treated in the newsletter are rampant rumors of *felini misteriosi* (mystery cats), *terremoto annunciato* (bogus earthquake prophecies), and organ-theft legends. A rash of exaggerated reports about gigantic "torpedo fish" (*pesce siluro*) terrorizing scuba divers are similar to American legends about giant catfish. The Italian legend center does an excellent job of documenting such urban rumors and legends as they circulate in oral tradition, in printed sources, and as part of radio and TV broadcasts.

Book-length collections of Italian urban legends continue to appear. Paolo Toselli published *La Famosa Invasione delle Vipere Volanti* (The Famous Invasion of Flying Vipers) in 1994, followed by *Di Boooa in Bocca* (From Mouth to Mouth) in 1996. Cesare Bermani published *Il Bambino è Servito: Leggende Metropolitane in Italia* (The Baby is Served: Urban Legends in Italy) in 1991 and *Spegni la Luce chè Passa Pippo* (Douse the Lights When Pippo Goes By) in 1996. A 1993 book by Titta Cancellieri was *E se Capitasse a Te?* (And If It Happened to You?), and one by Danilo Arona published in 1994 was titled *Tutte Storie: Immaginario Italiano e Legende Contemporanee* (Nothing But Stories: The Italian Imagination in Contemporary Legends). What is needed for Italian legend tradition to become better known is for some of these books to be translated into English.

As with the legends of so many countries, many familiar international stories are found in the Italian repertoire of urban legends. An English or American reader will easily recognize published stories that are known at home as "The Vanishing Hitchhiker," "Blue Star Acid," "The Mexican Pet," "The Hippy Baby-sitter," "The Spider in the Cactus," and many others. Here is a good example of the AIDS Mary legend as it is known in Italy, in the words of an Italian businessman who wrote it down in 1991 after hearing it from a colleague who swore that it happened to the daughter of a friend of his:

A sweet little sixteen or seventeen year old girl goes on summer vacation in Sardinia, and there she meets a handsome boy just a few years older and falls in love with him. After a few days she goes to bed with him, losing her virginity. They spend several more days together, and when she is about to go home, she asks him where he lives. He answers that he cannot tell her, but he will be in touch with her soon. And he gives her a nicely wrapped parcel, saying that she must not open it until she gets back home.

When she opens the parcel she finds a dead rat (or mouse, since in Italian we use the same word, *topo,* for both) inside, along with a note that reads, "Welcome to the club. Now you too have got AIDS."

Italian urban legends without a widespread international circulation include "The Mystery of the Blue Grapefruit" as reported in *Tutte Storie* (no. 4, April 1992). Back in 1988 rumors spread of poisoned grapefruit entering Italy from Israel; supposedly the tainted fruits all had a bluish stain on them. The story developed numerous bogus details and was much repeated both orally and in the press before it was debunked. Another false story reported in the press—even appearing in the *New York Times*—claimed that in Naples one could buy T-shirts printed with safety belts so that drivers could fool policemen into thinking they had their seat belts fastened. People regarded this, *Tutte Storie* reported, "as an example of the proverbial cunning of Napolitans [Neapolitans]."

An example of recent Italian urban legend research was brought to a wider public when Paolo Toselli attended the 1994 meeting of the International Society for Contemporary Legend Research (held in Paris) and gave a paper in English titled "Child Kidnappings and the Body Parts Black Market: Italian Rumors and Contemporary Legends in the Nineties." Toselli traced the development of these rumors and stories from 1990 when warnings circulated about a gang driving a black ambulance supposedly cruising through the country kidnapping children in order to steal their organs for transplants. By 1992, with a big boost from the Italian media, these stories reached a climax, and by 1993 "the well-known 'Kidney Heist' story arrived in Italy" and further variations on the theme began to circulate. Other ideas entering the tradition were the alleged kidnapping of children by gypsies and elements of legend known as "The Attempted Abduction." A distinctive motif in the Italian tradition of these stories was the notion of a mobile operating room built into a van or truck.

References: *Baby Train,* 247–249; Paolo Toselli, "An Italian Center for Collecting Contemporary Rumors and Legends," *FOAFtale News* no. 21 (March 1991): 6–7.

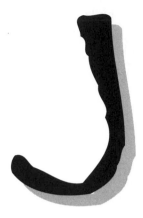

Japan

Awareness in Japan of the genre of urban legends arose following the published translations of books on the subject by Jan Harold Brunvand. All five of Brunvand's books were translated, from *The Vanishing Hitch-hiker* (1981, Japanese ed. 1988) through *The Baby Train* (1993, Japanese ed. 1997). The Shinjuku Shobo Company of Tokyo, publishers of the translations, also issued in 1994 a paperback selection of 20 English-language texts from *The Baby Train* with explanatory notes, for the use of Japanese students learning English. A similar teaching anthology drawn from *The Mexican Pet*, titled *New Urban Legends in America*, also containing 20 texts as well as notes, was published in 1992 by Asahi Press of Tokyo.

Japanese readers soon recognized not only the general concept of urban legends but also specific stories circulating in their own country that are legendary. A few letters from readers in Japan have found their way into American books on the subject, but it is hoped that eventually a Japanese folklorist will take up the systematic collection and study of the contemporary legends of this highly industrialized and advanced urban society. Doubtless there is a much richer tradition of urban legends in Japan than has heretofore been recognized.

Two well-known international urban legends reported from Japan are "The Vanishing Hitchhiker" and stories describing the abduction of young women into prostitution (so-called white-slavery legends in Western countries). In common with their foreign counterparts, the Japanese versions of these legends become highly localized. The hitchhiker, for example, in Japan is sometimes said to be a young woman asking to be taken to the University of Kyoto; she turns out to be the ghost of a girl who died after a terrible accident while being treated in Hakuaikai Hospital and whose spirit sometimes haunts Midoro Pond near the hospital. The abduction of the Japanese girl into prostitution is sometimes said to have happened to a student from Doshisha University who is vacationing in Thailand.

The theme of Japanese tourists abroad being harmed or murdered appears in other contemporary legends of Japan. Sometimes the victim is a recent bride, and the location of her attack may be Paris or New York City. In one version of "The Mutilated Bride" the woman is eventually spotted despite her badly wounded hands and feet being exhibited in a circus sideshow in the Philippines.

These few bits of urban-legend tradition from Japan only hint at the rich tradition of such stories that surely must exist in that country.

References: *Baby Train,* 250–251; *Curses!,* 85–87.

"The Jewish Secret Tax"

A baseless claim was circulated via printed fliers and word of mouth that the existence of a "Jewish secret tax on food" is coded into packaged food labels in one or more ways—either by a capital-letter *K*, a lowercase *u* inside a circle, or the word "parve." In reality, these common markings found on countless product packages are simply indicators that the contents were prepared according to Jewish dietary laws. (*K* indicates kosher, the *u* symbol refers to the Union of Orthodox Jewish Congregations, and "parve" means "neutral.") Sometimes the baseless tax claim is printed on small yellow stickers, which people are encouraged to attach to appropriate food packages on grocery shelves.

Articles in anti-Semitic publications frequently warn consumers to "Boycott the Kosher Tax!" But the actual cost to any consumer of whatever slight amount it may cost a manufacturer to gain rabbinical approval and affix the symbol to packages is miniscule, and the advantage of having products marked as kosher is a direct benefit to both consumers and manufacturers. In no sense may the markings be considered a tax.

References: *Mexican Pet,* 106–107.

"The Jogger's Billfold"

See "The Stolen Wallet"

Joke

A "joke" is defined as a brief, humorous folktale, usually containing only a single episode and ending with a punch line. Many classic traditional jokes may be recognized simply by their familiar punch lines, such as "That was no lady, that was my wife," or "I've never heard the pluperfect subjunctive of that," or "People who live in grass houses shouldn't stow thrones." Some jokes even seem to consist of nothing but a punch line, as in "Take my wife—please!" or "We can't go on meeting this way."

All folktales, by definition, are fictional oral narratives, and nobody would confuse the obvious fantasy of a fairy tale, a tall tale, a fable, or a joke with the claimed (and even possible) truth of an anecdote or a legend. However, many people do casually refer to any humorous quip, riddle, prank, or story as a "joke," unaware of the folklorists' more specific use of such genre terms.

In practice, some humorous urban legends are frequently told as jokes, with the teller indicating by performance style (tone of voice, facial expression, gestures, etc.) that he or she regards the story as mere fiction. The line between joke and legend blurs even further with urban legends that acquire a punch line ending. Examples include "Old Versus Young" (ending "that's what happens when you're old and rich"), "The Blind Man," (ending "okay, lady, now where do you want me to hang these blinds?"), "The Nut and the Tire Nuts," (ending "I may be crazy, but I'm not stupid"), and especially "The Nude Housewife" (ending "I don't know what game you're playing, lady, but I hope your team wins.")

See also Hoaxes, Pranks; State Police "Balls"; "Stuck on the Toilet"

Jumping to Conclusions

The "twist" in a number of urban legends is that someone jumps to an incorrect conclusion, thus setting himself or herself up for some kind of uncomfortable, often hilarious, downfall. In a classic example of this device, a cement-truck driver sees a new car parked in his driveway, then spots his wife speaking to a handsome stranger in the house; he immediately concludes that she is having an affair, so he fills the car with wet cement, only to learn later that the other man was a car dealer and his wife had just bought the new Cadillac (now the "Solid Cement Cadillac") for his birthday present.

In other urban legends based on people drawing quick and faulty conclusions, a Mexican rat is mistaken for a Chihuahua, an innocent stranger is thought to be a pickpocket, or a lump in a hotel-room carpet is believed to be a "bug" (i.e., an eavesdropping device). What helps to make such stories appealing and plausible is the realization that anyone could easily make such a mistake in judgment; indeed, many of us have surely jumped to the wrong conclusion at some time in our lives.

See also "The Air-Freighted Pet"; "The Brain Drain"; "The Hairdresser's Error"; "The Hare Dryer"; Human Nature; Mistaken Identifications; "The Package of Cookies"; "The Poisoned Pussycat at the Party"; Stupid Pet Rescues; "The Surpriser Surprised"; and "The Tube on the Tube"

References: *Too Good,* 26–46.

"The Kangaroo Thief"

The Australian version of "The Deer Departed" claims that a group of tourists in a rented car hits a kangaroo on the road. They stop and prop up the animal against a fencepost, dressing it in the jacket of one of the

men in order to take a gag photo. But the kangaroo was merely stunned, and when the tourists step back to focus the camera the animal revives and bounds away into the outback, still wearing the jacket, which contains the passport, travelers' checks, tickets, money, and other belongings of the owner.

This story has been attributed to a touring English cricket team, to the folksong group the Kingston Trio, and to various foreign yacht-racing crews competing in Australia. Australian folklorists have traced ancestors of "The Kangaroo Thief" as far back as 1902, identifying it as an old "bush yarn" that developed into a contemporary legend. A 1992 collection of Dutch urban legends describes how a group of tourists from the Netherlands suffered the "kangaroo's revenge."

References: *Baby Train*, 233–235; Amanda Bishop, *The Gucci Kangaroo* (Hornsby, NSW: Australasian Publishing Company, 1988), 26–32; Peter Burger, *De Wraak van de Kangoeroe* (Amsterdam: Prometheus, 1992), 35–37; *Mexican Pet*, 24–25; *Too Good*, 340–341.

"The Kentucky Fried Rat"

This is one of the best-known food-contamination stories, being circulated since the early 1970s. It describes how a customer of a national fried-chicken franchise allegedly found a batter-fried rat in a bucket of chicken. Usually, the victim has eaten some of the rat before noticing the rodent's tail and realizing that the meat is *not* chicken. Victims are most often women, and the setting tends to be one with low light, such as a candle-lit dining room or a drive-in movie. The story has spread abroad with the establishment of Kentucky Fried Chicken franchises in other countries.

There are some well-documented instances of rodents or rodent parts getting into food products, but none of these actual cases follows the plot of the legend. Rather than being merely faulty retellings of real experiences, "The Kentucky Fried Rat" represents an imagined account of what seems plausible in the fast-food outlets popular in our modern and highly urbanized society. To Americans, rats are particularly loathed vermin, whereas chicken is one of the most popular meats; the combination of the two creatures in a food-contamination legend seems inevitable.

Gary Alan Fine has discussed how contemporary-legend content "is responsive to environmental change and the psychological effects that are concomitant with this change." A predominant theme that he finds in the chicken/rat legends is that "the fast food establishments are settings of employee sabotage and corporate greed." Fine also comments that "the growth of fast food chains represents a change of function in the direction of profit-making enterprises and away from home cooking and the community or church supper."

See also Church's Chicken Rumors; "The Mouse in the Coke"

References: Gary Alan Fine, "The Kentucky Fried Rat: Legends and Modern Society," in *Manufacturing Tales*, 120–137 (chapter first published in 1980); *Too Good*, 177–179; *Vanishing Hitchhiker*, 81–84.

"The Kidney Heist"

Originating in 1991 in the United States and quickly spreading to other countries, the story has circulated about a person—usually a man traveling away from home—who is seduced and sedated by criminals who remove a kidney for use in an illegal organ-transplant operation. Here is a typical version as reported in 1992 by a man from Cincinnati:

> A friend told me that a friend of his was in Chicago on business, and decided to go out to a Rush Street bar. He picked up a beautiful young woman, and they eventually retreated to a motel. The next morning the man woke up with a splitting headache, and there was blood all over the bed sheets. The woman was gone. It doesn't take him long to discover a freshly stitched incision on his side, and by some means or other the man eventually reaches a local hospital where he finds that one of his kidneys has been removed. He is told by the hospital staff that the operation was performed very professionally, and that his kidney is probably headed for sale on the black market.

Some typical variations in this much-told legend are illustrated by comparing the above version with one reported from Los Angeles in 1993:

> Two married men were out of town on business and shared a hotel room. On the evening before they were to return home, they went down to the hotel bar for a drink. There they met two women, and after a couple of hours one man left with one of the women. The remaining man said goodnight and went up to their room alone. The next morning his friend had not returned, and he waited and waited, fearing they would miss their plane home. Just as he was preparing to leave for the airport, his phone rang. It was his friend, moaning and barely able to talk, saying "Help me, help me; I'm all bloody!" His friend gave an address and the man rushed to his friend's aid with the police and found him in a motel room in bed covered with blood. He was bleeding from a crudely cut and sutured incision from his chest to his abdomen, and it was discovered that one of his kidneys was missing. Apparently he had been duped by a gang of medically trained organ thieves who lure unsuspecting people to strange motel rooms where they drug them, then cut them open and steal organs to sell for transplants.

Countless changes in details occurred as "The Kidney Heist" spread via word of mouth, photocopies, faxes, and eventually the Internet. Legend-tellers differed as to how the victim was seduced, where he was discovered, in what part of the body the incision was made, and how the victim's rescue was carried out. Some people recognized the similarity of the opening scene to the earlier "AIDS Mary," but few seemed to question the idea that the kidneys of random strangers could somehow be matched to people needing a transplant, despite the elaborate official network of tissue-matching, waiting lists, and organ registration set up for transplant operations. Neither did they consider that the doctors who perform these operations are highly trained, well-paid professionals—unlikely candidates for corruption by a gang of kidney thieves.

"The Kidney Heist" furnished the plot of a televised thriller in 1991 and continued to show up regularly in oral tradition, newspaper columns, and Internet chatrooms through the 1990s. It provided the climactic moment in the 1998 film *Urban Legend*, with the intended victim being saved at the last moment. Foreign folklorists continued to report the legend in their countries, and a 1994 collection of Swedish urban legends was actually titled *The Stolen Kidney* (*Den Stulna Njuren*). Meanwhile, in Holland, the legend became known as *de gestolen nier.*

Some of the latest versions of "The Kidney Heist" circulating in the United States included the names of medical or law enforcement personnel (all of them phony) who had supposedly investigated the case. Although the details of the story seemed to grow ever more bizarre, people continued to circulate the bogus warnings. By the end of the decade, some versions claimed that *both* kidneys had been stolen and that the victim awoke in a postoperative state of shock sitting in a hotel bathtub full of ice cubes and with a note pinned to him saying "Call 911. You have lost your kidneys." How anyone could get enough ice down the hall to fill a tub without being noticed is never explained.

There is a grain of truth in the legend: Illegal organ sales and occasionally organ thefts have been documented in some Third World countries. But the detailed plot of "The Kidney Heist" is completely fictional.

The title piece, "Scar Vegas," of Tom Paine's 2000 collection of stories is based on recent versions of "The Kidney Heist." The book's review in the *New York Times* (January 13, 2000) suggested that "as an image of exploitation, stealing [the main character's] kidney seems so bizarre as to transcend ideology."

References: *Baby Train,* 149–154; Véronique Campion-Vincent, "Organ Theft Narratives," *Western Folklore* 56 (1997): 1–37; *Too Good,* 398–402.

"The Kilkenny Widow"

See "The Unexpected Inheritance"

"The Killer in the Backseat"

This is a classic automobile horror legend first noted by folklorist Carlos Drake in 1968 in texts collected by Indiana University (IU) students. Curiously, Drake's sample text came via a student from Utah who said the story was told about "a high-school girl who lived in a suburb of Ogden." Other examples from the IU folklore archive published the following year, and many further texts collected elsewhere, proved that the same legend had been told since at least 1964 and was known throughout the United States. Another Indiana folklorist, Xenia Cord, has pointed out that because the man lurking in the car is always detected and disarmed in the legends, a better title might be "The Assailant in the Backseat."

A capsule summary alludes to the two common variations of the plot: "Would-be killer lurks in back, detected by motorist or gas-station attendant." In all versions, the intended victim is a woman. In the versions in which another motorist spots the assailant, the driver notices that the car or truck following her keeps blinking his lights or shifting them to the high beam. When she reaches home—still followed by the blinking vehicle—the other driver rushes to her car and pulls out the lurking stranger. In the gas-station versions, the driver is asked by the attendant to come into the office because of some problem with her credit card. The attendant then locks the office door, tells her about the threat from behind, and calls the police.

"The Killer (or Assailant) in the Backseat," besides being widely told, has appeared as a cautionary anecdote in articles on crime prevention, has been repeated in at least one Ann Landers column, and provided the initial scare in the 1998 film *Urban Legend*. (In the film, however, the assailant does actually kill the driver.) David Letterman's telling of the legend as he heard it growing up in Indianapolis is included in *Too Good to Be True,* and the story also inspired the cover art of the book.

Although other car-crime legends are well known abroad, "The Killer in the Backseat" does not seem to have taken root very strongly outside

North America. In *Great Australian Urban Myths* (1995) Graham Seal can only recall "vague memories" of the legend from the 1960s, and he admits that he has not heard the story told recently Down Under. The Swedish version (*mördareni baksätet* [Killer in the Backseat], in Bengt af Klintberg's 1986 book *Rattan i Pizzan* [The Rat in the Pizza]) was told to af Klintberg by a Danish journalist who had heard the story in the United States.

The advice attached to most tellings of this legend—"Always check the backseat of your car before getting in!"—makes good sense, whether the story is true or not. And as Carlos Drake pointed out, the legend may have been inspired by a similar incident in real life.

See also "The Hairy-Armed Hitchhiker"

References: *Choking Doberman,* 214; Xenia E. Cord, "Further Notes on 'The Assailant in the Back Seat,'" *Indiana Folklore* 2 (1969): 47–54; Carlos Drake, "The Killer in the Back Seat," *Indiana Folklore* 1 (1968): 107–109; *Mexican Pet,* 58–59; *Too Good,* 97–100; *Vanishing Hitchhiker,* 52–53.

"Kitty Takes the Rap"

A trial lawyer told the story of his boyhood prank when he and his brother ate half of a Dutch apple pie, then pushed their pet cat's face into the remainder and told their mother that the cat had eaten the pie. Their mother immediately threw the cat out of the house and into a small stream that ran behind the house, and, the storyteller concluded, "That wasn't the last cat to be sent up the river on crummy circumstantial evidence."

The neat punch line to the story raises suspicions about its truth, and, indeed, the storyteller admitted that he had heard it from another lawyer and simply adopted it into his repertoire. His source, in turn, said that he had heard it from yet another lawyer, thus establishing the usual friend-of-a-friend pattern of urban legends.

"Kitty Takes the Rap" includes the same ploy as a more widely told legend ("Fifi Spills the Paint") further proving the traditional nature of this whole cycle of stories. Another version of "Kitty" appears in Toni Morrison's 1972 novel *The Bluest Eye.*

References: *Baby Train,* 25–27; *Too Good,* 61–63.

Ku Klux Klan Rumors

The Ku Klux Klan (KKK), the notorious racist secret organization, is credited in various rumors and legends with owning or controlling large corporations. Good citizens, especially African Americans, are urged to boycott these alleged KKK–influenced businesses or products, which are said to include Marlboro cigarettes, TROOP athletic wear, Tropical Fantasy soft drinks, and Church's Fried Chicken.

References: Gary Alan Fine, "Among Those Dark Satanic Mills: Rumors of Kooks, Cults, and Corporations," in *Manufacturing Tales,* 174–185; Patricia A. Turner, "Conspiracy I: 'They . . . the KKK . . . did it,'" in *I Heard It Through the Grapevine* (1993), 57–107.

"La Llorona"

"The Weeping Woman" is a well known traditional legend among Mexican Americans that occasionally merges with modern urban legends. The figure known as "La Llorona" is said to be the ghost of a mother bereft of her children, sometimes allegedly drowned by her own hand. She is seen along waterways—creeks, canals, rivers, and the like—crying and calling out for her lost children and sometimes threatening or harming those who encounter her. The legend often functions as a warning to young people not to linger after dark, especially in certain "haunted" sites. The specific appearance of La Llorona varies from place to place, ranging from a harmless spectral figure dressed in white to a female monster with long fingernails and sometimes the face of a horse.

In the heavily industrial Calumet region of northeastern Indiana, Philip Brandt George collected some versions of "The Vanishing Hitchhiker" that combined with an origin story about the hitchhiking ghost that borrowed from the "La Llorona" tradition. (The vanishing hitcher was said to be the ghost of a Mexican woman who had killed her children and was doomed to wander eternally in search of them.)

See also "I Believe in Mary Worth"

References: Philip Brandt George, "The Ghost of Cline Avenue: 'La Llorona' in the Calumet Region," *Indiana Folklore* 5 (1972): 56–91;

Joe S. Graham, "La Llorona," in Brunvand, *American Folklore: An Encyclopedia* (1996), 431.

"The Last Kiss"

A workman is caught in a piece of heavy machinery, his body horribly mangled. Although still alive, he will certainly be killed by any attempt to rescue him or if the machine is restarted. For a short time, then—as long as nothing is moved—the workman may say his farewells. He is given a heavy dose of pain killers, and his wife is rushed to his side to give him one last kiss. Then the machine is restarted and the man's crushed, lifeless body is removed.

A common American variant of "The Last Kiss" is "Caught in the Coupler," which describes a railroad accident. The plucky workman may even request a lantern so that he may personally signal the engineer when it is time to move the train. Other versions mention a subway train, steel-rolling machinery, or a piece of heavy military equipment. Sometimes it is said that the man's wife was simply called on a telephone to say her last good-byes and that the conversation was accidentally picked up on the company's public address system so that all his fellow workers heard the heart-rending farewells.

In New Zealand the same story is told about the Petone shingle-crusher, referring to a piece of machinery used in Petone, a city near Wellington, to crush larger rocks into gravel.

References: *Curses!*, 70–72; *Too Good*, 170–171.

"The Laughing Paramedics"

A typical ending motif of hilarious-accident legends is that paramedics summoned to assist an injured person, upon hearing how the injury occurred, laugh so hard that they drop the stretcher, further injuring the victim. This motif is a fixed part of "The Exploding Toilet" and "The Pet and the Naked Man," and it occurs sporadically in other legends about bizarre accidents that seem funny to everyone except the victim.

References: *Too Good*, 369–370.

Law Legends

Anecdotal traditions, mostly negative ones, abound concerning lawyers, judges, juries, and courts. As Robert M. Hayden has pointed out, "These stories are similar to urban folklore, [and] while data can be debated, who can counter a good anecdote?" Most of these widely circulated stories center on the notion that Americans are overly litigious—bringing countless frivolous law suits against companies and governmental institutions until the caseload clogs the legal system and excessively punitive monetary awards imperil the economy. "Arguing by anecdote," as Hayden calls it, occurs both by word of mouth and in the media, exploiting such stories as "The Psychic and the CAT Scan" or "The Ladder in the Manure," which turn out, upon investigation, to be inaccurate and misleading accounts of court cases and judgments.

Marc Galanter, the leading collector and student of legal legends, identified "a familiar factoid in the rhetoric of the 1992 [presidential] campaign" when Vice President Dan Quayle asserted in a speech that the United States is home to 70 percent of all the world's lawyers. This and another of Quayle's claims—that our legal system costs Americans $300 billion a year—were much repeated and discussed in the media, but both figures are wrong. Neither is the product-liability system "killing our economy," as other political pundits claimed. Neither are 80 percent of Environmental Protection Agency regulations challenged in court. And neither have law schools "been flooding the nation with graduates who are suffocating the economy with a litigation epidemic of bubonic plague proportions," as a leading economist suggested in 1991. All of these claims and stories plus many more, although often repeated, can be proven false. Yet they are believed because in their memorable anecdotal form they embody what Hayden calls the "cultural logic" of Americans' assumptions about their legal system. Doubtless there are similar stories circulating abroad as well.

See also Legal Horror Stories

References: Marc Galanter, "News from Nowhere: The Debased Debate on Civil Justice," *Denver University Law Review,* 71 (1993): 77–113; Marc Galanter, "An Oil Strike in Hell: Contemporary Legends about the Civil Justice System," *Arizona Law Review* 40 (1998): 717–752; Robert M. Hayden, "The Cultural Logic of a Political Crisis: Common Sense, Hegemony, and the Great American Liability Insurance Famine of 1986," *Studies in Law, Politics, and Society* 11 (1991): 95–117.

"The Lawn-Mower Accident"

This legal horror story is based on the notion of a product-liability lawsuit running amok. The plaintiff in the case wins his suit, despite the injury being clearly his own fault.

Supposedly, a man picks up his power mower while it is running, intending to use the machine to trim his hedge. Instead, the tips of all his fingers are cut off; his thumbs, being on the outside of the blade housing, are intact. He sues the manufacturer for failing to publish a warning about using the mower in this way, and he wins a large judgment. Sometimes two men are involved in the accident, losing all 16 of their fingertips.

Although this "case" is well known among insurance adjusters, lawyers, and power-mower manufacturers, no such accident was ever recorded, and no such suit was brought to court. Still, the story has appeared in advertisements and in at least one textbook used in college law classes.

References: *Choking Doberman,* 160–162; Jerry Geisel, "Case of the Missing Case: Ad about Lawn Mower Suit Doesn't Cut It," *Advertising Age* (October 31, 1977): 102; *Mexican Pet,* 164; *Too Good,* 163–164.

Leaning Towers

Besides other legends about architects' blunders (sinking libraries and shopping malls, backward buildings, switched campus buildings, etc.), occasionally one hears about a tall tower under construction that is leaning dangerously off center. The flaw is usually said to be caused by either (or both) design flaws or construction of the tower on shifting subsoil.

One example is the Oakbrook Terrace Tower, a 31-story office building erected in a Chicago suburb. Despite rumors that the building was leaning some four or five feet off of vertical, the tower was declared to be "perfectly straight" by the engineer in charge of the construction, and it opened on schedule in December 1987. The obvious comparison of this tower to another famous example was suggested in a local news story that debunked the rumors and then commented, "Oakbrook Terrace has no plans to adopt the Tuscany village of Pisa as a sister city. One leaning tower is enough." Two thoughts come to mind: First, Pisa's tower, despite its tilt, has stood for centuries; and second, there are, in fact, many other leaning towers in Italy and elsewhere, although Pisa's is an extreme example and certainly the best-known.

References: *Curses!*, 254–255.

"The Leashed Dogs"

When a family on vacation stops for a break, someone puts out a water dish for the family dog and ties the pet's leash to the back bumper of the car or camper. Unfortunately, the dog is forgotten when the family drives off again, and it is dragged behind the vehicle to its death.

Or a family member at home ties the dog's leash to the garage-door handle. Another member, driving home, while still a couple of blocks away, activates the remote control to open the garage door. The pet is lynched.

Although there are claimed witnesses to both pet tragedies—or at least to incidents that are very similar—most of the retellings are attributed to friends of friends and vary in their details. In the first-person tellings, the pet usually survives, while in the second-hand stories the pet almost invariably dies, sometimes (in the vehicle version of the story) not even being missed by the family until they arrive home from vacation. Speaking of which, the 1983 film *National Lampoon's Vacation* depicted a camper version of the legend.

References: *Curses!*, 149–150.

Legal Horror Stories

Legal horror stories are known among lawyers as "atrocity stories"; Marc Galanter defines them as "citation[s] of cases that seem grotesque, petty or extravagant." Many of these stories tell of huge judgments awarded in lawsuits brought by individuals, often in product-liability cases. Either the judgments described in the stories are fictional, or the facts of the case are misstated and exaggerated so as to cast a bad light on the whole field and to make court decisions look as unfair and unwarranted as possible.

Some legal horror stories have achieved the status of individual urban legends in their own right, widely known to many laypeople. Examples include "The Exploding Butane Lighter" and "The Lawn-Mower Accident." Other legends are better known among the legal profession than among the public at large. Some legend topics include, as Galanter has listed them, "the woman who sued when denied the right to breast-feed her infant; the child suing for parental malpractice; the suitor suing the date who stood him up; [and] the girl suing the little league."

See also Law Legends

References: *Choking Doberman,* 160–161; Marc Galanter, "Reading the Landscape of Disputes: What We Know and Don't Know (and Think We Know) about Our Allegedly Contentious and Litigous Society," *UCLA Law Review* 31 (1983): 4–71; *Mexican Pet,* 167–168.

Legend

See Definition of "Legend"

Legend-Tripping

A legend trip is a teenage ritual in which a group of friends visit a site associated with ghostly or otherwise frightening legends in order to tell stories, demonstrate their courage, and possibly experience some of the rumored manifestations of supernatural events associated with the site. The sites that are targets of legend trips are often named locally and well known to the community, where they may be regarded as unique. However, similar legends, sites, and trips are typically known in many places.

Travel on legend trips is usually by automobile to a spooky location that is remote from their own neighborhoods; drinking or other forbidden behavior is common. Legend trips function both as informal tests of the claims made in supernatural legends and as verification of the courage of the teens themselves, who may try to act out the legends they have heard by blinking the car lights a certain number of times, calling out for the ghost, or sitting on a cursed gravestone. Even if nothing happens, the stories associated with legend-trip sites continue to grow and develop as they are passed in the oral tradition of several generations of teens.

See also Ostension

References: Bill Ellis, "Adolescent Legend-Tripping," *Psychology Today* (August 1983): 68–69; Bill Ellis, "Legend Trip" in Brunvand, *American Folklore: An Encyclopedia* (1996), 439–440; Patricia M. Meley, "Adolescent Legend Trips As Teenage Cultural Response: A Study of Lore in Context," *Mid-America Folklore* 18 (1990): 1–26.

"The Lesson in Compassion"

Either an urban legend has suggested a psychological study, or (more likely) the study itself has inspired an urban legend. In either case, the background story is the parable of the Good Samaritan. John M. Darley and C. Daniel Batson's 1973 article describes how the test subjects were placed in a situation in which they encountered a stranger in need of help while hurrying to give an assigned talk. For some of the subjects the topic of their talk was the Good Samaritan; for the others it was a nonsignificant topic. The researchers concluded that "this made no significant difference in the likelihood of their giving the victim help."

The study was summarized in several psychology textbooks, and this may have suggested either the telling of similar stories or, possibly, teachers trying similar experiments with their own classes. The typical legend form of the story involves a college class studying ethics, religion, "the life of Christ," or the like; the students arrive for the final exam, only to find a note from the instructor saying that the room has been changed to one far across campus. En route to the new site, the students pass a person in need—in reality an actor placed there by the instructor. According to the story, not a single student stops to help, thus proving that they have not learned the lessons of the class. Alternatively, one student does stop to help and is the only one in the class to pass the test.

It should be noted that the Darley and Batson experiment was more complex than summarized above, both in experimental procedure and the processing of data. The legend version, in contrast, is simple, straightforward, and uncluttered with scientific jargon or methodology. Several people recall hearing variations of the story, but none, so far, has claimed to have been in the psychology class itself. A few individuals report having a similar "test" administered to them as part of a leadership training course. The whole tradition seems to be especially popular among Mormons.

References: *Baby Train*, 318–320; John M. Darley and C. Daniel Batson, "'From Jerusalem to Jericho': A Study of Situational and Dispositional Variables in Helping Behavior," *Journal of Personality and Social Psychology* 27 (1973): 100–108.

"A License to Practice"

A respectable, well-to-do American couple proudly (and smilingly) display in their home a certificate issued by police authorities in Mexico City, Paris, Rome, or elsewhere abroad that allows the American wife to work there as a prostitute. Sometimes the document is an identification card for registered prostitutes. The couple explain that on a recent vacation trip the wife was pacing back and forth in front of their hotel (or in the lobby) impatiently waiting for her husband to arrive. She was detained by the police, who suspected her of soliciting sex, and she was forced to acquire the inexpensive license or identification card in order to avoid arrest and a large fine.

In variations of the story, the wife has worn too flashy an outfit on the streets or has wandered into a particular bistro or cantina reserved for sex providers and their customers. It is claimed that phony prostitutes' licenses and ID cards are sold as tourist souvenirs in some countries, but proof is lacking. Although "A License to Practice" is usually told as a recent incident, the story has been known since at least the 1920s.

References: *Choking Doberman*, 141; *Too Good*, 151–152.

"The Licked Hand"

In this story, especially popular among American children and adolescents, several young girls have gathered at the home of one for a slumber party (also know as a sleepover). The parents are away, but the hostess has a large pet dog that they count on for protection against any possible danger.

Late at night, after all the girls have finally fallen asleep, the hostess is awakened several times by odd noises in the house. Each time, however, her dog licks her hand, and she is comforted and falls back asleep. In the morning she wakes to find all of her little friends murdered, the dog's body hanging in the bathroom or kitchen. Written in blood on the wall is the message, "People can lick, too."

This legend, sometimes called "The Doggy Lick," is also told as a college story in which the handwriting on the wall reads, "Aren't you glad you didn't turn on the light?"

See also "The Roommate's Death"

References: *Choking Doberman,* 73–77; *Curses!,* 203–205; *Too Good,* 58.

"Lights Out!"

Here is an example of this bogus warning, which began circulating via faxes, printed fliers, and on the Internet in 1993. The following version, quoted verbatim, was one of many being e-mailed throughout the country in the summer of 1999:

A police officer who works with the DARE program at an elementary school passed this warning on to us and asked that I share it with anyone who drives.

If you're ever driving after dark and see an oncoming car with no head lights turned on DO NOT flash your lights at them! This is a new common gang member initiation "game" that goes like this: the new member being initiated drives along with no headlights on and the first car to flash their headlights at him is now his "target." He is now required to chase that car and shoot at or into the car in order to complete his initiation requirements.

Make sure you share this information with your family and any one else you can!

Earlier versions of "Lights Out!" elaborated on the story, by adding references to families who had already been killed and giving the name of a nonexistent police officer who was said to have investigated one case. A specific weekend in September 1993 was said to have been designated "Blood Weekend" for the commission of this crime, but the dates passed without any incident of this sort occurring. Investigative journalists, police authorities, gang experts, and folklorists investigated the story and all determined that it was unrelated to any actual crimes or initiation rituals. "Lights Out!" clearly reflects the paranoia of some Americans about gang violence, and it suggests that the performance of a simple, well-intentioned driving habit may turn one from being a Good Samaritan into the victim of a random killing.

The revival of this story in 1998 was probably attributable to people finding copies of the older warnings posted on an uncleared bulletin board or stuffed into a desk drawer. Urban rumors and legends that have such printed or published texts often return without warning, or seemingly without any actual incident to spur their reappearance. The mention of an officer in the DARE program or some other authority figure repeating the warning indicates that people in such roles may sometimes use such stories as examples in their work without determining their authenticity.

References: *Too Good,* 393–395; *The Truth,* 95–107.

Linguistic Approach

Folklorist W. F. H. Nicolaisen advocates an "informed scrutiny of the structure of [the] language of narration" in urban legends, following the findings of William Labov's well-known study presented in his 1972 book *Language in the Inner City: Studies in the Black English Vernacular,* particularly as developed in Labov's last chapter ("The Transformation of Experience in Narrative Syntax"). Labov concluded that a "fully formed narrative" would have six structural elements: Abstract, Orientation, Complicating Action, Evaluation, Result or Resolution, and Coda.

When Nicolaisen applied these concepts to the 28 variant texts of "The Surpriser Surprised" collected in William Hugh Jansen's 1973 study of that legend, he found that three elements (Orientation, Complicating Action, and Resolution) were "normally the narrative core of the legend." (This finding seems similar to the old classroom definition of "plot" as necessarily including "a conflict resolved.")

What Nicolaisen found to be especially characteristic of urban legends as narratives was that often "a piece of vital information known to the narrator is left out of the Orientation section to be made known to the listener only after the telling of the Complicating Action has been completed." In "The Surpriser Surprised," for instance, the listener is only told at the end of the story that a surprise party has been arranged for the now-naked couple. Nicolaisen suggested that this "delayed orientation" is "an important structural feature of many [urban legends]." Furthermore, he concluded, "much of the success of legend-telling apparently depends on the clever handling of this device."

In other words, it makes no sense for a storyteller to announce at the beginning, "This one I heard is about Reggie Jackson on the elevator," or "Do you remember the one about the fingers caught in the Doberman's throat?" or "This woman wanted to sell her philandering husband's Porsche at a low price." The twist or resolution or explanation in these legends must come at the end for it to be an effective story.

In a follow-up study, Nicolaisen applied his approach to variant texts of "The Vanishing Hitchhiker"; here he concluded that the requirement of at least two narrative elements (Orientation and Complicating Action) was essential in this legend, along with the typical holding back of one important story element—in this instance the fact that the hitchhiker was a ghost.

In both of these studies, and especially in his 1992 article published in *Contemporary Legend,* Nicolaisen emphasized that full narrative texts, or at least "narratable" texts, were necessary in order to study the linguistic structure of legends. The work of writers who sometimes publish only summaries—in particular the author of this encyclopedia—was criticized in this essay. Ideally, for a linguistic-structural analysis, audible tape recordings of legends being told are preferred to even the most careful visual transcriptions made from tapes.

See also Structural Approach

References: W. F. H. Nicolaisen, "The Linguistic Structure of Legends," in Bennett, Smith, and Widdowson, *Perspectives on Contemporary Legend II* (1987), 61–76; Nicolaisen, "Linguistic Aspects of the Vanishing Hitchhiker," in Leander Petzoldt and Stefaan Top, eds., *Dona Folcloristica: Festgabe für Lutz Röhrich zu seiner Emeritierung* (Frankfurt am Main: Peter Lang, 1990), 187–199; Nicolaisen, "Contemporary Legends: Narrative Texts Versus Summaries," *Contemporary Legend* 2 (1992): 71–91.

Literature and Urban Legends

Folklorist Daniel R. Barnes announced a broad range of sources to be reported when he began publishing his survey of urban legends in literature in 1991. He proposed to identify "literary works ancient, modern, contemporary, popular and 'serious,' fictional and nonfictional, poetic and dramatic—that either allude to or employ in some degree . . . a recognizable contemporary legend." By the third installment of his checklist, with folklorist Paul Smith joining him in the effort, Barnes had cataloged some two dozen legend references, several of them occurring in multiple sources. The literary works cited ranged from children's books and modern detective novels to writings by renowned authors like Anthony Burgess, Carson McCullers, and Ernest Hemingway. (These three writers, respectively, made use of the legends known as "The Runaway Grandmother," "The Fart in the Dark," and a seldom-noted story that the compilers refer to as "The Voyeur in the Brothel.")

The study of urban legends in literature only begins with the identification of legend themes and plots found in published writings, but cataloging such examples is an essential first step toward analysis of the literary uses and functions of these traditional stories. The plots of urban legends themselves often seem too simple and undeveloped to have much literary interest; it is the ways that writers may elaborate them or integrate them into a larger work that become interesting to the literary critic.

Folklorist and literary scholar Bruce A. Rosenberg closely analyzed both the background legends ("The Killer in the Backseat," "The Vanishing Hitchhiker," and others) and a literary counterpart (Elizabeth Jane Howard's 1979 story "Mr. Wrong") to develop his discussion of the patterns and themes found in all of these narratives. He concluded that "Mr. Wrong" is a good example of "the lasting relationship between literature and folklore, more specifically between 'ordinary' people as tellers of stories and skilled artisans of tales."

Because some of the legends that we now refer to as "urban" and "contemporary" have a long history, we find allusions to the same material in much earlier periods. For example, Geoffrey Chaucer reworked a recognizable prototype of "The Mutilated Boy" from the medieval blood-libel tradition into "The Prioress's Tale" in his classic *Canterbury Tales*. Daniel Defoe and Charles Dickens were later English authors who referred to the oral traditions of legends of their own times, and Nathaniel Hawthorne in the United States displayed a similar awareness of folk legends in some of his works.

Other literature-legend connections may be found in this encyclopedia under the entries for "Alligators in the Sewers," "The Choking Doberman," "The Crushed Dog," "The Dead Cat in the Package," "The Elephant that Sat on the VW," "Kitty Takes the Rap," "The Loaded

Dog," "Not My Dog," and "The Package of Cookies." The fact that so many of these legends are about animals must be more than coincidence, but nobody has yet offered an explanation or an interpretation of this phenomenon.

References: Daniel R. Barnes and Paul Smith, "Research Notes—The Contemporary Legend in Literature: Towards an Annotated Checklist," *Contemporary Legend* 1, 2, and 3 (1991, 1992, 1993); Jan Harold Brunvand, "Urban Legends," in Mary Ellen Brown and Bruce A. Rosenberg, eds., *Encyclopedia of Folklore and Literature* (Santa Barbara, Calif.: ABC-CLIO, 1998), 676–679; Bruce A. Rosenberg, "Urban Legends: The Modern Folktales," in *Folklore and Literature: Rival Siblings* (Knoxville: University of Tennessee Press, 1991), 220–235.

"The Loaded Dog"

"The Loaded Dog," a short story written by Australian author Henry Lawson in about 1899, provides the common title for one variation of the legend generally known as "The Animal's Revenge." Lawson's "The

Loaded Dog" was an early example of the modern short story, but the general theme of "The Burner Burnt" had prototypes in an Aesopian fable and even in a biblical passage. In the Australian story a lighted high-explosive charge is thrown by a person, then retrieved by a dog, so that a large portion of a mining camp is blown up. Jack London wrote his version of this plot in his 1902 short story "Moon Face," and New Zealander Barry Crump published yet another in his 1960 book *A Good Keen Man.*

In modern tradition—both oral and published—"The Loaded Dog" may also be described as a rabbit, rat, raccoon, possum, hawk, coyote, or other animal. Often the creature is "wired" by a sadistic person, but the loaded animal runs or flies back to, instead of away from, its tormentor, thus "burning" the "burner." Graham Seal discusses an Australian text that he describes as "a modernised old bush yarn." A typical dog version from the United States was published in the sports section of the *Washington Post* on January 28, 1990:

> Attendees at this month's Shooting, Hunting, Outdoor Trade (SHOT) Show in Las Vegas brought back a ghastly tale.
>
> Seems a group of duck hunters went out on Tennessee's Reelfoot Lake during December's cold snap and, finding it frozen, decided to blow open a hole with dynamite. But when they threw the TNT out, fuse lit, their trusty Labrador retriever raced off, snatched it up and trotted dutifully back toward the blind as the men shrieked for it to stop.
>
> When it was 20 yards away, one hunter took it upon himself to shoot the dog. The dynamite went off and destroyed the front of the blind, but no one was injured.

References: Graham Seal, "The Loaded Rabbit," in *Great Australian Urban Myths* (Sydney: Angus and Robertson, 1995), 69–70; *Too Good*, 71–73.

"The Locked-out Nude"

See "The Nude Bachelor"

"The Locked-out Pilot"

This legend, told by airline personnel and passengers, describes how through a series of mishaps and misunderstandings both the pilot and copilot on a commercial flight leave the cockpit unattended. The door is closed and locked, either by turbulence or through force of habit by one of the pilots. Since neither pilot has brought the cockpit key with him, they are forced to break down the door with a fire ax in full sight of the horrified passen-

gers. The story is often attributed either to a foreign airline or to an early commercial flight.

Fearful air travelers should be reassured by the lack of eyewitnesses to this incident that it never actually happened. Furthermore, airline procedures and the design of modern airplanes would make "The Locked-Out Pilot" an impossible scenario.

References: *Curses!*, 48–50; *Too Good*, 278–279.

"The Lost Wreck"

An automobile-accident story debunked in an Edmonton, Alberta, newspaper in 1985 seems to incorporate a key motif borrowed from a Norwegian legend collected in 1835. In the Norse story a medieval village decimated by the bubonic plague is rediscovered in a remote overgrown forest when a hunter's arrow goes astray and clangs against the church bell. In the Canadian legend a car accident of the 1950s on a mountain road in which four people were killed is discovered decades later when highway workers push some large rocks into a ravine and hear the clang of the rocks striking metal. The newspaper reporter commented "this rumor seems to have sprung from a fertile imagination fed by the clean mountain air."

The similarity of the two audible "discovery" motifs strongly suggests that this element of the modern story was borrowed from Norwegian folklore, possibly coming from the memory of a Norwegian settler in Alberta. Accounts of real-life lost-wreck incidents, of course, do not contain this traditional folkloric motif.

References: *Curses!*, 99–100; *Too Good*, 235–236.

"The Lottery Ticket"

Ever since the creation of state lotteries (and before that with other kinds of gambling tickets), the story has circulated about a man who finds that he holds a ticket with the winning numbers. He's rich! The man is in a bar watching the numbers come up on television (or watching the race horses come to the finish line), so he decides to pass the ticket around so all his pals can see what a real winner looks like.

His winning ticket goes hand to hand all around the room and back to him again, except that when it arrives where it started it's a different ticket. (The legend does not take into account the fact that in order to cash in the winning ticket, the thief would have to reveal his identity.)

See also "Pass It On"

References: *Curses!*, 20; *Mexican Pet*, 142; *Too Good*, 332–333.

"The Lover's Telephone Revenge"

A young woman is disgruntled when her boyfriend dumps her; he orders her to move out of his apartment, and he leaves her there to pack. When he returns, somewhat fearful of what he will find, he discovers that the woman and her things are gone and everything else is untouched—except the telephone, which is off the hook. The man picks it up, hears some foreign language being spoken, shrugs, and replaces the receiver. Only when he gets his telephone bill does he learn that she had dialed the time and temperature number in Tokyo (or Hong Kong) and left the phone off the hook for the past several hours.

Sometimes known as "Dial R-E-V-E-N-G-E," this story and its satisfying ploy would not work, since the phone companies have an automatic shutoff for these calls. Other urban legends of lovers taking revenge include "The Philanderer's Porsche," "The Solid Cement Cadillac," and "Superglue Revenge."

References: *Curses!*, 216–217; *Too Good*, 79–80.

LSD Stickers, Transfers, and Tattoos

See "Blue Star Acid"

"The Madalyn Murray O'Hair Petition"

This bogus warning concludes with a letter that people are asked to sign in opposition to a nonexistent petition to the Federal Communications Commission (FCC) supposedly initiated by America's best-known atheist, Madalyn Murray O'Hair. O'Hair (all three of whose names are regularly misspelled in the warning fliers) is said to have submitted petition number RM-2493 (or RH-2493) demanding that the FCC ban religious broadcasting in the United States and "remove Christmas programs from the public schools." The statement that concerned Christians are asked to sign and send to the FCC typically reads like this:

> I am an American and proud of my heritage. I am also very much aware of the place religious faith has played in the freedom that we, as Americans, now enjoy. Therefore, I protest any human effort to remove from radio or television any program designed to show faith, GOD as a Supreme Being, or to remove CHRISTMAS SONGS, PROGRAMS AND CAROLS FROM PUBLIC SCHOOLS.

In responding to the bogus petition, O'Hair is sometimes quoted as claiming, "If this petition is successful, we can stop all religious broadcasting in America." Instead, she has been accurately quoted as saying, "I think it's fabulous. . . . This craziness seems to have life everlasting."

An actual petition numbered RM-2493 was filed by someone else in 1974 and did refer to broadcast licenses for religious educational stations, but O'Hair had nothing to do with this request, and it was denied by the FCC in 1975. Nevertheless, and despite her mysterious disappearance in the 1990s, O'Hair continues to be mentioned in the warning fliers. Literally millions of signed statements have flooded the FCC from about 1977 to the present. The FCC has denied the story and explained its apparent origin in press releases, interviews, and in a taped message on its telephone line, to little avail. Eventually the FCC received permission from the Post Office simply to discard mail with "Petition 2493" written on the envelope, which, conveniently, is exactly what most of these bogus warnings direct the concerned citizens to do when they send in their signed statements.

References: Paul F. Bolloer Jr. and John George, *They Never Said It: A Book of Fake Quotes, Misquotes, and Misleading Attributions* (New York: Oxford University Press, 1989), 101–102; Jim Castelli, "The Curse of the Phantom Petition," *TV Guide* (July 24, 1976): 4–6; *Choking Doberman,* 184; Eldon K. Winker, "Two Rumors That Refuse to Die," *Lutheran Witness* (December 1992): 8–9; *Too Good,* 407–408.

Mall Slashers

See "The Slasher Under the Car"

Malls

See Shopping Malls in Urban Legends

Malpractice Stories

Medical malpractice obviously does occur in real life, but a series of apocryphal or exaggerated stories also circulates describing the horrible consequences said to have struck anonymous friends of friends because of mistakes made in their medical treatment. Chief among the problems included are flopped X-rays, switched patients, and operations to remove the wrong organ or to amputate the wrong limb. Let the patient beware!

References: *Choking Doberman*, 98; *Too Good*, 202.

"The Man on the Roof"

This widely traveled story has been told since at least the 1960s. Here is a capsule version masquerading as a news item that was published as a "filler" in many newspapers in January 1980:

> CAPE TOWN (Reuter News Agency)—A man was badly injured Saturday when his wife drove off to go shopping and towed him from the roof where he had been fixing tiles.
>
> As a safety measure, the man had tied a rope around his waist and asked a boy on the ground to attach it to something secure.

Continuing the journalistic career of "The Man on the Roof," the tabloid *Weekly World News* expanded the story in 1988 to supply a name and age for the hapless South African and to explain that his nine-year-old son had tied the rope to the bumper of his wife's car. The tabloid version is reprinted in *Too Good to Be True*. Other versions of the story have the victim adjusting the TV antenna on his house or using the rope thrown over the rooftop as a means of climbing up when he lacks a long-enough ladder. Sometimes this legend combines with other hilarious-accident stories and concludes with the laughing-paramedics motif.

This modern urban legend may derive from traditional European folktales about a man who does his wife's housework (Types 1210 and 1408). At least the means of the man's injury is similar. The distinctive motif in the tales is number J2132.2 (*Numskull ties the rope to his leg as the cow grazes on the roof. The cow falls off, and the man is pulled up chimney*). In a popular Norwegian version of the folktale, the wife is inadvertently responsible for the man's further injury: She comes home from doing his farm work, sees the cow dangling from the roof, cuts the rope, and thus sends her husband head-first into a large pot that is bubbling on the hearth.

See also Motif; Tale Type

References: *Too Good,* 373–375; *Vanishing Hitchhiker,* 181.

Mary Worth

See "I Believe in Mary Worth"

Masturbating into Food

A disgruntled employee of a restaurant or café—usually a fast-food franchise—masturbates into the food before serving it or sending it out for delivery. Often the perpetrator is said to be a victim of AIDS who wants revenge against society for ignoring his plight or seeks revenge against his employers for mistreating or firing him.

This story has plagued businesses selling everything from donuts to coleslaw since at least the early 1980s, but in recent years it has focused especially on Burger King ("Hold the mayo!") and Domino's Pizza ("Hold the mozzarella!"). Other franchises also mentioned in the stories include Hardees, Taco Bell, and Pizza Hut.

Earlier versions of the story were little more than rumors along the lines of, "I heard that some guy was [doing something] . . . at [name of place]." Later the story acquired more narrative elements, such as a description of the man's motives and methods and an account of his telephoning the victims after their food has been delivered and admitting—anonymously—to his deed. The revenge of an AIDS sufferer is a motif also found in "AIDS Mary," and contamination of food is a widespread legendary theme with many variations.

References: *Choking Doberman,* 121; Janet Langlois, "'Hold the Mayo': Purity and Danger in an AIDS Legend," *Contemporary Legend* 1 (1991): 153–172; *Too Good,* 199–200.

McDonald's Rumors

McDonald's Corporation ("billions served"), because of its size and its market dominance, has been the magnet for a number of negative claims and stories circulating by word of mouth, all of them completely without foundation. Because of the early attachment of such traditions to McDonald's, the variety of the claims, and the longevity of some of them, McDonald's rumors may be considered a classic example of modern American anticorporate folklore.

Beginning about 1977, stories began to circulate claiming that the president of the company, the late Ray Kroc, was a member of the Church of Satan and that his success story with hamburger franchises could be traced to that connection, something that he had supposedly bragged about on a national TV talk show. Folklorist Gary Alan Fine has suggested that the company's phenomenal growth, as well as the foreign sound of the president's name and its *k* phoneme (which seems vaguely sinister), may have contributed to the believability of the stories. Eventually the alleged satanic links and the talk-show setting began to bedevil other companies, especially Procter & Gamble.

Also in the late 1970s stories began to circulate claiming that McDonald's was making burgers out of worms, with alternative versions mentioning kangaroo meat, horsemeat, sawdust, spider eggs, and cardboard. Fine identified this and other stories of food contamination by fast-food companies as being in part "responses to [the] loss of community control" as big corporations took over much of the inexpensive local restaurant business and people cooked at home less often.

Whether such stories actually harm big corporations is doubtful, at least in the long run and for any multinational company as a whole. A United Press International story of November 1978 reported that sales had dropped as much as 30 percent in Atlanta when the contamination stories hit that area, but business soon bounced back and, obviously, McDonald's has prospered since then.

The McDonald's response to rumors has been low-key and factual. After declaring the early rumors to be "too ludicrous to even think about," spokespersons stressed the quality control and purity of their materials and cooking methods without ever using the term "worm" in public. The fact that worms or kangaroo meat are much more expensive than beef was pointed out only by folklorists, one of whom, Susan M. Goggins of Georgia State University, even wrote a master's thesis about "The Wormburger Scare" in 1979.

See also The Goliath Effect; "Snakes in Playland"

References: Fine, *Manufacturing Tales*, esp. 147–151, 178–179; *Vanishing Hitchhiker*, 90.

Medical Student Pranks

Stories abound about medical students' pranks, and perhaps a few actual pranks have taken place. In such stories, as Frederic W. Hafferty has written, the students "physically (and thus symbolically) manipulate whole cadavers or certain cadaver parts." The most common tales involve removing a cadaver finger, hand, or penis and then hiding it in someone else's belongings or exposing it in a shocking manner. Sometimes the appendage is attached to a shade pull or a light switch or handed to a highway toll-booth operator. The penis pranks generally involve male versus female medical students.

The stories—seldom verified—are international and are regarded as true incidents by those who tell them. But the "reality anchors" used to support their alleged truth are generally just friend-of-a-friend formulas.

See also Cadavers; Toll-Booth Pranks

References: *Baby Train*, 315–317; *Choking Doberman*, 99; *Curses!*, 299–301; Frederic W. Hafferty, "Cadaver Stories and the Emotional Socialization of Medical Students," *Journal of Health and Social Behavior* 29 (1988): 344–356.

Memetics

The evolutionary biologist Richard Dawkins coined the term "meme" (rhymes with "cream") in 1976 to refer to units of replication by means of which specific aspects of human culture are transmitted. He suggested as examples of memes "tunes, ideas, catch-phrases, clothes fashions, ways of making pots or of building arches." And he outlined an analogy to genetic evolution: "Just as genes propagate themselves in the gene pool by leaping from body to body via sperms or eggs, so memes propagate themselves in the meme pool by leaping from brain to brain via a process which, in the broad sense, can be called imitation."

Dawkins's identification of memes as "the new replicators" caught on, and by 1998 when he wrote the foreword for Susan Blackmore's exploration of the new field of memetics Dawkins conducted a computer search for the name of this new science and turned up more than 5,000 mentions of it on the world wide web. The *Oxford English Dictionary* by then included this definition of "meme": "An element of a culture that may be considered to be passed on by nongenetic means, esp. imitation." Thus, as Douglas Hofstadter had commented earlier, "the very meme of 'memes' [was] taking hold and spreading through the human ideosphere."

Dawkins mentioned in *Unweaving the Rainbow* (1998) that "the genes build the hardware. The memes are the software." In the same book he commented on how avidly others had picked up his idea, remarking that "there seems to be some kind of religion of the meme starting up—I find it hard to decide whether it is a joke or not." Aside from the proliferation of semiserious websites, online articles, meme Internet chatgroups, and the like, there is a growing scholarly literature exploring the possibilities of memetics as a new tool for understanding how elements of culture develop and are retained.

The application of memetics to folklore transmission seems obvious, and even Dawkins's original short list of examples resembles a subset of folklore/folklife topics. Although folklorists themselves have been slow to apply the concept of memes to their studies, virtually every writer on memetics has alluded to folklore materials, often to urban legends. For example, in *Thought Contagion* author Aaron Lynch devoted a short section to "Folklore as Thought Contagion" and identified urban legends as "those plausible narratives regarded as true by most tellers and listeners—but generally found to be mythical after careful investigation." Lynch mentioned as examples the stories about "gerbiling," "The Elephant that Sat on the VW," "The Exploding Toilet," and the McDonald's "wormburger" rumors, offering a brief suggestion of how and why such traditions develop and are spread. In his 1999 article on "millennium thought contagion" Lynch referred to "writers and reporters [who] catch news memes from each other . . . everything from royalty scandals to urban legends."

Richard Brodie's *Virus of the Mind* (the title alluding to another of Dawkins's phrases), a book directed to a popular audience, also mentioned urban legends, asking "Why do some outlandish stories get endlessly perpetuated?" and pointing out that "a scary urban legend [is] full of juicy memes." Brodie's examples included the Craig Shergold legend, "The Procter & Gamble Trademark," stories about food contamination, and his own experience in tracking the legend "Lights Out!" as he traveled the country during a book-promotion tour.

The most comprehensive work on memetics to date, Susan Blackmore's *The Meme Machine,* also makes reference to folklore, particularly urban legends. Blackmore's opening generalization about what constitutes memes, like Dawkins's list, sounds a lot like folklore; her examples include "the stories you know, the skills and habits you have picked up from others and the games you like to play . . . the songs you sing and the rules you obey."

As an example of how memes replicate themselves via variation, selection, and retention, Blackmore reviews "The Microwaved Pet," a kind of story "that takes on a life of its own regardless of its truth." She proposes that through the process of selection "millions of people tell millions of stories every day but most are completely forgotten and only very few achieve urban-myth status."

So far, folklorists have only produced occasional conference papers with titles like "Legends as 'Mind Viruses'" and "Folkloric Transmission as Self-Replication." But memetics should provide a useful tool for deeper understanding of how traditions evolve, spread, and become varied in folk circulation. Urban legends in particular, since they are vivid, contemporary, ubiquitous examples of modern folk narratives, would seem to hold great promise as topics of memetic investigation.

References: Susan Blackmore, *The Meme Machine* (Oxford: Oxford University Press, 1999); Richard Brodie, *Virus of the Mind: The New Science of the Meme* (Seattle: Integral Press, 1996); Richard Dawkins, *The Selfish Gene* (New York: Oxford University Press, 1976); Aaron Lynch, *Thought Contagion: How Belief Spreads Through Society* (New York: Basic Books, 1996); Lynch, "The Millennium Thought Contagion," *Skeptical Inquirer* (November/December 1999): 32–36.

Mercantile Legends

The term "mercantile legends" was introduced by folklorist Gary Alan Fine as an "adjectival description" (not a new generic term) to be applied to contemporary legends that deal with "the economic and corporate implications" of modern business and economics. These legends "feature businesses and corporations as central images and actors," touching on such themes as food contamination, dangerous products, foreign imports, and the sinister goals of upper management. Seldom, if ever, do mercantile legends paint a positive picture of corporations.

See also Business Legends; Companies; The Goliath Effect

References: Fine, *Manufacturing Tales*, 142, 158–159, 160, 164–171.

"The Message Under the Stamp"

This European legend about hard conditions during World War I evolved into a more international story about atrocities during World War II. Journalist Irwin S. Cobb commented in his 1941 book *Exit Laughing*, "I don't know how we'd get along without that standby every time war breaks out in Europe."

In both periods a secret message is written underneath a stamp. In the earlier stories a letter comes to the United States from a relative in Germany who writes that everything is fine there and that the American cousins might want to steam the stamp off the envelope for "little Alf." But there is nobody named Alf in the family. When they follow the clue and steam off the stamp, the Americans find written underneath in tiny letters, "We are starving."

A few World War I versions of "The Message Under the Stamp" identified the source of the hidden message as a prison camp, and during World War II this became the standard version. A soldier held in a German or Japanese concentration camp sends a letter home with a similar request to "save the stamp for little Johnny." Under the stamp is written, "They have cut off my hands!" or "They have cut out my tongue!" The fact is, however, that prisoner mail during the wars was forwarded by the International Red Cross and did not require any postage stamps.

There is evidence that some families did employ the ruse of sending hidden messages under postage stamps during wartime. In her 1971 book *The Hiding Place*, for example, Corrie ten Boom, a Dutch woman who worked for the resistance, recounts her experience while in a German prison receiving a package of supplies from home. The handwritten address slanted upward and to the right, seemingly pointing to the postage stamp, so she soaked the stamp off and found the message, "All the watches in your closet are safe," a coded report that the Jews hidden in a secret room had escaped safely.

References: Gordon Allport and Leo Postman, *The Psychology of Rumor* (New York: Henry Holt, 1947), 171; *Curses!*, 73–75; Arthur Ponsonby, *Falsehood in War-Time* (New York: E. P. Dutton, 1928), 97–98.

"The Messenger Boy"

An Australian story about mistaken identification, probably of British origin, tells of a group of schoolboys lined up for punishment by their headmaster. The boys must hold out their hands, palm up, and the headmaster swats each hand a set number of times with a light cane. As suggested by the title of the story (also known as "The Caned Telegram Boy"), the lad at the end of the line is merely in the school to deliver a message. But before he is recognized by his uniform and the telegram in his other hand, the headmaster has given him the same number of strokes as the rest of the misbehavors.

References: *Baby Train*, 169–171.

"The Mexican Pet"

The versions of this legend that gave the story its usual name among folklorists were first collected in the early 1980s and had Mexico as their setting, as in this example reported in August 1984 from Garland, Texas:

I heard this last year here in Garland; it supposedly happened to a friend of a friend of my wife's. It seems that this friend was on a vacation in Acapulco, swimming at a deserted beach one morning, when she saw a Chihuahua in the water. After they both got to shore, she looked for the owner, but there was no one around. Not knowing what else to do, she took the dog to her hotel to feed it. Time passed, and she kept the animal with her in the hotel room for the rest of her stay in Mexico.

The dog was quiet, never barking or disturbing the other guests and she quickly learned to love it. When the time came for her to leave for home, she decided to smuggle her new pet back to the U.S. She hid it in her purse, and was lucky that it made no sound, either on the airplane or while passing through customs.

Once home, she kept it in her apartment, and since it never barked the neighbors never complained. One day she came home from work only to discover that the dog had fallen into the toilet. She rescued and dried it, but fearing for some possible illness, she took the dog to a veterinarian. After an examination, the vet asked her where she got the dog. She told him the story, but then asked why that was important.

Reluctantly, the vet explained that the animal was not a Chihuahua at all, but instead a Mexican Water Rat!

Numerous variations developed as the story circulated as to where the pet was found in Mexico, what tender care the tourist took of the pet, how it was smuggled home, in what ways it interacted with the American's other pets (often by killing them!), what the vet said, the breed of rat involved, and so on. Consistently, the theme of unsanitary conditions south of the border mingled with the image of the kindhearted but misguided American tourist adopting the cute little Chihuahua.

A good example of the pervasiveness and popularity that the legend achieved in the 1980s was given by journalist Reese Fant of the *Greenville* (South Carolina) *News* in a column published on August 21, 1988. He wrote,

My boss heard the story from his wife, who heard it at work. The person who told it there heard it from her husband, who heard it from a man who works here in Greenville. That man heard it from his mother, who heard the story from a friend of hers who works in Easley. This woman heard the story from her boss, who said the whole thing happened to a friend's daughter.

Reese's account describes ten links in the story's transmission—four family members, three coworkers, and three friends—perhaps a typical ratio of family members to others in a chain of urban-legend transmission.

Eventually "The Mexican Pet" migrated to American urban coastal settings (Baltimore, San Francisco, New York, Miami, etc.), and the illegal-immigrant creature became a clear symbol of Haitians, Chinese, and other "boatpeople" seeking to enter the United States through a backdoor. The rat/dog was always said to have come in on a ship from some

Third World country. In Europe, too, the story gained a foothold, whether describing Dutch tourists in Egypt, Germans in Spain, Italians in Thailand, or other such combinations. A typical justification for the tourist's mistake is something like "There's a breed of rat in Thailand that looks exactly like a Yorkshire terrier," as stated in one version about Spanish tourists in the Far East.

Now well into its second decade of circulation, "The Mexican Pet" (which might better be titled "The Rat Dog") continues to resurface. In August 1996, for example, the following highly doubtful news item appeared in the syndicated newspaper feature "Earthweek: A Diary of the Planet" and was widely reprinted under the title "False Terrier":

> Kiev's *Vseukrainskiye Vedomosti* (All-Ukraine Gazette) reported a tale of mistaken identity that endangered a child and left its parents "thunderstruck." Viktor R. returned from an unnamed foreign destination with what he thought was a bull-terrier puppy for his wife and son as a gift. At first, the animal ate normally and did not demand much attention. But the paper said that on the sixth day the parents were awakened by the screams of their three–year-old whose ear was being chewed off by the animal. The child was treated for minor wounds, and a veterinarian informed the parents that their pet was actually a rare species of Pakistani rat which in its early stage of development resembles a bull terrier puppy.

Although presented as an authentic news item, "False Terrier" is really no more specific or reliable than the versions of "The Mexican Pet" that have appeared in tabloids under such headlines as "Our New Puppy Is a Killer Rat!"

References: *Baby Train*, 15–16; *Mexican Pet*, 21–23; *Too Good*, 38–40.

Mickey Mouse Acid

See "Blue Star Acid"

"The Microwaved Pet"

Facetiously titled "Hot Dog!" when it was "discovered" by folklorists in 1979, the microwave version of this legend was preceded some 20 years earlier by accounts of family pets being cooked and often killed after either accidentally or deliberately by being left inside a conventional oven or a clothes dryer. As microwave ovens became popular in the late 1970s and early 1980s the legend was adapted to the new technology, generally describing misuse of the innovative kitchen appliance by either a very old or a very young user. There are, of course, real dangers associated with stray microwave emissions, but the legends are mostly fantasy.

Usually it was said that an old woman had been in the habit of drying her toy poodle after its bath by placing it on a towel on the open door of her oven and setting the heat at a low level. When her son gives her a new microwave oven for Christmas, the woman assumes that she can use it to dry her pet, as usual. But when she puts the wet dog inside the oven, shuts the door, and turns it on, the poodle explodes.

Other versions of the story mention a dog or cat being accidentally doused by a garden hose while children are playing. One child decides to dry off the pet in the microwave oven. Both versions are known abroad as well as in the United States.

French folklorist Jean-Bruno Renard used "The Microwaved Pet" as his major example of what he termed "the gremlin effect" in legends, noting that a creature is exploded in a microwave oven in the 1984 American film *Gremlins*. A gremlin is the imagined cause of otherwise unexplained mechanical failures, the term coming from U.S. Air Force slang and dating to World War II. Renard described three kinds of rumors and legends concerning microwave ovens and suggested that such stories go through distinct phases as a new product becomes better understood, cheaper, and more widely accepted.

A related cycle of urban legends is about babies being cooked in microwave ovens by drunk, demented, or confused caregivers.

See also "The Baby-Roast"; France; The Gremlin Effect

References: *Baby Train,* 241; *Choking Doberman,* 151–152, 215–216; Keith Cunningham, "Hot Dog! Another Urban Belief Tale," *Southwest Folklore* 3(1) (1979): 27–28; *Too Good,* 290–291; *Vanishing Hitchhiker,* 62–65.

Mikey

See "The Death of Little Mikey"

Military Legends

The American folklorist Richard M. Dorson wrote enthusiastically in 1959 that "volumes of floating lore swirl through the armed services . . . [and] the experiences of war spew up countless exploits and escapes enshrined in legend." However, few collections and studies have been made of military folklore since Dorson's Korean War–era survey, which mentioned only the stories of military snafus, greenhorn pranks, and horrors.

Recent studies reveal that many other kinds of military folklore exist, both in peacetime and wartime, and that the subjects of military legends in particular include stories about the home front, training, troop transport, survival, and technology. Much of the serious documentation of wartime legends dates from World War II and later, but all past military situations and engagements have generated their own body of rumors and legends. For instance, during the American Revolution a story circulated about scout Tim Murphy shooting a hidden Indian enemy by bending his rifle so that the bullet traveled in a curve around the tree or rock. And during the Civil War personal narratives about hardships and heroism became family legends passed down to later generations.

A typical example of a legend about individual survival during a war is "The Magic Bullet" in which a soldier's life is said to have been spared because of some bizarre and lucky way in which a bullet aimed directly at him was deflected or stopped, often by a bible or a packet of love letters in his breast pocket. Thereafter, the survivor carries the spent bullet as a good-luck charm representing "the one with my name on it." The miraculous survival of a particular site is the subject of a legend about the Mormon Temple in Hawaii, which supposedly attracted the attention of a Japanese pilot during the Pearl Harbor attack. Legends claim that he was unable to release his bombs over the temple but succeeded in dropping them on the military targets. After the war, when the pilot supposedly learned what the spared edifice actually was, he converted to Mormonism. Extensive research has failed to locate this Japanese convert or to verify his inspiring story.

Even the 1991 Gulf War—a short, high-tech, modern-day military engagement—quickly generated its share of rumors and legends. Stories circulated about massive unreported government orders of body bags and caskets, atrocities against Kuwaiti babies supposedly carried out by the Iraqis, amazing coincidences involving Iraqi Americans trapped during a visit home, as well as spectacular successes and dismal failures attributed to the advanced weapons employed by the United States and its Coalition allies. One persistent legend claimed that Saddam Hussein's forces were collecting return addresses from American soldiers' mail in order to target their relatives back home for terrorist attacks.

One of the oddest military legends, and one that circulates through all branches of the American armed services, is "The Tale of the Truck." The story claims that the metal ball atop military flagpoles (i.e., the truck) contains a match, a bullet, and a grain of rice. Supposedly these items are for the use of the last survivor of any military loss; he should eat the rice to provide the strength to burn Old Glory, then use the bullet to kill himself. Such claims are absurd (unless viewed as symbols of military pride and determination), and the term "truck" refers not to the decorative finial topping the flagpole but rather to the pulley mechanism below it by which the flag is hoisted.

See also "Grenadians Speak English"; "The Message Under the Stamp"; "The Veterans' Insurance Dividend"; "The War Profiteer"

References: Brunvand, "Some Oddities of Military Legendry," in *The Truth,* 149–159; Richard M. Dorson, "GI Folklore," in *American Folklore* (Chicago. University of Chicago Press, 1959), 268–276; Monte Gulzow and Carol Mitchell, "'*Vagina Dentata*' and 'Incurable Venereal Disease': Legends of the Viet Nam War," *Western Folklore* 39 (1980): 306–316; Graham Shorrocks, "'Body Bag Backlog': A Contemporary Legend?" *FOAF tale News* no. 20 (1990): 5; see also the entries Civil War, Gulf War, Korean War, Military Folklore, Revolutionary War, Vietnam War, and World Wars I and II in Brunvand, *American Folklore: An Encyclopedia* (1996).

Mint-Condition Vintage Vehicles

Wishful thinking combined with the dream of owning a classic automobile or motorcycle have for many years spawned rumors and legends about mint-condition vintage vehicles being available for a pittance. The specific details range from brand-new Model-A Fords discovered in an abandoned railroad freight car or unused U.S. Army Jeeps stored in a forgotten government warehouse to Harley-Davidson bikes still in their shipping crates stacked in some farmer's barn. Compounding the absurdity of these claims is the further notion that these vehicles are being sold for a ridiculously low price—$25 or $50—as if the person discovering such treasures would not have the sense to cash in on the situation.

The theme of these rather amorphous rumors continues in popular urban legends about fine cars that are offered for sale cheaply either by the mother of a soldier lost in combat, by a dealer who cannot rid a car of the smell of death, or by the disgruntled wife of a philandering husband.

See also "The Bargain Sports Car"; "The Death Car"; "The Philanderer's Porsche"

References: Ron Lawson, "In Search of the Warbike Motherlode: Harley's on Ice," *Cycle World* (January 1990): 34–35; *Vanishing Hitchhiker,* 178.

"Miracle at Lourdes"

A modern Irish legend tells of a woman from Dublin who visits the Grotto at the French shrine of Lourdes, famous for its stories of miraculous cures. Although in good health, the woman feels tired on the hot day of her visit, and she sits down in an empty wheelchair to rest, then falls asleep. Waking when a priest arrives to bless the visitors, the Irish woman jumps up from the chair and is immediately surrounded by crowds of other pilgrims crying, "A miracle! A miracle!" In the excitement the woman is knocked to the ground, and her leg is broken. So she returns home from Lourdes with her leg in a cast.

References: *Too Good,* 27–28.

"The Misguided Good Deed"

This story was summarized in a 1990 *New York Times* edition:

A woman on a subway sees an expensive-looking leather glove lying on the floor just as a well-dressed man is leaving the train. She snatches it up and throws it onto the platform before the train doors close.

The other passengers all stare at her, and then one of them, a mild-looking man, asks plaintively, "Why did you toss my glove out the door?"

The lack of specific details or a source for this funny story suggest that it may be a legend, as does the similarity to the following story—"The Through Train"—as reported in Paul Smith's 1986 collection of English legends, *The Book of Nastier Legends:*

Mr. Rowe boarded the last train of the day from London to travel up to Doncaster. In conversation with a fellow traveler he suddenly realized that he was on the wrong train—this one went straight through to York.

Having found himself in a similar position once before, Rowe enlisted the aid of the other passenger and it was agreed that if the train slowed down sufficiently at Doncaster he would attempt to jump off. As they approached the station the train slowed and, clutching his bag, he jumped out on to the platform and ran alongside the train so as to reduce his speed.

He had only gone a few yards when the following coach caught up with him and another passenger, holding the door open, yanked him in. "Well done," said the passenger "you nearly missed it. It was lucky I saw you running. Didn't you know, this train doesn't stop at Doncaster?"

References: *Baby Train*, 125, 230.

"The Missing Day in Time"

This fable, showing modern science being overcome by Christian religion, circulates in the form of fliers (anonymous, typed or computer-printed, photocopied) often titled "THE SUN *DID* STAND STILL." The fliers, as well as religious tracts reprinting them, tell the story of NASA engineers unable to account for "a day missing in space in elapsed time" as they attempt to calculate the positions of heavenly bodies several centuries in the future using a supercomputer. The engineers are stumped, but one "religious fellow" on the team remembers two passages in the Bible referring to the sun either standing still or moving backward; when the engineers factor in this data, the program runs perfectly. The fliers conclude, "Isn't that amazing? Our God is rubbing their noses in His Truth!"

The story is credited to "Mr. Harold Hill, President of the Curtis Engine Co. in Baltimore, Maryland, and a consultant in the space program," and indeed in Hill's speeches and writings various versions of the story do appear. But officials at the Goddard Space Flight Center in Greenbelt, Maryland, deny not only the story itself but also the underlying premises about celestial navigation upon which it is supposedly based. They also point out that Hill's relationship to the space program was peripheral and did not involve navigational computations.

A precomputer version of "The Missing Day" can be traced to Lieutenant C. A. Totten, an instructor in military science at Yale University from 1889 to 1892. Through a series of revisions and reprintings, both oral and published, the story came down to Harold Hill (who died in 1987 without ever retracting his story about the missing day or finding his original notes on the source, which he had promised to supply to inquirers). A version transcribed from a speech by Harold Hill appeared in the *Spencer* (Indiana) *Evening World* on October 10, 1969, and seems to be the source of all the many later reprintings. More than 30 years later "The Missing Day" continues to circulate.

References: *Choking Doberman,* 198–199; *Too Good,* 237–239; *The Truth,* 137–148.

"The Missionaries and the Cat"

Missionaries of the Church of Jesus Christ of Latter-day Saints (known more commonly as the Mormons) often teach lessons to potential converts in their homes using a low-tech visual aid—a flannel board or a flip chart. Two teaching missionaries one time had their illustrative materials attacked by the pet cat of the elderly lady they were visiting, so when their "golden contact" (as they're called) left the room to get milk and cookies for them, one of the missionaries just sort of snipped the cat hard on the nose with his forefinger. Unfortunately, he hit the cat just right, and it fell down dead.

Horrified by what he had done, the guilty missionary either pushed the cat's body under the couch or leaned it up against his pant leg and stroked it through the rest of the lesson. The missionaries managed to get out of the house without the crime being detected, and when they arrived a few days later for another lesson, the lady sadly informed them that her pet cat had died since their last visit.

This version of the story, popular among Mormons, illustrates how even the best intentions can lead to difficulties. A reverse message—retribution falling on the head of a disbeliever—is sent in the story of a woman confronted by two Mormon missionaries on her front porch. She angrily slams the door in their faces, breaking the neck of her pet cat or dog, which was standing beside her looking out curiously at the visitors.

In a similar story lacking the Mormon details, a piano tuner accidentally kills a pet cat by hitting it with a tuning fork. And in yet another related legend told in England, a nervous suitor struggles to carry on a conversation with his girlfriend's father while waiting for her to prepare for their date. The family's budgie (parakeet) has been released from its cage and is flying freely around the room; a cozy fire is crackling on the hearth. As the young man begins to relax, he casually starts to cross his legs, but when he raises his foot he accidentally strikes the parakeet in midflight, sending it straight into the fireplace to a fiery death.

See also "The Crushed Dog"

References: *Baby Train,* 276–277; *Too Good,* 360–361.

Mistaken Identifications

Several urban legends depict the experience, fairly common in everyday life, of either misidentifying or utterly failing to recognize someone. Often the misidentified person is a black or Hispanic celebrity assumed in these racist stories to be a lowly worker such as a bellhop, a parking valet, or a gardener. In a black-white confrontation in an elevator, a black sports star or pop idol and his entourage are unrecognized and thought to be muggers. The range of persons unrecognized in these legends, which border on jokes, goes from British royalty ("I'm the sister of the queen of England") down to the parent of a teacher's elementary-school student ("Sorry, I thought you were the father of one of my children").

The person making the misidentification may be misled by language: A naked woman just out of her shower asks "Who's there?" when her doorbell rings, and the reply, "Blind man," could have two meanings. Unfortunately, the woman chooses the wrong meaning and opens the door to the man from the window-blind company. When Eddie Murphy on an elevator says "hit four" or "hit your floor" to a white passenger, he is thought to have ordered, "Hit the floor!"

When a handsome male celebrity—a white one this time—*is* recognized in an ice-cream store, a woman becomes so flustered that she puts her ice-cream cone into her purse.

In terms of their basic psychology, these stories of mistaken identifications are another manifestation of the tendency in urban legends, and in life, for people to jump to conclusions.

See also "The Blind Man"; "The Elevator Incident"; Generation Gap Legends; "The Ice-Cream Cone Caper"; Jumping to Conclusions; "The Messenger Boy"; Stupid Pet Rescues

References: *Too Good,* 411–424.

"The Modem Tax" and "The E-Mail Tax"

The Federal Communications Commission rejected a proposal to place a surcharge on computer data transmission via telephone lines in 1988, but warnings about the supposed "modem tax" raced through the Internet via electronic bulletin boards and e-mail in 1990 and 1991. (The word "modem" refers to the devices that "*mo*dulate and *dem*odulate" computer signals so that they can be transmitted on telephone lines.)

The warnings urged computer users to "make it clear that we will not stand for any government restriction of the free exchange of information!" Even though no such legislation or regulation was even being considered, thousands of letters, calls, and petitions flooded government agencies and legislative committees. Most of the effective debunking of the modem tax was carried out on the Internet, with commentators frequently linking the stories to urban legends.

In 1999 a similar warning flashed through computer networks, claiming that Congress was considering a tax of five cents per e-mail message to support the United States Postal Service, which was said to be losing huge amounts of money because of its reduced first-class postage business. The warnings came complete with the name of the congressional sponsor, the number of the bill, the name of an attorney who is "working without pay" to fight the measure, and a reference to an article in the *Washingtonian* published in March of that year. Every one of these "facts" is wrong, and the story can be traced—complete with the same or similar names—to Canada, where it is equally fraudulent. However, Canadian sources claimed that the story began in Arizona.

Both of these stories seem to derive from computer users' feeling that the fast and inexpensive (often *free!*) communication via the Internet is too good to be true. Surely the government will find a way to tax this benefit.

References: *Baby Train,* 188–190; "FCC Scraps Plan to Charge for Computer Access to Phone Systems, Sources Say," *Wall Street Journal* (March 17, 1988): 6.

Mongolia

In 1990 the Polish folklorist Dionizjusz Czubala interviewed Mongolian academics visiting the University of Katowice in Poland, and in 1991 he conducted a research trip to Ulan Bator in Mongolia to collect legends. He classified his materials in five groups: legends involving automobiles, political legends, legends about Almas or manlike creatures, legends about UFOs, and miscellaneous. Although the Mongolian material was a small sample collected by an outsider under less than ideal conditions, it offers a rare opportunity to survey contemporary legends in a little-known part of the world, suggesting the promise of similar legend traditions existing in many other countries as well.

Although Czubala found the Mongolian legends to be "quite different from their European counterparts," a few familiar themes that emerged were vanishing hitchhikers, contaminated imports, the bad behavior of foreign visitors (especially Russians, Chinese, and Americans), and the stealing of body parts for illegal transplants. The most characteristic Mongolian contemporary legends seemed to be related to the hard facts of daily life, such as poor roads, shortage of consumer goods, high crime rates, and the political and economic influence on Mongolia from outside powers.

Drivers on the long stretches of extremely primitive Mongolian "highways" have supposedly been accosted by a man with half his hair shaved off, a naked girl or a girl in a red dress, or a man that changes into a dog. Any of these figures may race along beside the vehicle for miles, only to disappear when the driver stops. Other drivers are said to have seen blue fires flickering along the roadsides, although these do not seem to be dangerous. Legends about places where horses stop and refuse to move evolved into stories about places where cars mysteriously break down. Drivers who desecrate or steal from roadside shrines are stricken with illnesses that are not relieved until the sufferer returns to the shrine to make amends.

Many Mongolian political legends reflect actual depredations against people by foreigners, usually Russians or Chinese. Besides generalized accounts of rapes, murders, and thievery, stories tell of Russians leaving behind a child to be raised as a Mongolian when they return to their own country, and of the Chinese trying to poison people with infected silk goods and contaminated vodka. Other stories glorify the "founding fathers of modern Mongolia" in the 1920s and speculate about their eventual demise. Polish and American tourists, recent visitors, are said to have tried to smuggle valuable artworks or museum artifacts out of the country; other stories tell of Americans being robbed of up to $10,000 carried in cash. The Almas legends are similar to stories from abroad about Bigfoot, Yeti, and other such monsters; in Mongolia, encounters with Almas are said to have happened "in 1965," or "a few years ago," or "not so long ago." (A good comparative note on other apeman creatures follows Czubala's third report in *FOAFtale News*).

References: D. Czubala, "Mongolian Contemporary Legends" [3 parts], *FOAFtale News* no. 28 (December 1992): 1–5; no. 29 (March 1993): 1–7; and no. 31 (November 1993): 1–4.

"The Mother's Threat Carried out"

Here is an English example from this legend cycle, sometimes referred to as "The Inept Mother," quoted from Rodney Dale's 1978 book *The Tumour in the Whale:*

At the beginning of the war, a young mother sailed for Ireland with her two young children, a girl of five and a baby of two. She was trying to settle them in their bunks for the night so that she could go off for dinner, but the baby refused to stop crying. In desperation, she shouted: "If you don't shut up, I'll put you out of the porthole." This seemed to quiet the child, and she went for her meal. When she returned, the porthole was open, the baby was gone, and her daughter slept blissfully.

The porthole version is reminiscent of the Aesopian fable "The Nurse and the Wolf" in which the caregiver threatens a child: "If you make that noise again, I will throw you to the wolf." (Seeing the wolf waiting outside, the nurse closes the window.) Other contemporary legends, known internationally, describe the mother saying to the male toddler, "If you wet again, I'm going to cut it off." The older sister acts out the mother's threat when her younger brother wets. Yet another variation has the mother answering the girl's question about the baby's penis, "Oh, that's just something the doctor forgot to cut off."

These bloody legends are similar to a tale in the original 1812 collection made by the Brothers Grimm in Germany titled "How Children Played Butcher with Each Other," in which an older son cuts his brother's throat in imitation of their father butchering a pig. When the mother discovers the tragedy, she takes the same knife, stabs her son and then herself; meanwhile, the baby, whom she had been bathing, drowns in the tub. Some contemporary legends in this depressing group also incorporate the drowned-infant theme. Janet Langlois has interpreted these legends about domestic incompetence from sociopolitical, psychoanalytical, and metaphysical perspectives.

References: *Baby Train*, 68–71; Janet L. Langlois, "Mothers' Doubletalk," in Joan Newlon Radnor, ed., *Feminist Messages: Coding in Women's Folk Culture* (Champaign: University of Illinois Press, 1993), 80–97; *Mexican Pet*, 72–73; *Too Good*, 223–224.

#

A "motif," in general folkloristic usage, is defined as a traditional narrative unit such as a character, an incident, an object, or any other remarkable detail that occurs repeatedly in myths, legends, and folktales. The standard motifs of folk narratives the world around were compiled by Indiana University folklorist Stith Thompson, then classified and published in his six-volume work *The Motif-Index of Folk-Literature* (1955–1958 in its latest edition). Well-known motifs of traditional folklore include "The Unpromising Hero," "The Wicked Stepmother," "Sacrifices to a Dragon or Other Monster," "Magic Clairvoyant Mirror," and "Punishment by Being Thrown into a Briar Patch." Motifs in Thompson's system are listed by letters referring to general categories (e.g., Animals, Taboos, Deceptions, Rewards and Punishments, Traits of Character) followed by specific index numbers extended with decimal points followed by a title. Thus Motif G303.4.5.3.1 (*Devil detected by his hoofs*) occurs in chapter G, Ogres, and represents a sub-sub-sub-subtype (so to speak) of a large group of motifs dealing with how a supernatural creature may be recognized by its appearance.

Only a few contemporary-legend motifs appear in Thompson's index, which is devoted to documentation of the huge body of older traditional narratives. An exception is "The Vanishing Hitchhiker," which is an ancient enough theme to have its own number in chapter E, The Dead (E332.3.3.1). Another older motif, E422.1.11.5.1 (*Ineradicable bloodstain after bloody tragedy*), is believed to be the source of contemporary urban legends' smell-of-death motif found in "The Death Car."

Some details in modern urban legends are repeated often enough in different stories to constitute modern motifs. These include "Hair Turned White," "The Handwriting on the Wall," and "The Laughing Paramedics." So far, however, no index numbers have been established for these narrative elements, and they are referred to simply by their titles.

References: Brunvand, "Myths and Motifs," in *The Study of American Folklore*, 4th ed. (1998), 170–195.

"The Mouse in the Coke"

Of all the food-contamination rumors, one of the oldest and best known is "The Mouse in the Coke," a stomach-turning account of someone finding a dead mouse in the can or bottle of a soft drink. Following the so-called Goliath effect coined by Gary Alan Fine, the usual culprit mentioned in rumors and legends is the Coca-Cola Company, the market leader in soft drinks. Several lawsuits documented from the 1930s and later have proven that such a thing as mouse-in-Coke contamination has happened, *or* that it can be faked. But the stories circulating in oral tradition are seldom based on real court cases that the storytellers have researched or experienced. Instead, the legends are dramatized and localized accounts of the general notion that small rodents may get into a soft-drink container during the bottling process and escape all of the company's quality controls. The focus in these legends is usually on the horrified reaction of the person discovering the contamination and on the large monetary settlement awarded by the court. There are, of course, many other possible ways that foods of numerous varieties may be contaminated by all kinds of impurities, but the legends tend to focus on just a few possibilities, such as a mouse in a Coke or a chicken-fried rat.

Fine's analysis of the statistics involving court cases and legend occurrence on the mouse-in-Coke theme led him to conclude that some of the legends must have derived from actual incidents. Thus "polygenesis" (individual multiple origins of stories) followed by "diffusion" of the stories is a partial explanation for the profusion of such legends.

See also Cokelore

References: Gary Alan Fine, "Cokelore and Coke Law: Urban Belief Tales and the Problem of Multiple Origins," in *Manufacturing Tales,* 79–85; *Too Good,* 179–181; *Vanishing Hitchhiker,* 84–89.

Movies

See Film and Urban Legends

"The Mrs. Fields Cookie Recipe"

From about 1982 through 1989 the main focus of the expensive-recipe urban legend was the Mrs. Fields Cookie Company, founded in Palo Alto, California, in 1977 and later headquartered in Park City, Utah. Unlike the prototype legend "Red Velvet Cake," in which the customers are charged in person a rip-off price for a simple recipe, the Mrs. Fields version claimed that someone had telephoned the company asking for the recipe for her famous chocolate-chip cookies. The caller was allegedly told that the cost would be "two-fifty," and she put the charge on her credit card, only to discover when the bill arrived that it was for $250. As with "Red Velvet Cake," the customer was unable to avoid paying the bill, so in revenge she distributed the recipe as widely as possible.

The cookie recipe accompanied by the story circulated around the world via mail, publications, the Internet, and face-to-face transmission. Although the recipe did make decent cookies, it listed the odd ingredients of a cup of "blenderized" dry oatmeal and a single Hershey chocolate bar, along with the usual bag of chocolate chips. In a denial of the legend that was issued in interviews and printed on cookie bags and posters, the Mrs. Fields company insisted that the whole recipe, especially these two ingredients, was phony and that they had never revealed or sold the company's recipe, which was "a delicious trade secret." In her 1987 biography, *One Smart Cookie,* Debbi Fields wrote, "Of all the problems . . . that are going to be dropped on your doorstep if you run a large company, the worst, absolutely the worst, are the rumors."

By 1989 the expensive-recipe legend had shifted to the Neiman Marcus retail company, complete with the same spurious directions for baking the chocolate-chip cookies.

See also "Neiman Marcus Cookies"; "Red Velvet Cake"

References: *Curses!,* 219–226; *Too Good,* 260–261.

Music and Urban Legends

Rumors and legends spread mainly by Christian fundamentalist writers and preachers contend that "satanic" messages are coded into rock music; usually the messages are said to have been recorded in reverse on albums and compact discs by a process called "backward [or back-] masking." Supposedly the listener's mind perceives these messages subliminally, and the unaware adolescent is led to unsavory behavior and even suicide. There is scant evidence for any recorded backward masking except for a few deliberate pranks, and virtually no evidence supporting the theory of subliminal influences on the human mind. The irony is, as Tom McIver wrote, "that much of the music accused of harboring these demonic messages truly is an unhealthy influence on kids." However, the source of these influences is "the words and behavior of real people, not supernatural demons."

Besides the urban lore *about* music, there is a small body of popular music pieces inspired by urban legends. Perhaps the oldest such song, and a classic example, is Dickey Lee's 1965 recording "Laurie (Strange Things Happen)," which tells "The Vanishing Hitchhiker" in full detail. Another treatment of the same story is the bluegrass song "Bringing Mary Home" recorded by the Country Gentlemen and other groups.

And a related legend of a ghost trucker is retold in a song performed by Red Souvine titled "Big Joe and Phantom 409."

A legend that has had almost as much circulation in song form as in its story format is "The Dead Cat in the Package," immortalized in a popular folk piece usually titled "The Body in the Bag" and performed and recorded by numerous groups. Among sci-fi buffs the same dead-cat story has been turned into a "filk" song titled "Another Urban Legend," which itself is a parody of an earlier "Vanishing Hitchhiker" filk parody titled "Ferryman." (Such sci-fi songs are called "filk" songs because of a misprint years ago on a convention program that was announcing a *folk* song gathering; ever since, the term has been "filk song" among these fans.)

Probably there are many other songs in various genres with legend inspirations, but just two more might be mentioned here: a song called "Saguaro" performed by the Austin Lounge Lizards tells "The Plant's Revenge," and a John McCutcheon song heard on *A Prairie Home Companion* radio series in the 1990s takes "The Philanderer's Porsche" as its inspiration.

Not really an urban-legend piece but repeating a popular shorthand definition of the genre is the song "Too Good to Be True," performed by Tom Petty and the Heartbreakers since the 1980s. An older song with the same title, but completely different in words and music, was a favorite piece during the swing era and recorded by Benny Goodman (with Helen Ward singing), Roy Eldridge, and others. Echoing the proverbial expression "it seems too good to be true," the popular music versions refer to the singer's supposed love interest. In legend definition, the phrase refers to a plot that is too unlikely and coincidental to be taken as literal truth.

References: *Baby Train,* 21 (for a verse of "Another Urban Legend"); Tom McIver, "Backward Masking, and Other Backward Thoughts about Music," *Skeptical Inquirer* 13 (Fall 1988): 50–63; *Mexican Pet,* 52–53 (for lyrics of "Laurie").

Musicians and Urban Legends

Professional musicians in all genres—pop, jazz, classical, and others— are often the subjects of stories illustrating their talents or their supposed eccentricities. Some of these stories may be true; most belong to the genre of personal anecdotes; but some such stories acquire variant versions and attach themselves to more than one personality, thus entering the category of modern legends. For example, the story about jazz pianist Fats Waller's response to a woman asking him to define jazz usually concludes with the witty musician saying, "Madam, if you don't know by now, don't mess with it!" Several variations of the "don't mess with it" comeback have been applied to Louis Armstrong and Jelly Roll Morton as well, and there are different versions of how the question and the answer were phrased.

Rock musicians and groups in particular have many stories told about them, often accounts of their alleged outrageous behavior. Among the performers spoken of in these accounts are Buddy Holly, Elvis Presley, the Beatles, the Grateful Dead, Mick Jagger, Jim Morrison, Ozzy Osbourne, Rod Stewart, and Frank Zappa. Some of the stories concern a particular song closely identified with the performer, such as Phil Collins's "In the Air Tonight," claiming to reveal the "secret meaning" or the "story behind" that piece. Many such stories told about pop stars are difficult if not impossible to separate from the canned media hype and public-relations gimmicks that surround celebrityhood.

The traditional stories about classical music and musicians are known more within the circle of professional performers and their highbrow audiences than among the public at large. For example, several symphony musicians are said to have responded to a question about who was their favorite conductor by saying, "That's like asking a mouse 'Who is your favorite cat?'" Another symphony legend is "Start the Music":

> A famous pianist, whose identity varies—Rubinstein, or Graffman, or Serkin—is scheduled to perform a concerto as guest soloist with an equally famous orchestra, the identity of which also varies. The pianist has rehearsed the Rachmaninoff *Variations on a Theme of Paganini,* which begins with the orchestra playing alone.
>
> But the orchestra has prepared Rachmaninoff's *Piano Concerto No. 2,* which begins with the pianist playing alone. Evidently, the guest pianist and the orchestra have never rehearsed the work together. [Hardly likely, but this is a legend.]
>
> On the night of the performance both pianist and conductor waited patiently for the other to begin, for a very long time, each one assuming that the other would begin when ready.

A minor genre of musical folklore includes stories about things that naive students supposedly wrote in an assigned paper about classical music. It seems hardly likely that grade-school classes would even be given such an assignment, and the appearance of very similar lists in several times and places suggests that they belong to folklore rather than to reality. Some examples:

> "I know what a sextet is, but I'd rather not say."
> "A harp is a nude piano."
> "A virtuoso is a musician with real high morals."
> "Music sung by two people at the same time is called a duel."
> "An opera is a song of bigly size."

See also "The Dolly Parton Diet"; "The Youngest Fan"

References: *Baby Train*, 220–222 ("What Is Jazz?").

"The Mutilated Boy"

In this older and more horrible form of "The Attempted Abduction," a small boy is castrated or otherwise mutilated in the men's restroom of a shopping center while his mother waits outside wondering why he is taking so long. Often the criminals are said to be minority persons and/or gang members, and the mutilation is believed to be part of an initiation ritual. Unlike "The Attempted Abduction," in which the child is rescued, in "The Mutilated Boy" the child either bleeds to death or is permanently disfigured. The criminals are never caught, and both the nearby businesses and the local police are said to be suppressing the facts of the case.

"The Mutilated Boy" is a perennial urban-legend phenomenon, resurfacing again and again with local details that inflame the public with outrage and the desire to capture and punish the perpetrators. Despite the best efforts of law enforcement agencies, governmental authorities, folklorists, and sociologists to debunk these stories, they continue to arise anonymously and spread through word of mouth, especially near the Christmas season or other times of heavy shopping traffic. Sometimes the very efforts made to suppress the "Mutilated Boy" stories seem themselves to contribute to spreading the legend.

The modern elements in the legend—shopping center, gang violence, class conflicts, and so on—are deceptive. This story actually has a long history, including both classical and medieval prototypes. It derives from the anti-Christian blood-libel legends of ancient Rome, which evolved into anti-Semitic legends told in medieval Europe, one famous instance of which is Geoffrey Chaucer's "The Prioress's Tale." In place of the motif of disposing of the body down a well, the mall restroom has entered the story; and instead of religious rivalries, the modern legend deals with racial and class-based conflicts.

Viewing "The Mutilated Boy" psychoanalytically rather than historically, Michael P. Carroll noted that mostly women—especially mothers—seem to tell the legend and that the despised-minority theme is not as universal as other studies have suggested. Carroll cites Freud's idea that castration may be interpreted as an attempt "to disguise the wish being gratified" and (following other psychoanalytic theories) suggests that the story might be seen as a manifestation of penis envy and the gratification of women's unconscious desire to castrate males. Although some folklorists have been quick to reject such blanket Freudian readings of urban legends, to Carroll's credit it must be noted that he bases his conclusions not just on abstract psychoanalytic theory but also on a thorough review of variant versions, and he cites the published folklore studies concerning this legend. Further, he considers the context and audience for the stories as well as their content features.

See also "The Attempted Abduction"; "The Blood Libel"

References: Michael P. Carroll, "'The Castrated Boy:' Another Contribution to the Psychoanalytic Study of Urban Legends," *Folklore* 98 (1987): 216–225; *Choking Doberman,* 78–92; Bill Ellis, "*De Legendis Urbis:* Modern Legends in Ancient Rome," *Journal of American Folklore* 96 (1983): 200–208; *Mexican Pet,* 151–156.

"The Mutilated Shopper"

See "The Cut-Off Finger"

"The Mystery Trip"

An English travel-trouble story is told by Rodney Dale in *The Tumour in the Whale* (1978) as follows:

A couple went on holiday and thought it would be rather fun to spend a day on an advertised mystery coach [i.e., bus] trip. So they bought tickets and set off in high hopes, only to find that the mystery destination was their home town. So rather than paying exorbitant rates for the local food, they decided to pop home and cook themselves a meal there. And somehow, they managed to miss the coach back.

See also "The Day Trip"

References: *Baby Train,* 230.

Myth

"Myth," suggests folklorist C. W. Sullivan, "may be one of the most misused words in the language." The most common misapplication of the term refers to any beliefs that one considers to be false. Referring instead to specific traditions of ancient and modern storytelling, Sullivan defines a myth as a "traditional prose narrative that enables people to discuss preternatural topics." True "myths" are usually associated with the ancient traditions of the classical, Norse, Celtic, Slavic, Oriental, or other cultures, or to the myths told by native peoples. As such, myths are distinguished from *legends,* which have a close connection with belief, experience, and history, and from *folktales,* which are obviously fictional narratives.

There is little, if any, need for the term "myth" in urban-legend studies, since other words are more precise and more widely accepted in this area of folklore research. Still, journalists and the general public persist in calling contemporary legends "myths" or "urban myths"; thus, we must recognize and come to terms with this semantic confusion.

See also Definition of "Legend"

References: Brunvand, "Myths and Motifs," in *The Study of American Folklore,* 4th ed. (1998), 170–195; C. W. Sullivan III, "Myth," in Brunvand, *American Folklore: An Encyclopedia* (1996), 497–499.

Naive Computer User Stories

Although electronic computers perform wondrous tasks for modern people, they can also be difficult to master and frustrating for the beginner. As computers entered the workplace and home en masse starting in the 1970s, a cycle of naive computer user stories developed—both jokes and legends. Gradually, as computers became more familiar, these stories declined in popularity, perhaps replaced by the frequent scares of computer viruses (both real and imagined) that would alter or destroy one's work.

Many of the naive user stories describe supposed calls to the technical support lines of hardware and software companies. In these accounts, beginners overlook obvious problems like failing to plug in the machine or to connect the printer and the computer or to adjust the brightness knob on the monitor. Other stories claim that naive users failed to understand a direction in the program manual, such as "press any key"; they call tech support to say that there is no "any" key on their keyboard.

Stories that claim a naive user once put liquid whiteout over his errors on the screen are probably just jokes, whereas a story claiming that someone used a CD-ROM drive as a cupholder just may be believed by some people who tell it, or may even be true in a few special cases.

Similar naive user stories are told about other pieces of office equipment such as photocopiers and fax machines. (A new employee may photocopy a computer disk when asked to make backups, or request a paper company to fax the office some blank paper while they wait for the delivery of a full carton of paper for the machine.)

See also Computers

References: *Too Good,* 286–287.

Naive Hunter Stories

Hunters, usually from *outside* the state where the stories are told, are credited with shooting a horse, cow, or mule, unable to tell the domestic animals from the deer or elk they are seeking. (Mules may be confused with mule deer, which also have large ears.) Often the naive hunter— from California in Utah stories, from Utah in Wyoming stories, and so on—is caught when he passes through a check station set up by the state Fish and Game Department. The large animal's feet sticking out from under a tarp on his pickup truck

are obviously not those of a deer or elk; sometimes they are even shod with iron shoes. But the out-of-state hunter brags to the wildlife agent about the fine "elk" he has shot. Wildlife officials in several states, when asked about these stories, admitted that they had heard them but knew of no authenticated cases.

During hunting season, many ranchers and farmers are said to have painted "HORSE" or "COW" on their livestock in vibrant letters; a few livestock owners have actually done this.

References: *Curses!,* 138–139.

"Nasty Legends" and "Nastier Legends"

English folklorist Paul Smith in two popular collections of urban legends used these terms; Smith compiled *The Book of Nasty Legends* (1983) and *The Book of Nastier Legends* (1986). Clearly Smith did not mean to set up yet another new set of terms for the genre, since he consistently uses the label "contemporary legends" in the prefaces to these books and in all of his subsequent writings on urban legends. The "nasty" aspect of the stories in these books is suggested by the general topics of the chapters: embarrassment, contamination, death, revenge, and the like. Another English writer, Christie Davies, however, did adopt the term "nasty legends" for a survey of sick humor concerning the consumption of objectionable foods and concerning disasters involving modern technology.

References: Christie Davies, "'Nasty' Legends, 'Sick' Humour, and Ethnic Jokes about Stupidity," in Bennett and Smith, *A Nest of Vipers* (1990), 49–68

Native American Contemporary Legends

The slight amount of borrowing that has been documented between contemporary Native American and Anglo American legends is illustrated in two versions of "The Boyfriend's Death." In one variant of that popular urban legend told in New Hampshire, the haunted spot where the doomed teenagers park is said to be the site where the last white man of the region was killed by Indians. In a version of the same basic legend told by Navajo children in Arizona, the murderous entity at the haunted site is said to be a "hairy one," or skinwalker, a character from the Native tradition of legends. (Of course, in most tellings of "The Boyfriend's Death" there is no mention or influence whatever of Native Americans.)

Keith and Kathryn Cunningham of Northern Arizona University have collected a number of legends from contemporary Navajo, Hopi, and Zuni storytellers that seem to show a similar influence of the modern Anglo or Hispanic legend tradition, or at least the texts show some cultural references from other groups in the modern urban world. One typical theme—the dangerous stranger approaching women at a Squaw Dance, for example—is reminiscent of the devil-in-the-dance-hall stories.

In a survey of Anglo American urban legends known among the Navajos living around the old Mormon community of Ramah, New Mexico, the Cunninghams found that "The Vanishing Hitchhiker" was the urban legend most often recognized and most likely to be told there. These versions, too, however, often incorporated the theme of a Squaw Dance, and after the figure disappears sometimes it is said to have left behind coyote tracks. Studying borrowing in the reverse direction, Peggy E. Alford found that Anglo American retellings of skinwalker stories often set the action "on the road" (like the hitchhiker stories) rather than in the more traditional setting of a Navajo hogan.

These few published studies suggest that other Native American groups in other regions should also be investigated for their possible influence on or borrowing from contemporary Anglo American (or other) legends.

The following story told in 1995 by a man raised in Los Angeles is in the form of a contemporary legend that presents the Native Americans as tricksters who fool the modern scientific Anglos:

> In 1966 or so a NASA team doing work for the Apollo moon mission took a team of astronauts to the desert near Tuba City, Arizona, where the terrain of the Navajo reservation looks very much like the Lunar surface. With all the trucks and other large vehicles were two technicians dressed in full Lunar spacesuits.
>
> Nearby a Navajo sheepherder and his son were watching the strange creatures walk about, occasionally being tended by personnel. The Navajo gentleman did not speak English, so he sent his son to ask for him what these strange creatures were. The NASA workers told them that they were men preparing to go to the moon. The Navajo sheepherder asked if he could send a message to the moon with the astronauts.
>
> The NASA people, knowing a publicity coup when they saw one, thought this was a great idea, so they rustled up a tape recorder. And after the man recorded his message, they asked his son to translate, but the boy refused.

Later, NASA employees asked other people on the reservation to translate the message, but every person they asked would listen to the tape, chuckle, and refuse to translate. So NASA wised up and brought copious cash with them on their final translating attempt. Well paid, a resident of the reservation listened to the tape and then recited for the anxious NASA people the message, "Watch out for these guys; they come to take your land."

References: Peggy E. Alford, "Anglo-American Perceptions of Navajo Skinwalker Legends," *Contemporary Legend* 2 (1992): 119–136; Margaret K. Brady, *"Some Kind of Power": Navajo Children's Skinwalker Narratives* (Salt Lake City: University of Utah Press, 1984); Keith Cunningham, "It Was the (Untranslatable)": Native American Contemporary Legends in Cross-Cultural Perspective," *Folklore* 102 (1991): 80–96; Keith Cunningham and Kathryn Cunningham, "The Appearing Hitchhiker: Narrative Acculturation Among the Ramah Navaho," in Bennett and Smith, *The Questing Beast* (1989), 213–230; *Too Good*, 103–104 ("The Boyfriend's Death").

Needle-Attack Legends

Beginning late in 1998 notices began to circulate in large numbers on the Internet warning against contaminated hypodermic needles left in public places and infecting innocent people. Here is a typical example of these bogus warnings that was forwarded numerous times in November 1998 before reaching the compiler of this encyclopedia:

PLEASE READ IMPORTANT MESSAGE BELOW AND SEND TO ANYONE YOU KNOW

A very good friend of mine is in an EMT [emergency medical technician] certification course. There is something new happening that everyone should be aware of.

Drug users are now taking their used needles and putting them into the coin return slots in public telephones. People are putting their fingers in to recover coins or just to check if anyone left change, are getting stuck by these needles and infected with hepatitis, HIV, and other diseases. This message is posted to make everyone aware of this danger. Be aware! The change isn't worth it!

P.S.—This information came straight from phone company workers, through the EMT instructor. This did NOT come from a hearsay urban legend source.

The punctuation and random capitalization of the notices, the friend-of-a-friend source, the anonymity of the first-person voice, the mention of supposed authoritative proof, and the complete lack of any actual documentation all mark this as an urban legend of highly doubtful accuracy. Ironically, this text concludes with a disclaimer asserting that it is "NOT . . . from a hearsay urban legend source," but, in fact, it *is*.

Variations of the needle-attack warnings, which continued to circulate on the Internet for at least the first six months of 1999, included references to victims being stuck by contaminated needles left in the coin-return slots of soda machines or in theater seats. In spring 2000 yet another version appeared on the Internet, warning that infected needles had been affixed to "the underside of gas pump handles." Sometimes, in all versions, there was said to be a note attached to the syringe saying, "Now you have HIV," a detail reminiscent of the AIDS Mary legend. Other stories told of a stranger dancing with women at a nightclub, sticking them with a needle, and handing them a card with the same frightening message. Still other accounts claimed that the keypads on public telephones have sometimes been painted with "a mixture of LSD and strychnine." Sometimes the various attacks described in these bogus warnings were said to be gang-related, usually as part of an initiation. Although some of the warnings claimed that the Centers for Disease Control and Prevention (CDC) had verified the stories, CDC spokespersons interviewed by journalists branded the stories as hoaxes.

These modern-day needle-attack legends are not completely new. A few such warnings could be found in the mid-1980s, and using hypodermic needles to inject sedatives into young women was a standard motif of the white-slavery folklore of the 1920s and 1930s. Other rumors and stories circulating for years describe random needle or hatpin attacks directed against young women on the streets of large cities.

In a paper delivered at the Perspectives on Contemporary Legend conference held in St. John's, Newfoundland, in May 1999, Diane E. Goldstein pointed out that poisoned arrows, thorns, spindles, needles, and pins were familiar in older folktale traditions. (The story of Sleeping Beauty is one example.) Goldstein interpreted the latest needle-attack stories as "a disguised critique of medical authority" that implies the sentiment "a condom won't help me in the bedroom if the real danger is in theaters or from pay-phone slots."

See also "AIDS Mary"; "Blue Star Acid"; White-Slavery Legends

"Neiman Marcus Cookies"

The generalized American expensive-recipe story with its roots in the 1940s (perhaps even the 1930s) became the classic "Red Velvet Cake" urban legend in the 1960s, then shifted to Mrs. Fields Cookies in the early 1980s. By 1989 the legend shifted again, this time to the Neiman Marcus company, being circulated mostly on the Internet.

The typical story (which is circulated along with the recipe) describes in the first person how a woman and her daughter enjoy lunch in the café of the Neiman Marcus flagship store in Dallas. For dessert they have chocolate-chip cookies, the recipe for which, the waitress informs them, is "only two-fifty." When she discovers on her monthly credit card bill that this means $250 not $2.50, the woman demands a refund. Being refused, she promises to give the recipe free to as many people as possible, using e-mail as her major method of circulation. The recipe itself is nearly identical to the one circulated for years in the Mrs. Fields version of the story, and the shift in business targets may have gone from Mrs. Fields to Marshall Fields (a Chicago store) to Neiman Marcus.

The company in a good-natured way denies the story on its website (located at www.neimanmarcus.com), provides a free cookie recipe, and rightly compares the story to other urban legends: "Just like the poodle in the microwave story, certain urban legends have real staying power. One that has plagued us for years is the story of a woman who requested a cookie recipe." In another version of this posting the company mentioned "Red Velvet Cake" and the Waldorf Astoria hotel in New York.

See also "The Mrs. Fields Cookie Recipe"; "Red Velvet Cake"

References: *Curses!*, 225–226; Barbara Whitaker, "The $250 Cookie Recipe Exposed," *New York Times* (July 2, 1997).

The Netherlands

See Holland

"The New Identity"

See FBI Stories

New Zealand

The presence of urban legends in New Zealand has been reported by only a few Kiwi journalists, one American tourist, and a single trained folklorist from New Zealand, Moira Smith, whose interest in folklore began when she was a student at Victoria University in Wellington. Smith researched the "capping" (i.e., graduation) stunts of New Zealand students for her doctoral dissertation in folklore at Indiana University, discovering that many of the oral and published accounts of outrageous behavior were merely legends that circulated in several variants. Scouring old student newspapers for descriptions of stunts, Smith also found an article from 1938 describing a "white slavery" scare in Wellington that was clearly a legend along the lines of "The Attempted Abduction." Although Smith encouraged and assisted the author of this encyclopedia when he was in New Zealand for several months in 1988, she has since relocated to the United States herself.

Even before visiting New Zealand, I was able to report urban legends from that country conveyed in letters from readers of my books. Two people, for example, sent me versions of the package-of-cookies story in a local variation: a punk rocker is mistakenly believed to have eaten an old woman's Moro candy bar (a New Zealand brand of chocolate bar).

Other readers reported "The Blind Man" and "The Hairdresser's Error," these and others being duly reported in my published urban-legend collections along with other rumors and stories I learned while traveling there.

One of the most distinctive Kiwi adaptations of a well-known legend is "The Petone Shingle-Crusher," a variation of "The Last Kiss." In this version a worker in a town near Wellington is said to have been trapped in the gears of a machine used to crush large rocks into gravel; he lives just long enough for his wife to come and give him one last kiss before his body is extracted from the machinery. Another interesting localization is the story told about the statue of Robert Burns that stands in the main square (an octagon, actually) of Dunedin; as with so many other statues the world over (including a statue of Brigham Young in Salt Lake City), this one is described as facing toward a financial institution with its back to a church.

The New Zealand version of "Grandma's Washday" was also thoroughly localized. It was posted in an exhibit, with copies offered for sale, in the Lakes District Centennial Museum in Arrowtown on the South Island. According to a museum guide, these charming rules for doing laundry the old-fashioned way had originated with an actual pioneer in the region, but this is exactly what people claim all over the United States where virtually the same set of rules is found.

Good evidence that international urban legends reach New Zealand as quickly as any place is demonstrated by the case of "Superhero Hijinks" in 1988. When an Aukland journalist queried readers about new stories going around, a Superman version of this popular legend was submitted, and other versions surfaced in oral tradition and in a gossip column. The next year a story published in *The Penguin Book of Contemporary New Zealand Short Stories* contained a Spiderman version of the same legend.

Unfortunately, the documentation of urban legends from New Zealand seems to have gone no farther than October 1990 to March 1991, when *Challenge Weekly*, a Christian newspaper published in Aukland, ran a series of articles asking the question "Are angels hitchhiking around New Zealand to get a heavenly message across to Kiwi Christians?" The rumors and stories reported were clearly related to the vanishing-hitchhiker theme, and Brian Finn, the series author, concluded that the old urban legend was circulating anew in his country. The New Zealand versions of the legend were set along specific named highways, and the message said to have come from the disappearing hitcher was the standard promise that Jesus would be returning soon.

New Zealand clearly merits further collection and study of urban legends. Perhaps someday Moira Smith will take up the challenge when she is back to visit relatives, or possibly I could be persuaded to return by the triple lures of some of the world's best trout fishing, skiing in the "summer," and, last but not least, an unmined treasure of urban legends.

References: *Baby Train,* 38 ("Superhero Hijinks"), 45–46 ("Hairdresser's Error"); *Curses!,* 24–25 (Brunvand in NZ), 70–72 ("The Petone Shingle Crusher"), 206–207 ("White Slavery in Wellington"), 213–215 ("Blind Man"), 243–246 ("Grandma's Washday"), 258 ("Burns' Statue in Dunedin"), 301–304 (student pranks); *Mexican Pet,* 138–140 ("Package of Cookies").

Norway

Professor Reimund Kvideland of the Department of Folklore and Ethnology at the University of Bergen, Norway, took early and important notice of urban legends in his country with the publication in 1973 of his article about contemporary rumors and legends in the press, published in the Norwegian journal *Tradisjon* ("Det stod i avisa! Når vandrehistorier blir avismeldingar," vol. 3: 1–12; translated as "It Was in the Papers! When Migratory Legends Become News Items"). Kvideland's examples included versions of the cement-filled car and runaway-grandmother legends, among others. Kvideland and other folklorists in Norway have continued to collect and occasionally to publish contemporary legends, but no book-length work has resulted so far.

There is, of course, a long tradition of folklore study in Norway going back to the early nineteenth century, when the classic fairy-tale collections were compiled, and the traditional legend has hardly been neglected. Fortunately, a major work in this area—Christiansen's index of migratory legends based on the Norwegian versions—was published in English.

Handily for those who do not read Norwegian (actually, not a difficult language for an English- or German-speaker), Kvideland, in conjunction with the Norwegian American scholar Henning K. Sehmsdorf of the University of Washington, published a small selection of English translations of typical Scandinavian urban legends in their book *Scandinavian Folk Belief and Legend.* Of the 20 stories included, 11 are from Norwegian sources.

These sample stories are arranged in four groups representing major themes in Scandinavian urban folklore: Outsiders and Strangers, the Supernatural, Horror and Antitales, and Adulterers and Thieves. The Norwegian story texts include variants of "The Spider Bite," "The Vanishing Hitchhiker," and one about the spirit of a dead person showing up in a modern photograph. "Antitales" or "Antilegends," incidentally, is a term for humorous mock-horror stories usually told by children, a genre identified in a 1971 article in the journal *Indiana Folklore* (vol. 4: 95–140) by American folklorist John M. Vlach. But usually antilegends are not considered to belong to the genre of urban legends, being more akin to jokes than legends.

In general, we must agree with Kvideland and Sehmsdorf's judgment, expressed in the introduction to their anthology (see pp. 36–37), that many of the urban legends circulating in the Scandinavian countries seem to have originated in the United States. But whatever their origin, as the editors further insist, these stories do "often express a sense of insecurity and frustration with contemporary life, ranging from trivial concerns to more basic social problems." In comparing the traditional stock of Scandinavian legend with recent urban stories, the editors conclude that "on the whole the culture mirrored in contemporary legends differs radically from the stable rural world depicted in the older legend tradition."

One example of a modern legend that may have originated in Scandinavia and spread beyond is "Baby's Stuck at Home Alone." Even versions told in England and the United States often give the setting as Sweden or Norway for the horrifying tale of a baby left fastened into its highchair waiting for the baby-sitter to arrive while its parents leave for a vacation abroad. When the sitter has an automobile accident en route to the home, the baby starves to death while trapped in its chair. This horror legend first appeared in print in Norway in the early 1970s and became part of a serial novel published in a Norwegian magazine in 1978.

The obvious localization of an international urban legend to Norway is illustrated well by a version of "The Double Theft" published in a Norwegian magazine in 1975 and included in Kvideland and Sehmsdorf's anthology. Norwegians call this story (paraphrased here from the translation) "Free Tickets":

A wealthy couple in a fashionable suburb of Oslo look out the window of their villa one evening to see that their car, which was parked in front, is missing. They notify the police, while cursing "this miserable country of thieves."

The police cannot locate the car, but the next morning the couple see, to their surprise, that it has been returned. Oddly, the thieves have parked the car back where it was, with a note taped to the steering wheel: "We are terribly sorry that we stole your car. Can you forgive us? We filled up the gas tank, and we enclose two tickets to the Chat Noir for tonight. Please use them! Then we'll know that you are not angry anymore."

The owners feel better now, thinking, "There are still some sweet and honest people in this country after all." They use the tickets to attend the program that night at the Chat Noir, a popular music-hall theater in Oslo.

When the couple return home, they find their house has been stripped of all its valuables. Eventually it dawns on them: The car thieves had used the free tickets as bait to lure them away so they could burglarize their home.

See also "The Lost Wreck"; "The Well to Hell"

References: *Baby Train*, 196–197; Reidar Th. Christiansen, *The Migratory Legends: A Proposed List of Types with a Systematic Catalogue of the Norwegian Variants*, Folklore Fellows Communications No. 175 (Helsinki, 1958); Reimund Kvideland and Henning K. Sehmsdorf, eds., *Scandinavian Folk Belief and Legend* (Minneapolis: University of Minnesota Press, 1988), 375–392 ("Urban Folklore Today"); *Too Good*, 222–223.

"Not My Dog"

This story has been repeatedly told and published, attributed to various times and places, and often claimed as a first-person experience. Surely it could have happened—even more than once—but the multiple retellings with their varying details suggest also that the story has acquired a life of its own as, at the very least, a sort of semilegend. Here is the version published in Ed Regis's 1987 book *Who Got Einstein's Office*, quoted from Julian Bigelow, who was recalling his own 1946 trip to meet the computer pioneer Johnny von Neumann at the Institute for Advanced Study at Princeton:

"Von Neumann lived in this elegant lodge house on Westcott Road in Princeton," Bigelow says. "As I parked my car and walked in, there was this very large Great Dane dog bouncing around on the front lawn. I knocked on the door and von Neumann, who was a small, quiet, modest kind of a man came to the door and bowed to me and said, 'Bigelow, won't you come in,' and so forth, and this dog brushed between our legs and went into the living room. He proceeded to lie down on the rug in front of everybody, and we had the entire interview—whether I would come, what I knew, what the job was going to be like—and this lasted maybe forty minutes, with the dog wandering all around the house. Towards the end of it, von

Neumann asked me if I always traveled with the dog. But of course it wasn't my dog, and it wasn't his either, but von Neumann—being a diplomatic, middle-European type person—he kindly avoided mentioning it until the end." (p. 110)

The earliest published account of "Not My Dog" is in Lucy Maud Montgomery's 1924 children's book *Emily Climbs*, where the dog is a white chow and the punch line is, "Not your dog? Whose dog is he then?" A 1970 report from Florida says the dog was a beagle, with the punch line being, "My dog? Isn't that *your* dog?" A California version remembered from about 1975 claims that the dog was "large," the reaction being, "That's not my dog!" A version from England published in 1985 says that the dog was "large and friendly" and the host asked, "Aren't you going to take your dog with you?" Then there's another California version published in 1990 in which the dog is "big, old, and mangy" and inspires the reaction, "My dog? You mean he's not *your* dog?" The latest account of the story comes from Utah, published in 1991 and set at an unspecified time in the past: The dog is "a massive black Labrador" and the homeowner screeches, "My dog? My dog? My dear young woman, I thought that beast was yours."

Probably there are other versions of the story, and possibly some or all of them are true. If so, this is less a legend and more a personal-experience story, another form of modern folklore.

References: *Curses!,* 146–148; *Too Good,* 55–57.

"The Nude Bachelor"

When the delivered morning newspaper bumps against the front door of his home or apartment, the bachelor has just stepped out of the shower. Wearing only a towel or less, he cautiously reaches outside to get the paper, but the doorknob slips from his hand, and he is stranded outside. The man is naked, without a key, and usually has only the newspaper to cover himself with. In other versions the naked man may have been staying with his girlfriend or stepping out of his apartment to drop a letter down the mail slot or to dispose of garbage in a chute. In the versions when the man is locked out of his house, he may try to gain entry through a window, sometimes by climbing a nearby tree; neighbors, seeing a naked man lurking around, call the police.

"The Nude Bachelor" is documented in Europe, particularly Eastern Europe, since 1960 and was incorporated into literature and films there. The story became localized and well known in the United States by the next decade, and it was mirrored in a "Garfield" cartoon in 1987.

Several people report similar personal experiences. For example, in his 1969 book *Ambassador's Journal*, John Kenneth Galbraith described a very similar personal experience, which he said happened to him in 1960 in a hotel. Luckily, a friend of his was outside the room waiting for the elevator, and he loaned Galbraith his coat to wear while waiting for a hotel employee to arrive with a passkey.

References: *Too Good,* 147–149; *Vanishing Hitchhiker,* 138.

"The Nude Housewife"

Often told more as a joke than a legend, "The Nude Housewife" typically ends with a punch line. At least since the 1960s, the story has been frequently published in popular books and magazines as well as several times in Ann Landers's advice column, where it is invariably presented as true. Here is the version published in *Reader's Digest* in March 1961:

> A friend was doing her washing in the basement and on impulse pulled off the dress she was wearing and added it to the tubful. Then she saw a big

spider web. Not wanting to get dust or web in her hair, she put on the nearest headdress, her son's football helmet, and went after it with a broom. At that moment she heard a knock; in desperation she grabbed an old raccoon coat hanging nearby and opened the door.

The gasman gave her a quick look and went to read the meter. Then, as he left, he said, "Hope your team wins, lady!"

The raccoon coat is an unusual detail in "The Nude Housewife"; it may have been added either by *Reader's Digest* or the person sending in the story to cover her nudity but still retain the embarrassment of the situation.

Some versions of this story mention leaky pipes in the laundry room and the plumber arriving to fix them just at the moment that the woman has removed her dress. As anyone knows who has waited a long time for service persons to arrive, it *could* happen that they finally show up just as the homeowner has given up and is doing something silly.

See also "Waiting for the Ice Man"

References: *Curses!*, 15; *Too Good*, 376–377; *Vanishing Hitchhiker*, 139–140.

"The Nude in the RV"

A husband or wife on a hot day, while riding in the back of the family camper, motor home, or house trailer while it is being driven or towed by the other partner, removes all or most of his or her clothing before lying down for a rest. Some unexpected road hazard causes the driver to stop suddenly, and without thinking the nude or nearly nude partner steps out on the roadside to see what has happened. The driver proceeds, leaving the naked partner stranded. Sometimes the nude RV orphan—a man—manages to get home ahead of his wife, even though he is wearing only his boxer shorts. Thinking his garb looks enough like a bathing suit to get by, the man begins to water the lawn, which has dried out during their vacation. Just then his wife arrives at the wheel of the RV, and she is so surprised to see him standing there in his underwear that she drives straight through the closed garage door.

Much varied and often incorporated into published, filmed, and recorded media, "The Nude in the RV" has also been told in England, Germany, and Australia, where it is more typical for the wife to be left behind. The story may derive from an older railroad legend on the same theme known as "The Cut-Out Pullman."

See also "The Wife Left Behind"

References: *Too Good,* 378–381; *Vanishing Hitchhiker,* 132–136.

"The Nude Surprise Party"

See Comparative Approach; "The Surpriser Surprised"

Nudity

Being caught naked is a persistent theme in many urban legends. Besides the entries immediately preceding this entry, see also "The Blind Man"; "The Cat (or Dog) and the Nude Man"; "Come and Get It"; "The Cut-Out Pullman"; "The Dormitory Surprise"; "Superhero Hijinks"; and "Waiting for the Ice Man"

"The Nut and the Tire Nuts"

This story is variously told or published as a joke (ending with a punch line), as a brain teaser (asking for the solution to the problem), or as a legend (illustrating how native wit beats education). Winston Groom incorporated it into his 1986 novel *Forrest Gump* with the punch line, "Maybe I am an idiot, but at least I ain't stupid." Here is a verbatim text as collected in 1978 by folklorist Jens Lund from a man in Cairo, Illinois, and included in Lund's 1983 Indiana University folklore dissertation "Fishing as a Folk Occupation in the Lower Ohio Valley":

> My dad tol' me, when I was pretty small, he said, "Don't never think you know it all. Regardless of how foolish a man seems to be or anything or crazy," says, "he sets down and starts to give you some advice, you listen to every bit, 'cause somewhere along the line, some part of it's gonna help you," and I've found it to be true.

We got, as they say, a "bughouse" up here at Anna—asylum?—yeah, a state hospital. They's a fellow's drivin' along there one day and a wheel fell off o' his car. He was standin' there wonderin' what to do next. And this fellow's standin' there lookin' over the fence at him, you know? He says, "What's the matter, sir?" "Well, sir, my wheel fell off. They got no lug nuts on 'em, I gotta walk into town and get some." He says, "Well, you know sir, if it was me," he says, "I'd go aroun' the other wheels and take a nut off each one of 'em, put that wheel back on there and drive it into town."

That fellow says, "You know, you supposed to be outside and me inside." And so it works that way. Now, see, that fellow is supposed to have good knowledge and good brains, and that fellow's inside there 'cause supposed to been crazy. But he told that guy somethin' to help.

In most modern versions of "The Nut and the Tire Nuts" the driver is changing a flat tire when he accidentally loses the lug nuts. The most common punch line is, "I may be crazy, but I ain't stupid."

References: *Mexican Pet,* 63–64; *Too Good,* 113–115.

"The Obligatory Wait"

Numerous college and university students, and even a few professors and administrators, believe that a campus regulation specifies how long a class must wait for a late instructor to arrive in the classroom. Sometimes there is a sliding scale indicating the number of minutes to wait, depending upon the rank of the course's instructor—from five minutes for a graduate assistant up to 20 minutes for a full professor. Some campusfolk insist that the obligatory wait rule may be found spelled out in official college regulations, but so far nobody has located a copy of that particular rule.

It is true that some instructors do announce their personal policies regarding lateness of either students or themselves, but this is strictly an informal and unofficial action. New students generally learn about "The Obligatory Wait" via the grapevine from older students, some of whom will "prove" that the rule exists by citing either a friend of a friend or else instances when one of their classes decided to wait so-many minutes for a late professor.

See also "The Suicide Rule"

References: *Baby Train,* 296–298; *Too Good,* 426–427.

"Octopus Eggs Impregnate Swimmer"

A traditional motif found in English legends seems to make no sense physiologically. The motif is B784.1.4 (*Girl swallows frog spawn: an octopus grows inside her with tentacles reaching to every part of her body*). Obviously, the infestation here should be baby frogs or tadpoles, not an octopus. More reasonable, though still doubtful, the modern versions of the story seemingly derived from this motif usually sound more like the following brief example, as published in a New Zealand newspaper in 1990.

Years ago a young woman complained about gripping pains in her stomach. When operated upon, a young octopus was discovered.
The explanation? She swallowed an octopus egg while swimming.

"Octopus Eggs Impregnate Swimmer" belongs to the bosom-serpent tradition concerning various amphibians or fishes growing inside the human body, and the story resonates with fears of unwanted pregnancy.

See also "The Bosom Serpent"; Motif; "Sperm in the Swimming Pool"

References: *Choking Doberman*, 110–111.

"Old Versus Young"

Sometimes called "Revenge of the Rich," this story tells of a wealthy person (often a woman), driving an expensive car (typically a Mercedes) who is beaten to a parking place in a crowded lot by a young man in a compact car or a small sports car (sometimes a Corvette); he zips into the last open spot just ahead of her. The young man grins at the woman and says, "That's what happens when you're young and fast." The woman calmly backs off and rams her Mercedes repeatedly into the sports car, saying, "And that's what happens when you're old and rich."

The story is also told in Europe (Rolls-Royce versus a "Mini," BMW versus a VW, etc.), where, as in the United States, it is localized to a particular city or company parking lot. Verification for the incident, of course, is purely of the friend-of-a-friend variety, and there is considerable variation in the quoted comments of each driver. Searches by insurance adjusters have failed to turn up any actual example of this incident.

"Revenge of the Rich" was told as a true story from Hershey, Pennsylvania, on a Paul Harvey radio broadcast in 1987, and it was incorporated as a staged incident in the 1991 film *Fried Green Tomatoes*.

References: *Mexican Pet*, 67; *Too Good*, 81–82.

"The One-Word Exam Question"

The professor's question in this classic tricky Q-and-A story, usually set in a philosophy class, is simply "Why?" The clever student's winning answer is generally either "Why not?" or "Because." This legend has been widely told on college and university campuses, both American and foreign, for years, and it may have been acted out by more than one professor, although there is no evidence that any actual course grades were based on the one-word question.

The story was given a political twist in a 1992 "Shoe" comic strip and then made a fictional medieval appearance in a 1995 "Prince Valiant" strip. In 1991 and again in 1992 the story appeared as a query to the "Ask Marilyn" feature published Sundays in *Parade* magazine.

In a related college story the students are asked to write their own final examination question; one student writes "Write your own final examination question" as his response. In yet another college story, applicants are asked to write a question about themselves and then answer it; one student writes "Do you play the tuba?" and answers "No." Tradition says that both of these clever answers to tricky questions won the students the professor's or the college's approval.

See also "Define 'Courage'"; "Which Tire?"

References: *Curses!*, 286; *Too Good*, 445–447.

"The Open-Book Exam"

Another tricky Q-and-A story from the college campus: Students are told that they may use anything they can carry into the classroom for the final examination, which is "open book." One clever student carries in a graduate student from the same department to write his examination for him.

References: *Curses!*, 284–285.

Organ Thefts

Although there is some truth in the stories about thefts or sales of human organs in Third World countries for use in transplants, the persistent rumors and legends about organ-theft crime rings at work in other countries are simply urban legends. Medical ethics, the registration and assignments of organs for transplanting, the need for proper tissue, and blood-type matches and several other factors all argue against the theft of organs from random victims. The legend-form of this notion is usually called "The Kidney Heist."

References: Véronique Campion-Vincent, "Organ Theft Narratives," *Western Folklore* 56 (1997): 1–37; Todd Leventhal, "Traffic in Baby Parts Has No Factual Basis," letter to the *New York Times* (February 26, 1992).

Ostension (or Ostensive Action)

Borrowing a term from the field of semiotics, Linda Dégh and Andrew Vázsonyi proposed that "ostension," specifically "ostensive action," be regarded as an alternate means of legend transmission. Semiotics (or semiology) is the study of signs and of sign systems in human communication; "ostension" in this context refers to direct presentation of "the thing, the situation, or event itself," rather than using a conventional sign (such as a cross) to represent something else (in this case Christianity). An example of ostensive action as simple communication might be someone holding up a single cigarette to signal a friend some distance away to buy another pack of cigarettes.

The concept of ostension applied to the study of urban legends recognizes that sometimes people actually enact the content of legends instead of merely narrating them as stories. As Dégh and Vázsonyi phrase it, this form of legend transmission involves "presentation as contrasted to representation (showing the reality itself instead of using any kind of signification)." Thus a person could lead a group's visit to a supposedly haunted site and try to raise the spirits versus simply telling others the story of the place.

Halloween offers many examples of ostensive action serving to transmit legends. Trick-or-treating, wearing costumes, putting up seasonal decorations, building spook houses, and the like are all based more or less on legends, but these Halloween activities directly involve people in acting out some parts of the stories. Rumors of tainted Halloween treats have a slender basis in fact, but the exaggerated stories themselves about Halloween sadists became partial reality when a few copycats began acting out the crimes. Dégh and Vázsonyi showed that "not only can facts be turned into narratives, but narratives can also be turned into facts."

True ostensive action may be illustrated, Bill Ellis showed, in actual incidents of people forming satanic groups and practicing rituals based on stories they have heard, as well as carrying out mutilations, sacrifices, murders, or other crimes. "Pseudo-ostension," in contrast, would be the term appropriate for something like teenagers dressing as the grim reaper to scare other teens visiting a legend-trip site. Yet another variation, which we can refer to as "quasi-ostension," might be the appropriate term for a situation in which observers interpret some puzzling information (such as cattle mutilations) not as a likely result of natural causes (like the work of predators) but as resulting from cult activity or visits from extraterrestrials, as described in rumors and legends.

See also Halloween Sadists; Legend-Tripping; Redemption Rumors; "Roaming Gnomes"; Satanic Panic; "The Solid-Cement Cadillac"

References: Linda Dégh and Andrew Vázsonyi, "Does the Word 'Dog' Bite? Ostensive Action: A Means of Legend-Telling," *Journal of Folklore Research* 20 (1983): 5–34; Bill Ellis, "Death by Folklore: Ostension, Contemporary Legend, and Murder," *Western Folklore* 48 (1989): 201–220; Fine, *Manufacturing Tales,* 205–208; Wendy Leeds-Hurwitz, "Semiotic Approach," in Brunvand, *American Folklore: An Encyclopedia* (1996), 656–657.

"Out of the Mouths of Babes"

A persistent story that has been associated with various American and European TV shows since the 1950s has these usual components, according to French folklorist Jean-Bruno Renard, who traced the story:

> A child discloses indirectly and in public that one of his parents is unfaithful to the other one, when the latter is not at home, with a close relative.

Here is a summary published in 1993 of typical versions of the story, as told in Italy about the popular TV show *Piccoli Fans:*

Sandra Milo [presenter of the show] asked a child: "And what about you, sweetheart? What will you do when you grow up?" The child immediately replied, "What Mum and Uncle Giovanni do when Dad isn't in." Someone is then slapped; depending on the version, it is either the husband who slaps the wife, or the wife who slaps the boy or even Sandra Milo who boxes the ears of the innocent boy.

In France the story has been associated with the popular TV show *L'École des Fans,* while in the United States it has been told about the programs *Strike It Rich* and Art Linkletter's long-running show *Kids Say the Darndest Things.* Renard hypothesized that the story most likely "developed independently on both sides of the Atlantic," but he pointed to possible prototypes in such traditional folktales as Aarne-Thompson Type 1358* (the asterisk indicates a subtype of another story) summarized in the index as "Child Unwittingly Betrays His Mother's Adultery."

Besides noting the sexual and moral implications of "Out of the Mouths of Babes," Renard also mentioned the role of television, which, he suggested "has grown into a dreadful modern form of the eye of God which sees and judges every single thing." Other modern legends, such as "Bozo the Clown's Blooper" and "The Videotaped Theft," also concern crimes or moral shortcomings revealed by television or some other recording medium.

It hardly needs to be added that nobody has, so far, exhibited an actual audio or video recording of the supposed incident described in these legends, and neither has any eyewitness come forward.

See also Tale Type

References: Jean-Bruno Renard, "'Out of the Mouth of Babes': The Child Who Unwittingly Betrays Its Mother's Adultery," *Folklore* 106 (1995): 77–83.

"The Package of Cookies"

Known as "The Packet of Biscuits" in England, where the story was first publicized in the 1970s, this legend has many variations, all based on the same essential plot element. The premise of the legend is that someone mistakenly believes that a stranger has started eating his or her food, usually in a train or bus station or an airline terminal. The shared food is often a package of cookies (or biscuits, as they are called in England) but may also be a candy bar or even a salad or a main course ordered in a cafeteria. The aggrieved person retaliates in some way before realizing his or her error.

Here is a typical version as published in the *Amarillo (Texas) Globe-Times* in 1993; it was told by a man who got it from his wife who heard it on the telephone from a woman calling her to order tickets:

> The woman, in an airport between flights, bought a newspaper and a Snickers candy bar. She sat down in one of those chairs linked to its fellow seats by a common table and began reading her paper. Suddenly, she saw the man in the next seat pick up the Snickers from the table and take a big bite. Stunned, she broke off the end of the candy bar, hurled it down and stalked off.
>
> Later, still fuming, she saw the same man just sitting down in the airport snack bar. On his plate was a bagel. On the spur of the moment, she

walked over, picked up the bagel and took a big chomp. The astonishment on his face made her feel very good.

She continued feeling self-satisfied until she'd boarded her plane. She sat down and opened her purse for something. Nestled inside was the untouched, still-wrapped Snickers she'd purchased at the airport and stuffed into the purse with her change.

"The Package of Cookies"— perhaps better titled "Who's Sharing What with Whom?"— was adapted for Douglas Adams's 1984 book *So Long, and Thanks for All the Fish.* Two short films of 1988 and 1990 were also based on the legend, and it pops up regularly in other media, particularly newspaper columns, both in the United States and Europe as well as in Australia and New Zealand. One popular conduit for the story's transmission is among ministers and missionaries who tell it as an example of how jumping to conclusions may lead to unseemly behavior.

References: *Choking Doberman,* 191–193; *Mexican Pet,* 137–140; *Too Good,* 30–31.

"The Packet of Biscuits"

See "The Package of Cookies"

Panthers on the Loose

See Big Cats Running Wild

Parodies of Urban Legends

Increasing public awareness of urban legends as a genre of modern folk narratives in the 1980s and 1990s provided fertile ground for the invention of urban-legend parodies. The success of any parody depends upon the audience's familiarity with the material being referred to, so the existence of these parodies of modern legends is a clear sign of their coming of age as a recognized folklore genre.

Newspaper columnists, who frequently receive "news tips" from readers that turn out to be rumors or legends, sometimes mock or parody these themes. For example, in 1988 Gerald Kloss of the *Milwaukee Journal* wrote a column pretending to share with readers some of the latest legends he had collected. One of them was a hilarious parody of "The Nude Housewife" in which Kloss reversed the situation and told of "a 275–pound defensive tackle for a pro football team who was surprised by a female gas-meter reader as he was repairing a faucet leak while wearing only his football helmet. The meter-maid commented, "I hope you win the game Sunday, mister," and Kloss's punch line for the story was a parody of the kind of stereotyped replies pro athletes give to questions from the press: "Our running game's shaping up and if our pass defense holds up, I think we've got a good chance of going all the way."

Especially with the growth and popularity of the Internet, urban-legend parodies have proliferated and may almost be considered a separate subgenre of legendry. One common form of parody circulated on the Internet is a combination of a number of different urban legends into a single massive, bizarre story. Another popular parody-form adds an absurd conclusion to a well-known story, as in this example from Harvard Lampoon's 1991 book-length parody of college life *A Harvard Education in a Book:*

> Did you hear about those two kids who were making out in a car in the woods? They heard these weird sounds coming from right outside and got nervous, so the guy stomped on the gas and drove away. When they got out of the car, hanging from the passenger door handle was a bloody hook. *The very same one that the girl had lost the week before.*

Yet another parody format alluding to urban legends is a mock warning against a computer virus. Some of these parodies merely mock the notion of viruses, but one text titled "The Gullibility Virus" supposedly causes Internet users to believe weird things—"every groundless story, legend, and dire warning that shows up in their inbox or on their browser." The examples listed, of course, are mostly urban rumors and legends.

References: *Too Good,* 376 ("The Nude Housewife"), 473–480.

"Pass It On"

A drug-awareness official giving a warning lecture at a high school passes around a plate with two marijuana cigarettes on it so the students can view and sniff the real thing and know how to identify one when they encounter it. The official cautions the students, "There had better still be *two* joints on the plate when I get it back!" When the plate has been around the room and is returned to the official, there are *three* marijuana cigarettes on it.

The nondrug counterpart to this story is "The Lottery Ticket."

References: *Choking Doberman,* 163; *Too Good,* 331.

"Paul Is Dead"

Andru J. Reeve's definitive (if somewhat obscure) book on the subject of this rampaging rumor, which surfaced during the Beatles' heyday, contains the following concise summary as part of the jacket blurb:

> For a scant four weeks in the fall of 1969, Beatle-watchers held their collective breath as the rumored death of Paul McCartney became the bizarre focus of attention in countless broadcast studios and newsrooms worldwide.

Although not an urban legend in the usual sense of the term, the Paul-is-dead rumor spread so quickly and so widely, and it eventually included so many details about "clues" to the popular musician's supposed demise, that folklorists and other scholars for a brief period gave the stories their close attention. Reeve's investigation proved that the story began as a spoof by Midwestern American college students based on slender rumors that were flying about. Reeve's book contains the best and longest (plus fully illustrated) account of the numerous musical and pictorial clues from recordings and from record covers that were cited by true believers in the rumor.

References: Donald Alport Bird, Stephen C. Holder, and Diane Sears, "Walrus Is Greek for Corpse: Rumor and the Death of Paul McCartney," *Journal of Popular Culture* 10 (1976): 110–121; Hal Morgan and Kerry Tucker, *Rumor!* (New York: Penguin, 1984), 82–87; Andru J. Reeve, *Turn Me On, Dead Man: The Complete Story of the Paul McCartney Death Hoax* (Ann Arbor [48106] Popular Culture, Ink [P.O. Box 1839], 1994); Ralph L. Rosnow and Gary Alan Fine, *Rumor and Gossip: The Social Psychology of Hearsay* (New York: Elsevier, 1976), chap. 2; Barbara Suczek, "The Curious Case of the 'Death' of Paul McCartney," *Urban Life and Culture* 1 (1972): 61–76.

Penis Captivus

The technical medical term for a couple becoming "stuck together during intercourse." See "The Stuck Couple."

Performance of Urban Legends

The term "performance" in folkloristics refers to the presentation of folklore as a form of "artistic communication" by the tellers and doers of all kinds of traditions. Analysis of verbal folk performances involves observing a host of details, including the "frame" in which a performance occurs, the verbal and gestural style of presentation, and the social context of the performance. From a performance perspective, the presentation of an urban legend might be seen more as a drama, a game, or some other interactive strategy rather than as a simple situation of one person telling a story to others.

Gillian Bennett applied a performance approach to contrast the telling of legends by two individuals, the first "an apparently believing narrator" and the second "an apparent skeptic." The former told the "absolutely true" story of "The Wife Left at the Roadside" (i.e., "The Nude in the RV"), while the second told the story, which he characterized as "nonsense," of "The Hairy-Armed Hitchhiker." Bennett showed in detail how each performance was characterized by specific features that supported the teller's viewpoint toward the truth or falsity of the story. The believing narrator tended (among other things) to assert directly the truth of the material, to be specific about details, and to maintain "a lively air of conviction and performative energy." The skeptical narrator, in contrast, tended to use a formulaic opening, to be vague about details, and to project "a 'distanced' performance strategy."

In her analysis of the "playful chaos" of a story-swapping session among a group of English university students, Bennett observed how apparently disjointed and confusing the session was. Still, her extracts from the tape recordings made of the event demonstrated how:

> The group is having fun, remembering a past occasion, recalling the stories which were told then, squeezing the maximum entertainment out of the familiar plots by drawing attention to their inherent unlikeness, and exploiting the processes of narrative to increase the sense of relaxed togetherness, consensus, joking communication and the general silliness of the mood.

Performance analysis moves a long way beyond the simple recording of "texts" of traditional stories; and it goes a long way toward a full understanding of what Bennett calls "the dynamic interaction of the story-*telling*."

See also Collecting Urban Legends; Context; Style of Urban Legends

References: Gillian Bennett, "Legend: Performance and Truth," in Bennett and Smith, *Monsters with Iron Teeth* (1988): 13–36; Gillian Bennett, "Playful Chaos: Anatomy of a Storytelling Session," in Bennett and Smith, *Questing Beast* (1989): 193–212; Elizabeth C. Fine, "Performance Approach," in Brunvand, *American Folklore: An Encyclopedia* (1996), 554–556.

"The Pet and the Naked Man"

See "The Cat (or Dog) and the Nude Man"

"The Pet Nabber"

A small pet—often a Chihuahua, a miniature dachshund, or a toy poodle and usually belonging to tourists—is snatched by a large bird, generally an eagle, an owl, or a pelican. Such things *do* happen, although the more likely predators on pets in many regions might be coyotes. In Australia the pet-

nabber story has become so prevalent that folklorist Bill Scott titled his 1996 compilation *Pelicans and Chihuahuas and Other Urban Legends*.

In 1993 the Associated Press distributed a doubtful story datelined Valdez, Alaska, about an eagle carrying off a "Chihuahua-like" dog belonging to a tourist couple traveling in a camper during a gas stop. Supposedly, while the wife was lamenting the loss of her pet, the husband stood on the other side of the camper chopping his hands in the air and muttering "Yeah! Yeah!" Yet another version of the story describes the demise of a small dog held by a tourist at a Marineland show; when a piece of meat is tossed into the tank during the shark feeding time, the dog leaps from its master's arms into the tank and is gobbled up before their eyes.

References: *Curses!*, 129–131; *Too Good*, 358–359.

Pets

See Animals in Urban Legends

"The Phantom Clowns"

Persistent rumors that spread all across the United States and became known as well in Great Britain maintained that groups of people dressed as clowns and traveling in vans painted a certain color (often black or blue) were abducting and murdering children. Most of the rumors circulated among young children themselves, some of whom claimed to have seen the clown-vans lurking near their schools or even driving off with victims inside. Investigations by adult authorities failed to discover any of the clowns, which therefore may be labeled "phantoms" until proven otherwise.

The first documented outbreak of the phantom-clown stories was from 1981, as reported by Loren Coleman. The scare of that year raged from New England through the Midwest and described clowns in a variety of disguises who were supposedly driving vans of many colors and wielding

swords, knives, or guns. Coleman suggested a possible connection to the stories of the Pied Piper of Hamelin; other commentators recalled the old fears about gypsies lurking around trying to abduct children.

A miniscare of killer-clown stories surfaced briefly in Phoenix, Arizona, in 1985, and the rumors returned in full force again in 1991 with reports ranging from New Jersey to Chicago and often likening the alleged threatening figure to the character Homey the Clown from the TV series *In Living Color*. The same year a phantom clown scare also hit Glasgow, Scotland. Besides Homey, other possible influences on the clown rumors may have been the Stephen King novel *It* and a video based on it, or the crimes of John Wayne Gacey, who in the late 1970s killed 33 boys near Chicago and was known to have entertained children at times wearing a clown suit. Although there is no record that Gacey ever used the clown disguise actually to entice children, he was dubbed "Killer Clown" by the media.

Educational and police authorities have thoroughly investigated claimed clown sightings, and newspapers have publicized the lack of findings. Here is the beginning of a typical report, one that indicates the considerable variations in detail, quoted from page one of the *Montclair (New Jersey) Times* of June 6, 1991:

Parents, Cops Quell False Rumors of "Killer Clown"

By Lucinda Smith

Someone dressed as Homey the Clown is not in Montclair trying to hurt children.

Someone dressed as Bart Simpson was not arrested for shoplifting in Montclair.

And none of the following has been seen in a van attempting to kidnap children in Montclair: Homey, Bart, Krusty the Clown, the four Teenage Mutant Ninja Turtles, the Smurfs, Bugs Bunny, the Little Mermaid, Barbie, Ken.

But nasty rumors about all of the above raged through Montclair elementary and middle schools last week, with gruesome stories spread quickly and widely among young children.

In neighborhoods and playgrounds, kids compared what they heard and wondered about its truth.

There is *no truth* to any of it.

Still the scary talk persisted.

Montclair police received about 50 telephone calls from parents, who "did the right thing to call us," said Deputy Chief John Corcoran.

"Most of the calls were about a so-called killer clown on the loose," he said. "But there were not real incidents of any kind, just unfounded rumors."

The motif of adults dressed as clowns also appears with a myriad of other themes in stories about supposed satanic ritual abuse. Tales about criminals cruising in black vans have circulated for years throughout Europe. But the phantom clowns tradition involving vans seems to be exclusively a part of childlore, perhaps reflecting children's actual distrust and even fear of clowns, who, ironically, are thought by adults to be invariably amusing to youngsters, most of whom would undoubtedly prefer a large, friendly, purple dinosaur to a clown any day.

References: *Baby Train*, 101–104; Loren Coleman, *Mysterious America* (Boston: Faber and Faber, 1983); chap. 19, 211–217.

"The Phantom Coachman"

This popular supernatural legend of the 1940s and 1950s incorporated the dream-warning motif—that is, a nightmare comes true. Although the legend has not been reported by folklorists since the 1950s, its appearance in a 1961 *Twilight Zone* TV episode kept the story alive as a subject for conversation. The following version of the story replaces the typical coach driver of the dream with a hearse driver; it was told by an Indiana University student in 1945 and published in the journal *Hoosier Folklore* (vol. 6, 1947: 58–59):

> This story was told to me by a middle-aged woman who was giving an account of a true story concerning a dream and its relation to an important incident. This is the dream and the incident as she told it to me:
>
> One of my friends in New York City had this horrible dream one night. She dreamed she was in the downtown section of new York City when suddenly she noticed a funeral procession passing by. It was one of the longest she had ever seen. She particularly noticed the driver of the hearse. He was a tall, rather sharp-featured man who sat very erect in his seat.
>
> The next morning, when she was preparing to go downtown to shop, she recalled the dream she had had the past night. The image of the driver came clearly into her mind once again, and she continued to think of him as she went to do her shopping. She entered a department store and was ready to step into the elevator when she noticed the operator. He was a tall, sharp-featured man resembling the man in her dream. It startled her, and she hurried to leave the elevator just as the door was closing. The elevator reached the third floor when she heard a screeching sound ending with a crash. The elevator had fallen, and everyone had been killed.

Because of the elevator accident at the end of most versions of this legend, and echoing a line often attributed to the sinister elevator operator, the story is sometimes called "Room for One More." Some versions of the legend were set in Chicago, and at times the driver of an already crowded taxi cab offers the dreamer a ride, saying (of course), "Room for one more!"

References: *Too Good,* 229–231.

"The Phantom Hitchhiker"

See "The Vanishing Hitchhiker"

"The Philanderer's Porsche"

Of the various stories involving people's fantasies about finding a highly desirable automobile for sale at an unbelievably low price, possibly the most popular example incorporates the revenge theme in which a wife gets back at her estranged or philandering husband. Variations of this legend have been widely passed in oral tradition and published by Ann Landers, as well as by numerous local newspaper columnists. The story was told on the air by Johnny Carson, among others, and rendered in song form by John McCutcheon.

The sale prices usually range from $10 to $500, and the makes and models of luxury vehicles mentioned are apparently unlimited. Thus

"The $50 Porsche," as the story is sometimes called, is something of a misnomer.

Here is a version of "The Philanderer's Jaguar" as published in the May 1995 issue of *Michigan Living,* an Automobile Club of America regional magazine. The story was used as a lead-in to a discussion of insurance rates in Michigan:

Drive Away with a Deal

The newspaper ad read: "For Sale: 1994 Jaguar convertible, $1. Thinking it a misprint, one reader called. "No," said the woman who answered the phone. "It's legitimate. Fork over $1 and the Jaguar is yours." Clearly aware of a good value when he saw one, the reader handed over the buck and drove away in a brand-new, luxury sports car. The catch? There was none.

Most people know a good value when they see one. . . .

[The article continues with its discussion of insurance rates, then concludes—]

For those of you wondering why someone would sell a Jaguar for $1, the answer is simple: the woman was recently divorced and was instructed by her ex-husband to sell his car. She did.

The Jaguar detail is actually more common in England, where as early as the 1940s tales were told of a husband's luxury car (sometimes a Rolls-Royce) that was sold cheaply by a bitter wife for anything from five to 50 pounds. Some British versions of the story claim that the terms of the late husband's will were to sell the car and give the money to his mistress.

See also "The Bargain Sports Car"; "The Death Car"; Mint Condition Vintage Vehicles

References: *Too Good,* 77–79; *Vanishing Hitchhiker,* 22–24.

Photocopy Lore

See Xeroxlore

"The Pig on the Road"

A popular American radio newsman became one more of many who have publicized this story, claiming it to be true, when he broadcast his version in January 1988. Here's how the Associated Press reported the incident shortly afterward:

WAURIKA, Okla. (AP)—One Waurika business has placed pig warning signs out front and residents are squealing about national attention their town got this week from radio commentator Paul Harvey.

As Harvey told it, Oklahoma Highway Patrolman Bill Runyan was driving down a rural road when he saw a farmer jumping up and down on the side of the road. While the trooper drove past, the farmer shouted "Pig, pig!"

Not to be insulted without retort, Harvey related, Runyan yelled back "Redneck, redneck!" But when he topped the hill, he ran into a 300–pound hog in the middle of the road.

Runyan insists it is nothing more than a story.

"Were the story true, I would have had to make an accident report," Runyan said. He did not file a report.

Runyan said the source of the story is a cousin who is a newspaper editor and that they often trade war stories based loosely on their experiences.

Actually, "The Pig on the Road" is told in Great Britain, Australia, and France with local variations, and it was published as far back as 1970 (by Bennett Cerf, who said it was an English story), and again in 1982 (by Leo Buscaglia), and in 1983 (by Robert Morley). Some people claim to remember it as being even older, perhaps from the 1950s.

Most foreign versions—and some American ones—lack the detail of the insulting term "pig" referring specifically to a police officer. Sometimes the loose animal, rather than being a road hog, is a sow or a cow. In his autobiography *A Kentish Lad* (New York: Bantam, 1997), Frank Muir tells an elaborate English version of the legend, identifying it as "my pig story" and humorously threatening a lawsuit against anyone who repeats it without credit. However, Muir admits that he found this "true" story "in a letter to a newspaper forty years ago."

References: *Curses!*, 127–128; *Mexican Pet*, 62; *Too Good*, 115–116.

"The Plant's Revenge"

This represents a true story, attested by local newspaper reports, similar in its general plot to "The Animal's Revenge," specifically "The Loaded Dog." Instead of a "wired" animal returning with its explosive load to kill or badly injure its tormentor, in this story a giant cactus wreaks revenge upon the man who was defacing it.

In February 1982, as two Phoenix, Arizona, newspapers reported the incident, one David Grundman was killed by a toppling giant saguaro cactus at which he had been shooting his rifle. The shots so weakened the plant that it fell, landing directly atop Grundman. The incident gained notoriety both locally and nationally with some variation of details occurring, thus making it legendlike, if not technically a legend. The death was celebrated in song by the Austin Lounge Lizards in their number titled "Saguaro," appearing on their 1984 album *Creatures from the Black Saloon*.

A suspicious story from another region tells of a hunter in Vermont killed by a porcupine's quills when he shoots the animal out of a tree and it falls directly onto him.

References: *Curses!*, 44–46; *Too Good*, 73–74.

Poetic Justice

Several urban legends illustrate the idea that people receive just what they deserve, whether punishment for bad behavior or (less commonly) rewards for doing good. A typical scenario in such stories is that a thief steals something of presumed value and ends up with something that is completely worthless and even shocking. Three examples involving theft: a nicely wrapped package that is snatched contains a cat's corpse; the tempting load on a stolen car's roof turns out to be a dead grandmother; the liquid contents of a stolen whiskey bottle is only a urine sample.

In "The Loaded Dog" and "The Plant's Revenge," a person who tortures an animal or destroys a plant is injured, or even killed, by the object of his attack. "The $50 Porsche" and several other stories depict an act of revenge against an offending spouse or a companion, and "The Videotaped Theft" and "Urban Pancake" depict thieves being detected and then receiving their just deserts. Pride preceding a fall, a variation of the poetic-justice theme, is illustrated in legends like "The Unstealable Car" and "The Blind Date," although the latter might also be considered to show how bad behavior may be punished.

Among the legends that illustrate good works being rewarded are "The Will" and "The Unexpected Inheritance," in both of which a person gains a valuable inheritance from some random act of kindness or affection.

Of course, there are many other legends in which no rewards or punishments are meted out, but someone merely becomes the victim of crime, an accident, or some other threat. The people hurt in "The Kidney Heist," "AIDS Mary," "Lights Out!" or "The Double Theft," for example, can hardly be said to deserve their fates for merely showing poor judgment or being careless.

See also Revenge in Urban Legends

References: *Too Good*, 66–88 ("Just deserts").

"The Poinsettia Myth"

Although folklorists generally reject the term "myth" for urban legends, the story of the supposedly deadly but popular Christmas plant is so often debunked by other writers under the rubric "myth" that this has become the shorthand way to refer to the tradition. In a nutshell, the claim is made that poinsettia plants are deadly poisonous and, thus, extremely hazardous to both animals and humans, especially children.

Possibly contributing to "The Poinsettia Myth" is that the name of the plant sounds somewhat like the word "poison," but the usual justification (if any) for the myth is some reference to a published 1919 account of an incident in which an army officer's son in Hawaii supposedly died after eating poinsettia leaves. This diagnosis was later disproved, but the erroneous first report has been repeated many times since in a variety of sources.

An Ann Landers column of March 1987 contained a letter from a distraught woman whose house cat supposedly died from eating poinsettias that had been sitting around since Christmastime. In her retraction published in May 1987, Landers cited government and university studies that had conclusively disproved the poinsettia's reputation as a killer. For example, research done at Ohio State University in 1975, when a proposal was made to put warning labels on poinsettias, concluded that a 50-pound child could eat more than 500 poinsettia leaves without becoming seriously ill. The *AMA Handbook of Poisonous and Injurious Plants*, a standard physicians' reference book, states that "*Euphorbia pulcherrima* [the poinsettia's scientific name] has been found to produce either no effect (orally or topically) or occasional cases of vomiting." Still, the *Handbook* indicated that poinsettia plants were consistently among the top eight plants about which people inquired to poison control centers.

Joining her sister Ann in debunking the myth, Abigail "Dear Abby" Van Buren wrote in a December 1988 column that "the beautiful poinsettia plant rates a clean bill of health—and comes out smelling like a rose." Here is the sensible comment on the question given in a pre-Christmas column on caring for poinsettias in the Salt Lake City *Deseret News* in 1998:

Like other nonfood items, the poinsettia may cause stomach discomfort if ingested, but nothing more.

Poinsettia poisoning is an "urban legend" that has long been associated with this plant. The best advice is to enjoy them as a plant and not as food, and you will not suffer any harmful effects.

References: *Mexican Pet,* 91–92.

"The Poison Dress"

One of the earliest urban legends to be noted by American folklorists, "The Poison Dress" (or "Embalmed Alive") was discussed in folklore collections and journal articles in the 1940s and 1950s, sometimes recalling the story being told in the 1930s. Ernest Baughman assigned Motif Z551 (*The poisoned dress*) to the modern versions; Stith Thompson describes Greek classical prototypes of the story (like "The Nessus Shirt") and assigns Motif D1402.5 (*Magic shirt burns wearer up*). Here is the plot summary from Baughman's index, based on versions published in 1945:

> Girl wears new formal gown to dance. Several times during the evening she feels faint, has escort take her outside for fresh air. Finally she becomes really ill, dies in the restroom. Investigation reveals that the dress has been the cause of her death. It had been used as the funeral dress for a young girl; it had been removed from the corpse before burial and returned to the store. The formaldehyde which the dress has absorbed from the corpse enters the pores of the dancing girl. [Note: Variants of the story usually mention a certain well-known store at which the dress was supposedly purchased; this circumstance suggests the possibility that the story is used as adverse publicity to discredit a certain business.]

Paul Smith reports that "this morbid legend has enjoyed increasing notoriety on both sides of the Atlantic." The legend continues to be told long after its initial popularity, with "embalming fluid" (a substance harmless to the living if merely applied topically) usually replacing the formaldehyde of earlier versions, but with specific department stores still mentioned by name. However, there is no evidence of rival businesses using such scare stories to generate adverse publicity, as Baughman speculated. The classical prototypes for "Embalmed Alive" mentioned either poisoned or burning garments given to a person as an act of revenge. Also related to the poison-dress theme are stories of contaminated blankets distributed to native peoples by colonists.

See also Motif

References: *Choking Doberman,* 112–114; "The Poisoned Dress," *Hoosier Folklore Bulletin* 4 (1945): 19–20; Adrienne Mayor, "The Nessus Shirt in the New World: Smallpox Blankets in History and Legend," *Journal of American Folklore* 108 (1995): 54–77; Adrienne Mayor, "Fiery Finery," *Archaeology* (March/April 1997): 54–58; J. Russell Reaver, "'Embalmed Alive': A Developing Urban Ghost Tale," *New York Folklore Quarterly* 8 (1952): 217–220; Smith, *Nastier Legends* (1986): 49; *Too Good,* 196–197.

"The Poisoned Pussycat at the Party"

Recalled by some tellers as being known in the 1930s and 1940s, "The Poisoned Pussycat" has been a favorite legend of journalists and other storytellers for at least 60 years. The *San Francisco Chronicle* columnist Herb Caen repeated it in 1969, and the *Chicago Tribune* columnist Mike Royko told his version in 1986. The story showed up once again in print in John Berendt's 1994 best-seller *Midnight in the Garden of Good and Evil.* Yet another version appeared in the 1989 film *Her Alibi.* The story is well known abroad as well, including versions from England, Australia, and Germany, and even one collected in Romania by this writer in 1981.

This legend exploits the jumping-to-conclusions theme, specifically by depicting a family's assumption that when their cat dies suddenly it must have been poisoned. Here is a typical version as told by an Ohio woman in 1991 (complete with a delightful dangling modifier opening the second paragraph):

My sister's boyfriend knows a family who had this unfortunate incident happen to them. They were the hosts of a backyard barbecue, and were grilling fish. The hostess found their cat sampling the fish before it was served to the guests, and subsequently chased it away. The guests, of course, were never told.

Upon finishing the meal, and preparing to return home, the cat was found dead in the driveway. The hostess notified all that the fish must have been tainted, as the poor kitty had tasted some, and met his maker. The host and hostess and all the guests made a beeline for the local emergency room where they all had their stomachs pumped.

Upon returning home, the host of the ill-fated barbecue found a note on his door from the neighbor which read, "Please accept our apologies for running over your cat. We will be happy to replace him."

The cat's demise, the stomach-pumping, and the note from the neighbor are consistent features of the legend, while the exact food that was nibbled varies from seafood or a casserole to mushrooms, pizza (with anchovies), or a stew. In the German version, the apparently dying kitty turns out to be delivering kittens and she is contentedly purring with her new babies when the queasy family returns from its hospital ordeal.

This and other urban legends about cats have led some journalists to dub all doubtful stories "Dead Catters."

References: *Too Good,* 44–45; *Vanishing Hitchhiker,* 111–112.

Poisonous Tomatoes?

Popular writers frequently assert that our American ancestors regarded the tomato as poisonous. One well-known encyclopedia claimed that "the tomato was introduced into cultivation in Europe during the 16th century, but in the United States was grown only as a curiosity for a long time because the fruit was thought to be poisonous." A supposed justification for this idea is the fact that the tomato is a member of the nightshade family, which includes some toxic plants.

The notion of poisonous tomatoes, if ever widely held, had certainly been dispelled by 1829 when the

Englishwoman Frances Trollope (1783–1863) traveled in the United States and wrote this tomato-blurb in her famous book *Domestic Manners of the Americans* (1832): "From June until December tomatoes (the great luxury of the American table in the opinion of most Europeans) may be found in the highest perfection in the market for about sixpence the peck."

Folklorist Warren E. Roberts gathered references from 1816 to 1855 that demonstrated "unequivocally that some Americans, at least, ate tomatoes well before the Civil War." He concluded his report with the hypothesis that "some people in the United States at some places and at some times may have considered tomatoes poisonous." But he guessed that the compilers of reference works might have extended a regional distrust of tomatoes to the whole country, and he applied this to the vague period of "a long time."

References: Warren E. Roberts, "Were Tomatoes Considered Poisonous?" *Pioneer America* 11 (1979): 112–113.

Poland

The urban legends of Poland began to be documented in the 1970s and 1980s; fortunately, there are several publications in English or with English summaries, and one good survey in German, to which the non-reader of Polish may turn for information. Among the contemporary-legend themes well covered in these sources are "The Black Volga" and other child-abduction and atrocity stories, rumors about food contamination, "The Poison Dress," and legends about the spread of AIDS. As Dorota Simonides commented in her 1990 survey of the collected material, "Those unusual stories which make one's blood run cold and sound even incredible prevail," but she added that "both tragic and very humorous events" appear in Polish urban legends (which is also true of many non-Polish variants on the same themes).

Dr. Dionizjusz Czubala of the University of Silesia in Katowice, Poland, has been the primary collector and publisher of Polish urban legends. His small 1985 book *Opowiesci z Zyci* (Tales Taken from Life) contained stories collected over many years by Czubala and his students, but the book came to the attention of American folklorists only in a 1993 review (see *Baby Train*, below), aided by the very concise English summary included in the original. Many of the legends in this collection, not surprisingly, deal with situations during World War II and the postwar communist era. Others are in the horror genre familiar in urban legends the world over.

"The Black Volga," a legend told since the 1970s in various versions in Russia as well as Poland (and perhaps elsewhere in Europe), combines the themes of child abduction and organ theft. It is said that people disguised as priests or nuns try to lure small children into a large black or red limousine (often a Russian Volga model) intending to drain the blood and steal the organs of the victims.

Rampant rumors of AIDS infection in Poland have circulated for years. The stories describe supposedly infected barbers, dentists, doctors, and even whole hospitals and prisons that people are advised to avoid for fear of catching the dreaded disease. Among Czubala's collected stories concerning this "black plague of the twentieth century," as he calls it, is the following exchange recorded from two students at the University of Silesia in May 1990:

> M.M.: I have a couple of friends in those circles (i.e. drug users), so I heard that a lot of them are sick. They all got the virus from a girl that had come from Warsaw. She slept around with a few guys from Katowice, and she got paid with dope. When she was leaving, she told them jokingly about her disease. Quite possible that she did this on purpose.
>
> A.K.: I heard a similar story. A girl slept with a guy and did not ask for money; instead she left a farewell message on the mirror. When the boy woke up, he read, "Welcome to the AIDS club." [See the entry "AIDS Mary"]

In 1996 Czubala published his major collection and study of Polish urban legends, *Nasze Mity Wspolczesne* (Our Modern Myths), containing 135 examples of "narrative threads" (i.e., individual stories) organized into nine chapters by subject matter. Although the book contains only a general summary in English, professor John Gutowski of Saint Xavier University, in Chicago, prepared an English summary of each chapter's topics especially for this entry. Here are the general topics, with the total number of stories for each category, along with three sample stories (citing, when possible, the familiar titles used in English) from each category:

1. *Komiczne* [13] (Jokes), including "The Exploding Toilet," "The Ski Accident," and "The Unlucky Contact Lenses."
2. *Wygrana* [12] (Gambling), including "The Lucky Lottery," "Bad Winnings," and "Two Rings for One."

3. *Ekscesy seksualne* [18] (Sexual Excesses), including "The Stuck Couple," "Sex with a Dog," and "A Father Raped His Own Daughter."

4. *Medyczne* [16] (Medical Stories), including "The Poison Dress," "Allergic to her Own Husband," and "AIDS at the Hairdressers."

5. *Obrzydliwosci* [9] (Disgusting Things), including "The Accidental Cannibals," "Roasted Rat," and "The Mouse in the Bottle."

6. *Zwierzeta atakuja* [19] (Animal Attacks), including "The Spider in the Cactus," "The Animal's Revenge," and "Ticks Inside the Body."

7. *Dzieci bez opieki* [7] (Abandoned Children), including "The Foolish Mother," "The Mock Hanging," and "A Chain of Misfortunes."

8. *Makabryczne* [10] (The Macabre), including "Worms in the Nose," "Little Hands Chopped Off," and "Blinded by a Razor Blade."

9. *Samochodowe* [31] (Automobiles), including "The Vanishing Hitchhiker," "The Wallet on the Roof," and "The Nude on the Highway."

As further examples of typical Polish urban legends, here are two stories from Czubala's latest book in translations prepared by his colleague, Anna Milerska:

A Mercedes for a Syrena

I heard about two smart students at the Technical University in Gliwice. They were desperate to have a car, but also short of money. So they bought an old Syrena [a Polish car that has not been produced for some 20 years], or maybe it was a Trabant [an East German car, also no longer manufactured]. They barely managed to drive the old car across the border into Czechoslovakia.

They spent a day or two in the Czech Cieszyn, drinking beer. Then they called the Czech customs officers and told them to watch out for a Syrena that would soon be returning to Poland, as its owners would be smuggling drugs.

When they approached the border, customs officers were waiting for them, and they searched the whole car. They simply took it to pieces. But no drugs were found, and then nobody could put all the parts together again. As a result, the Czechs had to buy them a new car, and they got a Mercedes! [Two other variants were collected.]

Blinded by a Razor Blade

This happened in Czestochowa. A girl was walking along, and a man caught her and ripped a gold chain off her neck. She kept walking, but now she was crying too. Another man met her in the street and asked why she was crying. She told him about that stolen chain, so he asked if she would recognize the thief. When she said she would, he took out a razor blade and cut her eyes. [Four other variants were collected.]

See also "AIDS Mary"; Revenge in Urban Legends

References: *Baby Train*, 242–244; D. Czubala, "The 'Black Volga': Child Abduction Urban Legends in Poland and Russia," *FOAFtale News* no. 21 (March 1991): 1–3; D. Czubala, "AIDS and Aggression: Polish Legends about HIV-infected People," *FOAFtale News* no. 23 (September 1991): 1–5; Dorota Simonides, "Moderne Sagenbildung im polnischen Großstadtmilieu," *Fabula* 28 (1987): 269–278; D. Simonides, "Contemporary Urban Legends in Poland," in Lutz Rörich and Sabine Wienker-Piepho, eds., *Storytelling in Contemporary Societies* (Tübingen, Germany: Gunter Narr Verlag, 1990), 45–50.

Police

Law enforcement officials, particularly local and state police, frequently figure in urban legends, not surprisingly most often in legends about crime. A police presence is typically introduced, for example, into such legends as "AIDS Mary," "The Baby-sitter and the Man Upstairs," "The Body in the Bed," "The Choking Doberman," and "The Hare Dryer." Even "The Vanishing Hitchhiker" mentions the police as the authorities to whom the mysterious disappearing figure is reported. When actual rumor panics strike a community, the police must become involved in investigating, and usually debunking, such stories as those about big-cat sightings, Halloween sadists, alleged satanic ritual abuse, and phantom clowns. Sometimes the stories have become so pervasive and disturbing to the public that the police must show a presence at the supposed sites of crimes in order to reassure people that they are safe.

Typically, bogus warnings about crime and other dangers will supposedly be validated by reference to the police as a source of information. See, for example, many of the warning fliers about "Blue Star Acid" and the "Lights Out!" crimes. Most often in such instances the police deny any part in distributing the warnings, although on occasion law enforcement personnel themselves have encouraged the rumors, often merely by suggesting that such crimes have been committed in other nearby communities but not in our own city—yet. The psychology involved in heeding the bogus warnings is "better safe than sorry."

Everyday police work is referred to in "The Arrest," a legend in which a police cruiser is accidentally stolen by a driver stopped for speeding. Similarly, "The Colander Copier Caper" deals with routine police interrogation, although the method described seems to be more a matter of rumor than of fact. "The Danger of Drugs Lecture" (or "Pass It On") is another legend depicting typical police activity. Such examples suggest that the police themselves must share a body of legendary lore.

Police corruption is implied in a few legends circulating mostly outside law enforcement circles. In general terms, it is often said that the police suppress information about crimes involving businesses (like shopping malls and department stores) in order to spare the companies any loss of revenue. A worse claim of corruption occurs in "The Sheriff's Daughter" (also called "The Cop on the Beach") in which officers trade sex with a suspect for dropping charges, only to discover that one of the young women involved is the daughter of one of the arresting officers.

See also Crime; FBI Stories; "The Hunter's Nightmare"; "The Pig on the Road"; "The Slasher Under the Car"; State Police "Balls"

References: Kenneth V. Lanning, "Satanic, Occult, and Ritualistic Crime: A Law Enforcement Perspective," *Police Chief* 56 (1989): 62–83; Kenneth V. Lanning, "Ritual Abuse: A Law Enforcement View or Perspective," *Child Abuse and Neglect* 15 (1991): 171–173; *Too Good*, 302–303.

Pop Rocks Cause Death

See "The Death of Little Mikey"

Popular Culture and Urban Legends

Urban legends are pervasive in contemporary popular culture. Because international culture is so media-dominated and technologically advanced, it is inevitable that there would be a strong overlap with modern folklore. In fact, legends and popular culture have intersected for centuries, ranging in time and topic from the distribution of lurid traditional ballads via sixteenth- to nineteenth-century printed broadside sheets to the ubiquitous circulation of modern legends on the Internet.

The distinction between folk and popular culture in this sense is that the "folk" traditions tend to be anonymous and variable as they are passed from person to person, whereas the "popular" versions derive from a known source (usually a commercial one) and tend to be more fixed in their form and content.

Urban legends are frequently alluded to in print-media stories and columns as well as in comic strips and cartoons, films and TV programs, advertising, popular music, and even in such "fringe" media as T-shirts, bumper stickers, and pins. Although a rich *oral* tradition of urban legends continues to flourish, these modern folk stories also circulate via print and broadcast media and especially on the Internet as frequently forwarded e-mail messages.

Popular culture provides the subject matter of many urban legends, including especially those about celebrities, the media, companies, fast foods, and various other institutions, products, and services.

See also Celebrities; Comics and Urban Legends; Computers; Film and Urban Legends; Internet Resources; Literature and Urban Legends; Music and Urban Legends; Musicians and Urban Legends; Radio and Urban Legends; Tabloids and Urban Legends; Talk Shows and Urban Legends; Television and Urban Legends; Xeroxlore

References: Paul Smith, "Contemporary Legend and Popular Culture: It's the Real Thing,'" *Contemporary Legend*, 1(1991), 123–152.

"Postcards for Little Buddy"

The story of "Little Buddy"—the alleged leukemia (or cancer) victim and postcard collector from Paisley, Scotland—was the prototype for the Craig Shergold legend and several other similar appeals to send inexpensive items for a sick child's collection. Starting in 1982 as a story circulating on citizens-band radio, the appeal claimed that Buddy's dearest wish was to see his name entered in the *Guinness Book of World Records* for amassing the largest collection of postcards. There was at that time no such record, and the child and his wish were mythical as

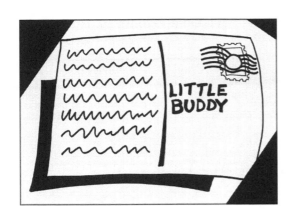

well, but the story grew and evolved into a version that continues to haunt Craig Shergold, who did, in fact, establish the record for collecting postcards as recorded in the 1989 edition of the *Guinness Book*. For more details, including the aftermath of Craig's feat, see the entry "Craig Shergold Legend."

References: *Curses!,* 227–232; Mark Schumacher, "The 'Little Buddy' Story," *American Philatelist* (November 1988): 1104–1105.

Pranks

Pranks and practical jokes are traditional customs in which a trickster attempts to lure others into believing or behaving foolishly. Such prankish behavior is a valid area of humorous folklore in itself. Familiar examples of "folk" pranks are "The Snipe Hunt" and "The Fool's Errand" (sending a new worker to fetch a nonexistent item). Besides April Fool's Day, a typical context for playing pranks is when initiating a newcomer, welcoming a foreigner, or introducing some other outsider to an occupation or a group. Pranks themselves are not legends, but when stories *about* pranks circulate and acquire variations, they may be considered a part of modern legendry.

One of the best-known prank legends concerns the cadaver's hand that was extended out of a car window to a highway toll-booth collector by waggish medical students. Probably this actual prank has seldom been performed, but lively accounts of supposed instances with varying details have circulated widely for decades. Other legends about student practical jokes describe activities like stealing garden ornaments and sending them on vacation, competing in prankish exploits with a rival college, and leading the general public to believe an outrageous lie (such as that urine samples should be brought to post-office branches on a certain day to test for a suspected epidemic).

There are some claimed instances of pranksters actually creating urban legends that have caught on with the public; some of these accounts may be true, especially in the modern age of e-mail and the Internet, which facilitate the rapid spread of stories.

See also "The Butcher's Prank"; Hoaxes; "Roaming Gnomes"; "Toll-Booth Pranks"

References: *Curses!*, 302–304; Moira Smith, "Prank," in Brunvand, *American Folklore: An Encyclopedia* (1996), 587–589.

"The Pregnant Shoplifter"

A news story circulated nationwide in February 1985 claimed that a pregnant woman in Arlington, Virginia, had been detained and searched by a sporting-goods store's personnel under suspicion of attempting to steal a basketball by concealing it under her clothes. To some journalists and folklorists this seemed too neat, too much like a legend, and, in short, "too good to be true." The story appeared to be an obvious variation of the legend about "The Shoplifter and the Frozen Food" in which a would-be thief conceals frozen food under his or her hat but is caught when either the product begins to melt or the thief faints from the cold while standing in the checkout line to buy an inexpensive item.

However, "The Pregnant Shoplifter" proved to be an authentic news story, eventually well covered in the press with names, dates, and other validating details furnished. The woman filed suit against the store for false arrest and negligence, seeking both compensatory and punitive damages. As reported in the *Washington Post* (November 19, 1986), she lost in court, but that does not mean her case is a genuine urban legend. (Still, a word-of-mouth story telling of a woman trying to steal a watermelon from a supermarket by hiding it under her dress and claiming to be pregnant has *not* been verified. Life and legend come very close together in such incidents and stories.)

References: *Curses!*, 177–179; *Mexican Pet*, 144; *Too Good*, 451–452.

"The Price of Cabbage Memo"

See "The Wordy Government Memo"

"The Procter & Gamble Trademark"

A bogus warning circulating since 1981 as a photocopied flier claims that the president of Procter & Gamble (P&G) bragged on a national TV program that his company donated a portion of its enormous profits to the Church of Satan and that "there are not enough Christians in the U.S. to make a difference." Supposedly the company's famous trademark—an encircled man-in-the-moon facing 13 stars—is a satanic symbol. The fliers list numerous P&G products and interpret the trademark's details, finding sinister meanings in the number of stars, the "horns" on the man's head, and the possible appearance of the "mark of the beast" (the number 666) in the stars and the man's beard. The fliers are usually distributed by fundamentalist Christians, and they urge readers to boycott P&G products. The idea is to prove to the president of P&G that there are enough Christians to "put a very large dent into his profits." Indeed, the company claims that lost sales and image deterioration have been considerable problems since the warnings emerged.

Despite the best efforts of folklorists, P&G officials, prominent religious leaders, and the TV talk-show hosts named in the fliers to debunk the story, it has persisted. True believers in these charges do not seem fazed by the facts that the TV programs sometimes named in the fliers are no longer on the air, that there is no identifiable "Church of Satan" to which donations could be made, and that P&G has removed the trademark from its products, explaining each one of the trademark's details as innocent design features that had been used for decades. P&G has even brought lawsuits against some individuals and companies who have spread the story. But the fliers continued to appear through the 1990s and may be expected to pop up again. Part of the reason for this is the mysterious nature of the trademark, which seems to have little connection with P&G's products; another reason is that old copies of the printed fliers may surface at any time from a desk drawer, a rack of religious tracts, or a cluttered bulletin board. Then it is a simple matter for a concerned citizen, unaware of the truth, to begin reproducing and circulating the fliers anew.

Procter & Gamble's latest lawsuit was brought against the Amway Corporation in 1995 after an Amway distributor in Ogden, Utah, spread the satanic rumor on the company's phone-message system. In March 1999 a federal judge in Salt Lake City dismissed the suit; P&G appealed that decision and was continuing to pursue other suits against Amway and individuals.

"The Procter & Gamble Trademark" provides a case study in the endurance of bogus warnings, the damage that may result when a leading company is targeted, the futility of trying to counter such stories, the willingness of some people to believe unlikely and undocumented claims, and the power—whether positive or negative—of a company's image-building trademark.

References: Dana Canedy, "Advertising: After Two Decades and Counting, Procter & Gamble Is Still Trying to Exorcise Satanism Tales," *New York Times* (July 29, 1997); *Choking Doberman*, 169–186; *Too Good*, 404–406.

"The Proctological Examination"

A generalized medical horror story told among laypersons describes the death of a patient whose colon exploded during examination when a spark from the examining device ignited intestinal gasses. Probably such stories derive from journalistic reports of actual, although rare, cases that are occasionally described in the medical literature.

Marc-Andre Bigard et. al. (1979) reported a case from the central university hospital in Nancy, France, from 1977, describing it as "the first reported colonic explosion during colonoscopic polypectomy." But United Press International had reported a similar case that occurred in Garden City, New York, in 1974; it resulted in a lawsuit, which the attending physician lost.

Although exploding creatures may safely be identified as an urban-legend theme (e.g., "The Death of Little Mikey"), this particular version does have a basis in fact, however rare the actual incidents. Changes in operating procedures and in the equipment used have now eliminated the chance of such accidents occurring again.

See also Exploding Animals

References: Marc-Andre Bigard, Pierre Gaucher, and Claude Lassalle, "Fatal Colonic Explosion During Colonoscopic Polypectomy," *Gastroenterology* 77 (1979): 1307–1310; *Choking Doberman,* 98–99.

Professions

See Academe, Legends of; Business Legends; Government Legends; Law Legends; Legal Horror Stories; Musicians and Urban Legends

"Promiscuity Rewarded"

See "The Unexpected Inheritance"

"The Promiscuous Cheerleader"

A female high school or college cheerleader faints during a game and is rushed to a hospital. It is discovered that she had performed oral sex on all the members of the men's football (or other) team, and an amazing amount of semen must be pumped from her stomach. Gary Alan Fine and Bruce Johnson analyzed the psychological and social functions of 29 versions of the story collected in Minnesota, in particular noting its popularity among male adolescents during the early 1970s, often told to belittle members of a rival school.

The female student fainting for a reason only revealed at the hospital is reminiscent of the spiders-in-the-hairdo legend, and revealing sexual misbehavior is a common theme in many urban legends. Pumping semen from someone's stomach is also described in contemporary legends about certain male rock stars.

References: Gary Alan Fine and Bruce Noel Johnson, "The Promiscuous Cheerleader: An Adolescent Male Legend," in Fine, *Manufacturing Tales:* 59–68 [chapter originally published in 1980].

Proto-Legend

Rumors, beliefs, experiences, news stories, bits of film and TV plots, and even jokes may constitute the raw material of legends and are sometimes termed "proto-legends." As the Finnish folklorist Leea Virtanen commented, while contemplating the possibility of observing "the birth of a protoform" in modern folklore, "It is possible to imagine that our environment is bristling with narratives that are potential primordial cells for folklore." Proto-legend versus "true" legend is not a very precise distinction, but certainly for a text to be identified as a legend it must have clear narrative elements plus some variations in details created by people's unself-conscious repetition of the story.

References: Brunvand, "Some News from the Miscellaneous Legend Files," in *The Truth:* 160–169; *Vanishing Hitchhiker,* 174, 194; Leea Virtanen, "Modern Folklore: Problems of Comparative Research," *Journal of Folklore Research* 23 (1986): 221–232.

Pull-Tab Collecting

See Redemption Rumors

"Push-Starting the Car"

This legend of technical incompetence regarding automobiles dates back to the introduction of automatic transmission in the 1950s and was sometimes earlier applied to cars equipped with Hydromatic, Fluid Drive, or Dynaflow. In every case, such cars, if stalled with a dead battery, needed to be brought up to a particular speed in order to be push-started. Typically—and stereotypically—the person who misunderstood the intent of this requirement was a woman. In July 1954 *Reader's Digest* published a short item mentioning "more than 100" claimed reports of this incident from all across the United States and even the Canal Zone.

Here is the usual scenario: A man's car is stalled on a highway, and he flags down a woman motorist to ask for a push-start. He explains that since his car has automatic transmission, she will have to get it up to 35 miles per hour to start it. She agrees, and they both get back into their respective cars. After a longish pause, the man looks into his rear-view mirror just in time to see the woman's car, which she has backed several yards away, coming at him at 35 miles per hour. Both cars are badly damaged.

Other legends of automotive technical incompetence concern misunderstanding either cruise control or the gear indicators on shift levers or push buttons.

See also "Cruise Control"; "'R' Is for Race"

References: *Choking Doberman,* 65; *Too Good,* 294–295.

Queensland Folk

Legendary Australian folklorist Bill Scott published a series of short articles about urban legends from Down Under in *Queensland Folk*, the journal of the Queensland Folk Federation, starting in 1986. The subjects and relevant issues of six of these, published from 1988 to 1991, are described as entry number 140 in Bennett and Smith's *Bibliography* (1993). Most of this material was later incorporated into Scott's popular books of yarns and legends.

See also Australia

"The Queensland Poet" (James Brunton Stephens)

See Australia

"The Queer Roommate"

See "The Gay Roommate"

"'R' Is for Race"

A technologically challenged driver is confused about the meanings of the letters marked on the gear shift of his new car. He interprets "D" for "Drag," "L" for "Leap," and "N" for "Nothing." Then, while racing on the highway with another hot new car, he shifts into "R" for "Race," and his transmission blows up. In a variant version, the driver selects "P" for "Pass." ("R" actually denotes "Reverse," and "P" denotes "Park.")

This incident is often attributed to a young driver, a woman, or to a minority person who is supposedly unfamiliar with automotive advances. In one version the driver is the chauffeur for a southern state official. The story was popular as a legend when automatic transmission was a relatively new option, and a few early models actually had reverse placed between drive and low. In later years, the story was told more as a joke than a legend. The southern comedian Brother Dave Gardner, popular in the 1950s and 1960s, told it as a regular part of his standup routine. Yet another variation of the story describes a man teaching his wife to drive; she asks if "D" is for "Dirt Roads" and "P" is for "Pavement."

References: *Curses!*, 117.

Racism in Urban Legends

The same taint of racism found in superstitions, jokes, parodies, and other forms of folklore is evident in some urban legends. "The Elevator Incident" is a good example, when—invariably—the white passengers on the elevator assume that the large black man with the dog must be a mugger. The race of the man, who is really a celebrity, is emphasized in the story when tellers imitate the dialect speech of his request "Hit fo!": (Hit four! [i.e., for the fourth floor]), misunderstanding his request as "Hit the floor!" Another popular urban legend with a frequent black character, this time one who is mistaken for a thief, is "The Package of Cookies." Several other legends about mistaken identifications similarly deal with blacks or Hispanics believed to be menial workers when, in fact, they are celebrities.

Another strain of racism is evident in "The Choking Doberman" versions in which "black fingers" are a detail simply added to the legend by many who retell the basic story of the dog that defends the home against a burglar. Similarly, in "The Mutilated Boy," many contemporary versions convert the anti-Semitism of the medieval prototype into the racial stereotyping more typical of modern crime narratives.

See also "Lights Out!"; Mistaken Identifications; Social Class in Urban Legends; Talk Shows and Urban Legends

References: Venetia Newall, "The Black Outsider: Racist Images in Britain," in *Folklore Studies in the Twentieth Century: Proceedings of the Centenary Conference of the Folklore Society* (London: The Folklore Society, 1980), 308–311.

Radio and Urban Legends

Radio disc jockeys and talk-show hosts play a significant role in eliciting urban legends from listeners, and sometimes in spreading the stories further via the airwaves. (For accounts of some specific urban legends circulated in this way, see *The Baby Train*, pp. 15–17 and 159.) Even radio newscasters may repeat doubtful rumors and tales; although generally debunking such stories, the newspersons' explanations may not be remembered as well by listeners as are the legendary material itself. Some on-air personalities—notably Paul Harvey on a national scale—seem to have a particular affinity for odd stories and weird "news," some portions of which have proven to be urban legends.

Amateur radio, especially citizens-band broadcasts, may also disseminate urban legends. "Postcards for Little Buddy" evidently first made the rounds on citizens-band radio, then later spread to the public at large.

The background story for "Bozo the Clown's Blooper," a TV-based legend, is the much older tale "Uncle Don's Blooper," concerning a mishap during a live radio broadcast. The legend about "The Madalyn Murray O'Hair Petition" concerns a supposed attempt to ban religious broadcasting both on television and radio.

Railroads

See "The Baby Train"; "The Bedbug Letter"; "The Cut-Out Pullman"; "The Last Kiss"; "The Misguided Good Deed"

"The Rape Trial"

See "The Witness's Note"

"The Rat in the Rye Bread"

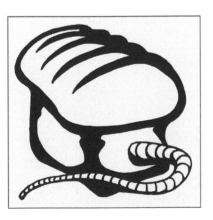

A popular legend of the 1940s told both in Canada and the United States claimed that a bakery—always specified as a specific local company—had accidentally baked a rat into a loaf of rye bread. The bread was bought unsliced, and the rat was discovered when the loaf was sliced at home. Perhaps rye was considered more folksy, or just more "natural," than white or wheat loaves. Often it was said that the bread buyer actually bit into the rodent, then reported the contamination. It was sometimes claimed that when the bakery that produced the loaf was inspected later on, numerous health violations were discovered. Allegedly the victim won a large monetary settlement in the case.

"The Rat in the Rye Bread," although occasionally remembered by older people, is not told often nowadays. Instead, the rodent-infested-food theme appears in the legends "The Mouse in the Coke" and "The Kentucky Fried Rat."

References: *Choking Doberman*, 120–121; *Too Good*, 176–177.

"The Rattle in the Cadillac"

As a prank, or because of some disgruntlement with management, an assembly-line worker at a luxury-automobile factory sabotages a new car by putting something inside a door panel that will rattle annoyingly when the car is driven. He adds a note taunting the owner, should he ever locate the source of the rattle. The car is not always a Cadillac, and the wording of the note varies (e.g., "So you finally found it, you SOB!" or "Aha! You found me!"). The stowaway objects may be a pop bottle, nuts and bolts, or miscellaneous trash, sometimes being suspended inside the panel on a string. There are some claims that the prank has actually been carried out, but it is certainly so much idle talk around automobile factories rather than a frequent real occurrence. Some versions of the story conclude with the wealthy car owner framing the junk and the note, displaying them in his plush office, presumably as a sort of trophy commemorating his victory over the blue-collar worker-saboteur.

Other urban legends involving some kind of car crime and a note are "The Dishonest Note," "The Double Theft," and "The Unstealable Car." A luxury car is also the subject of legends like "The Bargain Sports Car," "The Death Car," "The Philanderer's Porsche," "The Solid Cement Cadillac," and others.

References: *Choking Doberman*, 62–63; *Too Good*, 275–276.

Razor Blade Sabotage

The most common claim of the Halloween-sadists rumors are that people plant razor blades or needles inside apples or other treats given to children on the holiday. Razor blades are also sometimes said to have been planted on amusement park rides and other attractions—particularly water slides. Decades of annual X-raying of children's Halloween treats, and repeated searches of amusement rides, have failed to detect any such actual sabotage, although there is always the chance of copycat crimes—even if there was no original crime to copy.

See also Amusement Park Dangers; Halloween Sadists

"Red Velvet Cake"

The prototype story for various expensive-recipe legends was "Red Velvet Cake," an American legend that emerged in the 1960s and soon became attached to the Waldorf-Astoria hotel in New York City. Supposedly a diner in the restaurant there asked for the secret recipe for a delicious red cake with white frosting, and he or she was billed an outrageous amount for it (from $25 to $100, usually). The "secret" proved to be merely adding a large amount of red food coloring to a normal white cake recipe. The diner was unable to avoid paying the demanded price, so in revenge he or she circulated the recipe for free. Copies of the recipe that supposedly brought about the scam have been widely distributed for decades, person-to-person and also via mail and e-mail. These recipes make a decent cake that many people find appealing and delicious, and somehow the existence of actual red velvet cakes seems to convince some that the legend is true.

A taste for various kinds of red cakes is documented back to the early part of the twentieth century, while expensive-recipe stories were told about a variety of dessert foods at least by the 1940s. One of the early companies to exploit the recipe in advertising was the Adams Extract Company of Austin, Texas, which has long linked the cake to its own brand of red food coloring. The Waldorf-Astoria, in contrast, up to about 1979, consistently denied the story and disputed the idea of ever having served a bright red cake in their restaurants. Later, however—yielding to the power of legend—the hotel began sending out a free copy of their supposedly "authentic" red velvet cake recipe to anyone who inquired.

The luxury reputation of the large and famous Waldorf-Astoria and the regal suggestions of "red velvet" contrast in this legend with the negative image of a large company overcharging an unwary customer. The unusual color of the cake and the guarded "secret" of its production, along with the holiday association of red foods (with Valentine's Day and

Christmas especially) all contribute to the appeal of the story. Folklorist Keith Cunningham found another reason to focus on this legend when he parodied Freudian interpretations of folklore in an essay that described the product as a "sexy cake" and claimed to find sexual symbolism even in the frosting, the cutting, and the serving of the cake.

By the mid-1980s the expensive-recipe legend had shifted to cookies and fixed itself first upon Mrs. Fields Cookies and later on the Neiman Marcus company.

See also The Goliath Effect; "The Mrs. Fields Cookie Recipe"; "Neiman Marcus Cookies"

References: Keith Cunningham, "Reflections and Regurgitations," *Folklore Forum* 5 (1972): 147–148; *Curses!*, 221–224; *Too Good*, 257–259; *The Truth*, 62–75; *Vanishing Hitchhiker*, 154–160.

Redemption Rumors

Huge collections of otherwise useless items are saved under the mistaken notion that a large corporation will redeem the items by providing health benefits to the needy. The most common pattern is to save great quantities of aluminum pull tabs from soft-drink cans believing that they can be exchanged for time on kidney dialysis machines. The collecting points for pull tabs in schools, churches, and workplaces often display a notice mentioning some pathetic case of a poor child awaiting dialysis treatment, presumably in a local hospital. The belief persists, and pull-tab collecting goes on and on, even though kidney dialysis is paid for by insurance or government programs and nobody is providing dialysis in exchange for pull tabs, which are worth exactly their weight in aluminum. (Some, however, claim that the aluminum on a can's top is "purer" and thus worth more.) It would be far more effective, but apparently not as satisfying, for people to recycle the whole cans, or in certain states to collect the can deposits, and then donate the returns to charity.

Gary Alan Fine traced prototypes for the pull-tab beliefs in earlier campaigns to save useless things like empty cigarette packages or tea-bag tabs, supposedly to help provide seeing-eye dogs, wheelchairs, or iron lung treatment to unfortunate sufferers. Fine suggested that both companies and individual collectors are imagined to "redeem themselves" by these rumored good deeds for having produced or used unhealthy products.

The early design of the pull-tab can was eventually altered so that drinks could be opened without detaching the tab. Even though more effort is now required to remove these tabs, the collecting-for-charity rumors continue. Newspapers have reported scores of examples of well-meaning local individuals and groups amassing gargantuan collections of pull tabs, only to learn that no hospital anywhere is accepting them as payment for kidney dialysis or any other health benefit.

In 1988 Reynolds Aluminum and the National Kidney Foundation launched an ambitious "Keep Tabs on Your Cans" campaign debunking the stories, but to little avail. The misguided collections have continued, and beginning in the late 1980s various institutions, especially Ronald McDonald House, have launched campaigns urging people to send in their pull-tab collections for recycling, with the proceeds going to support the program. Queries to the company about why the whole cans are not recycled, and pointing out the relative worth of pull tabs versus the cost of mailing them, have all been met with ill humor directed toward those who would "spoil the fun" and specious arguments about "health concerns" and the supposed inconvenience of saving whole cans. The trademarked slogan of these campaigns is "Help pick up the tab for the Ronald McDonald House," and small, house-shaped collecting boxes (provided by Coca Cola) have been widely distributed. Thus legend, to some extent, has become reality.

References: Gary Alan Fine, "Corporate Redemption," in Fine, *Manufacturing Tales*, 189–208; *Mexican Pet*, 169–174; *Too Good*, 264–266.

Reebok Rumors

Reebok International, an American corporation best known for its line of popular athletic shoes, is rumored among African Americans either to be owned by the Ku Klux Klan or to be headquartered in South Africa and using its profits to support the white minority there. This conspiracy story was one of several dealing with popular brands of clothing that began to circulate in the late 1980s; other brands of athletic wear sometimes mentioned were TROOP Sport and the import line British Knights.

The name itself—a reebok is a common variety of gazelle in South Africa—may have some bearing on the rumors, although the company does not manufacture or market its products in that country. Even so, the rumor was common and convincing enough to cause some African Americans to stop wearing Reebok sneakers, and the company launched a campaign to dispel the stories.

Patricia Turner has discussed how the rumors relate to the symbolic significance of certain athletic wear, the rising costs of much-desired brands, the perceived "meanings" of names and trademarks, and misinformation concerning company ownership and policies. She suggested that a high product price associated with some risk in acquiring the desired product (i.e., stealing money or shoes, and diverting one's limited income to buy expensive gear), combined with the limited utility of the products, is a likely formula for generating such rumors.

See also Church's Chicken Rumors

References: Patricia A. Turner, *I Heard It Through the Grapevine* (1993), 127–136, 172–176.

"The Relative's Cadaver"

An actual incident of a female student's own late great aunt being one of the cadavers (*not* the one she was dissecting) assigned to the student's gross anatomy class was reported in a letter published in the *Journal of the American Medical Association* in 1982. The case drew wide attention from the media and seemed to confirm the truth of the urban legend about a relative's cadaver being assigned to a medical student for dissection. However, the legend is much older, and it invariably involves the student's own close relative (usually a sibling, mother, father, or grandparent) being recognized as the assigned study object. No such incident has ever been reported, although many variant versions of the story circulate among medical students as well as the general public.

As Frederic W. Hafferty pointed out in his survey of medical students' cadaver stories, usually the discovery of the relative's cadaver is said to have occurred on the first day of the anatomy lab, although sometimes it occurs near the end of the class when "nothing was left to do except the head and neck dissection." The shocked student—generally a male—may suffer great emotional or even physical upset, but usually he is described as able to work through his distress and return to complete his studies. Thus the legend is a sort of parable illustrating how medical students must prepare themselves to work with human subjects.

A similar story was told about the body of the English novelist Laurence Sterne, who died in 1768, being delivered to the Cambridge University medical school where it was recognized by a friend. This tale has been rejected by Sterne's most recent biographers as nothing but a legend.

References: *Choking Doberman,* 99–102; Frederic W. Hafferty, "Cadaver Stories and the Emotional Socialization of Medical Students," *Journal of Health and Social Behavior* 29 (1988): 344–356; "Her Relative Was the Cadaver," letter published in the *Journal of the American Medical Association* 247 (1982): 2096, signed by Drs. E. George Salter Jr. and Clarence E. McDanal Jr. of the University of Alabama School of Medicine; *Too Good,* 208–209.

Religion and Urban Legends

Sometimes a specifically religious detail is inserted into an otherwise secular (although perhaps supernatural) urban legend, as when the mysterious disappearing hitchhiker is revealed to be a heavenly messenger or even Jesus Himself. Similarly, Billy Graham has suggested that "The Ghost in Search of Help" might be interpreted as being an angel. Other examples of motifs related to religion in contemporary legends include the ministerial presence at the conclusion of "The Nude Surprise Party" and the taboo against looking back (as in the biblical story of Lot's wife) in "The Boyfriend's Death."

Anti-Semitism is an overt theme in "The Jewish Secret Tax," and it lurks in the background of "The Mutilated Boy" with its roots in the ancient blood-libel story. The legend about "The Lesson in Compassion" makes the point that Christians' actual behavior may sometimes be at odds with everyday life decisions, a point also made in a more benign way in the legend of "The Missionaries and the Cat."

Fundamentalist Christians in the modern world seem to specialize in circulating a number of legends concerning conspiracies, spreading the word via broadcasts, publications, tracts, preaching, and word of mouth. Some favorite topics are "The Communist Rules for Revolution," "The Madalyn Murray O'Hair Petition," "The Missing Day in Time," "The Procter & Gamble Trademark," "The Well to Hell," and stories falling into the category "Satanic Panic." (Each of these topics has a separate entry in this encyclopedia.)

Within religious groups various faith-promoting and inspirational stories also circulate, some of them with doubtful claims to truth. One collector of such stories calls them "evangelegends," with reference to such parables as one about a young woman protecting herself from muggers by shouting a biblical verse at them, except she garbles the wording and actually succeeds in frightening them off only by her "crazy" behavior. Other such stories describe the miracle of helpful dolphins answering prayers and rescuing a drowning child, a Catholic boy punished for not swallowing the Host at communion, and instant conversions of wicked persons brought about by their seeing a Gideon bible in their motel room.

See also "Buried Saint Sells Property"; "The Holy Place"; "Miracle at Lourdes"; Music and Urban Legends; Talk Shows and Urban Legends; Tricky Questions and Answers

Restaurants

See Chinese Restaurants; Church's Chicken Rumors; Contamination; "The Dog's Dinner"; "The Eaten Pets"; Fast Food; "The Grocery Scam"; "The Kentucky Fried Rat"; Masturbating into Food; McDonald's Rumors

"The Resubmitted Term Paper"

A student submits as his or her own work to a college course a term paper that he or she has plagiarized, or bought from a company supplying such papers, or found in the college's "crib" files, or otherwise acquired in violation of the rules. Sometimes it is a paper that has been submitted time and again by students at that college, always with minimal changes, and heretofore always earning a passing grade from the instructor.

This time the instructor's grade is higher (or lower) than before, and the comment indicates the instructor's awareness of the scam. Typical comments include, "I've read this paper four times now, and I like it better each time"; or, "I liked it better with the whale"; or, "This is a paper I myself wrote as an undergraduate, and I always thought it deserved a better grade."

See also Tricky Questions and Answers

References: *Curses!*, 286–87; *Too Good,* 441–442.

"The Resurrected Rabbit"

See "The Hare Dryer"

Resusci Anne Legend

See CPR Annie Legend

Revenge in Urban Legends

In a 1982 paper published two years later, the Swedish folklorist Bengt af Klintberg contrasted the bloody, aggressive, and gleeful personal revenge depicted in a Greenland Eskimo legend from the early twentieth century with the symbolic revenge theme found in certain modern urban legends. He suggested that since "it is no longer considered a social duty to take personal revenge," feelings of revenge have become taboo, and the treatment of the theme in contemporary legends has changed. He discussed three examples that illustrate "how deviators from socially accepted norms attack the security of normal citizens and are punished in return." This punishment (in "The Hook," "The Severed Fingers," and "The Choking Doberman"), he pointed out, comes not from the victims but from the aggressors themselves or from an animal.

A fourth example offered by af Klintberg is "The Solid Cement Cadillac" in which—depending upon the version told—the husband either gains revenge against his wife's actual lover or punishes *himself,* duped into mistakenly filling his own car with cement, believing it to be a rival's car when there really is no lover.

Although we may accept af Klintberg's general conclusion that some modern legends demonstrate how feelings of revenge are repressed and the punishment is symbolized or comes from the aggressor himself, there is no shortage of urban legends depicting direct and personal revenge. The most obvious examples are titled for their major theme: "The Animal's Revenge," "The Lover's Telephone Revenge," "The Plant's Revenge," "The Roughneck's Revenge," "The Wife's RV Revenge," and so forth. Other legends with similar themes are "Indecent Exposure," "The Package of Cookies," "The Rattle in the Cadillac," and "The Unfortunate Gas Thief."

The parties involved in the revenge theme in urban legends may be husband and wife, feuding lovers, workers and employers, rich and poor, criminals and victims, members of different races or social classes, and the like. Sometimes the revenge motive is obvious and even stated, as in "AIDS Mary" and the needle-attack stories, whereas in other cases like "The Dead Cat in the Package" and "The Runaway Grandmother" it is merely implied that the aggressor got what he or she deserved, and thus the victim's revenge was accomplished.

An actual desire for revenge is enacted in "Red Velvet Cake" when the characters in the legend distribute the expensive recipe in order to retaliate for having to pay an outrageous price in the first place. When other people pass on the story and the recipe, they are participating in the revenge against big business, although it must be remembered that no incident of any business actually charging for the recipe has occurred. In a similar way, people who distribute the Procter & Gamble trademark fliers are hoping to encourage revenge against the supposedly offending company by asking for a boycott of its products. Other boycott efforts based on rumors and legends have been directed against clothing designers, fast-food companies, sports-gear manufacturers, and other big businesses.

Modern legends about personal, aggressive, physical revenge are not entirely lacking. Examples include "Superglue Revenge" and "Old Versus Young" (or "Revenge of the Rich"), the former depicting a lover's harmful response to infidelity and the latter an incident of road rage. A legend from Dionizjusz Czubala's 1996 collection from Poland illustrates that the theme of "primitive" bloody revenge was still alive as recently as 1979 in that country (as it surely is elsewhere); this example and two further variants of the story were collected:

> It happened in Zabkowice, near the water reservoir. A group of gypsies was just camping there at the time. One of their kids ran on to the road and was

knocked over by a truck. Since the child was alive, the truck driver stopped some cars and they took the child to the nearest hospital. On the road he left the truck with his small daughter inside. As he came back, he saw his daughter's head on the hood of his truck. The gypsies had killed her in revenge. He said nothing to that, just took his truck to their camp and destroyed it all, killing forty-two gypsies. It happened this week, on Friday, I believe.

See also "Bikers Versus Smokers"; "The Robber Who Was Hurt"; "Truckers and Bikers"

References: Bengt af Klintberg, "Why Are There so Many Modern Legends about Revenge?" in Smith, *Perspectives* (1984), 141–146.

"Revenge of the Rich"

See "Old Versus Young"

"Roaming Gnomes"

First reported in 1986 in England and Australia, "Roaming Gnomes" depicts the student prank of stealing a garden ornament and sending it on "vacation," with snapshots and postcards mailed home to its owners before the ornament itself is eventually returned. The first targets were the small plaster or plastic garden gnomes that were popular as yard decorations in Great Britain and Down Under. Whether the actual pranks or merely the stories describing them came first cannot be determined, but certainly in later years the prank itself has been perpetrated many times in several different countries. Examples are well documented in newspaper and magazine articles, complete with examples of photographs of the wandering artifact.

Among the many items that have been stolen and taken on tour are various other elf and dwarf figures, plastic flamingos, a wooden rabbit, a stone frog, metal jockey-boy statues, and decorative plastic snowmen and other Christmas decorations (including baby Jesus from a manger scene). The mere snatching of a yard ornament is not the "tradition" here; the authentic prank requires that the figure be taken on a tour and photographed at different sites, then returned unharmed to its home. Also, the postcards and/or photos are an essential ingredient. Probably "Roaming Gnomes" is an instance of the publicizing of a practical joke leading to more and more people deciding to enact the prank themselves.

See also Ostension

References: *Curses!,* 305–310; "On the Road: Heigh-Ho, Heigh-Ho, It's Far, Far Off We Go; or, Grumpynappers Give a Cement Dwarf a Joyride," *People* (June 26, 1989): 100–101.

"The Robber Who Was Hurt"

In the modern legend on this theme, a woman, often elderly, is home alone when she hears or sees somebody trying to gain entry through the front door of her home or apartment. The door is fastened with a chain, and a hand is seen reaching in, attempting to open or force the lock. (Sometimes the door is actually opened, but the intruder is disguised with a ski mask.) The woman drives away the intruder by burning his hand, sometimes with the hot iron she was using at the time, or in other versions snatching up a hot poker from her blazing fireplace. After the man runs screaming from her door and the porch or hallway is quiet, the woman goes to her next-door neighbor to tell her about the attempted forced entry. But the neighbor stops her, saying, "I'm sorry, but I can't talk now; my husband just came home with his hand badly burned, and I have to take care of him."

"The Robber Who Was Hurt," a popular urban legend in Britain that seems to be told less often elsewhere, has been identified as an updating and rationalizing of a much older legend, "The Witch Who Was Hurt." The prototype story corresponds in part to the traditional folktale "The Clever Maid at Home Kills the Robbers," which is Tale

Type 956B. In the earlier story the intruder is a witch who is able to take animal form—usually as a dog or cat—while preying upon her neighbors. One day someone manages to injure the demon-animal on a front paw; the next day an old woman in the neighborhood is seen with the corresponding hand bound up with a bandage. (Sometimes a paw is cut off, and the witch is seen with her hand missing.) The older supernatural motif is, thus, rationalized into its modern urban form, as Jacqueline Simpson showed in her 1981 discussion of several variants of these legends.

In the United States "The Robber Who Was Hurt" has occasionally been told in combination with "The Double Theft," with the original theft being an unsuccessful ruse to get the woman out of her home. Staying home the night of the intended burglary, the woman is able to rout the robber by the usual means—a hot iron or poker—learning later that her neighbor's husband had suffered a burned hand that same night. A recent American version of the legend has the crime victim dissuade the attacker by rubbing his fingers with sandpaper.

See also Tale Type

References: *Baby Train,* 121–121; *Choking Doberman,* 37–41; Jacqueline Simpson, "Rationalized Motifs in Urban Legends," *Folklore* 92 (1981): 203–207; *Too Good,* 309–311.

Rolls-Royce Legends

Arguably "the world's best car," the Rolls-Royce is certainly one of the most expensive, most meticulously assembled, most reliable, and most conservative and stodgy of luxury cars. As such, the Rolls-Royce and its British manufacturers have inspired numerous stories about their legendary reputation.

In 1969 in a pioneering article on urban legends Stewart Sanderson listed 11 items of Rolls-Royce folklore that he had collected. Typical themes of these stories were that several mechanical parts of the cars were sealed to prevent owners from tinkering, that the company prevents owners from doing any kind of modifications to the cars' design, that the noisiest thing in a Rolls-Royce is the dashboard clock, and (the most common breakdown story) that the company quickly replaced a broken axle or other major part, then refused to charge for the repair or even to acknowledge that any such incident had occurred.

In his 1984 article, David Buchan revisited Rolls-Royce folklore and collected several variations on these themes. In the United States Buchan heard that "Rolls-Royce engines are machined so well that they don't use gaskets" and that "once you buy a Rolls-Royce, you're guaranteed a perfect car for life," but that "no one can own a Rolls-Royce unless screened by the company." In California, Buchan collected this version of the never-breaking-down legend:

> A friend of a friend of mine bought a Rolls-Royce and took it on a very rough trip. He took it through many rocky and unpaved roads, and in general, drove it like a Land Rover. After several weeks of hard driving, the car's brakes need adjusting (or some other minor thing) and he took the car in for servicing. He received a new Rolls-Royce and the words "Rolls-Royce's brakes never need adjustment."

Buchan commented on how the "magnificent benevolence on the part of the company" was "balanced by a snobbish paternalism." He also noted that while an attitude of humor accompanies most of the British versions of Rolls-Royce legends, American versions often tend to be "delivered straight," giving the impression of the Rolls-Royce representative as "a starry-eyed lunatic, an inscrutable European far from the wholesome scrutability of your ordinary Chevy dealer."

References: David Buchan, "Modern Traditions and the Rolls-Royce," in Smith, *Perspectives* (1984): 99–107; Mike Fox and Steve Smith, *Rolls-Royce—The Complete Works: The Best 599 Stories about the World's Best Car* (London: Faber and Faber, 1984), 143–160 ("Apocrypha"); Stewart Sanderson, "The Folklore of the Motor-car," *Folklore* 80 (1969): 241–252.

Romania

As a visitor to communist-era Romania in the 1970s and 1980s, although officially there to study folk architecture, I was able to collect good examples of modern folklore, including many political jokes and a few urban legends. Undoubtedly there is a rich tradition of modern folk stories continuing to circulate in Romania, as in other Eastern European countries, awaiting only its native collectors and interpreters.

The existence of the classic urban legend "The Vanishing Hitchhiker" in Romania was attested by the story's appearance in two popular novels published in 1973 and 1979. Oral versions circulating at about the same time contained the same three distinctive elements of the Romanian tradition: *two* female hitchhikers were given a ride, the driver accidentally left some personal item in their apartment, and upon returning the next day to claim his property he found the apartment sealed and learned that the hitchhikers had been dead for several weeks.

Romanian versions of "The Accidental Cannibals" were still remembered from World War II days in the 1970s when I was there. As in most other European countries, the story circulated about how postwar food packages from the United States led to a gruesome confusion. When one package arrived containing an unlabeled dark powder, people assumed it was some kind of instant soup or drink, or perhaps a condiment. Only after most of the powder had been consumed did a letter from the United States arrive explaining that the powder was the ashes of their emigrant grandmother who had died during the war and who wanted her remains returned to Romanian soil.

The most characteristic truly "modern" legend that I encountered in Bucharest in the 1980s described two self-proclaimed "air samplers" who canvassed large apartment blocks, going door to door asking for a clean bottle or jar in which to take a sample of the interior air for analysis. The men wore badges or uniforms of some kind and claimed to be from a city health office. Each glass container was swished around in the apartment's air, then capped and labeled with a piece of paper and some string. After gathering all the bottles and jars they could carry, the men simply took them to a local bottle-return depot and collected the deposits. (In some parts of the city it was said that the men were posing as water inspectors.)

The rich and well-documented traditional folk culture of Romania and the harvest of modern folklore already begun in Poland and well under way throughout Western Europe all suggest that urban legends in abundance will eventually be collected in Romania.

References: *Baby Train,* 75–76 ("Accidental Cannibals"); *Choking Doberman,* 196–197 ("Air Samplers"); *Mexican Pet,* 49–51 ("Vanishing Hitchhiker").

"Room for One More"

See "The Phantom Coachman"

"The Roommate's Death"

In what might be termed the "classic" version of "The Roommate's Death," first noted by American folklorists in the 1960s, two female college roommates are left alone in their dormitory during a school vacation. One girl leaves the room to use the restroom, get some food, or go on an errand while the other stays behind. After a long time the girl in the room hears a thumping in the hallway and a scratching on her door. Terrified, she remains locked in the room until morning; then she summons help from a mailman or deliveryman by shouting out the window. Her roommate is found outside the dorm-room door, stabbed to death, lying in a pool of blood, sometimes with a hatchet embedded in her head. Long scratches had been carved into the door by her fingernails during her dying agonies.

"The Roommate's Death" has been told on numerous college campuses since at least 1961, and it has been a favorite among folklorists intent upon tracing themes and variations, noting the contexts of narration, and especially for interpretive readings. In her reading of the legend, for example, Beverly Crane suggested that the series of significant oppositions in the story (male/female, home/away, intellectual/emotional, life/death, victim/killer, etc.) suggest that the overall symbolic meaning of the legend is that if women "choose to venture into the realm of equality with men, they must become less dependent, more self-sufficient, more confident in their own abilities and, above all, more willing to assume responsibility for themselves and others."

Later versions of "The Roommate's Death" included some significant alterations and additions to the plot. There are still two female college roommates, one of whom leaves the room, but now the victim becomes the girl left behind. When the absent roommate returns late at night, she tiptoes into the room without turning on the light, believing that her roommate may have her boyfriend in bed with her. Despite some sounds of heavy breathing and movements from across the room, the girl falls asleep. In the morning she finds her roommate lying dead in her bed in a pool of blood, and written in blood (or lipstick) on the wall is the message, "Aren't you glad you didn't turn on the light?" (This version was enacted in the 1998 film *Urban Legend*.)

Terming the older versions "TRD$_1$" and the later ones "TRD$_2$," Michael P. Carroll asserts that the images of the girl "pierced, 'split,' and bleeding" in TRD$_1$ are intended "to express in a disguised manner [young women's] fears and anxieties about the damage and pain they associate with their first experience of heterosexual vaginal intercourse, fears and anxieties they are reluctant to confront directly." The changes in TRD$_2$, Carroll suggests, confirm this reading of the legend by including explicit references to sexual intercourse. He quotes an even more vivid example of this theme in a third variant (TRD$_3$) in which the murdered girl's head (literally, the "maiden head") is discovered lying in the lap of the insane killer who is sitting in a rocking chair.

See also Handwriting on the Wall

References: Michael P. Carroll, "Allomotifs and the Psychoanalytic Study of Folk Narratives: Another Look at 'The Roommate's Death,'" *Folklore* 103 (1992): 225–234; Beverly Crane, "The Structure of Value in 'The Roommate's Death': A Methodology for Interpretive Analysis of Folk Legends," *Journal of the Folklore Institute* 14 (1977): 133–149; Lara Maynard, "Locked Doors: Bearer–Centered Interpretation of 'The Roommate's Death' and Other Contemporary Legends of Special Relevance to Females," *Contemporary Legend*, New Series 1 (1998),: 97–115; *Mexican Pet*, 202–204; *Too Good*, 432–434; *Vanishing Hitchhiker*, 57–62.

"The Roommate's Suicide and the Four-Point Grade"

See "The Suicide Rule"

"The Roughneck's Revenge"

A roughneck (i.e., oil-drilling laborer) accidentally drops a tool down a deep hole that was just drilled. Expending a great deal of time and effort, the crew finally manages to retrieve the tool. The toolpush (i.e., the drilling foreman) hands the tool back to the roughneck, saying, "You're fired!" The roughneck replies, "Fine, then I won't be needing this hammer [wrench, etc.] again," and he drops it back into the hole.

Told in virtually every oil patch (drilling site) in the world, "The Roughneck's Revenge" is one of several urban legends about the revenge of workers against management or against the wealthy consumers of the products turned out by their labors.

See also "Fifi Spills the Paint"; "Fixing the Flue"; "The Rattle in the Cadillac"

References: *Baby Train,* 163–165; *Too Good,* 276–277.

Rumor

Rumors are similar to urban legends in that they circulate orally in different versions and usually concern contemporary persons and events. Also, in common with urban legends, rumors are generally anonymous and may penetrate popular culture and even be reported in the press or via commercial broadcasting. However, in general rumors do not last as long in tradition as do legends; neither do they have a well-developed plotline. A legend is an actual *story* of doubtful truth, whereas a rumor is just an unverified *report.* Here is how Elon A. Kulii defined the genre in a recent essay:

> Rumor. Unverified information of uncertain origin often spread by the oral tradition, as well as by phone, fax, broadcasting, or computer. Although rumors may be malicious or idle, they thrive in most societies worldwide, in both urban and rural settings. Rumors affect all facets of human experience, and almost every person has participated at one time in either the simple form of rumor (gossip) or the more complex form that is closely akin to the legend.

Rumors become especially common during periods of crisis—wars, epidemics, natural disasters, political destabilization, and the like. At such times governments may even establish information hotlines and rumor-control centers in an attempt to defuse public fears.

Rumors have been studied more by sociologists, psychologists, political scientists, and mass-media analysts than by folklorists, even though these unverified reports clearly seem to behave much like other informally circulated traditions. Furthermore, rumors frequently interact with legends about such topics as sex, scandal, crime, and celebrities; in some instances it appears that rumors have developed into full-scale narrative legends. Thus most urban-legend scholars tend to give rumors equal weight with legends in their studies.

Some European scholars, the French in particular, prefer the term "rumor" to "legend," and the former word certainly has a longer history of usage for studies of contemporary traditions abroad. Jean-Noël Kapferer suggests that "a proliferation of concepts is undesirable" and regards so-called modern urban legends as "part of the general family of rumors," which he defines simply as "unofficial information circulating in society." At times, however, even Kapferer coins a new definition in referring to urban legends as "migratory rumor stories."

In the United States, rumor scares often adopt the same subjects as urban legends, particularly crime. Thus we hear rumors closely related to stories like "The Attempted Abduction," "Blue Star Acid," "The Slasher Under the Car," "Lights Out!" and many others. Similar spates of rumors have surrounded such themes as immigrants and ethnic minorities, the Procter & Gamble trademark stories, the notion of sinking malls and leaning towers, and such college subjects as "The Obligatory Wait" and "The Suicide Rule."

See also Big Cats Running Wild; Campus Rumor Scares; Celebrities; Halloween Sadists

References: Joan Noël Kapferer, *Rumors. Uses, Interpretations, and Images* (New Brunswick, N.J.: Transaction Publishers, 1990) [originally published in French in 1987], Elon A. Kulii, *Rumor* in Brunvand, *American Folklore: An Encyclopedia* (1996): 642–643; Patrick B. Mullen, "Modern Legend and Rumor Theory," *Journal of the Folklore Institute* 9 (1972): 95–109; *Vanishing Hitchhiker*, 12–13, 17.

"The Runaway Grandmother"

The legend of the grandmother who is stolen, vanishes, or "runs away," as she is most often described, seems to have arisen in Europe during World War II then spread worldwide, becoming especially popular in the United States. Allusions to the well-known legend range from scenes in John Steinbeck's *The Grapes of Wrath* (1939) and in Anthony Burgess's *The Piano Players* (1986) to another enacted in the film *National Lampoon's Vacation* (1983). Prototype stories in Europe from as far back as the Renaissance possibly link the modern legend to early variations of "The Accidental Cannibals" and "The Relative's Cadaver."

At least two foreign collections of modern urban legends, one Finnish and one Australian, have featured a title (or subtitle), as well as cover art, referring to this legend.

In common with "The Dead Cat in the Package" (which is likely a legend of American origin), this one also involves the unwitting theft of a dead body. In earlier versions, the grandmother's corpse was lost as the family fled the Nazis or was escaping from Eastern Europe; later the story concerned a tourist family whose grandmother died on a trip abroad and whose body was stolen along with their car. The typical American version has the family driving in Mexico (less commonly in Canada) when the grandmother dies. They tie her body to the roof rack and start home, but when they stop for a meal the car with Granny on top is stolen from the restaurant parking lot. (In versions mentioning Canada, the body may be placed in a canoe on the car's top or in a boat being towed behind.)

Here is how "Granny on the Roof Rack" is summarized in a version from Australia given in Graham Seal's 1995 collection, a book that took its subtitle from this legend:

> A family took off on their annual holiday, the car packed with Mum, Dad, the kids and Granny. But out in the middle of nowhere on the Nullabor Plain, Granny died. Distraught and miles from anywhere, the family decided to bundle Gran's body up and lash it to the roof rack. They then drove off in search of the nearest police station to report the death.
>
> Eventually they found the police station and raced inside, leaving the car with the body still on the roof rack. When they returned with the sergeant, the car had disappeared. The stolen car and Granny were never recovered.

Seal identifies this as "one of the world's most popular holiday horror stories." He gives a second Australian version in which the body of a couple's "aged great aunt" is stolen along with their car while the couple rest from their ordeal in a motel on the way home. In Australian versions there is, of course, no national border to cross, but instead the vacationers' car crosses, as Seal explains, "the considerable physical and psychological 'border' of the Nullarbor plain."

Seeking meanings of this well-known modern legend, Seal relates it to "the peculiarly modern custom of the family automobile holiday," usually into unfamiliar places where unexpected crises may occur. Linda Dégh connected the legend with "the fear of the return of the dead" and emphasized the family's concern that their grandmother should be returned home for a proper burial. Alan Dundes, in a psychological interpretation, suggested that the grandmother is depicted as being old and in the way, "a burden whether alive or dead"; he felt that the family's major concern after taking their aged relative "for a ride" (i.e., on her death journey) seemed to be securing their inheritance of their grandmother's money.

In December 1999 "The Runaway Grandmother" reappeared in worldwide media disguised as a news item and circulated by the Associated Press. Here is the complete text:

> CHISINAU, Moldova (AP)—Thieves who made off with a rug reportedly got more than they bargained for. They also ended up with the body of a Moldovan woman.
>
> The incident happened after two impoverished Moldovan cousins bundled up their grandmother's corpse in a rug because they couldn't afford a coffin, the daily Observator reported.
>
> The men strapped the body to the top of their car and headed south from Ukraine to bury her in northern Moldova, the paper reported. En route, they stopped to eat in the Ukrainian town of Spikovo, 190 miles northwest of Kiev.
>
> When they left the restaurant, they discovered that the rug and the grandmother's body were missing, the newspaper said.
>
> The two men notified Ukrainian police and returned to Moldova, performing a burial service without the body.

Probably the only reliable information in this news item is that a regional paper called *The Observator* had published the story, most likely from a local oral source. But that hardly makes this familiar urban legend true, since every key detail of this version clearly marks it as apocryphal. (One wonders how two impoverished cousins could afford a car and restaurant meals, but not a coffin, which in a traditional Eastern European village would likely have been made by a local carpenter.)

References: *Choking Doberman*, 219; *Curses!*, 14–15; Linda Dégh, "The Runaway Grandmother," *Indiana Folklore* 1 (1968): 68–77; Alan Dundes, "On the Psychology of Legend," in Hand, *American Folk Legend* (1971), 21–36; *Too Good*, 76–77; *Vanishing Hitchhiker*, 112–123.

"The Runaway Patient"

An elderly patient, partially paralyzed and unable to speak, was put into a wheelchair and wheeled onto an elevator to go to a therapy session on another floor of the hospital. But nobody in the therapy section had been notified that the patient was coming, and no one on the elevator questioned whether the patient knew where he was going or was capable of getting there on his own.

Supposedly, the wheelchair-bound patient simply rode up and down in the elevator until he was missed back in the ward and a staff member there figured out what happened and went to rescue him. By then the patient was dead, or else weak and severely dehydrated from riding unattended for so long.

Anne Phipps of the Indiana University School of Nursing collected variations of this legend from personnel at five Veterans Administration and university hospitals in the Midwest. Another version was reported by actor Harry Morgan, who played Colonel Potter on *M*A*S*H*, in a 1983 interview published in *TV Guide*. Phipps also discovered newspaper accounts of a similar incident reported from a Chicago-area hospital in 1975.

References: Anne Phipps, "The Runaway Patient: A Legend in Oral Circulation and the Media," *Indiana Folklore* 13 (1980): 102–111; *Too Good*, 214.

Russia

The folkloristic categories of *spletni* and *tolki* (gossip and rumors), as the Polish folklorist Dionizjusz Czubala has shown, were of interest to certain Russian writers even before there was a well-established "science of folklore" in that country. Furthermore, several other named categories of Russian folk narrative appear to overlap with the English term "contemporary legend," and these genres have long been noted by writers in that country. Unfortunately for nonreaders of Russian, we have little more than Czubala's short reports in English to consult about this interest.

The earliest account of such materials reported by Czubala may be found in the writings of P. A. Viazemskii (1792–1878) who advised, "Collect all the silly rumors, fables, nonrumors, and nonfables that have been spread through the streets and houses of Moscow. . . . This is our oral literature." The journalist and literary critic Nikolai Dobroliubov (1836–1861) referred to similar traditions as *slushki* ("things heard," i.e., rumors) and wrote, "They are life with its swift events, sufferings, delights, disillusions, passions in all its beauty and truth. A week of such life can teach us more than seven volumes of statistics."

Another window into the early life of a legend on the streets of a Russian city was opened by Slavicist William B. Edgerton's discovery of an extended discussion of the ghost-in-search-of-help legend in five different Petersburg newspapers in December 1890. The basic story was reported, retold, sought in variants, and analyzed without any of the writers ever being able to trace it to a source or validate any details. One journalist, after a lengthy investigation and frustrated at his failure to track down anyone who had firsthand information about the story of a miracle that was sweeping the city, wrote, "I ran into monstrous obstacles deliberately placed in my way by gentlemen who were convinced, or who convinced others, that they knew the truth. . . . If all this really is true, then why are the people who know keeping quiet?!"

The earliest "purely scientific article about contemporary legends in Russia" that Czubala was able to find was written by S. N. Chernov in 1934. The article described a notebook containing rumors and sensational stories from 1825 to 1826 found in a Moscow archival source; the notebook referred to contemporary rumors that "reveal the mood of the society from which they come."

However, urban-legend studies did not flourish in Russia until the 1970s, when writers began to note the influence of rumors and gossip on literary works and to record such stories as the popular one that claimed that Czar Alexander I after his sudden death in 1825 had actually been poisoned. Supposedly, his body had turned black and could not be exhibited in such a state, so a wax cast was fashioned to surround the body for the viewing and the funeral. (In the United States the idea of a wax image of a celebrity substituting for the actual body is sometimes told about Elvis Presley.)

An example of an urban legend appearing in a recent Russian literary work occurs in Yevgeny Yevtushenko's novel *Wild Berries* (1981, tr. 1984). Here a group of workers sitting around a campfire out on the *taiga* (the swampy coniferous forests of Siberia) are exchanging stories. One of them tells a detailed version of "The Dead Cat in the Package" set in Leningrad. This time the unwitting theft of the cat's corpse is said to have happened to the narrator while riding a commuter train. Following the story, the book's narrator comments, "There is a peculiarity of the *taiga* camp story: Even the storytellers themselves don't know exactly where the truth ends and invention begins."

In documenting Polish legends about abductions of children in order to steal their organs, said to have been done by criminals driving black

Volgas (a Russian car), Czubala also found some variations of the story told in the Soviet Union. Texts that he collected in 1989 and 1990 were recollected by their tellers from several years earlier and were known in Russia, Ukraine, and Byelorussia. One example:

> Many such stories I heard from villagers and from the people of Minsk. They told them mainly in 1980. Later they returned to the topic from time to time. One of these stories was said to have happened in the place where I was born. A boy was walking along the road; a car was going by and the passengers asked him the way. They asked him to get in and show them the way. He got in and they went away.
>
> Later he was found in the wood without kidneys. He had been put to sleep by chloroform and then they cut out his kidneys. When he awoke they were gone. He was immediately taken to a Moscow hospital by air. He survived because he was very strong. He gave all the details of the kidnapping, what the people looked like. There was a special gang of people who delivered different body organs to hospitals.

The continuing circulation of urban rumors and legends in Russia is demonstrated occasionally when odd bits of dubious "news" find their way to the rest of the world via travelers' conversations or unverified press reports. What is needed is for Russian folklorists—or Russian-speaking folklorists from abroad—to record and document these items in a systematic way.

See also "The Bug Under the Rug"; "The Flying Cow"; "The Kidney Heist"

References: *Baby Train*, 245–246 ("Dead Cat"); D. Czubala, "Earliest Accounts of Contemporary Legends in Russia," *FOAFtale News* no. 18 (June 1990): 6–7; D. Czubala, "The 'Black Volga': Child Abduction Urban Legends in Poland and Russia," *FOAFtale News* no. 21 (March 1991): 1–3; William B. Edgerton, "The Ghost in Search of Help for a Dying Man," *Journal of the Folklore Institute* 5 (1968): 31–41; *The Truth*, 123–136.

Satanic Panic

Claims that well-organized cults devoted to Satan have existed for generations; related stories that they practice ritual abuse of innocent people have long circulated, periodically erupting into mass hysteria. The latest such "satanic panic" began in the 1980s following the publication of *Michelle Remembers* (1980) and other popular accounts by claimed "satanic survivors" and self-proclaimed former participants in ritual abuse. The panic about satanic ritual abuse in the United States and Europe eventually led to a large number of accusations and some arrests of day-care workers, teachers, foster parents, and even parents themselves who were charged with abuse, often either by children telling fantastic stories of mistreatment or by adults claiming to have recovered suppressed memories. A major example of the lengths to which these accusations went was the McMartin Preschool case brought in Manhattan Beach, California, in 1983. An example of the range and number of articles about supposed satanic ritual abuse in just one country may be found in two long listings of press accounts on the subject from Great Britain published in numbers 22 and 24 of *FOAFtale News* in 1991.

The details of the claims are truly horrific, supposedly involving sexual perversions, torture, sacrifices of humans and animals, nudity, eating of feces, and elaborate rituals always cleverly covered up by the participants. Rumors circulated that blonde, blue-eyed virgins were being kidnapped for sacrifice and that black cats were being adopted from humane societies for the same purpose. Eventually, since physical evidence was lacking, a backlash developed among investigators; numerous debunkings of most aspects of the satanic panic were published by investigative journalists, anthropologists, folklorists, psychologists, criminal justice specialists, and sociologists.

Kenneth V. Lanning, an FBI expert on cults, wrote, "After all the hype and hysteria is put aside . . . most satanic/occult activity involves the commission of NO crimes [or else] relatively minor crimes such as trespassing, vandalism, cruelty to animals, or petty thievery." Investigators reminded us that just because some youths adopt the symbols or clothing styles associated with Satanism does not prove that they are involved in sacrifices or other rituals. Another crack in the satanic-panic stories was opened by the identification of false-memory syndrome as a psychological reality.

Some of the stories and claims circulated in Satanism seminars or in the media were truly bizarre. Some "experts" even said that the name "Santa," being an anagram of "Satan," represents the Antichrist; thus parents should not teach their children about Santa Claus. Others insisted that the pentacles (five-pointed stars) on the American flag are occult symbols chosen by heretical Freemasons and Deists. They recommended that the blasphemous banner be redesigned without the stars. Further claimed satanic influences on American teenagers were rock music, the game Dungeons and Dragons, and the peace symbol introduced in the 1960s.

An early review of the American panic published in 1989 by anthropologist Phillips Stevens Jr. made the sweeping statement that "it is all folklore, of a particularly insidious and dangerous form; moreover, it fits classic and easily recognized patterns." However, as studies continued, the link to folk traditions seemed less solid, and scholars identified other important influences coming from self-styled satanic experts, well-meaning but deluded reformers, sensational journalism, and especially from alleged victims who were found to be suffering various degrees of mental illness (often encouraged by counselors and investigators who asked them leading questions).

The specific links of the satanic-panic material to urban legends have been seen differently by individual scholars. Certainly there is some overlap of the details of satanic ritual abuse on certain modern legends, particularly those stories dealing with child abductions and mutilations, mall attacks on women and children, organ thefts, drug-trafficking (as in "Blue Star Acid"), and the various rumors of corporate donations to "churches of Satan." The scapegoats in urban legends, however, in most cases are ethnic and racial minorities, homosexuals, Jews, or simply common criminals rather than Satanists. And as Bill Ellis has pointed out, the "ostensive traditions" of legend-tripping may involve dabbling in satanic symbols and customs that do not actually involve any ritual activity or abuse. However, it should also be noted that anecdotal evidence of supposed ritual abuse circulates informally, in part by word of mouth, and usually in variant versions, much like urban rumors and legends. Thus to some degree the satanic panic *is* folklore.

Sociologist Jeffrey S. Victor has made the clearest case for the influence of urban legends on satanic ritual abuse claims, stating in general that "contemporary legends create self-fulfilling processes whereby the rumor stories are sometimes acted out or used to provide 'accounts' of behavior." Victor analyzed several rumor panics and discovered how they developed in different regions. He concluded that "the blood ritual myth and similar subversion myths usually arise at times when a society is undergoing a deep cultural crisis of values, after a period of rapid social change which causes disorganization and widespread social stress." (Victor's 1993 book provides the most detailed summary of satanic-panic attacks in the 1980s and early 1990s as well as up-to-date resources and advice for combating these claims, including names and addresses of specific experts in the field.)

Another view of the relationship of legends to claimed Satanism, however, was presented by psychologist George B. Greaves (in D. Sakheim and S. Devine's 1992 book), who contrasted most urban legends with the recorded accounts given by ritual abuse survivors. Unlike urban legends, the survivors' accounts are told in the first person with strong emotional involvement; they may be accompanied by the display of actual body scars and are long and detailed narratives that do not include the whimsical or humorous touches that are characteristic of many urban legends.

See also "The Blood Libel"; Halloween Sadists; "The Procter & Gamble Trademark"; White-Slavery Legends

References: Bill Ellis, "The Devil-Worshippers at the Prom: Rumor-Panic As Therapeutic Magic," *Western Folklore* 49 (1990): 27–49; Robert D. Hicks, *In Pursuit of Satan: The Police and the Occult* (Buffalo, N.Y.: Prometheus Books, 1991); Debbie Nathan, "What McMartin Started: The Ritual Sex Abuse Hoax," *Village Voice* (June 12, 1990); 36–44; James T. Richardson, Joel Best, and David G. Bromley, eds., *The Satanism Scare* (New York: Aldine de Gruyter, 1991); D. Sakheim and S. Devine, eds., *Out* *of Darkness: Exploring Satanism and Ritual Abuse* (New York: Lexington Books, 1992); *Skeptical Inquirer,* vol. 14, nos. 3–4 (Spring and Summer 1990; several articles on satanic cult claims); Phillips Stevens Jr., "Satanism: Where Are the Folklorists?" *New York Folklore* 15 (1989): 1–22; Jeffrey S. Victor, *Satanic Panic: The Creation of a Contemporary Legend* (Chicago: Open Court, 1993).

"The Sawed-off Fingers"

A factory worker operating a power saw or another piece of heavy equipment accidentally saws or slices off a finger. When someone asks him how it happened, he gestures toward the machine and says, "Like this!" and he loses a second finger or a thumb. The number of fingers lost varies, and sometimes it is toes removed by a posthole digger.

Also referred to as "Give Me a High Three," this story has been around since at least the turn of the century. Sometimes the worker is distracted by a pretty woman who is on a factory tour; she asks him how he lost his finger, and he demonstrates. Told as a joke rather than a legend, the same story may be narrated in an immigrant dialect, often Swedish ("Voops! Dere goes anudder vun!") and set in a Midwestern sawmill.

See also "The Cut-Off Finger"; "The Lawn-Mower Accident"

References: *Baby Train,* 178–180; *Too Good,* 162–163.

SCA Legends

The Society for Creative Anachronism (SCA), a medieval re-creationist group founded in 1966, has developed its own set of "folk" traditions (customs, ballads, pranks, jokes, slang, etc.), including legends. The legendary stories always describe a costumed SCA participant somehow interacting with the outside community, as in the one about "The Barbarian at Burger King" who shows up in full costume and orders his hamburger "raw!" In other encounters, the SCA member deflects an attacker's knife with his chain mail or matches an assailant's

knife with his sword; in one popular legend an SCA group faces down a gang of Hell's Angels.

From her detailed analysis of SCA legends in context, Donna Wycoff determined that "these contemporary legends seem to function as 'as needed' rituals for dealing with the ambiguities and anxieties that result when ideologies and practices of the SCA microcosm come into contact with potentially incompatible elements of the mundane realm of the twentieth century."

References: *Baby Train,* 207–209; Donna Wyckoff, "Why a Legend? Contemporary Legends As Community Ritual," *Contemporary Legend* 3 (1993): 1036.

Scandal

Scandalous behavior, often of a sexual nature, is a staple topic of rumors and gossip, so it is no surprise that scandal is a common theme in urban legends as well. Stories of scandal may be found in all categories of legends, but most specifically in the "sex and scandal" genre.

Typical scandal topics in urban legends include being caught in the nude ("The Nude Housewife" and "The Dormitory Surprise"), caught in the act ("The Shocking Videotape" and "The Stuck Couple"), or simply being embarrassed publicly ("Green Stamps" and "Superhero Hijinks"). Some other popular sex-related scandal legends are "The Blind Date," "Buying Tampax," "The Hairdresser's Error," "Sex in Disguise," "Waiting for the Ice Man," and many others.

A legend in which a character dramatically reveals a scandal at a wedding is "The Bothered Bride"; another story of wedding scandal in which the revelation comes somewhat later is "The Videotaped Theft." The whole family and community are scandalized in a sudden revealing moment in "The Nude Surprise Party."

See also Celebrities; Zipper Stories

Scary Stories

"Scary stories" is a self-evident, folk-generic category of oral and written narratives. Children and adolescents seem to enjoy telling stories intended mainly to scare listeners, especially in such contexts as slumber parties, campfire circles, baby-sitting, parking, and long bus trips. One folklorist has suggested calling some of these stories "humorous antilegends" because they are told as legends but really function more as jokes. In fact, scary stories are more likely to be jokes, or at least obvious fictions, than believed legends per se.

The term "scary stories" has been adopted by compilers of spooky, eerie, mysterious, and otherwise frightening tales into scary-story anthologies. Some of these narratives drawn from the world of urban legends are "The Hook," "The Boyfriend's Death," "The Killer in the Backseat," and "The Baby-sitter and the Man Upstairs." In retelling such legends as scary stories, the compilers emphasize the atmospheric details of sounds, sights, and settings in order to pump up the chilling effect while maintaining a semiserious attitude that assures listeners that "this is only a story."

Contemporary storytellers, both amateur and professional, tend to trade scary stories with each other and then re-create them to fit their own personal narrative styles. Thus scary stories may also be thought of partly as a storytellers' genre enjoying special circulation among members of what might be considered a modern folk group. As for the children and adolescents who enjoy telling or reading scary stories, Richard and Judy Dockrey Young point out:

> While the stories . . . may seem bloody and gruesome to adults, they are less terrible than the evening news with its stories of wars and starvation around the world. If kids can face and master their fear of the horrible things [in scary stories], they will be better prepared to face the things we all actually fear, from crime to toxic waste pollution.

The same point could be made for urban legends that deal with horrible and frightening topics.

See also Horror Legends

References: John M. Vlach, "One Black Eye and Other Horrors: A Case for the Humorous Anti-Legend," *Indiana Folklore* 4 (1971): 95–140;

Richard and Judy Dockrey Young, *Favorite Scary Stories of American Children* and *Scary Story Reader* (Little Rock, Ark.: August House, 1990 and 1993).

Scotland

The first modern academic interest in the urban legends of Scotland was taken by Alexander "Sandy" Hobbs of Paisley College of Technology, who published notes and articles on the subject beginning in 1966. His 1978 article "The Folk Tale as News" (*Oral History*, vol. 6, no. 2: 74–86), however, called attention to a much earlier source of information. In Robert Chambers's 1825 book *Traditions of Edinburgh*, Hobbs discovered a concise version of a legend we might call "The Drunk at the Door," which incorporates an early example of the severed-finger motif that is now found in several modern urban legends, including "The Choking Doberman." Hobbs also investigated the nineteenth-century story "Downie's Slaughter (or "Downie's Slauchter"), which had been much discussed in Scottish periodicals from the 1880s though the first decade of the twentieth century. Hobbs concluded in his 1973 survey that the story of a fatal prank played on an official at the University of Aberdeen was a predecessor of the modern fatal-initiation legend, and that the "Downie" incident could neither be confirmed nor denied in any definitive way.

As the study of contemporary legends developed in Great Britain and beyond, Sandy Hobbs has continued to contribute to the field, often with theoretical and analytical articles not necessarily based on Scottish examples. However, his investigation (reported at a 1985 legend conference) of an incident that occurred in 1954 in Glasgow focused again on local legendary material. Hobbs and coinvestigator David Cornwell reviewed the case of hundreds of Glasgow children claiming to be out "hunting a vampire with iron teeth" in a local cemetery. Although press accounts from 1954 attempted to link this "monster" hysteria to horror films and comic books, no specific links to these pop-culture media were identified. Instead, Hobbs and Cornwell found that the iron-teeth motif was common in early-nineteenth-century stories of bogeymen used by adults to frighten children. A poem on the topic from 1879, "Jenny wi the Airn Teeth," had even been included in literary anthologies. Also supporting the tradition of hunting a monster or vampire was the well-documented custom of so-called children's hunts.

The other noteworthy documenter of Scottish urban legends has been Gordon McCulloch. At the first Perspectives on Contemporary Legend conference in 1982, McCulloch presented his research on the turkey-neck legend (summarized in this volume under that title as well as under "Comparative Approach"). Here is one version of the story exactly as McCulloch collected it from a woman in the mining village of Clelland, near Motherwell, Scotland. In this instance the turkey's neck is replaced by "the giblet," and the heavy Scottish dialect contrasts with the modern details of a friend of a friend at work and the turkey defrosting in the kitchenette:

> A fellah I work wi . . . lives up in Clelland. Aye, he went aboot tellin' it that the woman he gies a lift tae tae work . . . broke her arm. She was always rushin' aboot an' he took it . . . she'd fell that way. An' her pal says, "Ye'll never believe how she broke it."
>
> [Question: This was in Motherwell was it?]
>
> Clelland. An' . . . they burst out laughing. Seemingly her man comes in drunk every Saturday night. Falls asleep in front o' the fire. An' he's a bit o' a moan when he's got a drink in him, so . . . she jist switches off and goes tae bed. But the two sons came in later on. . . . An' they've got tae go intae the living-room tae get intae the kitchenette. Of course, when they put oan the light he starts his, "Nyehhh" .. . . girnin' and' groanin'. So here when he goes through the mother's got a turkey defrostin' . . . an' the giblets lyin' outside o' it. So the younger son says, "Ah'll gie him . . . know . . . gie a fright in the mornin.'" So he goes in an' he puts the giblet in front o' the fly o' his troosers. An' of course when the mother gets up in the morning . . . she sees the cat chowin' away at it an' she faints an' . . . [laughs] . . . that's how she breks her airm.

At the 1983 Perspectives conference McCulloch presented his findings on Scottish versions of the suicidal sculptors and architects legends. McCulloch collected 18 versions of these stories from Scotland, seven of them then current in Glasgow. They included stories of sculptors or architects supposedly committing suicide because their designs were constructed incorrectly, either "back to front" (such as the Kelvingrove Art Gallery in Glasgow), or incompletely (such as the tongueless lion of Murdostoun estate's gate). The continued currency of such Scottish legends was confirmed when in 1988 when the *Glasgow Herald* (May 14) began a story about "tall stories without foundation" with this lead paragraph:

> Every Glaswegian knows that the Art Gallery and Museum at Kelvingrove was built back to front. The architect took it very badly; on the opening day

he leapt to his death from the top of his travestied masterpiece, a martyr to the carelessness of the building trade.

Among other urban legends mentioned in the article are stories about pets cooked and served in a local restaurant, the "satanic" trademark of Procter & Gamble, and McDonald's wormburgers. The article concluded with another "queer example" of the genre heard by the writer from a friend of a friend:

[She said that] the combination of red and white flowers has long been thought unlucky, supposedly deriving from Roman funeral customs. A nurse was asked why this superstition is still respected in hospital wards.
"The colours," she said. "Blood on a sheet."

Following a lull in reports of Scottish urban legends, the world awaits more—perhaps the distinctive contemporary legends about haggis, golf, Scotch whiskey, or English tourists. Who knows what further themes and topics may emerge?

See also "The Flying Cow"; "Postcards for Little Buddy"; Satanic Panic

References: *Choking Doberman,* 44–46 ("The Drunk at the Knocker"); Alexander Hobbs, "Downie's Slaughter," *Aberdeen University Review* 45 (1973): 183–191; Sandy Hobbs and David Cornwall, "Hunting the Monster with Iron Tooth," in Bennett and Smith, *Monsters with Iron Teeth* (1988): 115–137; Gordon McCulloch, "'The Tale of the Turkey Neck': A Legend Case-Study," in Smith, *Perspectives* (1984): 147–166; Gordon McCulloch, "Suicidal Sculptors: Scottish Versions of a Migratory Legend," in Bennett, Smith, and Widdowson, *Perspectives on Contemporary Legend II* (1987): 109–116; *Mexican Pet,* 129–131 ("The Turkey Neck").

"The Scuba Diver in the Tree"

The legend about the scuba diver supposedly picked up by a fire-fighting plane or helicopter when it scoops water from a lake has been told since the mid-1980s in the United States, Europe, and Australia; it has also been widely spread in the media. The story's popularity abroad was confirmed in Peter Mayle's book *A Year in Provence* (1989) in which a character comments, "Every time there's a fire someone starts a rumor like that." The legend was also alluded to in a 1996 "Sherman's Lagoon" comic strip. It was a major plot element in the novel *Barney's Version* (1997) by Canadian Mordecai Richler, and the story circulated again on the Internet in 1998 and 1999 masquerading as a news account:

> Fire authorities in California found a corpse in a burnt out section of forest while assessing the damage done by a forest fire. The deceased male was dressed in a full wet suit, complete with a dive tank, flippers, and face mask. A post mortem examination revealed that the person died not from burns but from massive internal injuries. Dental records provided a positive identification. . . .

> On the day of the fire, the person went for a diving trip off the coast—some 20 miles away from the forest. The firefighters, seeking to control the fire as quickly as possible, called in a fleet of helicopters with very large buckets. The buckets were dropped into the ocean for rapid filling, then flown to the forest fire and emptied. You guessed it.

One person who forwarded this item added the comment, "I've heard it or read it a hundred times already." The film *Magnolia,* released in January 2000, contained yet another telling of "The Scuba Diver in the Tree."

References: *Curses!,* 47–48; *Too Good,* 168–169.

"The Second Blue Book"

At least three different ploys are described in the legend about the college student who fakes his way through an essay exam by using a second blue book. In all three versions there are two essay questions, and in the first two versions the student can answer only the second.

In the first ploy, he writes an incomplete sentence in a book marked "No. 2" and then answers the second question fully. His instructor later apologizes for losing the first book.

In the second ploy the student writes an answer in book No. 2, then takes a second blue book back to his dorm and writes an answer in "No. 1," using his notes and textbook. He has a friend turn it in, saying he had found it on the floor of the classroom later in the day.

The third ploy is the most elaborate. The student cannot answer either question, so he writes a letter to his mother praising the course and saying he learned so much that he finished early and had time to write to her while waiting for the end of the class. He hands in the blue book with the letter, writes two essays in another blue book after class in his dorm room, and mails that second blue book to his mother. When the instructor calls him, he claims to have mailed the wrong book home, and the instructor and the student's mother exchange blue books.

Supposedly, in all three versions the student gets a high grade in the course. This consistency, as well as the formulaic requirement for exactly two essay topics, mark the stories as highly unlikely. Add to this the fact that the first story was remembered from 1937, the second from 1959, and the third from at least the 1970s, and that all three are occasionally still told today. The proof that these are merely legends of academe is assured.

See also "Do You Know Who I Am?"

References: Lew Girdler, "The Legend of the Second Blue Book," *Western Folklore* 29 (1970): 111–113; *Mexican Pet,* 196–200; *Too Good,* 447–448.

"The Second Death"

Told by a mortuary employee as something that happened to a friend of a friend in a similar job, this story begins when a hearse is sent out for the body of an elderly woman who died at night. A noise from the back of the hearse alerts the driver that the woman was actually in a coma and had revived while being driven on a bumpy street. The hearse driver telephones a hospital from which an ambulance is dispatched, but the two vehicles collide as the hearse races toward the hospital. The woman is killed in the accident and so dies for a second time in the same night.

References: *Curses!,* 66–68.

"The Secret Ingredient"

In the 1970s and 1980s the story spread, especially among fundamentalist Christian groups in the United States, that collagens taken from fetuses of aborted babies were being used in the manufacture of cosmetics. It was claimed that these "youth-preserving" products depended upon the slaughter of millions of unborn babies annually in foreign countries and that the resulting beauty products were sold widely in the United States.

The flood of pamphlets, letters to newspapers, and broadcast talk shows making the secret-ingredient claim became so great that in 1985 the Food and Drug Administration issued a statement denying the rumors and stories and explaining that while protein substances are sometimes collected from placentas ("the after-birth of normal childbirth)" or from animals, no use of human fetuses as a source was documented, either in the United States or abroad.

Prodded by readers, the advice columnist Ann Landers wrote three columns debunking the secret-ingredient story in 1985. Her conclusion—that the story lacked "a shred of truth" and was "unadulterated garbage"—probably succeeded in killing the claims for good.

References: *Mexican Pet*, 93–98.

Severed Fingers

See "The Cut-Off Finger"; "The Lawn-Mower Accident"; "The Sawed-Off Fingers"

"Sex in Disguise"

Sometimes referred to as "The Halloween Party" and "Sex with the Wrong Partner," this story often circulates via photocopy. It tells of a married couple who have rented costumes to wear to a neighbor's party. The husband has not seen his wife's costume, and after he is dressed and ready to go she informs him that she has a splitting headache and does not feel up to it. She urges him to go without her, and he does.

An hour later, having taken an aspirin and a nap, the wife feels fine again and decides to put on her costume and go to the party. There she spots her husband in costume and, without identifying herself, dances and flirts with him. Eventually they end up in an upstairs bedroom having sex, still without unmasking. The wife leaves first and is back in bed when her husband returns home. She's very curious about how he will describe his night out.

When she asks him how he enjoyed the party, he says, "I never danced at all; some other guys were stag, too, and we just went into the den and played poker all night. But the guy who borrowed my costume had a hell of a good time!"

A variation on the same theme tells of two married couples on a camping trip, each couple in a separate tent. The husbands decide to switch tents and try out each other's wife, unaware that the wives had already switched tents on their own. Thus each man ends up with his own wife.

References: *Curses!*, 209–211; *Too Good*, 132–133.

Sex in Urban Legends

Urban legends about sex follow a number of themes, including aphrodisiacs, contraception, sex education, nudity, homosexuality, deviance, promiscuity, revenge for sexual misbehavior, and sexually transmitted diseases. Besides the legends that focus primarily on sex, there are also some sex-related legends involving automobiles, crime, business, and academic life.

A typical sex legend describes a scandalous situation in which participants are caught in the act; examples of this genre are "Filmed in the Act," "The Stuck Couple," and "Superhero Hijinks." Another popular topic involves some kind of misunderstanding about sex, as in "The Hairdresser's Error," "The Surpriser Surprised," and "The Witness's Note." People's supposed propensity for having sex whenever the opportunity presents itself is illustrated in "The Baby Train," while embarrassment about one's sexual nature is shown in legends like "The Blind Date" and "Buying Tampax."

Sexually inspired horseplay leads to problems in "The Unzipped Mechanic" and "The Turkey Neck." Yielding to sexual temptations results in serious trouble in "AIDS Mary" and some versions of "The Kidney

Heist." A fantastic notion of how sexual impregnation might occur is the subject of "The Bullet Baby," which was originally a hoax story.

See also Scandal; "The Sheriff's Daughter"

"Sex in the Classroom"

Various rumors and stories circulate about sex-education classes and sexy comments or situations occurring in high school or college classes. There are claims that some teachers have demonstrated sexual behavior to students, or have had students "practice" having sex. Another charge is that sex education has led to sexual experimentation or even sex crimes. A more developed story concerns an instructor who asks a double-entendre question deliberately to embarrass female students: "What part of the body is wet with hair around it and expands when needed?" The "correct" answer is the eye. Yet another variation on the theme has an instructor playfully calling his pop quizzes "quizzees"; a female student comments, unthinkingly, "Well, I'd hate to see your 'testees.'"

The sex-in-the-classroom story with the longest documented history can be traced to an anecdote about a Cambridge University anthropologist who died in 1940. Supposedly he was lecturing about a native group's customs and mentioned that women propose marriage in their traditions. When a group of female students from an affiliated college rose to leave in order to catch their bus, he quipped, "No hurry, there won't be a boat for some weeks." This was eventually converted into a very well known story told on countless other professors both in England and abroad about a lecturer mentioning the extraordinary size of the penises of men in a certain African tribe. ("The boat won't leave for Africa until next week.")

References: Jan Brunvand, "Sex in the Classroom," *Journal of American Folklore* 73 (1960): 250–251; Brunvand, "Further Notes on Sex in the Classroom," *Journal of American Folklore* 75 (1962): 62; *Choking Doberman,* 132.

"The Sheriff's Daughter"

Sometimes referred to as "Dear Old Dad" or "The Cop on the Beach," this is a sex legend about mistaken identification (or perhaps one should call it *delayed* identification.)

Two patrolling policemen, a rookie and a veteran, stop to check out a tent that is pitched illegally on a beach or a car that is parked in a cemetery or some other illegal spot. The rookie cop reports back to his partner in the squad car that there's a young couple inside "making out." The veteran instructs him to tell the couple that they will get only a warning if both cops can have sex with the girl. The couple, terrified, agree. The rookie cop takes his turn first. When the veteran cop approaches the car he discovers that it is his own daughter inside.

Another version of the story tells of a traveling businessman who discovers that the prostitute he had summoned to his hotel room is his own runaway daughter; sometimes the girl blackmails her father. Yet another variation describes a couple who exchange sexy talk anonymously on the Internet; when they finally meet in person discover that they are father and daughter.

References: *Choking Doberman,* 145–146; *Too Good,* 121–122.

"The Shocking Videotape"

A home video of a couple who taped themselves having sex is accidentally made public, usually because they returned the wrong tape in a rental box. The couple are either husband and wife and prominent socialites, or an unmarried couple cheating on their spouses. Often the pairing is a teacher with his or her student or a coach with a team member. Sometimes the tape is being shared around a TV station when it is accidentally broadcast.

Unverified rumors and stories about amateur X-rated videotapes going public have been around nearly as long as home camcorders have been available. Few people who repeated the claims had actually seen the tapes. But there are also some well-documented cases of actual incidents of this kind, and such tapes definitely do exist. One such incident involving a law enforcement officer was reported from Kansas by *Time* magazine in its October 29, 1990, edition; another involving a University of Minnesota coach was covered in detail by the Minneapolis *Star Tribune* with the resolution of the case described in the edition of May 20, 1998.

See also "Filmed in the Act"

References: *Baby Train,* 61–64.

"Shooting the Bull"

Here is a good version of this legend about a hunter's prank as told by Don Boxmeyer of the St. Paul, Minnesota, *Pioneer Press and Dispatch* in his column for October 7, 1985:

A colleague here at the paper just told me a story she heard from a friend. The friend swore it happened to someone he knows:

Three hunters drove into a farm yard and one of them went up to ask the farmer's permission to hunt his fields. The farmer gave his permission, on one condition: That the hunters shoot an old bull he had been planning to get rid of.

The hunter went back to the car and pulled a little gag on his buddies. He said the farmer was a rotten old coot who refused them permission to hunt, and had the driver stop when they passed the bull. Then he got out of the car, shot the animal and said, "That'll take care of that rotten old coot," whereupon his two companions each shot a cow, commenting "That'll REALLY take care of that rotten old coot."

Boxmeyer mentioned that soon after hearing that story he was told it again by visitors from South Africa who also claimed that it was true.

"Shooting the Bull" (sometimes depicting the target as a horse, cow, or mule) has been published as a local story since the 1940s and 1950s, but it is probably even older. In some versions the trickster, having shot the farmer's animal, then announces that he wonders what it would feel like to shoot a man. When he turns his rifle toward his companions, they shoot at *him* in panic.

This legend is often told about celebrities, especially professional athletes, and it may indeed represent a prank that has actually been played. Among the people named in versions of the story have been former Texas Governor Coke Stevenson hunting with legislators and a lobbyist, baseball players Billy Martin hunting with Whitey Ford and Mickey Mantle, and football coach Tom Landry hunting with coach Mike Ditka. Author Tobias Wolff drew on the legend as the basis for a short story published in his 1981 book *Garden of the North American Martyrs*.

References: *Curses!*, 138–141; *Too Good*, 342–343.

"The Shoplifter and the Frozen Food"

In the versions of this story told in Europe since the 1970s, a person is caught trying to smuggle a frozen chicken out of a supermarket by hiding it under his or her hat. The shoplifter is caught either when the bird

begins to thaw, sending rivulets of blood down the neck, or else when he or she faints from the chilled brain. In American versions of the story the item stolen may be some other kind of frozen food or a steak, and the thief is often described as a poor person, often elderly.

Another legend in which food on the head leaks out is "The Brain Drain." Prototypes for that legend, plus other stories about stolen goods hidden in one's hat, suggest that both stories may be derived from much older narratives.

See also "The Pregnant Shoplifter"; Sweden

References: *Curses!*, 178–179; *Mexican Pet*, 143–144; *Too Good*, 312–314.

Shopping Malls in Urban Legends

Shopping malls and department stores, particularly their parking lots or garages, are often the scenes described in urban legends about crime. For examples of such legends, see "The Attempted Abduction," "The Dead Cat in the Package," "The Hairy-Armed Hitchhiker," "The Mutilated Boy," "The Slasher Under the Car," and "The Wrong Car." For a noncrime mall legend, see the entry Sinking Shopping Malls.

Shopping malls are prominent fixtures of the contemporary business scene—popular with masses of people ranging from parents with tots to teens and senior citizens—and offering a wide range of goods and services in a familiar and seemingly safe environment. Thus it is ironic and upsetting that, at least according to legends, they are also the settings for death and danger. Another disturbing aspect: It is often asserted that the mall or law enforcement authorities are covering up the crimes in order not to hurt business. The legends, therefore, illustrate a supposed dark side to these familiar gathering places. Compounding this theme is the fact that often the mall-crime legends flourish in a community during the Christmas shopping season. New shopping malls also tend to attract such legends at the time of their grand openings.

"Shrink-to-Fit Jeans"

Supposedly a teenager was squeezed to death when he or she sat in a bathtub filled with water wearing a new pair of Levi's jeans, hoping to shrink them to a snug fit. The family won a huge cash settlement from the company.

References: *Choking Doberman,* 154.

Sinking Libraries

In a typical "architect's blunder" legend, college and university libraries across the country are rumored to be sinking because the architect forgot to figure the weight of all the books into his design. The problem is supposedly worsened, according to some versions, because the library was built on swampy or unstable land. Among the best-known sinkers are the libraries at Northwestern, Yale, Colgate, Syracuse, and Brown, as well as the Rensselaer Polytechnic Institute, the U.S. Naval Academy, and, in Canada, the Universities of Toronto and Waterloo. Occasionally the same story is told about public libraries. The fact that there are always some blank spaces on the library shelves where books are checked out seems to encourage belief in the story; people say that the library

can never be filled to its planned capacity without its beginning to settle deeper into the earth. Sometimes various design features of the library—pillars, ramps, overhangs, and the like—are explained as units introduced later in order to negate the problem.

The sinking-library story has circulated orally and on the Internet concerning the Indiana University Main Library on the campus in Bloomington. For a time library officials were receiving at least one query per month about the problem, many coming from alumni who were concerned about the safety of the structure. The university's chief architect finally published a statement in *IU Alumni Magazine* explaining that "five feet below the Bloomington campus is a 330–million-year-old 94-foot thick layer of limestone." Obviously, neither the library nor any other campus building was in any danger of sinking.

References: *Baby Train,* 299–301; Stacey Hathaway-Bell, "Satan's Shelving: Urban Library Legends," *American Libraries* 29 (1998): 44–49; "Oh, That Sinking Feeling," *The Source* (newsletter of Indiana University Bloomington Libraries) (Fall 1998): 4–5; *Too Good,* 435–436.

Sinking Shopping Malls

Newly opened shopping malls are sometimes the subjects of rumors and legends claiming that the mall, because it was constructed on reclaimed or unstable land (or sometimes because of an architect's faulty design), is sinking into the ground. Some mall shoppers claim to feel a quivering or vibrating motion that proves that the mall is indeed sinking, despite management's assurances to the contrary.

Among the publicized sinking malls of recent years have been the Town Centre Mall in Greensboro, North Carolina; the Danbury Fair Mall in Connecticut; the Emerald Square Mall in North Attleboro, Massachusetts; and the Carousel Center in Syracuse, New York. When the Irondequoit Mall of Rochester, New York, opened in March 1990, the developers, Wilmorite, Inc., ran a full-page advertisement in local newspapers headlined "Thank you for all your support." After describing the successful opening days of the mall, officials added this:

> There has been one ongoing negative that we feel must be addressed . . .
> that being the rumors that have been perpetrated about the building mo-
> tion and more unpleasant rumors about "sinking." Both questions that
> have been raised and repeated are without merit. Our normal motion at
> certain points at the upper level is built-in as part of the mall's structural
> engineering and was so designed for safety and structural integrity. Ru-
> mors about sinking are not only totally incorrect but have no basis in fact.

See also Leaning Towers; Sinking Libraries

References: *Curses!*, 253–254.

"The Ski Accident"

Since the winter of 1979–1980 (at least) the "true" story has circulated annually about a female beginning skier who has an accident with a comical twist at a major ski resort. On her first attempt at skiing from the top of the mountain, the woman gets off the lift and realizes that she needs to use the restroom before descending. Seeing no lodge or other facilities up top, she decides to ski behind some trees and take care of the problem. She leaves her skis on and lowers her pants, only to slip backward down the moun-tain at an ever-increasing speed until she collides with a tree, breaking her arm.

Rescued and treated by the ski patrol, she is bruised and embarrassed but other-wise unhurt when another injured skier is brought into the first-aid room. He is a ski instructor, still wearing his logo jacket. "How could you have hurt yourself?" the woman asks him. He replies, "I was riding up the chair this morning to meet my class, and a woman went by underneath, skiing backward with her pants around her ankles. I leaned over for a better look and fell out of the chair. How about you?"

The silly skier in these stories is always identified as to her home-town and the resort visited (e.g., an Ohioan at a New York resort, a Californian at Aspen, an Oklahoman at Vail, an Atlantan at Squaw Valley, a Chicagoan at Alta, a Missourian at Sun Valley, etc.). Several newspapers and at least one ski magazine have published the story, sometimes debunking it, sometimes not. Some versions of the story circulate in photocopied form (often titled "So, How'd You Break Your Arm?") and the story is a favorite of after-dinner speakers during the winter months.

"The Ski Accident" is also told about skiers from Canada, England, New Zealand, and probably anywhere else that has either skiing tourists or ski terrain. In 1985 the story appeared—as absolutely true, of course—in a magazine distributed to riders on the Swedish national railway; this time the plot concerned *en kvinna i Leksands slalombackar* (a woman at the Leksand slalom hill).

This is the favorite urban legend of the compiler of this encyclopedia.

References: *Mexican Pet,* 117–120; *Too Good,* 164–166; *Vanishing Hitch-hiker,* 181.

Slapstick Comedy in Urban Legends

Many urban legends are funny, and some of these humorous stories feature the ingredients of slapstick comedy, including emphasis on physical humor, ridiculous situations, a series of mishaps, and a cast of somewhat dimwitted characters. Although some of the situations depicted in slapstick legends may be dangerous or even life-threatening, the style of their telling keeps the plots in the mode of cartoon encounters, similar to Wile E. Coyote versus the Roadrunner and Tom versus Jerry. This kind of humor led one newspaper columnist to dub such legends "Mack Sennetts" with reference to the director of the old Keystone Kops films. The term "slapstick" itself derives from the loud "slapping" sound effect that was used to accompany inane jokes told or enacted on the vaudeville stage.

The motorcycle version of the exploding-toilet legend is a good example of the slapstick genre. The hapless husband toying with his new motorcycle on the patio starts the series of mishaps by accidentally driving through a plate-glass window. While he is being treated in the hospital for cuts and bruises, his wife mops up the spilled gasoline and deposits it into the toilet. The husband returns home and uses the toilet while smoking a cigarette, thus setting off an explosion and requiring a second call to the paramedics. When they return and hear about his second accident, they laugh so hard that they drop the stretcher, causing the man yet another injury. It's like something straight out of a slapstick routine on stage or from an Abbott and Costello movie.

The dropped-stretcher motif is a favorite ending for accident legends including "The Pet and the Naked Man" and "The Man on the Roof." Other legends with a slapstick style include "Stuck on the Toilet," "The Exploding Bra," and "The Nude Housewife." But perhaps "The Stunned Deer" is the best example to illustrate slapstick comedy, because the heart of the legend is a dramatic dialogue supposedly carried out between the hapless driver and the police (or 911 operator) as the man reports his comical mishaps involving a deer, his dog, and his car.

References: *Too Good,* 367–383.

"The Slasher Under the Car"

Stories of men hiding under women's cars in shopping mall parking lots intending to slash their ankles when they return to their vehicles have broken out time after time in America. No such crimes have ever been documented, but starting in about 1984 some two dozen rumor scares involving ankle-slashers have erupted periodically in at least 20 different states. The attackers were said to be aiming at the Achilles tendon with a knife or a tire iron, intending to immobilize their victims so they could rob or rape them. Such stories tend to surface during the Christmas season, with the added motive of stealing women's gift purchases. Sometimes the stories link the attacks to gang initiations.

Among the cities where the story has run rampant are Birmingham, Alabama; Phoenix, Arizona; Tacoma, Washington; and Winston-Salem, North Carolina. A typical rationalization for not seeing news reports of the crimes is that "the authorities are covering them up to avoid bad publicity." Rumors and stories of "The Slasher Under the Car" have been so disturbing to shoppers in some cities that police had to set up field stations in the named malls, not with the expectation of arresting any actual slashers but simply to offer shoppers a sense of security. Although most of the numerous local newspaper articles about the story have debunked it, Abigail "Dear Abby" Van Buren expressed no disbelief whatever in commenting on a reader's letter she published in her column in 1992.

Yet another version of the slasher theme began to circulate as an e-mail warning in 1999 under the title "BE ALERT AT GAS STATIONS." After summarizing the "Killer in the Backseat" legend first, the warning continued:

> It has become "ritual" of gang members to take one body part from women as an initiation into gangs. The rule is that it has to be in a well-lit area and at a gas station, so be careful. They tend to lay under the car and slash the female's ankles when she goes to get in her car, causing her to fall and then they cut off a body part and roll and run. . . . It may sound bizarre and gross but the bigger the body parts the higher the initiation they receive.

The "validation" of this rumor included in the warning was typically vague. "This info. was communicated by a female law enforcement person that works in the South."

References: *Baby Train*, 134–138; *Too Good*, 105–106.

"The Small World Legend"

The bit of folk wisdom embodied in the well-known proverb "it's a small world" sums up what sociologists and mathematicians have proven in their studies: that in a surprisingly small group of people, one may discover connections between oneself and others. Often there is a further link to some famous person who happens to be connected via a mutual friend. In folk expression, this phenomenon is sometimes stated as something like this: "Do you realize that there may be only two [or three] links between yourself and any famous person I can name?" Anecdotal evidence seems to confirm the truth of this axiom, although it must be remembered that nobody ever recounts the instances when the two-link or three-link theory did not work out.

Experiments with what researchers call "The Small World Problem" usually measure the number of intermediate links between a volunteer in one part of the country and a target person living far away. One statement of the typical research question was this: "Starting with any two people in the world, what is the probability that they will know each other?" Volunteers were given a message with instructions to mail it to someone they know who lived in the direction of the target individual. The friend did the same thing and so on, until the message was delivered. In most trials of the experiment there was an average of five or six links between volunteers in the Midwest and target persons in the East. The shortest chains were just two links long. These are surprising enough results in themselves, but not quite up to the level of the "folk" versions of the story.

People seem to have converted information about these carefully controlled sociological experiments into a story about researchers sending jokes or legends by word of mouth from one coast to the other, usually "in just three days." Such a procedure, however, would be impossible to control scientifically, considering all the people who hear and tell such stories, and especially with the "interference" caused by such channels as telephones, print media, broadcasts, and e-mail. Furthermore, there have been no reported small-world experiments using urban legends as the messages being transmitted, orally or otherwise. (It might be noted here that the story about an experimenter spreading a legend is, in fact, an urban legend about an urban legend.)

Small-world problems are a serious concern of scientists who are ever refining their theories on the subject and creating abstract mathematical models to describe the phenomenon. Simultaneously, unscientific small-world legends and anecdotes continue to be a staple of conversational folklore. What the scholars call "shortcuts" (i.e., when someone you know actually knows a highly placed government official) facilitate the surprising situations of very few links between a given citizen and famous folk. These same shortcuts help sustain belief in "The Small World Legend."

(A personal footnote: The author of this encyclopedia has appeared on *Late Night with David Letterman* several times. The author's brother, Tor Brunvand, once played golf with former President Gerald Ford, and the author's daughter, Dana Williams, once shook the hand of Prince Charles when he visited her exchange school in New Zealand. Surely these shortcuts must link me to most of the famous people of the twentieth century. And that's no legend. Try it with your own family!)

References: Sandra Blakeslee, "Mathematicians Prove That It's a Small World," *New York Times* (June 16, 1998); *Curses!*, 314–317; Charles Korte and Stanley Milgram, "Acquaintance Networks Between Racial Groups:

Application of the Small World Method," *Journal of Personality and Social Psychology* 15 (1970): 101–108; Stanley Milgram, "The Small World Problem," *Psychology Today* 1 (May 1967): 60–67; Jeffrey Travers and Stanley Milgram, "An Experimental Study of the Small World Problem," *Sociometry* 32 (1969): 425–443.

"The Smashed VW Bug"

Two giant semi trucks collide and, from the force of the accident, are literally fused together. The trucks are hauled away in one big piece to a wrecking yard. Days or weeks later when the debris is separated to reclaim the scrap metal, a Volkswagen Beetle (nicknamed the "Bug") is discovered smashed between the two trucks with the flattened remains of a driver and sometimes more individuals inside. Versions of the story vary as to the location of the accident, the direction the trucks were traveling, the number of victims, and how the deaths were discovered (sometimes from a terrible odor emanating from the wreck).

In another variation of the story a VW is struck by a large truck without the truck driver noticing. The VW is found hours later still stuck like a real bug to the front of the other vehicle. Both versions of the smashed-Bug story are found in Europe and the United States. These gruesome yarns, which reflect a modicum of truth about actual accidents, serve to underscore the relative safety of large heavy vehicles versus compact cars in highway accidents. The focus on the popular Volkswagen Beetle rather than some other small car suggests the influence of the "Goliath effect," although perhaps considering the size of the car it might better be called the "David effect" in this instance.

See also "The Body on the Car"; "The Lost Wreck"

References: *Curses!*, 89–91.

"The Snake (or Spider, etc.) in the Bananas (or Greens, etc.)"

While actual infestation of organic products (food, potted plants, etc.) by potentially dangerous insects and other creatures is certainly a possibility, and genuine critter/customer encounters have occurred in stores from time to time, most of the stories told about people bitten by such creatures while shopping are unverified. The apocryphal accounts tend to follow typical patterns like "a tarantula in the bananas" or "a snake among the greens" or "a baby cobra or pygmy rattler in the onion bin." Usually these rumors and stories concern imported or "ethnic" foods, and frequently the alleged victims are said to be themselves members of an ethnic or national minority suggesting that such dreaded contaminations may be the fault of immigrating creatures or citizens. Other versions, typical of the Southern American states, attribute the infestation to "greens" or some other "folk" food type. The stories sometimes claim that the victims won large sums of money in a lawsuit, and that local authorities tried to suppress the details of the incident to protect business interests.

Among the scares of this kind reported in recent years—all of them thoroughly debunked by local investigators—were these: a viper in greens in Vicksburg, Mississippi (June 1990); a cobra or other snake among imported pineapples or bananas in Houston, Texas (July 1990); a snake in the onions in Memphis, Tennessee (October 1991); a rattlesnake among collard greens in Sumter, South Carolina (November 1991); baby cobras in the vegetables sold in an Asian grocery store in Chicago (January 1992); and the unusual variation of snakes in a market that was selling meat to Navajos in Gallup, New Mexico (April 1992).

Swedish folklorist Bengt af Klintberg traced Scandinavian versions of similar stories that he collected from 1973 to 1977. The infestation in a banana was first said in Sweden and Finland to be a poisonous snake, then a dangerous spider, and finally a worm (or worms). The contamination motif was generally included in a story about parents giving a child a banana to eat; the child complained that something was moving or biting him or her from the banana, but the parents ignored the complaint until the child was actually seen being bitten by the snake, spider, or worm. Versions of the story were published in Scandinavian newspapers, and some accounts claimed that a child had actually died from the bites. One suggested remedy was to peel bananas completely before eating them and to cut a small piece from each end of the peeled fruit.

Swedish hospitals had absolutely no reports of such attacks or deaths, even though one newspaper headlined a story *"Hela Uddevalla talar om det: Flickan, bananen och ormen"* ("All Uddevalla is talking about it: The girl, the banana and the snake"). A poison information hotline in Stockholm reported that their telephone rang "almost incessantly" in August 1975 with inquiries about the snake- or spider-bite stories.

See also "The Snake in the Store"

References: *Baby Train*, 288–290; Bengt af Klintberg, "Legends and Rumours about Spiders and Snakes," *Fabula* 26 (1985): 274–287.

"The Snake in the Store"

Sometimes called "The Snake at Kmart," "The Snake in the Store," "The Snake in the Blanket," or "The Snake in the Coat," this legend is invariably attached to an actual store, or to a chain of stores, usually ones that feature discount pricing. The infested product is often said to be imported, frequently from an Asian country. Thus "The Snake in the Store" suggests that dangers may lurk in both imported goods and low-priced bargains.

A shopper may have been running her hands over a blanket, a rug, or yard goods—or trying on a garment in the store (or at home)—when she feels a pinprick. Later she collapses, and hospital attendants determine that she was bitten by a poisonous snake. The bite is traced back to the store. In other scenarios the snake (or snake eggs) may be sewn into the lining or a pocket of a garment. Other variations on the story include the eggs hatching when a contaminated electric blanket is first used, the pinprick then being attributed to a price tag or perhaps a loose wire in the blanket. Sometimes—fortuitously—an Asian doctor happens to be on duty in the hospital where the victim is brought, and he immediately recognizes the bite of a particular snake and knows the antidote.

When "The Snake in the Store" was first noted by American folklorists in numerous versions in 1968 and 1969 it was speculated that perhaps the message of the legend was revenge coming from Southeast Asia in retaliation for the American military involvement in Vietnam. However, Vietnam was only one of many places mentioned as the supposed source of the contamination (which included Mexico and South America as well), and the story continued to circulate long after the American withdrawal from Vietnam. Gary Alan Fine suggests that "the primary mistrust [in this legend] is economic," since the nations named in the legend are generally those that export to the United States goods which were once made here. Discount stores, of course, are typically where many of these cheaper imported products are marketed in the United States.

Other kinds of contaminated-product stories circulate in Europe and elsewhere abroad, but "The Snake in the Store" seems to be particularly an American form of this theme.

See also "The Contaminated Comforter"; "The Snake (or Spider, etc.) in the Bananas (or Greens, etc.); "The Spider in the Cactus."

References: Gary Alan Fine, "Mercantile Legends and the World Economy: Dangerous Imports from the Third World," in *Manufacturing Tales* (1992), pp. 164–173; *Too Good*, 185–187; *Vanishing Hitchhiker*, 160–171.

"The Snake in the Strawberry Patch"

In the summer of 1987 a localized version of the old "bosom serpent" legend spread through North Carolina and Virginia, as reported in several regional newspapers. Supposedly, a baby had been fed some milk, then left sleeping by the side of the field while its mother picked strawberries. A snake, attracted by the smell of milk on the baby's breath, crept up to the child and slithered down its throat, strangling the baby. Both the supposed attraction of snakes to milk and the snake's approach occurring when the victim is asleep in the outdoors are motifs found in the older legend, which must have migrated to the United States from Europe where it has been well known for centuries.

References: *Curses*, 82–84; *Too Good*, 349–351.

Snakes

Besides the entries with entries mentioning snakes first, see also "The Bosom Serpent," "The Can of Snakes," "The Cat (or Dog) and the Nude

Man," "The Fatal Boot," "The Hapless Water-Skier," "The Incautious Swimmer," "The Wrong Rattler," and Viper-Release Legends. The fear and loathing that many people feel toward snakes is augmented in legends by the further association of snakes in religion with original sin and in psychology with phallic symbolism. Many urban legends, both American and international, contain references to snakes, invariably with negative associations.

In contrast to the general public's dislike of snakes, some people keep snakes as pets. When these pets get loose and are found in unexpected places, publicity about the incidents is considerable, and it tends to feed into legendary lore about snakes in toilets, coiled around water pipes, in heating vents, under floorboards, inside hollow walls, and so on.

Bengt af Klintberg suggests that "the rarity of spiders and snakes in the modern urban environment has had the consequence that they have come to assume mythical proportions in our narrative tradition." Two possible symbolic readings are that they represent, as he puts it, "the wildness and potential danger of the Third World" or that they may reflect "ambivalent female feelings towards male sexuality."

References: Bengt af Klintberg, "Legends and Rumours about Spiders and Snakes," *Fabula* 26 (1985): 274–287.

"Snakes in Playland"

Starting in 1993 a story began circulating that a child had been bitten by a snake (or snakes) hidden among the plastic balls at the "playland" of a fast-food outlet. Specifically, the attack was said to have occurred at a local McDonald's playground area. Parents are warned not to allow their children to jump into the large bins filled with colorful plastic balls lest they, too, are snake-bitten. An article bylined Lori D. Roberts in the Columbia, South Carolina, newspaper *The State* (May 14, 1993) furnished a typical local debunking:

> Spartanburg County's coroner, Jim Burnett, hears plenty of rumors. Oddly enough, he said, snakes get in on a lot of them.
>
> "Snake stories are always good stories, you know that," he said. "People just love snake stories."
>
> But snake bites are rarely fatal and it is unlikely a snake would hang out at a McDonald's Playland.

"Reptiles, especially snakes, are very much afraid of people and they do not like to be around inhabited areas, and this goes doubly for rattlesnakes," said Scott Pfaff of Riverbanks Zoo. "They like to live in the woods, in fields, places like that, so I would not expect any kind of snake to be living at a McDonald's."

See also "The Snake in the Store"; "Snakes in the Tunnel of Love"

"Snakes in the Tunnel of Love"

Snakes and other creatures hidden in amusement rides is a major theme in legends (see the entry "Amusement Park Dangers"). Watersnakes—especially water moccasins (or "cottonmouths")—are said to infest the streams through which little boats move, as in the tunnel of love, the log flume, and similar rides. Often it is said that a rider has dangled his or her hand over the side into the water, where it is bitten by a snake with fatal results. The couple emerge from the tunnel at the end of the ride with one party dead.

See also "The Can of Snakes"; "The Hapless Water-skier"; "The Incautious Swimmer"

References: *Curses!*, 37–39; *Too Good*, 348–349.

Social Class in Urban Legends

Some urban legends clearly reflect the contrasts among—and the conflicts between—different social classes. For example, the legend called

"Old Versus Young" (or "Revenge of the Rich") depicts as much a competition between members of different social classes as between an older and a younger person. Automobiles are also the markers of status in "The Solid Cement Cadillac" (in which a blue-collar worker believes his wife is being unfaithful to him with the owner of a new Cadillac) and "The Rattle in the Cadillac" (in which an assembly-line worker sabotages a luxury car, leaving a mocking note for the owner to find). The legend "Cruise Control," depending upon the details, may characterize either a woman, a young person, or an immigrant as unable to understand an automotive feature.

Two legends in which laborers oppose their employers are "Fifi Spills the Paint" and "Fixing the Flue." A similar story in which a laborer (termed a "roughneck" in this story) outsmarts his foreman is "The Roughneck's Revenge," a legend from the oil-drilling business. In "The Barrel of Bricks" a contrast is drawn between a manual laborer and an office worker when the laborer's written report of a serious accident seems laughable to the person processing requests for sick leave. (The report might also be seen as the laborer's ironic response to the need for detailed paperwork to "prove" his right for a leave.)

Legends about crime often stereotype the perpetrators as belonging to a lower social class and, frequently, also to a racial or ethnic minority. This is true of stories like "The Mutilated Boy," "Car Stolen During Earthquake," and "Lights Out!" When the motif of possible gang activity (usually initiations) is included in a legend, this may be taken as an indication of membership in some despised lower class. The same is true of "Indecent Exposure," which explicitly states that the native staff of a resort hotel has violated the guests' privacy and health, even leaving behind (so to speak) a photograph to mock their victims.

See also Racism in Urban Legends

Society for Creative Anachronism

See SCA Legends

Sociological Approach

Describing a sociological approach to folklore in general, Gary Alan Fine wrote:

> A sociological perspective emphasizes the central position of social structure or interaction processes. The question "What does a text mean?" can only be answered through an examination of the broader contexts in which narrators and audiences operate.

Fine listed four approaches typical of sociological study that have also been applied to folklore: (1) impression management and performance, (2) group dynamics and the creation of folk groups, (3) social control and social conflict, and (4) nation-building and social change.

The application of sociological theory and methods to folklore has been fruitful in all four areas; however, for urban legends in particular there has been relatively little research, including that done by Fine himself and presented in his 1992 book (subtitled *Sex and Money in Contemporary Legends*). He noted that legends "hold a mirror—a distorted one—to the social and economic conditions of modern, Western, industrial society," and he suggested that "at least in theory [contemporary legends have] some power to influence social structure and the ordering of society." In these terms, he studied such legends (or legend themes) as "The Promiscuous Cheerleader," "AIDS Mary," "The Kentucky Fried Rat," Cokelore, and redemption rumors, as well as defining "mercantile legends" and identifying "the Goliath effect." Declaring that narratives "reside in a structural surround," Fine studied folklore diffusion through interactive social networks (the title of chapter 5 of his book), showing how a set of folk stories about exploding Pop Rocks spread and became varied through specific communicative conduits in networks of relationships existing among groups of preadolescent boys and girls in a Minneapolis suburb. The links of transmission were influenced by such factors as schools attended, team memberships, friendships, and grade levels. He described one situation among girls of simple diffusion of a single version of the story versus an instance among a male group of more complex diffusion of multiple versions.

Taking a different sociological (or social-psychological) approach, Sandy Hobbs responded to the "lack of an adequate definition" of contemporary legend by pointing out that in terms of the psychological processes involved the telling of a legend is "for the teller, an aspect of his or her behaviour, and for the listener, an aspect of his or her environment." In terms of the truth or falsity of legends (an aspect often mentioned in attempts at definition), Hobbs made the astute observation that "a 'good' story may triumph at the expense of a 'true' one." (As another truism phrases it, "The truth never stands in the way of a good story.")

Hobbs proposed describing various functions that legend telling might fulfill and, by way of experiment, devised six possible "function categories," including "I am in the know" (i.e., "The Economical Car") and "normal behavior in inappropriate settings" (i.e., "The Fart in the Dark"). Of course, many urban legends have more than one function, and different tellings of the same legend may serve different functions. When Hobbs scored the contents of two general urban-legend collections against his list, the three leading functions expressed were *anxiety justified* (i.e., "The Boyfriend's Death"), *poetic justice* ("The Solid Cement Cadillac"), and *expressing inappropriate feelings* ("The Runaway Grandmother," which is also an instance of poetic justice). Hobbs's function with the lowest score in his experiment was *permanent representation of feelings* ("The Death Car").

Although one must agree with Sandy Hobbs that "it would be difficult to overemphasize the tentative nature of this theory" (i.e., that the leading three functions named in his essay may be the principal ones in most urban legends), his approach deserves further thought and application to other bodies of data. It may turn out, as Hobbs concludes, that urban legends may eventually be definable as part of some broader category of social-psychological process.

Jeffrey S. Victor's review of the use of the concept of urban legends by sociologists revealed that out of 37 introductory textbooks published between 1987 and 1992, five of them included a section on contemporary legends. Furthermore, a 1992 textbook on collective behavior devoted an entire chapter to the subject. In general, these sociologists agreed that urban legends are closely related to rumors as "collective, cultural products with a 'life' of their own, and not psychological expressions of personality dynamics." Sociologists regard urban legends as "always emergent out of interaction and never finished" and thus never reducible to any original authentic "text." (In this regard, sociologists are certainly in agreement with most contemporary folklorists.)

Victor suggested three major theoretical frameworks for the sociological analysis of urban legends, each furnished with citations of sample studies: (1) *symbolic interaction theory* (identifying cultural symbols in legends "as metaphors for the construction of social reality"; example: studies of Halloween sadists); (2) *social conflict theory* (identifying social groups' vested interests that are promoted by legends; example: Studies of the baby-parts legends); and (3) *social functionalist theory* (identifying the purposes of contemporary legends; example: studies of anti-Semitic rumors in France).

Victor pointed out that his own study of satanic cult legends employed all three forms of sociological analysis, concluding that "sociologists and folklorists have much that they can offer each other, and it is time that we begin to work together."

See also Memetics; Satanic Panic; "The Small World Legend"

References: Gary Alan Fine, "Sociological Approach," in Brunvand, *American Folklore: An Encyclopedia* (1996), 675–677; Fine, *Manufacturing Tales;* Sandy Hobbs, "The Social Psychology of a 'Good' Story," in Bennett, Smith, and Widdowson, *Perspectives on Contemporary Legend II* (1987): 133–148; Jeffrey Victor, "The Sociology of Contemporary Legends: A Review of the Use of the Concept by Sociologists," *Contemporary Legend* 3 (1993): 63–83.

"The Solid-Cement Cadillac"

A venerable automobile legend—the story of an expensive car being filled with wet cement by a jealous husband who drives a ready-mix truck—was first noted by American folklorists in the spring of 1960. The husband, on the way to a delivery, happens to drive through his neighborhood when he spots the car in his own driveway and sees his wife inside the house talking to a strange man. The husband learns later that the man was a car dealer delivering the new convertible ordered by his wife as a birthday present for him. Technically, what he dumps into the car (any of several makes) is *concrete* (cement plus aggregate [sand and gravel] plus water), but the legend is usually called "The Solid Cement Cadillac."

This attempted-revenge legend quickly spread to England, Germany, Scandinavia, and beyond, sometimes in a variation in which the wife is actually caught in bed with another man and the ruined car becomes a

VW Beetle with a sunroof. An English version published in 1978 describes a cemented Triumph convertible and ends when "a foxy little man came out of his house, climbed on to a bicycle, and pedaled briskly away in the opposite direction." An Australian version recorded by Graham Seal ends with the wife saying, tearfully, "I won the Porsche at an Art Union. A young man had just delivered it when some bastard filled it up with concrete."

An incident of someone actually filling a car with concrete was reported in the *Denver Post* in August 1960, but there was no jealousy motive, and the car itself was an old Desoto belonging to a coworker at the ready-mix plant. Evidently the perpetrator in this instance was imitating the legend. The headlines of three successive news stories about this event and its resolution were as follows: "Driver 'Blows Stack' 5 Tons of Concrete Dumped Into Auto" (August 5); "Friendship Crushed by Concrete Mended" (August 6); and "Neighbors Have a Carnival: Petrified Auto Carted Away on Trailer."

This popular and appealing legend has inspired many illustrations and a number of interpretations. At one level, the story highlights the class distinction between the blue-collar worker (the truck driver) and his supposed rival (a man with an expensive car). Even the actual car dealer or salesman seems to reside on a social step above the trucker. Another obvious theme in the legend is poetic justice: The husband receives an appropriate punishment (ruining his own car) for distrusting his loving and generous wife. Several folklorists have also offered symbolic interpretations of the legend, viewing the open car as either (or both) a symbol of potency or a direct reference to the wife's vagina; as the Swedish folklorist Bengt af Klintberg expressed the idea, "The filling of the empty car with wet cement is nothing but an enormous symbolic ejaculation."

In his *Dynamics of Folklore*, Barre Toelken describes hearing this legend from an academic colleague as something that was "actually true." When Toelken described variations on the story, mentioned its long history, and summarized the sexual-symbolic interpretation, he was met with an angry reaction and invited to "step outside and settle the matter." Toelken then realized that his colleague "was telling me the story not because I was a folklorist, but because I was a man and we were sitting with a group of men." (See "The Cultural Cement Truck Driver," pp. 316–318.)

References: Louie W. Attebery, "It Was a Desoto," *Journal of American Folklore* 83 (1970): 452–457; *Choking Doberman,* 220; *Too Good,* 29–30; *Vanishing Hitchhiker,* 125–132.

South Africa

South Africa can boast one of the most fascinating and well-documented vanishing-hitchhiker traditions known anywhere. The seed for the local version of this legend was sown on Easter Sunday 1968 near the town of Uniondale when a girl named Marie Charlotte Roux was killed in an automobile accident. Beginning in 1973 and for years thereafter, according to press reports and several claimed eyewitnesses, on the anniversary of her death Marie's ghost appeared to drivers along that stretch of road. The spirit seemed to be simply a girl hitching a ride home, but (in the manner of all such roadside ghosts) she vanished from the moving vehicle (sometimes a car, at other times a motorcycle) after giving her address. A comprehensive press report by journalist David Barritt in the South African *Sunday Times Magazine* of March 29, 1987, was reprinted in *FOAFtale News* number 13 with subsequent discussion of the case in numbers 17 and 19 (1989 and 1990). Folklorist Sigrid Schmidt concluded a review of the case thus:

> The South African press played its role in the game of legend-telling perfectly. It transformed the legend into an official report . . . [until] a nationwide Uniondale legend was formed by the press, and people were left expecting the ghost girl to hitchhike at the same spot next Easter.

One of the writers who had publicized the case, however, insisted that rather than simply repeating press accounts he had "followed this up personally." Cynthia Hind, who wrote about the ghost sightings in *Fate Magazine* in 1979, informed *FOAFtale News* readers that she had interviewed several of the claimed participants in the experiences and had found them to be credible witnesses, even though some of their "facts" could no longer be verified and there were some obvious variations of their stories circulating locally.

When Arthur Goldstuck, a Johannesburg journalist, became interested in urban legends, one of his first concerns was to investigate the Uniondale ghost girl. In his 1990 book *The Rabbit in the Thorn Tree*, Goldstuck reviewed all of the published material about the international hitchhiker legend and also asked writer David Barritt to recheck his own records and memories on the local case. Barritt, while admitting that there were some discrepancies in the stories told by his interviewees and stating firmly that he did not himself believe in ghosts, pointed out that the stories "weren't second-hand . . . [but] were the first-hand testimony of three highly credible people who didn't have any reason to make up a story." Goldstuck himself preferred the conclusion of another researcher, English writer Michael Goss, who had written this:

> We can still dismiss the thing: police involvement or not, there is still absolutely no guarantee that the witness was speaking the truth. And even if he was, the truth as he perceived it may not correspond with the truth of what actually happened.

Although the Uniondale ghost is certainly, as Goldstuck put it, "the best-known South African ghost story," there turned out to be many more international urban legends circulating in that country, including a high percentage of indigenous rumors and stories. Goldstuck's first book is titled after "the archetypal South African political urban legend," which sprang up when Barclays Bank changed its name to First National Bank and adopted a logo depicting a thorn tree silhouetted against a rising sun. The logo was said to be "a symbol of life, strength, hope." By coincidence (or so the bank claimed) the tree branches formed an outline of the map of Africa, and some people believed they also saw a leaping rabbit in the branches, which rumors claimed to be a symbol of the still-banned African National Congress. When other such "symbols" were rumored to exist in the logo as well, the bank redesigned the thorn tree so as to remove all of the images while continuing to maintain that no such symbolism had ever been intended or included.

Besides the rabbit-in-the-thorn-tree legend, Goldstuck's first book documented many of the urban legends familiar to people around the world existing in South Africa as well. These included "The Attempted Abduction," "The Choking Doberman," "The Double Theft," "The Hairdresser's Error," "The Hook," "The Mutilated Boy," "The Nude Surprise Party," "Satanic Panic," "The Spider Bite," "Superhero Hijinks," and many others, including this localized version of a Chinese-restaurant story, "one of the most popular food legends in South Africa":

> Now this really did happen, but you can't write about it, because there was a court case and the chap had to pay a fine. I think he can sue you if you write about it now.
>
> What happened was a family went to eat in one of those Chinese restaurants at the bottom of Commissioner Street—you know, near John Vorster Square. The wife ordered chicken, and she was still busy eating when a

bone got stuck in her throat. She was rushed to the hospital, and the doctor managed to get the bone out. He examined it, and then asked her what she had been eating.

She said "Chicken." He said, "Let me ask you again what were you eating?" She again said, "Chicken."

He replied: "I'm afraid not, lady. This is a cat bone." She sued the restaurant and I think she was awarded R20,000 [rands].

Reviewing the whole South African urban-legend scene during his 1991 visit, American folklorist Gary Alan Fine declared the country to be "a Republic of Rumor," replete with numerous unverified and varying claims and stories, many of them simply localized versions of international urban legends but given a political, organizational, or antigovernment slant. For example, at the "dawn" of postapartheid society, dramatically signaled by the release from prison in February 1990 of Nelson Mandela, countless stories predicted a "white apocalypse"—the fear that on a specific planned day blacks would take up arms and depose whites from their homes and jobs. Arthur Goldstuck recounts hearing at a dinner party in 1990 about one guest's upsetting "experience of friends of her daughter-in-law's parents":

These friends of friends who apparently lived in Pretoria had a domestic servant who was not terribly well disposed towards her employers. One day she announced to them, out of the blue, that she would soon own their home. "And how do you expect to do this?" they enquired, being *au fait* with the details of her breadline wages. "I'm paying the ANC a rent of R10 a month, and when they take over the country, they'll give me the house," she explained quite earnestly.

Despite other oral versions of the story, plus mentions of similar incidents in the press, no such plan and no such employer-employee conversation could be documented; in fact a similar rumor had circulated in Namibia as that country moved toward independence one year earlier.

As South Africa experienced the end of apartheid and the rise of democracy, the themes of black-white conflicts, fears, and stereotypes became stronger in hearsay and the popular press, as documented in Goldstuck's second and third books of urban legends, *The Leopard in the Luggage* (1993) and *Ink in the Porridge* (1994). Contrary to all the scare stories, however, the elections of April 1994 and the following dramatic change of government occurred in relative peace and harmony. Perhaps the proliferation of scare stories served as a safety valve for emotions rather than inciting unrest.

Even though the new South African political and social climate seems to discourage belief in many of the older claims of coming racial violence, localized versions of international urban legends continue to thrive in that small country. Arthur Goldstuck's latest collection, *The Aardvark and the Caravan: South Africa's Greatest Urban Legends* (1999), takes its title from a local version of "The Animal's Revenge." Goldstuck, South Africa's "Mr. Urban Legend," continues to work on a history of his country's ghost legends while keeping the outside world updated via his website: www.legends.org.za/arthur/welcome.html.

An excellent example of Goldstuck's research methods and findings was posted on his website in 1996 when the story of a supposed series of bizarre and mysterious deaths in a South African hospital circulated worldwide on the Internet. By comparing press accounts of the incident, Goldstuck demonstrated how the original highly suspicious and poorly documented story was magnified and standardized by newspapers, then finally began "feverishly circulating on the Internet" in a new and thoroughly legendary form.

See also "The Baby Train"; "The Graveyard Wager"

References: Gary Alan Fine, "Rumors of Apartheid: The Ecotypification of Contemporary Legends in the New South Africa," *Journal of Folklore Research* 29 (1992): 53–71; Michael Goss, *The Evidence for Phantom Hitch-Hikers* (Wellingborough, Northamptonshire: Aquarian Press, 1984), Cynthia Hind, "'I Followed This up Personally': Additional Notes on the South African Hitchhiker," *FOAFtale News* no. 19 (October 1990): 3–4; Sigrid Schmidt, "The Vanishing Hitchhiker in South Africa: Additional Notes," *FOAFtale News* no. 17 (March 1990): 1–3; "Vanishing Hitchhiker Update: South Africa," *FOAFtale News* no. 13 (March 1989): 3.

 Spain

With its rich background of traditional folklore and folklife, Spain, not surprisingly, turns out to have an equally impressive stock of contemporary legends. However, very little of this modern material was known to nonspeakers of Spanish until recently. Only passing references to the international legends "The Cut-Off Finger" and "The Cadaver Arm" as these stories appeared in Spain were noted in an English-language book.

Inspired by reading about urban legends abroad, the Barcelona writer and translator Josep Sampere began in the mid-1990s to record every "presumed legend" he came across in Spain, and when his friend Antonio Ortí, a journalist from Valencia, became aware of the collection he wrote in 1998 an article for the Sunday supplement of the leading Spanish newspaper *La Vanguardia*. Ortí's piece caused a sensation and inspired the Barcelona publishing house Ediciones Martinez Roca to commission a book by the two friends and amateur legend researchers. Sampere and Ortí's impressive collection (*Leyendas Urbanas en España*, 2000) contains the results of the compilers' thousands of questionnaires circulated in libraries and universities all over Spain as well as material from interviews, literature, and pop-culture sources. The Spanish materials are annotated with reference to the international scholarly studies of urban legends and analyzed with reference to contemporary Spanish life and times.

Many of these newly recognized Spanish urban legends are familiar to folklorists. Such stories as "The Vanishing Hitchhiker," "The Runaway Grandmother," "Spiders in the Cactus," "The Scuba Diver in the Tree," "Welcome to the World of AIDS," and numerous others are clearly international stories. Other widely told legends seem to have unique Spanish features, such as the local versions of "The Hare Dryer" in which the disinterred pet is a parrot rather than a rabbit. The Spanish version of the helpful-celebrity story describes not Elvis or Evel Knievel but King Juan Carlos himself out riding a motorcycle who stops to help a stranded motorist.

Some legends in the Spanish collection are better known (or sometimes *only* known) in European rather than American sources. This seems true of the viper-release stories, for example, as well as those about airplanes that steal rain, the Italian hypnothieves, and disappearing honeymooners.

One typical example of a recent legend from Spain that reflects a typical Spanish custom—while preserving the very old fatal-wedding theme—is "The Wedding Chainsaw Massacre," as retold in English by Josep Sampere:

> After a wedding breakfast, a friend of the groom proceeded to perform the ritual "Cutting of the tie." He wanted to play a joke, so instead of using a pair of old-fashioned scissors, he produced a king-sized chain saw! While another friend was holding the end of the necktie, the joker walked to the groom with the chain saw at the ready.
>
> Some "witnesses" said that he stumbled because he had drunk too much; others said that the chain caught on the tie. The outcome of the joke was that he buried the chain saw in the groom's chest. The horrified

guests couldn't do anything, and the groom bled to death in front of them. The joker suffered a nervous breakdown, ran out of the restaurant, got into his car, and crashed right into a tree, dying on the spot. The bride killed herself by jumping off her balcony the next day.

To demonstrate the style of Spanish modern legends, and as a practice text for readers who know the language, here is a version from Barcelona of "The Mexican Pet" legend, in this instance describing a German "mutant rat" adopted by tourists who think it is a stray dog:

El perro extranjero

Una pareja se fue con su perro a Alemania. Allí encontraron a otro perro abandonado, muy débil. Decidieron traerlo a España. Poco a poco se fue recuperando. Un día volvieron a casa y vieron que su perro estaba destrozado: se lo había comido el perro quo recogieron. Lo llevaron al veterinario y resultó que no era tal, sino la mutación de una rata. Me lo contó una amiga; le habia pasado a unos amigos de una conocida.

The popularity of *Leyendas Urbanas en España* brought about several reprintings in the first few months after publication, and a flood of new stories came in from readers, mostly via e-mail. At the time of this writing, Josep Sampere was already planning a sequel.

References: *Baby Train*, 122 ("The Cut-Off Finger"), 316 ("The Cadaver Arm").

"Sperm in the Swimming Pool"

As in the similar legend "Octopus Eggs Impregnate Swimmer," a young woman who swears she is a virgin becomes pregnant after swimming. In this instance, she supposedly received sperm that was ejaculated by males using the same swimming pool. This is yet another modern bosom-serpent story with a long history: Sir Thomas Browne's *Vulgar Errors* of 1646 mentioned a woman becoming pregnant after immersion in a warm bath in which a man had recently been. Browne characterized the incident "a new and unseconded way in History to fornicate at a distance."

References: *Choking Doberman*, 110.

"The Spider Bite"

A young woman from England (or Scotland, Scandinavia, Holland, New York, etc.) goes on a vacation to Africa (or Spain, Portugal, Mexico, South America, etc.), where she is bitten on the cheek by a spider while sunbathing on the beach. The bite swells into a large boil, and she rushes home for medical treatment. When the doctor lances the boil, hundreds of tiny spiders come running out. Sometimes the sufferer—always female—goes insane from the shock.

In another version, the woman takes a bath and the boil bursts, releasing scads of spiders into the water. Occasionally the story is told about a vacation in one's own country (e.g., a Midwestern woman is bitten in Florida). In all cases, the implication is that southern locales are less clean and more dangerous than one's home turf. When the story is told, the details are quite specific: "A friend of a friend of mine knows this Minneapolis woman who went to Miami Beach, and. . . ."

"The Spider Bite" seems to have emerged as a modern legend in Europe in the late 1970s, but it clearly echoes much earlier manifestations of the bosom-serpent story type, with all kinds of creatures being said to enter the body and sometimes to reproduce there.

See also Ants or Termites Invade the Body; Earwig Stories

References: *Choking Doberman,* 108; *Mexican Pet,* 76–77; *Too Good,* 192–103.

"Spider Eggs in Bubble Yum"

In 1977 a new Life Savers product called Bubble Yum (a soft chewing gum) was the target of rumors that the gum was contaminated with spider eggs. The manufacturer spent large amounts of

money, including full-page newspaper advertising, to combat the stories, which faded in about a year. Some people said the contaminant was "spider *legs*," though both eggs and legs seem most unlikely items to be either introduced or detected in a chewing gum. Others claimed that the new gum would cause cancer. The fact that the rumors stuck to Life Savers and not other gum manufacturers was seen an instance of the "Goliath effect."

See also "The Death of Little Mikey"; McDonald's Rumors

> **References:** John E. Cooney, "Bubble Gum Maker Wants to Know How the Rumors Started," *Wall Street Journal* (March 24,1977): 1; Fine, *Manufacturing Tales,* 153–154; *Too Good,* 193–194; *Vanishing Hitchhiker,* 89–90.

Spiders

Besides the other entries that relate to spiders, see also McDonald's Rumors and "Superhero Hijinks" (for a Spiderman reference). In urban legends spiders are said to have taken up residence in cactus plants, food products, beehive hairdos, and even inside the human body. All varieties of spiders are loathed by many people, but especially poisonous ones (like black widows) or large hairy ones (like tarantulas) are most often featured in legends. The 1990 film *Arachnophobia* exploited this fear. Spider webs are a standard part of the decor of horror films, suggesting neglect and the threat of some kind of frightening attacks. Perhaps it is because of their two extra legs that spiders seem even more fearsome than other insects.

Bengt af Klintberg has suggested that "the rarity of spiders and snakes in the modern urban environment has had the consequence that they have come to assume mythical proportions in our narrative tradition."

> **References:** Bengt af Klintberg, "Legends and Rumours about Spiders and Snakes," *Fabula* 26 (1985): 274–287.

"Spiders in the Cactus"

A woman brings into her home a large cactus plant that was either purchased at a nursery or dug up in the desert. She plants it in a large pot, and every time she waters it the cactus quivers or shakes and a strange buzzing or humming sound is heard. She calls the store (or a library, a botanist, etc.) to ask about this strange behavior of her plant and is told to get out of her house at once. Shortly after a detoxification team arrives, wearing protective gear; they remove the cactus to the backyard and torch it, whereupon a horde of generic spiders, tarantulas, or scorpions come running out of the charred plant.

In the early 1970s this legend became well known in Europe. A typical English version claimed that tarantulas infested yucca plants that had been imported from Africa for sale at Marks and Spencer department stores. Echoing this version, a 1990 German collection of urban legends compiled by Rolf Wilhelm Brednich is titled *Die Spinne in der Yucca-Palme* (The Spider in the Yucca Palm). In the United States the story became popular between 1989 and 1995, sometimes being attached to either Frank's Nursery and Crafts stores or Ikea, a home-furnishings chain. This story reflects people's dread of spiders, and it shares the motif of a telephone warning to leave the house with several other contemporary legends.

References: *Baby Train*, 278–287; *Mexican Pet*, 83–84; *Too Good*, 194–196.

"Spiders in the Hairdo"

Dating from the 1950s when the piled-up and lacquered hairdo called the "beehive" was popular, the legend about spiders infesting such a 'do is one of the best-documented and most-often anthologized and discussed American urban legends about contamination and hygiene. Usually it is said that a high-school girl wearing her hair in a "beehive" passed out in class. A trickle of blood was observed on her neck, and when her hair was washed and combed out at the hospital, spiders (often black widows) were found to be nesting there. Long after such hairdos were popular, people continued to refer to the legend and its warning against vanity in a nostalgic way. The enduring popularity of the story is indicated by a Gary Larson "Far Side" cartoon of 1990 and a popular anthology of urban legends titled *Spiders in the Hairdo* (Holt and Mooney, 1999).

The moral of the legend—"wash your hair or die"—was suggested in a 1976 *Esquire* article, "Folklore of the Fifties," but discovery of an apparent medieval prototype story provided another perspective. In a thirteenth-century English exemplum a vain woman who was habitually late for mass because she spent too much time arranging her hair was visited by the devil in the form of a spider that attached itself to her coiffure. Medievalist Shirly Marchalonis commented that in the updated version of this ancient story "cleanliness has replaced godliness as the operative force." "Spiders in the Hairdo" was also the target of a parody of Freudian legend analysis in which folklorist Kenneth Clarke claimed to find both phallic and womblike attributes to the hairdo as well as significant double meanings to the sometimes-mentioned presence of cockroaches in the beehive.

References: *Baby Train*, 16; Kenneth Clarke, "The Fatal Hairdo and the Emperor's New Clothes Revisited," *Western Folklore* 23 (1964): 249–252; Shirley Marchalonis, "Three Medieval Tales and their Modern American Analogues," *Journal of the Folklore Institute* 13 (1976): 173–174; *Too Good*, 191–192; *Vanishing Hitchhiker*, 76–81.

"St. Joseph Sells Real Estate"

See "Buried Saint Sells Property"

State Police "Balls"

Although reported several times as true in different American and Canadian locations, this story sounds more like a joke than an incident or even a legend. A beautiful young woman is stopped for speeding by a state patrolman. She pleads, "Couldn't you just sell me a couple of tickets for the policeman's ball instead of writing a ticket?" He replies, "State policemen don't have balls." Embarrassed by this admission, the policeman lets her go with merely a warning.

Another legend that includes an unintentional sexual double-entendre is "Buying Tampax." A college joke tells of a professor who refers to his pop quizzes as "quizzees"; one day a female student comments, "If these are your quizzees, I'd hate to see your testees."

References: *Choking Doberman*, 139.

Stolen-Corpse Legends

See "The Dead Cat in the Package"; "The Runaway Grandmother"

Stolen Kidney Legends

See "The Kidney Heist"

"The Stolen Specimen"

Reported since the mid-1930s and still popular in several variations is the story of the urine specimen collected in an empty whiskey or perfume bottle that is stolen while the patient is on the way to his or her doctor for a checkup. Older versions told in Great Britain and the United States described the theft taking place in a bus or tram, or else from the basket of the bicycle upon which the person is riding. Later—especially in the United States—the bottle is said to have been stolen from a parked car, either through an open window or by opening an unlocked door. Sometimes the person whose sample it is sees the thief running away with the specimen but does not bother to pursue him. The latest versions of the story begin in a way similar to "The Biscuit Bullet": Someone sees a pregnant woman sitting in a car, bent forward and shaking. The story continues when the onlooker asks if she needs help; the pregnant woman says, "No, I'm not sick or having the baby. I'm on the way to a doctor appointment and someone just stole my urine sample." Other versions of the story describe the theft of dog droppings carried for later disposal in an old handbag by a conscientious owner taking his pet for a walk.

The implied outcome of "The Stolen Specimen" is similar to that in legends about stolen corpses like "The Dead Cat in the Package" and "The Runaway Grandmother." The thief gets just what he deserves.

Ingesting urine—or pretending to—is also a theme in a prank story about a patient in a doctor's waiting room ("This specimen looks a little thin; I think I'll run it through again"—gulp!) and also in a story about an instructor demonstrating how to detect sugar in urine by a taste test (but he switches fingers and has not actually tasted the urine, a fact that his students fail to notice).

References: *Choking Doberman,* 127–130; *Mexican Pet,* 89–90; *Too Good,* 83–84.

"The Stolen Speedtrap"

A signed letter to the editor of *The Guardian,* a London newspaper, reported this "true" story on July 19, 1986, in these words:

> Sir,—This story may, in time, assume the apocryphal, but I know it to be true, as the son of the lady in question told it to me.
>
> A law-abiding lady was driving along a 30 mph road when she suddenly saw a microwave oven in the kerb. Being socially conscious *and* honest she pulled to a halt and picked the microwave up, putting it in her boot with the intention of taking it to the nearest police station. She drove off carefully and half a mile down the road was overtaken by a police patrol car, in full stereo lighting.
>
> The bobbies flagged her down and a discussion ensued, the gist of which was that she had been doing at least 70 mph in a built-up area. "We have registered you at a minimum of 70 mph," says the constable politely. "But I've never exceeded a speed restriction in my life," says the lad's mother.
>
> Further discussion reveals all. What his Mum had picked up was the aft end of a radar speed trap, designed to work on the assumption that it remains in a stationary position, which due to the honesty of Mother, plus her inability to recognise the difference between a microwave oven and a you know what, did not happen. —Yours honestly, [name and place of writer given].

The friend-of-a-friend attribution and the unlikely technical explanation make this report seem already apocryphal. Furthermore, a London reader forwarding a clipping of the letter to this writer pointed out that a variation of the story had been told on a BBC program about one week earlier. This version claimed that the woman's husband was an electrical repairman, and the wife knew that he could fix the "microwave oven." When the police stopped her, she was wracked with guilt.

By 1991 yet another variation of the story began circulating on computer bulletin boards across the United States, without naming an exact site, but implying that it had happened in the United States. This version is described as "a true story told by a friend of mine that happened to a girl she knew." The girl supposedly stopped in desperation along a highway to relieve herself behind a trash dumpster when no other rest stop is in sight. She spots what appears to be a microwave oven on top of the bin, and she puts it in her car so her husband can fix it later. State police spot the device in her car and stop her, charging her with theft of government property.

Although much evidence of an active oral tradition of "The Stolen Speed Trap" is lacking, the vague sources, the variations in detail, the doubtful technology, the stereotype of an unaware female driver, and the wide distribution of the story all suggest that it has a life of its own quite apart from any possible prototype incident.

References: *Curses!*, 111.

"The Stolen Wallet"

A classic urban legend about an unwitting theft and the ensuing embarrassment, this story—often called "The Jogger's Billfold"—has a long history. The typical American version describes a Manhattan businessman taking his morning run through Central Park on the way to his office. Another runner bumps him, and the businessman suddenly realizes that his wallet is missing. Determined not to be a victim, he catches up to the other runner and demands, "Give me that wallet!" With a frightened look, the runner hands over a wallet, and the businessman hurries to his office to clean up, calm down, and start work. Then his wife calls and says, "I hope you can borrow some lunch money or whatever you need today; you left your wallet on the dresser this morning."

In this form "The Stolen Wallet" has been widely told, sometimes as a joke, and became part of the 1975 film *The Prisoner of Second Avenue* based on a play by Neil Simon. Sometimes the action takes place in a bus or a subway train, and the object stolen may be a watch. Another American version has a Spanish-speaking runner protesting in vain "*¡Es mio! ¡Es mio!*" while in Germany the businessman exclaims, after realizing what he has done, "*Mein Gott, ich bin ja ein Taschendieb!*" (My God, I'm a pickpocket!). An American comic strip of 1935 and a book about an English traveler in Russian published in 1918 are but two of several bits of evidence that the story is quite old indeed. Hungarian American folklorist Linda Dégh recalls hearing a version about "Uncle Peter's gold watch," which was discovered to be missing when he was on a ferry boat; later her uncle later found that he had *two* gold watches in his pocket.

The English legend called "The Five-Pound Note" (see the entry "The Accidental Stickup") is based on the same essential misunderstanding.

See also Stupid Pet Rescues

References: *Baby Train,* 264–266; *Choking Doberman,* 188–191; Linda Dégh and Andrew Vázsonyi, "The Memorate and the Proto-Memorate," *Journal of American Folklore* 87 (1974): 225–239; *Too Good,* 37–38.

"Stripping the Car"

Here is how G. Gordon Liddy presented this story in his article "Security" published in a 1991 issue of *Forbes* magazine, complete with a cartoon illustrating the incident:

> Owner fraud is so prevalent in our major cities that street punks, seeing a car at the side of the road being worked on, just assume they're witnessing fraud or theft and jump in to help themselves, it never occurring to them that a legitimate repair may be in progress.
>
> Recently, in New York City, an owner had a flat. He was still jacking up the front wheels when he noticed that the rear of the car was starting to rise. Someone else was already starting to claim the rear wheels and tires! When the owner protested "Wait a minute; this is *my* car!", the automatic assumption was fraud, and the bargaining began: "Okay, just let me have the radio."

Certainly the car-stripping incident could have happened, but when, where, and exactly how? The same general situation had been described as long as five years earlier, and the locales mentioned included the Long Island Expressway, the Bronx River Parkway, and various unspecified stretches of freeway in the eastern United States. Different concluding lines spoken by the car-stripper were "Take it easy! There's enough here for the both of us!"; "Hey, man, I ain't gonna hassle you. You can have the engine, I'm just wantin' the wheels." and "It's OK. You take the back wheels, and I'll take the front. We'll split it, OK?"

The story seems to have taken on a life of its own and become an urban legend.

References: *Curses!*, 111–112; *Too Good,* 319.

Structural Approach

The application of structural analysis to folklore began in the 1920s with the work of Vladimir Propp analyzing Russian fairy tales. In the 1960s, with the English translation of *Propp's Morphology of the Folktale* and subsequent application of his theories to a broader range of folk narratives—eventually to other forms of folklore and folklife—structuralism gained a following among folklorists in the West, particularly in the United States, where it was stimulated by the research and writings of Alan Dundes, Elli Köngäs-Maranda, Pierre Maranda, and others. In Dundes's modification of Propp's system the minimal structural units of folk narratives (Propp's "functions") are termed "motifemes" (analogous to "phonemes" in linguistic analysis); the specific details that fulfill each such unit in actual folk narratives are termed "allomotifs." Thus "lack/lack liquidated" is a motifemic pattern whose allomotifs in a specific story (in this case an ancient myth) might be "lack of fire/the use of fire is revealed or discovered." Another typical motifemic pattern is "interdiction/violation/consequence," as in a story in which the command "Don't look back!" is followed by a person violating the command and looking back, only to see a horrifying spectacle that causes her to lose her mind (as in "The Boyfriend's Death").

Structural analysis has only occasionally been applied to urban legends, probably because by the time folklorists began to give major attention to this genre of folk narratives the general interest in structuralism had somewhat faded. However, some application of structuralist principles has occurred in studies of urban legends from a primarily Freudian or linguistic position. Certainly there are many different structural patterns in urban legends from those identified by folklorists in traditional legends, myths, and fairy tales.

Drawing directly from Dundes's work in both Freudian and structural analysis of folk narratives, Michael P. Carroll took "another look" at the well-known international legend "The Roommate's Death." Given that allomotifs in any story may be regarded as substitutions for the same basic motifemes (the structural units of the story), Carroll argued that all the allomotifs (the varying details) in different versions of an urban legend may be viewed as *"symbolically equivalent* in the minds of those telling and hearing the stories in which these allomotifs appear" (italics in original). By identifying and comparing the allomotifs in three distinct variations of "The Roommate's Death," Carroll confirmed the essentially sexual nature of the legend, in particular its emphasis on "male violence against women" and on young women's fears of "the first experience of vaginal intercourse."

Tackling the problem of how to deal with "truth" and "belief" in legend definition, Gillian Bennett applied a structural approach to specific recorded performances of the legend "The Wife Left at the Roadside" (or "The Wife Left Behind"). She found that "storytellers who wished to be believed structure their accounts with the precision of courtroom testimony," and she demonstrated how a narrator moved "in orderly fashion through six stages—abstract, orientation, complication, evaluation, resolution, and coda." Once this pattern was recognized, Bennett noted how individual legend-tellers departed from the usual structure in order to emphasize elements of belief or disbelief. Bennett then developed a "checklist of linguistic clues to performance strategies" that may allow a folklorist to recognize a narrator's intention of telling a legend "for true" versus telling it "for laughs."

The value of a structural approach to urban legends seems well established from the few studies done so far; it remains for more scholars to apply such theories and methods to a larger body of data, including not only texts but also contexts and performances of urban legends. As Robert Georges points out, structural analysis is "reductionist" (i.e., reducing folklore texts and other data to patterns and formulas). But as the studies of Carroll and Bennett demonstrate, a structural method can also be useful in studying matters of psychology, symbolism, and belief.

See also Linguistic Approach; "The Roommate's Death"; "Superglue Revenge"

References: Gillian Bennett, "Legend: Performance and Truth," in Bennett and Smith, *Monsters with Iron Teeth* (1988), 13–36; Michael P. Carroll, "Allomotifs and the Psychoanalytic Study of Folk Narratives: Another Look at 'The Roommate's Death,'" *Folklore* 103 (1992): 225–234; Alan Dundes, "From Etic to Emic Units in the Structural Study of Folktales," *Journal of American Folklore* 75 (1962): 95–105; Robert A. Georges, "Structural Approach," in Brunvand, *American Folklore: An Encyclopedia* (1996), 691–692.

"The Stuck Baby"

See "Baby's Stuck at Home Alone"

"The Stuck Couple"

A couple become stuck together during sexual intercourse in a small sports car; they are discovered in this embarrassing situation either by police or casual by-passers. The car must be dismantled and medical help summoned in order to free them. One widely circulated version ends like this: "The distraught woman, helped out of the car and into a coat, sobbed, 'How am I going to explain to my husband what has happened to his car?'"

Although claimed as an actual incident that occurred in London in the 1970s, the trapped-lovers story has several variations and many different localizations—both British and American—as well as prototypes in classical myths and legends. Popular books and magazines have frequently presented the story as "true." Dubbed *penis captivus* or *vaginismus* in the medical literature, the condition of becoming "stuck" during sexual intercourse is regarded by scientists (in Taylor's words) as "a rare but also a relatively transient symptom with consequences that are less sensational than those fabricated by rumour." The best-known (and supposedly validated) instance of a stuck couple has been proven to be a hoax perpetrated in an 1884 article by the Canadian doctor Sir William Osler writing under the pseudonym "Egerton Y. Davis."

Despite being easily debunked, the "myth" of *penis captivus,* as Benjamin Beit-Hallahmi calls it, "has attained a special popularity among medical personnel, physicians and nurses." Most versions of the story, this researcher discovered in his surveys, include the elements of surprise (causing the "captivity") and punishment (for their illicit intercourse).

References: Benjamin Beit-Hallahmi, "Dangers of the Vagina," *British Journal of Medical Psychology* 58 (1985): 351–356; Sidney W. Bondurant and Stephen C. Cappanari, "Penis Captivus: Fact or Fancy?" *Medical Aspects of Human Sexuality* 5 (1971): 224, 229, 233; *Choking Doberman,* 142–145; Richard Roberts, "Penis Captivus," *British Medical Journal* 2

(1979): 1591; F. Kräupl Taylor, "Penis Captivus—Did It Occur?" *British Medical Journal* 2 (1979): 977–978; *Too Good*, 122–123.

"The Stuck Diver"

The story is told among divers in the United States, Great Britain, Australia, and probably other countries that a scuba diver reaching into a rock crevice to catch a large crab or lobster is trapped when the creature swells up and pins his hand inside the crevice. Sometimes the diver simply dies; in other versions he uses his diving knife to hack off his own hand. Another variation of the story describes a man hunting abalone or other creatures along the shore who is trapped before the incoming tide by the same means and drowns when his cries for help are not heard.

There are various traditional folk-narrative motifs about people's hands, feet, noses, beards, and the like being caught in cracks or clefts (usually in a split log or in the mouth of a stone statue), but none seems to be exactly like the version in this modern legend.

See also "The Scuba Diver in the Tree"

References: *Baby Train*, 72.

"Stuck on the Toilet"

Two separate legends concern someone becoming stuck on a toilet. Both may owe something to the traditional folk-narrative Motif D1413.8 (*Chamber-pot to which one sticks*). The first story occurs in a home, usually to a baby-sitter who unwittingly uses a toilet with a freshly varnished or painted seat and becomes stuck fast. Discovered in that helpless condition by her employers, the stuck sitter must be taken to the hospital with the seat still attached for its surgical removal. Rendering the story sometimes more a joke than a legend, a doctor at the hospital, when asked about her plight ("Have you ever seen anything like this?") replies, "I've seen a lot of these in my time, but never framed."

Some versions of this first story describe the employers themselves becoming injured as they struggle to extricate the baby-sitter from her predicament. A few even conclude with the laughing-paramedics motif.

There is some evidence of people actually becoming stuck to toilets as a result of a prankster putting glue on the seat of a public facility.

The second story is really about someone becoming not merely stuck but eviscerated on a toilet, either on a jet airplane or a cruise ship. According to this one, a very fat woman uses the toilet, and the vacuum system that flushes the device, plus the smooth plastic seat, produces such a suction that a portion of her insides are drawn out. Published reports in various tabloids and even major news media seem to substantiate such an incident, and Dr. J. Brendan Wynne's 1987 letter describes one occurring on a Greek-registered cruise ship in full detail. This report, in its turn, received wide news coverage, sometimes with varying details and implying (probably falsely) that this was a recurring situation on ships and planes.

See also "The Exploding Toilet"; Motif

> **References:** *Too Good,* 372–373; J. Brendan Wynne, DO, "Vacuum Toilet Evisceration," *JAMA* 257 (March 6, 1987): 1177.

"The Stuck Santa"

A man required by business to be away from home during Christmas suddenly, and to his great pleasure, learns that his trip has been cancelled. He decides to dress as Santa Claus and surprise his family by coming in through the chimney on Christmas Eve. But he becomes stuck and dies in that situation, being discovered only when the family lights the Yule log and the smoke backs up into their home.

Although unverified versions of this story have circulated for years, two very similar incidents of this kind did actually occur, both of them in January 1993. One victim was a Cornell University student found suffocated in the chimney of a fraternity house; the second was a burglary suspect who became caught in the chimney of a house in Oceanside, California. Associated Press stories about the latter case included a photograph of the stuck "Santa."

> **References:** *Baby Train,* 74.

"The Stuffed Baby"

Here is how this horrendous legend began appearing in e-mailed warnings in 1999; the quotation is verbatim, except that paragraphing was added:

My sister's co-worker has a sister in Texas who with her husband was planning a weekend trip across the Mexican border for a shopping spree. At
the last minute their baby-sitter canceled, so they had to bring along their
two year old son with them.

They had been across the border for about an hour when the baby got
free and ran around the corner. The mother went chasing, but the boy had
disappeared. The mother found a police officer who told her to go to the
gate and wait. Not really understanding the instructions, she did as she was
instructed.

About 45 minutes later, a man approached the border carrying the boy.
The mother ran to him, grateful that he had been found. When the man
realized it was the boy's mother, he dropped the boy and ran himself. The
police were waiting for him and got him. The boy was dead, in less than 45
minutes he was missing, cut open ALL of his insides removed and his body
cavity stuffed with COCAINE. The man was going to carry him across the
border as if he were asleep.

A two year old boy, dead, discarded as if he were a piece of trash for
somebody's cocaine. If this story can get out and change one person's mind
about what drugs mean to them, WE are helping. Please send this E-mail
to as many people as you can, if you have a home PC send it out there too.
Lets hope and pray it changes a lot of minds. The saddest thing about the
whole situation is that those persons who suffer are innocent and people
we love. . . .

God Bless you in this united effort to spread the word. You just might
save a life!

One might wonder how a Mexican drug smuggler could hope to carry
a sleeping Anglo baby across the border without having a passport for it.
Or how the Mexican police knew exactly what he would do. Or why this
dreadful crime has not been publicized in the national media. Instead,
all we have to verify it is this anonymous e-mail message attributed to a
friend of a friend with the concluding appeal to "spread the word." It
certainly sounds like an urban legend—and it is!

Back in 1985 the same basic story was published in the *Washington
Post* and repeated in *New Republic* magazine. The *Post* quickly re-
tracted the story, quoting a U.S. Customs Service spokesman who said
the unverified story had been around since at least 1973. Other versions
of the story (sometimes said to have occurred within the United States
or at the Canadian border) continued to circulate, both orally and in
print, even finding its way into a *National Geographic* article about
emeralds in July 1990. The e-mailed variation of the rumor has further
details added to make it more of a legend, plus standardized opening
and closing formulas common in other bogus warnings.

References: *Baby Train,* 109–112; *Mexican Pet,* 145–146; Mary Thornton, "Drugs Making Miami Synonymous With Crime," *Washington Post* (March 25, 1985), and "Corrections" (March 30, 1985); *Too Good,* 224–225.

"The Stunned Deer"

See "The Hunter's Nightmare"

Stupid Pet Rescues

Following the theme of jumping to conclusions, in particular mistaken identifications, are several stories describing the return of the wrong pet. A look-alike dog or cat is returned to its owner by a helpful friend or neighbor—except that it's *not* the right pet. Usually the animal is left tied or penned in the yard with an explanatory note. In one variation on the story, a real-estate agent showing a house for sale obeys the owner's instructions in a note: "Please do not let cat out." The agent finds a tom cat lurking outside the front door, assumes that the homeowner's cat was let out by another agent, and locks it inside after showing the house. The tom is found consorting with the owner's prized Persian when the owners return; they recognize it as the neighbor's cat.

A published version of "The Stolen Wallet" from a small-town California paper in 1928 concluded with the writer being reminded of "an actual occurrence" in which a woman saw a stranger carrying "her" dog, a small spotted terrier. She demanded the dog from the stranger, took it home and chained it in the yard, only to find her own look-alike dog lying next to it the next morning. Both stories, obviously, play on the idea of an unwitting theft.

See also "The Bungled Rescue of the Cat"; "The Hare Dryer"; "The Mexican Pet"; "The Wrong Rattler"

References: *Baby Train,* 262–266.

Style of Urban Legends

"Style" in folklore has been defined concisely as "textual pattern, or the exploitation of available patterns within given contexts" (Nicolaisen, 1997) and as "a characteristic mode or manner of expression" (Bauman and Schacker-Mill, 1998). These general statements are easier said than proven or grappled with, for, as Nicolaisen adds, the concepts of *style* and its study (*stylistics*) "are slippery intellectual commodities . . . multifaceted . . . [and possibly] indefinable." For the purpose of this entry, however, "style" refers simply to patterns of expression that are evident in the exact wording of traditional texts, but it does not refer to the larger "stylistic" aspects of context and performance. Textual style has been much analyzed by folklorists, including in such areas as gender-based speaking patterns, oral formulaic composition, and ethnopoetics. But the styles of telling urban legends have barely been identified, let alone studied in any detail.

Even without having analyzed contemporary legend narrating style, folklorists have for a long time admired the skills and appeal of such storytelling. The English folklorist Stewart F. Sanderson, for example, in a 1981 lecture (also quoted in the entry for "England") echoed the sentiments of others, saying:

> What strikes me as perhaps its most outstanding feature is the creativity, imagination, and virtuosity brought to its performance by all kinds of people, old and young, well read and barely literate, educationally privileged and educationally deprived.

Although sometimes the verbatim words used by the tellers of urban legends may appear bland, repetitious, and relatively unstructured when transcribed on the written or printed page, the power of the narrative is projected effectively to listeners by the narrator's facial expressions and inflections, his or her attitude of belief (or of neutrality, or even of disbelief), and the feedback from the audience. As people tell urban legends they often emphasize key points, insert commentary, repeat major sections of the plot, and incorporate or respond to listeners' reactions. Frequently, in fact, the telling of an urban legend is more a group effort with several persons supplying details or variations than it is a standup performance with one teller addressing one or more listeners. Concerning published legend texts, I wrote in the first chapter of *The Vanishing Hitchhiker*:

> Even the bare printed texts retain some earmarks of effective oral tradition. Witness in the [quoted] Kansas text [of "The Boyfriend's Death"] the artful use of repetition (typical of folk narrative style). . . . The repeated use of "well" and the building of lengthy sentences with "and" are other hallmarks of oral style which give the narrator complete control over his performance, tending to squeeze out interruptions or prevent lapses in attention among the listeners.

Other aspects of style considered in the above source included the description of the setting, the use of sound effects, the dramatic roles of characters in the story, the quotation of dialogue, and the timing of a shocking ending that is similar to the actual contexts in which this particular legend is often told.

To professional storytellers and actors, the urban legends circulating in "folk" oral transmission often seem flat and uninteresting. As David Holt and Bill Mooney wrote in their popular anthology *Spiders in the Hairdo* (1999; see bibliography), "Most often, just the bare bones of the story are related, but, as with any intriguing tale, the plot can be expanded and embellished to suit the teller and the audience." By way of example of this notion, one might compare a typical everyday telling of "The Hook" with Holt and Mooney's embellished version. One text collected from a 19-year-old Texas woman (quoted in *Choking Doberman*, p. 213) begins:

> Once there was a couple and they were dating and they went out to a . . . they were out in the middle of the woods by a lake, parking. And they were making out and they had their radio on.

Another bare-bones version, this one from South Africa, is quoted in the entry on "The Hook." Here is how Holt and Mooney begin their retelling of the same legend:

Billy leaned over to kiss Jennie. He had been dreaming all week about this moment. He had finally talked his father into letting have the car for the night. Billy and Jennie had driven up Mulholland Drive, overlooking all of Los Angeles, and now Jennie was in his arms.

As Billy leaned over to kiss her, Jennie pushed him away. "Wait, Billy," she said. "Please. I don't feel good about being here."

"But we've both been looking forward to this time together."

"I know, but I just don't like being up here alone. It's creepy."

Whether such expansion of legend cores into "short stories" is more or less effective than the "folk" versions is a matter of personal taste, or perhaps it is just a matter of oral versus written style. At any rate, urban legends—usually elaborately retold ones—have become very popular among professional storytellers in the 1990s.

Lately, as urban legends have begun circulating commonly on the Internet, there would seem to be less in the way of "style" to observe in the texts. After all, most such legends (often being bogus warnings rather than narratives per se) are simply forwarded electronically without change or comment. However, even e-mailed rumors and legends have some stylistic aspects, using such devices as all capital letters, strings of exclamation points, parenthetical comments, citation of supposed verification, appended remarks (e.g., "THE FOLLOWING IS TRUE AND NOT A JOKE!!!"), and symbols to suggest an attitude, like the familiar mark :-) (which is a "smiley," used to indicate a joke).

See also Collecting Urban Legends; Context; Linguistic Approach; Performance of Urban Legends; Structural Approach

References: Richard Bauman and Jennifer Schacker-Mill, "Style," in Mary Ellen Brown and Bruce A. Rosenberg, eds., *Encyclopedia of Folklore and Literature* (Santa Barbara, Calif.: ABC-CLIO, 1998), 629–632; W. F. H. Nicolaisen, "Style," in Thomas A. Green, ed., *Folklore: An Encyclopedia of Beliefs, Customs, Tales, Music, and Art,* vol. 2 (Santa Barbara, Calif.: ABC-CLIO, 1997),776–777; *Vanishing Hitchhiker,* 4–10 ("The Performance of Legends").

Suicide

See "The Failed Suicide"

"The Suicide Rule"

This piece of American college folklore—more a rumor than a legend proper—combines, as William S. Fox of Skidmore College in Saratoga Springs, New York, pointed out, "three long-standing student concerns: grades, roommates, and death. Its most common expression is 'If your roommate commits suicide, you get a 4.0 [i.e., a perfect grade average] that semester.'" Fox made a comparative study of data collected in 1985 via surveys at his own and one other area college. He found, as other folklorists also have elsewhere, that the belief is well known among students, and it exists in several variations as to conditions that supposedly must be met to merit the 4.0 and alternate "compensations" (e.g., a better dorm room, a trip home for the rest of the semester) for the trauma of losing a roommate to suicide.

Although it is true that schools and colleges do usually provide special counseling and other support to students following some personal tragedy, no institutional rule for dealing with suicides by awarding a perfect grade has ever been introduced into any kind of official procedural manual. As a result, whenever "The Suicide Rule" surfaces at a college, the student or other local newspaper is likely to investigate the claim and publish a debunking.

In 1998, after the film *Dead Man on Campus* (based on the legend) was released, a story in the Mansfield, Ohio, *News Journal* quoted an Ashland University (Ohio) junior:

> My boyfriend's sister knew a girl whose roommate killed herself, and she got a 4.0 (grade-point average) for the year. It was at Bowling Green. It happened last year or two years ago.

But the article continued by explaining that there was no such rule documented anywhere, despite other students' insistence that it had happened "about six years ago" or that a "dead man's clause" existed in the regulations of some other university.

See also Comparative Approach

References: *Curses!*, 295–298; William S. Fox, "The Roommate's Suicide and the 4.0," in Bennett and Smith, *A Nest of Vipers* (1990): 69–76; *Too Good*, 427.

"Superglue Revenge"

Two popular writers on rumors and legends, Hal Morgan and Kerry Tucker, refer to this legend as "an engaging story, and it just might have happened somewhere, sometime." Marking it merely "unconfirmed" rather than "not true," Morgan and Tucker summarize "Superglue Revenge" thus:

> A woman who discovered that her husband was being unfaithful to her glued his penis to his leg with "superglue" while he was sleeping. He had to have an operation to get it unstuck. (1980)

Despite the real possibility of serious mishaps with the fast-bonding adhesives known generally as "superglue," as Morgan and Tucker admit, nobody has ever discovered a verified superglue-revenge incident, and the story sounds like a female counterpart to the male-oriented revenge legend "The Solid Cement Cadillac." In the superglue story the tying up of the sex partner is literal, whereas in the cemented-car story it is symbolic.

Mark Glazer, analyzing 22 versions of "Superglue Revenge" from the Lower Rio Grande Valley of Texas, distinguished versions in which the wife symbolically castrated her husband with superglue versus wife's-revenge versions in which she literally castrated her husband with a knife or razor. He found the stories equally well known among Mexican Americans and Anglos, told always by people over 20 years old, and circulated mostly by women; the peak year of popularity in Glazer's sample was 1979.

Interpreting the legends, Glazer took what he termed a "structuralist model," noting the binary opposites of nature versus culture in the stories. In "Superglue Revenge," he asserted, "culture plays a secondary role to nature," since in the legends when social/cultural norms are defied (i.e., husband is unfaithful, wife takes revenge) the "passions of nature" prove to be stronger than culture, and a cruel revenge is enacted. A second binary opposition that Glazer identified is between marital infidelity and revenge. Both aspects, he pointed out, "lead to a no-sex situation for both husband and wife." Thus the "moral of the story," Glazer suggested, may be that "over-indulgence in 'natural' behaviour to the extent of ignoring social norms will lead eventually to an inability to enjoy nature at all."

Curiously, another structural analysis was offered in a parody form in British author Adam Mars-Jones's short story titled "Structural Anthropology." Mars-Jones described five sets of oppositions, beginning with nature/culture and proceeding through limp/stiff, food/drug, and private/public all the way up to comedy/tragedy. His story concluded, "Just below the surface of story, like the succulent separate threads beneath the skin of a perfectly cooked vegetable-spaghetti, lies the tangled richness of myth."

See also "The Lover's Telephone Revenge"

> **References:** *Choking Doberman,* 146–149; Mark Glazer, "The Superglue Revenge: A Psychocultural Analysis," in Bennett and Smith, *Monsters with Iron Teeth* (1988), 139–146; Adam Mars-Jones, "Structural Anthropology," in *The Penguin Book of Modern British Short Stories* (1987); Morgan and Tucker, *More Rumor!* (1987), 199–200; *Too Good,* 212–214.

"Superhero Hijinks"

On October 7, 1994, the *Los Angeles Times,* in a column of short humorous items, published this anonymous version of "Superhero Hijinks":

> Where's Robin when you need him?
>
> The story, as we heard it, involved a husband and wife who recently decided to add a little excitement to their sex lives, somewhere north of Ventura Boulevard.
>
> So one night, he tied her to their bed and left the room. Moments later, he barged through the door in a Batman costume, executed some karate kicks and began trampolining on the bed. Alas, he bounced up and hit his head on a ceiling fan. Luckily, the fixture was turned off. But he still managed to render himself unconscious. His wife's screams alerted the neighbors, who called police. They untied her and revived the Conked Crusader, who no doubt wished he could hide in one of the manholes of L.A.

"Superhero Hijinks" was first published in Paul Smith's 1986 anthology of urban legends from Great Britain; the text described the husband wearing a Superman outfit, but an illustration pictured the couple in Batman garb hanging upside-down. Variations of the story were told in the United States through the 1980s and early 1990s, featuring both of these superheroes as well as Spiderman and Tarzan. Usually the story begins with a neighbor hearing cries for help coming from an apartment or house. The story was being told in New Zealand in 1988 and 1989, and it popped up in a Paul Harvey radio broadcast in 1989 and in an Ann Landers advice column in 1990.

See also "The Boy Who Played Superman"

> **References:** *Baby Train,* 38–43; Smith, *Nastier Legends* (1986), 103–104; *Too Good,* 130–131.

Supernaturalism in Urban Legends

Few of the stories classified by contemporary folklorists as "urban legends" involve the supernatural, although most of them certainly contain bizarre, unusual, and generally *un*natural aspects. Exceptions to this general rule are a few contemporary ghost stories like "The Vanishing Hitchhiker," "The Ghost in Search of Help for a Dying Person," and "The Phantom Coachman." These three, however, arc all updates of traditional supernatural legends, just as "The Ghostly Videotape" derived from earlier legends about the images of long dead persons becoming visible in modern photographs. Beyond these few examples, the only other group of contemporary legends that might be called "supernatural" has a basis in religion, as in "The Devil in the Dance Hall," "The Missing Day in Time," and "The Well to Hell."

It would appear from these few examples that the supernatural is mainly a phenomenon of past folk traditions and that most modern legends are based on natural, if unusual, situations. However, folklorist Linda Dégh has disputed that view, asserting that her fieldwork has convinced her "that modern industrial society fosters and nurtures irrationality of which the legend is the perfect manifestation." Dégh cites the increasing numbers of contemporary sects, cults, and alternative religions; the flourishing traditions about haunted properties and the return of the dead; the continuing attention to supernatural themes in television, tabloids, and other popular media; and the proliferation of popular publications about occult themes as evidence for her view. Thus she asks, "Why is there so much preoccupation with horror stories under the title of 'urban legends,' creating the impression that they are more typical and popular than ghost stories?"

The answer to Dégh's questions would seem to be related to the more secular than supernatural interests of many modern folklorists, as well as to the sheer numbers of nonsupernatural legends that have been collected. Also, by calling their subject "modern," "contemporary," or "urban" legends, folklorists would seem to be deliberately relegating the survivals of an older supernatural legend repertoire mostly to the realm of *traditional* or *rural* folklore.

Dégh's response to the question "What is the legend after all?" in her 1991 article was to restore the supernatural as an aspect of the subject. Thus she proposed (in part) that "the legend is a story about an extranormal (supernatural or its equivalent) experience attested by situational facts. It happens to average people within their cultural realms but contradicts accepted norms and values of society at large."

See also "The Devil in the Dance Hall"; "The Ineradicable Bloodstain"; Satanic Panic

References: Linda Dégh, "What Is the Legend After All?" *Contemporary Legend* 1 (1991): 11–38; *Too Good*, 227–250 ("Strange Things Happen").

"The Suppressed Product"

The best-known manifestation of this theme in urban legends is "The Economical Car" in which an advanced experimental automobile that gets phenomenal mileage is accidentally sold, then recovered by the manufacturer and kept out of production so as to preserve profits for big oil companies. A variation on this theme claims that a pill has been developed that will extend gas mileage or even render a tank full of water usable as fuel in a gasoline engine. Other suppressed products mentioned in rumors and legends include razor blades, light bulbs, and batteries that never wear out.

References: Morgan and Tucker, *Rumor!* (1984), 123–125.

"The Surpriser Surprised"

In his classic comparative study of this legend complex, William Hugh Jansen distinguished three versions of the story in which a planned surprise party turns out to be most surprising for the surprisers themselves. In the first version ("Why I Fired My Secretary"), a businessman misunderstands his secretary's invitation to her apartment as a seduction and is discovered wearing "nothing but my socks" when his family and office staff rush in to surprise him for his birthday. The second version ("The Nude Surprise Party") describes an engaged couple left alone in her home; they have stripped for action when they are summoned by telephone to do an errand in the basement, where they find a large family gathering ready to surprise them with an engagement party. The third version ("The Fart in the Dark") is described in its own entry above.

The businessman story, sometimes titled "The 49th Birthday," is often told in first person and circulated as photocopy lore, perhaps more typically as a joke than a legend. The engaged-couple story is the best known as a legend and has circulated both in the United States and abroad since at least the 1920s. As well known as "The Nude Surprise Party" is, a reader was able to pass off a first-person version as an actual experience and became runner-up in *New Woman* magazine's contest for "most embarrassing moments" (February 1995, pp. 66–67).

See also Comparative Approach; "The Fart in the Dark"; Linguistic Approach

References: *Choking Doberman,* 221–222; William Hugh Jansen, "The Surpriser Surprised: A Modern Legend," *Folklore Forum* 6 (1973): 1–24, reprint in Brunvand, ed., *Readings in American Folklore* (New York: Norton, 1979), 64–90; *Too Good,* 32–36; *Vanishing Hitchhiker,* 140–146.

"The Swallowed Contacts"

See "The Unlucky Contact Lenses"

Sweden

A popular collection of Swedish contemporary legends, *Sanna Historier?* (True Stories?) was published in 1970, compiled by Stig Nahlbom and Leendets Lindh; but the systematic study of the genre began with the work of Swedish folklorist Bengt af Klintberg, who in 1974 circulated a questionnaire about "Rumors of Our Time" among adults and teenagers in Sweden and collected some 2,000 pages of material. From that time on, af Klintberg has been the leading scholar of urban legends in Sweden, having written many articles—both academic and popular—and having compiled two popular books of urban legends complete with source information and comparative notes. So well known has he become for this work in his native country that Swedes now sometimes refer to urban legends as "Klintbergers."

Bengt af Klintberg's legend collections, each containing 100 examples, are *Råttan i Pizzan* (The Rat in the Pizza, 1986) and *Den Stulna Njuren* (The Stolen Kidney, 1994). His first book was translated into Norwegian, Danish, and, perhaps most helpfully, into German in 1990 (as *Die Ratte in der Pizza*). Besides the title stories (which should be recognized by any reader of this encyclopedia), the international legends from Sweden include "The Vanishing Hitchhiker," "The Runaway Grandmother," "The Death Car," "The Cooked Baby," "The Mexican Pet," "The Solid Cement Cadillac," and many others. The characteristic Swedish elements seem to be more a matter of detail and style than of actual legend content.

Fortunately for those who do not read Swedish or German, some of the most important articles by Bengt af Klintberg, whose command of English is impeccable, have been published in that language. The most basic of these essays, "Legends Today," first appeared in a Swedish journal in 1976 and then in an English anthology in 1989. Here af Klintberg surveys the characteristic themes of contemporary legends, giving examples mostly from Sweden. His topics include ethnocentric legends about the supposedly bad behavior of foreign or unsophisticated neighbors, food-contamination rumors and stories, horror stories like "The Boyfriend's Death," and legends like "The Hot-Rodder and the Bicycle-Chain" (or "The Severed Fingers") that depict clashes among members of different social classes. In this article and another published in *Arv* in 1981, af Klintberg gave particular attention to modern legends that have wide circulation through publication in daily newspapers. Among other topics related to urban legend that af Klintberg has studied are spiders and snakes, AIDS, and the presence of revenge in so many modern stories.

Besides all the good work by Sweden's leading urban-legend scholar, a scattering of essays about "Klintbergers" by other writers has appeared only in Swedish, and six sample texts of Swedish legends translated into English were published in the 1988 compilation by Reimund Kvideland and Henning Sehmsdorf (listed in the references below). The topics of these stories include food contamination, negative images of outsiders, a horror legend, and this characteristic European version of the "Shoplifter and the Frozen Food" story from Stockholm:

One day a woman went to Åhlen's grocery store to shop. After walking around the store for a while, she stopped by one of the deep freezers and took out a frozen turkey and stuffed it in her hat without anyone noticing. It was a big broad-brimmed hat. Then she put it back on and continued to shop as if nothing had happened.

But there was a line for the cashier, and she had to wait. While she was standing there, she suddenly passed out. Her hat fell off, and the turkey rolled out onto the floor. The cold turkey had been too much for her, and therefore, she had lost consciousness.

See also "The Ski Accident"; "The Snake (or Spider, etc.) in the Bananas (or Greens, etc.)"

References: Bengt af Klintberg, "Modern Migratory Legends in Oral Tradition and Daily Papers," *Arv: Scandinavian Yearbook of Folklore* 37 (1981), 153–160; af Klintberg, "Legends Today," in Kvideland and Sehmsdorf, eds., *Nordic Folklore: Recent Studies* (Bloomington: Indiana University Press, 1989), 70–89; af Klintberg, "Do the Legends of Today and Yesterday Belong to the Same Genre?" in Lutz Röhrich and Sabine Wienker-Piepho, *Storytelling in Contemporary Societies* (Tübingen, Germany: Gunter narr Verlag, 1990), 113–123; Reimund Kvideland and Henning K. Sehmsdorf, eds., *Scandinavian Folk Belief and Legend* (Minneapolis: University of Minnesota Press, 1988), 375–392 ("Urban Folklore Today").

"Swiss-Charred Poodle"

This is San Francisco columnist Herb Caen's nickname for "The Dog's Dinner." In his version, found circulating as a Reuter's news item in 1971, a Swiss couple dining in Hong Kong accidentally give directions to have their pet poodle cooked and served to them. Other journalists have called the story "Roast Rosa" or "Chow Mein."

Switched Campus Buildings

An architect's or planner's blunder leads to plans for campus buildings at two separate universities being switched. Each institution's structure is erected on the other institution's campus. Usually the legends are quite specific: The University of Virginia's chapel plan is said to have been switched with one intended for Notre Dame University (or Cornell University), and the Oberlin (Ohio) College library was built from a plan intended for the University of Florida. Some versions of the story claim that plans for dormitories were switched between a northern and a southern school with the result that one group of students is perpetually freezing in their underinsulated and poorly heated building while the other group is sweltering in a dorm designed for wintry weather. Lack of air-conditioning or of adequate ventilation is often attributed to the switched-building theory. In an extreme version of the story an entire campus is said to have been originally designed for another region and climate.

See also Backward Buildings and Statues; Leaning Towers; Sinking Libraries; Sinking Shopping Malls

References: *Baby Train*, 302–304; *Too Good*, 434–435.

Symbolic Approach

Some urban-legend researchers have suggested that certain striking details in the stories should be interpreted as symbols of psychological states of mind or of character's or storyteller's disguised intentions. Usually these symbolic readings are sexual in nature—chiefly Freudian—as when the hookman's prosthesis is regarded as a phallic symbol or the cement-filled car is viewed as the husband's way of symbolically preventing his wife's adultery.

There are many nonsexual possibilities of legend symbolism, only a few of which have been much explored. Questions about this aspect of interpretation might include these, among many others:

Are alligators, big cats, snakes, and spiders in urban legends symbols of "the wild"?

Should workers versus employers in urban legends be regarded as symbolic of whole social classes and the power struggles between them?

Can pets in urban legends usually be interpreted as standing in for family members?

Does the automobile in legends about adolescent drivers represent an escape from the constraints of parents or of society in general?

Are women in urban legends consistently stereotyped as helpless, or at least in need of male rescue?

Does feminism ever provide an alternative view of women in urban legends?

Shouldn't the persistence of the gang-initiation motif in crime legends be seen as a reference to the larger concern about random violence in contemporary society?

See also Analysis and Interpretation; Freudian Approach; The Goliath Effect; "The Mexican Pet"; "The Solid Cement Cadillac"; "Superglue Revenge"; Xenophobia in Urban Legends

Tabloids and Urban Legends

Because urban legends are often sensational in subject matter yet at the same time plausible, and also because the basic plots are not copyrighted or otherwise "owned," tabloids sometimes rewrite these traditional stories as pseudo news items for publication. But because libraries and archives seldom (if ever) save and index tabloids (the lowest of lowbrow journalism), the urban legends that appear in these sensational sources are seldom noted and even less often preserved. Here are a few examples from American tabloids of urban legends turned into supposed news stories:

"My Neighbor's Dog Fingered Intruder," *Globe,* November 10, 1981. Published as this issue's "Liveliest Letter," the item purported to be a firsthand account of "The Choking Doberman" experienced by a woman in Lansing, Michigan. The neighbor's dog "Tiger" was found to be choking on two fingers bitten off an intruder who was discovered by the police "cowering in the closet" minus two fingers. A Lansing journalist later learned that the woman's name had been changed for publication of her letter and that she had actually heard the story in a beauty parlor, not from her neighbor.

"Bride's Wedding Shocker," *Weekly World News,* December 24, 1985. "Stunned wedding guests" at "a posh California ceremony" were shocked when the bride turned from the altar before the ceremony began and announced that she was calling off the wedding because she knew that her maid of honor had slept with the groom the night before. A photograph of a woman dressed as a bride but with her face covered was captioned, "The identity of the bride was withheld to save her from any further embarrassment." See "The Bothered Bride" entry for variations of this legend.

"Man Yanked Off Roof by Safety Line," *Weekly World News,* September 19, 1988. A 32-year-old man in Cape Town, South Africa, was pulled from the roof of his home where he was making repairs when his wife drove away in the family car to which the man had tied his safety rope. The man's name was said to be David Willis; his wife was Michelle. Seemingly this was a perfect re-creation of "The Man on the Roof."

"Our New Puppy Is a Killer Rat!" *Weekly World News,* October 4, 1988. In a revision of "The Mexican Pet," Henri and Catherine Fritz, aged 84 and 82 respectively, of Innsbruck, Austria, were reported to have adopted a Chihuahua-size creature found on their doorstep. It turned out to be a rat rather than a small dog, and it attacked and killed their cat "Missy." A composite picture of a large rat looming over a cute cat wearing a collar appeared with this story.

"Brick Blunder Made Me a Human Yo-Yo," *National Enquirer,* February 11, 1992. Robert Ranahan of Lakeville, Massachusetts, is described and pictured in a color photograph after having suffered the barrel-of-bricks accident that is well known as an urban legend. The alleged victim is shown with a cast on his right arm and foot while his left hand still grasps the rope attached to the barrel (really a metal trash can in this photo), out of which several bricks are spilled. This story was on a page containing three other do-it-yourself disasters consisting of a woman who glued herself to her toilet seat, another who caused an explosion while spray-painting her oventop, and a man who blew up his septic tank by pouring yeast into a toilet hoping to unplug it.

Such stories share with legitimate folklore the fact that many of them came to the tabloids from readers who submitted their own versions of stories they had heard. These legends, however, are invariably processed by the tabloid writers who invent names, ages, places, dialogue, and other details typical of authentic news stories.

There is little evidence that tabloid versions of urban legends ever influence the oral tradition, or that other staples of tabloid news such as celebrity gossip, extraterrestrial invaders, and miracle cures ever pass into the oral folk tradition.

References: Paul Smith, "'Read All about It! Elvis Eaten by Drug-Crazed Giant Alligators': Contemporary Legend and the Popular Press," *Contemporary Legend* 2 (1992): 41–70.

"Take My Tickets, Please!"

In an American city with a losing professional team (usually football or baseball), a man has two tickets to the next game but no real desire to watch another debacle. He places his tickets in plain sight on the dashboard of his car and leaves the window open as he shops at a mall, expecting that someone will steal the tickets. However, when he returns to his car he finds that someone has left two more game tickets next to his own. The number of tickets may vary, and sometimes the story is told about a college team.

References: *Too Good,* 330.

Tale Type

The plots of many traditional folktales (i.e., animal tales, fairy tales, fables, tall tales, jokes, formula tales, and the like) have been cataloged and numbered by folklorists as an aid to archiving texts and performing comparative studies. The Finnish folklorist Antti Aarne devised an index of European tale types in 1910, and his work was translated and expanded by the American Stith Thompson in 1928. The latest edition of Thompson's *The Types of the Folktale* (Folklore Fellows Communications No. 74) was published in 1968 and remains a useful reference tool for folk-narrative studies. This "Type Index" is cross-referenced to the "Motif Index" and has been the model for a number of other such indexes focusing on the narratives told in many different countries.

Although the plots thus indexed are mostly those of clearly fictional stories (such as "The Three Little Pigs," "Cinderella," and "The House That Jack Built"), a few legends, and even fewer urban legends, do have affinities to these tale types. For example, the story included in the index as "The Faithful Animal Rashly Killed" (Type 178) is a prototype of "The Choking Doberman," and "The Clever Maiden Alone at Home Kills the

Robbers" (Type 956B) is related to the contemporary legend "The Robber Who Was Hurt."

A proposed "Type-Index of Urban Legends" was included in Jan Brunvand's *The Baby Train* (1993), with each story given a title, a summary, and a list of references but no "official" type numbers.

See also "The Climax of Horrors"; Folktale; "The Graveyard Wager"; Motif

> **References:** Brunvand, "Folktales," in *The Study of American Folklore,* 4th ed. (1998), 229–268.

Talk Shows and Urban Legends

Whereas radio talk shows serve urban legends mainly as venues where the stories may be retold and discussed, TV talk shows have become a significant part of the subject matter of some legends. A typical theme is that a show's famous host once made a racy and tasteless remark to a female guest. For example, Johnny Carson was long claimed to have said something overly sexy on the air to Zsa Zsa Gabor, Ann-Margaret, Raquel Welch, and Arnold Palmer's wife, and many people claim to know friends of friends who saw the actual program. Had the incident really occurred, however, it surely would have made the highlight shows time and again, but it never did. (For a definitive debunking, see <www.snopes.com/radiotv/tv/zsazsa.htm>.)

Another common TV talk-show legend says that a celebrity guest made some surprising announcement on a broadcast. These alleged revelations range from disclosures about the star's sexual orientation to giving out the person's telephone number or credit-card number so that fans may make free long-distance calls. Never happened.

Two similar legends about guests on TV audience-participation shows share a racist angle, since the foolish remark is invariably attributed to a black contestant. Both of these stories have the "punch-line" style of jokes yet are presumed by some white tellers to be true stories. The first is about *The Newlywed Game* hosted by Bob Eubanks. The host asks some female contestants the question, "Where is the strangest place that you and your husband ever made love?" A black woman supposedly answered, "That'd be in the butt, Bob." The second story claims that Tom Selleck was a contestant on *$10,000 Pyramid* and was paired with a black partner. The word to be guessed was "deer" or "buck" (or the topic was Bambi or "forest animals"). Selleck gives the clue "doe," hoping to elicit the right word, but the black man responds with "knob." The story concludes by saying that the entire cast and crew broke out laughing and that the black contestant sued the network when he realized they were mocking him. Needless to say, nobody really ever saw these episodes, either in the studio or as a broadcast.

One of the most persistent talk-show legends is that a high-placed business official appearing on a nationwide program revealed some sordid truth about his or her company. The classic example of this theme is the claim that the founder, president, or CEO of Procter & Gamble admitted on *Donahue* (or *Merv Griffin* or *60 Minutes*) that the company had made a pact with the devil to ensure its profits and was donating a percentage of same to the "Church of Satan." The second most common claim—and equally bogus—is that a major American clothing designer (Liz Claiborne or Tommy Hilfiger, usually) had said on *Oprah,* or another major talk show, that she/he did not design clothes for blacks and would prefer that no blacks ever buy or wear them. Absolute nonsense. In fact, none of the named persons has ever appeared on any of the named talk shows.

Two examples of urban legends told on the air by national TV talk-show hosts are transcribed verbatim in *Too Good to Be True;* these are Johnny Carson and Michael Landon telling "The Hare Dryer," and David Letterman telling "The Killer in the Backseat." Surely many other such stories have been told by both hosts and guests, but the texts are very difficult to catch on the fly. By the time the story is recognized, it's too late to set the VCR.

See also "The Celebrity's Telephone (or Phone Card) Number"; Radio and Urban Legends

References: *Choking Doberman,* 203–208; *Curses!,* 233–235; Scott Heller, "With a TV Appearance, a (Bleep) (Bleep) Professor Becomes Part of the Urban Folklore That He Studies," *Chronicle of Higher Education* (May 13, 1987): 17, 24; Morgan and Tucker, *Rumor!* (1984), 90–92; *Too Good,* 40–43, 97–100.

Tapeworms in Diet Pills

Yet another variation of the bosom-serpent theme claims that diet pills that suppress one's appetite really contain tapeworms or tapeworm eggs.

This is discovered after a woman has been taking the pills for some time and a tapeworm crawls out of her nose. In a variation the government inspects the pills and finds the head of a tapeworm inside each pill.

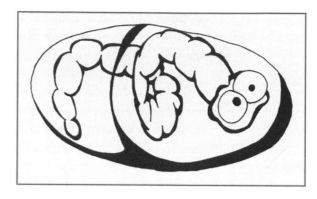

References: *Choking Doberman,* 111–112; Elizabeth Tucker, "The Seven-Day Wonder Diet: Magic and Ritual in Diet Folklore," *Indiana Folklore* 11 (1978): 141–150.

Technical Incompetence
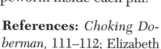

A favorite theme in contemporary legends is that of a technically challenged person failing to understand how some modern device works, which leads to dangerous results that are often humorous as well. Often the naïve user is said to be an especially young or old person, a woman, a minority member, or an immigrant. The implication is that "normal" white male Americans are perfectly capable to using technology properly, whereas "others" are stereotyped as being baffled by technology.

The devices that baffle the challenged individuals range from computers, microwave ovens ("The Microwaved Pet"), and tanning beds ("Curses! Broiled Again!") to automatic transmission ("Push-Starting the Car") and cruise control. The victims in these legends may suffer a computer crash, the loss of a pet, a deadly cancer, or an automobile accident. Other devices about which a few doubtful rumors and stories circulate are ATMs, remote controls, keyless entries, smoke alarms, and fax machines.

See also "The Barrel of Bricks"; Bungling Brides; "The Colander Copier Caper"; Computers; "Dial 911 for Help"; "The Ice-Cream Car"; "The Lawn-Mower Accident"; Naive Computer User Stories; "'R' Is for Race"; "The Sawed-Off Fingers"

References: *Curses!,* 189–192; *Too Good,* 285–298 ("Baffled by Technology").

"The Technology Contest"

As told in the United States, an American company's engineers are inordinately proud of their technical abilities. They ship a "wispy wire" of unbelievably tiny circumference in a special, velvet-lined box to a company in

Germany (or Switzerland, Japan, etc.) and very quickly receive it back apparently unchanged. But when the engineers inspect the wire closely with a jeweler's eyepiece or a microscope they discover that the foreign engineers have drilled a hole through it from end to end. Variations on the theme include producing a tiny machine screw and nut that the rival engineers modify by "drilling the screw, castellating the nut, and inserting a tiny cotter pin." Occasionally the rival engineers work for two different American companies.

Backgrounds for these stories include the tale about Robin Hood shooting an arrow that splits his rival's arrow already stuck in the bull's-eye, accounts of a Western gunman firing a bullet into the hole left by an earlier shot, the story of Victorian artisans being one-upped by Chinese craftsmen who hollow out the finest English needle, and legends describing Renaissance or Classical painters producing ultra-lifelike portraits and still-life paintings that fool the viewer into believing the subjects portrayed are real. (Another painter created a picture of a curtain so realistic that his rival tried to lift the curtain to see the painting beneath.)

References: *Baby Train*, 174–177; *Too Good*, 291–292.

Telephones in Urban Legends

The telephone, according to legend, poses a problem for a naive user in "Dial 911 for Help," and it functions as an instrument of retaliation in

"The Lover's Telephone Revenge." In "The Choking Doberman" a call from the veterinarian warns a dog owner that a dangerous criminal is hiding in her home. A similar instance of this telephone-warning motif occurs in "The Baby-sitter and the Man Upstairs," a legend in which repeated ringing of the phone and frightening messages heard from it create suspense and evoke horror.

Telemarketing ploys, telephone pranks, answering machines, and actual scams carried out via telephone sometimes become the topics of urban rumors and legends, most of them of the bogus-warning variety.

See also "The Celebrity's Telephone (or Phone Card) Number"

Television and Urban Legends

Television series based on suspense, ranging from yesterday's *Twilight Zone* to today's *Unsolved Mysteries* and *X-Files* series, have from time to time borrowed material from urban legends of crime and horror. Lighter legendary fare has appeared on television in such formats as the offhand allusions to "The Hook" and "The Batter Fried Rat" on *Seinfeld* and the sight gag based on "The Elevator Incident" in the classic *Newhart* episode "Sit, Whitey!" from 1973. One full-scale legend/TV adaptation (among several that might be cited) was the episode based on "The Kidney Heist" used as the major plot element on a 1991 episode of *Law and Order.*

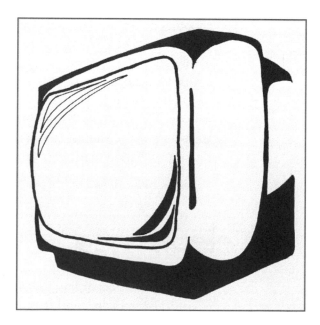

An updated version of the old TV series *In Search Of* went into production by the Fox television network in autumn 2000. One full-hour urban-legend episode was planned, along with others on such sensational topics as Bigfoot, voodoo, ancient astronomers, and the Loch Ness monster. Among the experts interviewed on camera for the episode were folklorists Moira Smith and Linda Dégh as well as the compilers of some popular legend anthologies, the creators of an urban-legend website, and a director of horror films. As of this writing (January 2001) air dates for *In Search Of* had not been announced, but information about the ongoing project was available at www.insearchofonline. com where it is described as "the most comprehensive analysis of urban legends done for television" (where, one recalls, hardly any analysis of urban legends has *ever* appeared!).

Life cereal TV ads introduced in 1971 became the basis for the legend "The Death of Little Mikey." Ads for other products shown on television have sometimes borrowed ideas from urban legends, but these are difficult to document because of the rapidity of change in advertisers' campaigns and the specific targeting of ads to particular regions and audiences. Among products and companies that have used "urban-legend ads" are Natural Lite beer, Kmart stores, and Levi's jeans.

TV news and features sometimes play a role in investigating and usually debunking urban legends, the latter effort helping to offset the influence of some talk shows where legends are uncritically repeated without qualifying comments. Unfortunately, the coverage of contemporary legends is too often made confusing by the broadcast journalists' tendency to intermix the terms "legend," "tale," "myth," and "rumor."

Besides TV broadcasts, home videotaping has become a legend theme in such examples as "The Ghostly Videotape," "The Shocking Videotape," and "The Videotaped Theft."

See also "Bozo the Clown's Blooper"; Talk Shows and Urban Legends; "The Unsolvable Math Problem"

References: *Too Good*, 419–420 ("Sit, Whitey!").

"The Telltale Report"

In an anecdote reported by Samuel Eliot Morison in *Three Centuries of Harvard: 1636–1936* (Harvard University Press, 1936), a student cut classes one winter in the 1880s and went to Havana for a break. He left behind a set of postdated letters to his parents for a friend to mail, but their housekeeper posted the whole lot together, alerting the parents and the university of his absence. The same ploy with a similar outcome is part of the legendary history of Mormon missionaries, who serve a two-year stint away from home and are required to stay on the job, shunning recreational activities. When two missionaries sneak off to a sports event or for a vacation, they leave a series of postdated letters addressed to the folks at home. But their landlady either mails the letters out of sequence or sends the entire set at one time. (Alternatively, the missionaries may be caught in the act when they are spotted by their supervisor on television attending the Olympics or another notable event.)

It seems likely that the Harvard story—both anonymous and unverified as Morison tells it—while not surviving among students in this more liberated age, has reemerged as a legend popular among Mormon missionaries, illustrating their reaction against their own restricted lifestyles.

References: *Curses!*, 292–294; *Too Good*, 438.

Theft in Urban Legends

Roughly half of the urban legends about crime involve theft in some form, always with some kind of twist beyond simply describing someone illegally snatching an item. For example, in "The Helpful Mafia Neighbor" stolen goods from a home are returned anonymously after the crime boss living next door helps out, and in "Indecent Exposure" the thieves mock their victims with a revealing photograph. Other typical theft legends include "The Robber Who Was Hurt," "The Lottery Ticket," and "The Videotaped Theft." A subcategory of these legends involves unwitting thefts, as in "The Stolen Wallet" and "The Accidental Stickup." Another popular group of theft legends involves the stealing of food, as in "The Grocery Scam," "The Package of Cookies," and "The Shoplifter and the Frozen Food."

Several automobile legends involve thefts or attempted thefts. For example, "The Unstealable Car" describes a foiled strategy to safeguard one's car, and "Car Stolen During Earthquake" illustrates poetic justice striking the car thief. An unwitting car theft is illustrated in "The Arrest," and the work of expert thieves is depicted in "The Double Theft," "Stripping the Car," and "The Two Hitchhikers," among other stories. Perhaps the ultimate well-deserved punishment for stealing from a vehicle is the subject of "The Unfortunate Gas Thief."

See also "The Dead Cat in the Package"; "Dog's Corpse Is Stolen"; "The Kangaroo Thief"; "The Kidney Heist"; Organ Thefts; "The Runaway Grandmother"; "The Stolen Specimen"; "The Stolen Speedtrap"

"The Through Train"

See "The Misguided Good Deed"

Toll-Booth Pranks

The most commonly mentioned cadaver prank attributed to medical students is that of removing an arm from a cadaver in the dissection class and

using it to extend a coin out a car window at a toll booth. The entire arm with the coin held in the fingers is left with the toll taker, who either faints or dies from the shock. The prank is claimed to have been carried out by students enrolled in schools all across the United States and in several foreign countries, always at some specific bridge or highway. Not surprisingly, first-hand (so to speak) versions are rare.

American accounts of toll-booth pranks have circulated since at least the 1930s, and there is an older version in which a student offers the cadaver arm for a handshake in the 1928 book by Spanish novelist Pío Baroja titled *The Tree of Knowledge*.

References: *Baby Train,* 316; *Curses!,* 299–301; *Too Good,* 116–117.

"The Toothbrush Photo"

See "Indecent Exposure"

Tourist Horror Stories

Many urban legends describe dire fates suffered by people while traveling. Even "The Vanishing Hitchhiker" and "The Mexican Pet" might be so classified, and the cross-references below are but a sampling of other candidates for the genre.

There also exists a special group of stories about outrages perpetrated upon Western tourists in exotic or Third World countries, including Turkey, Afghanistan, India, China, and various countries in Africa and Asia. Often the object of the foreigners' desire is a young, beautiful, and usually rich female tourist. The victim may end up dead, mutilated, or forced into prostitution.

The Japanese tell a distinctive version of the tourist horror stories in which a recent bride is abducted on her honeymoon in a large Western city and later shows up badly disfigured in a circus sideshow in the Philippines. "The Mutilated Bride" thus reflects Japanese distrust both of Western criminals and Asian opportunists; possibly there is also an echo in the legend of a fear of revenge wished against the Japanese by their enemies and victims from World War II.

See also "AIDS Mary"; "The Body in the Bed"; "The Dog's Dinner"; "The Kangaroo Thief"; "The Kidney Heist"; "The Runaway Grandmother"

References: *Choking Doberman,* 92; *Curses!,* 85–87.

"The Trained Professor"

Applying B. F. Skinner's technique of "operant behavior" as a practical joke, a college psychology class conspires to condition its instructor to adopt certain absurd behavior as he lectures. By smiling, nodding, and showing attention to the instructor's lecture at some points and feigning lack of interest at other points, the class manages to train the professor to stand in a certain part of the room, gesture in a specific way, or even to stand on an overturned wastebasket as he teaches.

Although most accounts of this application of behavioral psychology in the classroom can be considered apocryphal, or at least exaggerated, textbooks often mention the use of similar reinforcement techniques and even imply that complex conditioning has occasionally been successful in the classroom and elsewhere. Joan Chrisler's 1988 report of an attempt to duplicate the "anecdotes about groups of students conditioning their professors as a practical joke" concluded that his students' experiments "are often successful and fun." However, Chrisler's method was somewhat different from that described in the legends in that she was herself the subject of the attempted conditioning and the class was working together on an assigned project.

References: Joan C. Chrisler, "Conditioning the Instructor's Behavior: A Class Project in Psychology of Learning," *Teaching of Psychology* 15 (October 1988): 135–137; *Curses!*, 311–313; *FOAFtale News* no. 21 (1991): 3–4; and no. 24 (1991): 5–6; *Too Good,* 326–327.

Tricky Questions and Answers

Stories abound of students using ingenious methods to undermine the testing procedure by means of tricks, ploys, and even outright cheating. Some of the stories, of course, are probably true, but others seem doubtful, especially since they have been told and retold in many different places over a long span of time and with varying details. In a reversal of the student stories, other legends describe an instructor's own tricky exam question. For specific plots and ploys, see "The Barometer Problem," "The Bird-Foot Exam," "Define 'Courage,'" "Do You Know Who I Am?" "A Lesson in Compassion," "The One-Word Exam Question," "The Open Book Exam," "The Second Blue Book," and "Which Tire?"

There are two versions of the story of a supposed response a tricky student made to the assignment "Write your own question and then answer it." In one version it is a final-exam topic, and the student simply repeats the question: "The best possible final exam question is 'Write your own question and then answer it.'" The second version describes the situation as an entrance exam essay topic to which the student responds by writing, "Do you play the tuba? Answer: No."

References: *Too Good,* 444–447.

"Truckers and Bikers"

In the legendary rivalry between truck drivers and motorcycle riders, the former group always seems to win. Usually in these legends a group of Hell's Angels or members of another motorcycle gang are harassing a truck driver in a roadside café. He tolerates their behavior silently, then leaves. "He wasn't much of a man, was he?" one biker comments. The counterman or waitress replies, "No, and he wasn't much of a driver either," pointing out that the trucker had backed his big rig over the row of Harley Davidsons parked outside.

See also "Bikers Versus Smokers"

References: *Baby Train*, 213–214; *Vanishing Hitchhiker*, 178–179.

True Urban Legends

By definition, urban legends are *told as true* (as least by some tellers some of the time) but are *not literally true* (at least not in every last detail and certainly not in all the places where they are repeated). Sometimes an actual event seems so bizarre that it is mistaken for an urban legend (see, e.g., "The Pregnant Shoplifter"). In a famous instance of life becoming legend (see the entry "Craig Shergold Legend"), an English child has been unable to suppress the stories told about him.

The "truth" in most urban legends lies in their reference to specific details of everyday life and in their depiction of believable human psychology. Also, the lessons many legends teach may be quite reasonable and worthwhile, whatever the literal truth or falsity of the stories' plots. The two best examples of widespread legends that could be traced to actual incidents are detailed under the headings "The Heel in the Grate" and "The Unsolvable Math Problem." The important role of the mass media in modifying and spreading both stories should be noted.

See also "The Bullet Baby"; "Green Stamps"

References: *Too Good*, 449–472.

"The Tube on the Tube"

A New York City clerk needs to dispose of a burned-out fluorescent tube from his office. Unable to find a Dumpster as he walks to the subway, he still has the tube in his hand as he boards his train for home. Since he is holding it upright, other people on the train take hold of the tube, thinking it is a support pole. The man gets off at his stop, leaving the tube in the hands of his fellow riders.

Occasionally told and sometimes attributed to an unverified published source, this amusing story may or may not be an actual legend. The title suggested here makes it sound British, but there is no evidence the story is told overseas. The story is included in this compilation because it's a favorite of the compiler, and (as Paul Harvey sometimes says) "for what it's worth."

References: *Too Good,* 31–32.

"The Turkey Neck"

Reported and studied by Gordon McCulloch, this Scottish contemporary legend purports to explain how a woman broke her wrist, as she explains herself to coworkers the morning after the accident. Her husband had come home drunk and fell asleep downstairs on the floor or on a sofa. The wife leaves him there and goes to bed. Later their children return home and, as a prank, unzip their father's fly and insert the neck from a roasted turkey in the fridge. When the wife comes back downstairs to check on her husband, she sees the family cat nibbling on what appears to be his penis protruding from his pants fly. She faints, breaking her wrist in the fall. (Sometimes the wife herself inserts the turkey neck, but the cat's behavior still upsets her.)

A sample text of this legend is given in the entry for Scotland, and a brief discussion of McCulloch's analysis is included in the entry "Comparative Approach."

References: *Mexican Pet,* 129–131.

"The Two Hitchhikers"

Reported, so far, only in a 1983 version from Washington state and one remembered from the 1930s in Utah, this story has the ironic twist, if not the proven wide distribution, of a genuine legend. A single motorist driving on a long, lonely stretch of highway picks up a hitchhiker for company. But the man's rough appearance and demeanor alarm him, so he picks up a second, younger, and neater-looking hitchhiker, who gets into the backseat of the car. The younger man pulls a gun and orders the driver to stop and the other two to get out of the car.

But as the holdup man gestures toward the door with his gun, the older hitchhiker dives into the backseat and disarms him, knocking him cold with one quick blow. He removes the holdup man's billfold and offers to split the take with the driver, commenting, "I've been in this business 20 years, and I don't make dumb mistakes any more like pointing with a gun." Seeing the driver's horrified expression, he adds, "Oh, don't worry. I'm not working today, just going over to [wherever] on a visit."

A somewhat similar situation occurs in a story about a motorcycle gang coming into a small grocery store and paying in full for their purchases. A couple of clean-cut college students enter next and hold up the storekeeper, taking all the money spent by the bikers.

The English writer Jasper Maskelyne in a 1938 book told a first-person version of a related story involving just one hitchhiker. He described picking up a rough-looking hitchhiker who not only backed up his own lie to a policeman who had pulled him over for speeding but also picked both the policeman's and his own pocket, giving the "two fat wallets" back when he left the car later. Maskeleyne claims that he removed the policeman's notes on the incident and returned the rest of the notebook and wallet anonymously.

All of these and several other legends display what many people conceive of as the quirky criminal mind.

References: *Curses!*, 108–110; *Too Good*, 306–308.

"Uncle Don's Blooper"

"Uncle Don" was the name adopted by Don Carney (whose original name was Howard Rice) to use for his avuncular persona as the host of a popular children's radio program that ran from the mid-1920s until 1947. Legend claims that in signing off the air one day Uncle Don made an indiscreet and out-of-character remark, believing that his microphone had been cut off. Usually the statement is quoted as, "That ought to hold the little bastards for another day." Supposedly, the radio series was abruptly canceled.

However, the Uncle Don program was never yanked from the schedule but stayed on the air until its appeal dwindled; everyone associated with the program denied the swearing story. "Blooper" records and tapes purporting to contain a copy of the actual incident exist in at least three different versions, none of which can be verified. (Significantly, some of the "Blooper" versions are introduced with the phrase "a legend is Uncle Don's remark. . . .) Furthermore, the tradition of a children's radio-show host swearing on the air existed earlier, and stories of similar bloopers have been attached to different personalities many times over. Most early live radio shows were not recorded anyway.

"Uncle Don's Blooper" seems to be the background story for the legend about a children's TV-show host entitled "Bozo the Clown's Blooper."

References: *Mexican Pet*, 185; *Too Good*, 329; *The Truth*, 84–94.

"The Unexpected Inheritance"

Referred to generically as "Promiscuity Rewarded" and in a distinctive Irish version as "The Kilkenny Widow," this legend describes two men staying overnight at a small hotel or rooming house owned by a beautiful young widow. One man slips off to the bedroom of the widow, at her invitation, where he spends the night. Some months later, the other man receives word that the widow has died and left him a considerable fortune. It turns out that the first man had used the second man's name during his romantic rendezvous.

Variations of this story were told in Ireland in the early 1980s, published in *Reader's Digest* in August 1989, and appeared in a *New York Times* article in 1985. In the first of these versions the incident is credited to a small hotel in the village of Kilkenny. The second version describes two American tax agents having a car breakdown in an unspecified rural area, and the third sets the incident in a sleeping car on an Italian train in which a married *woman* gives another person's name to the man with whom she spends the night.

See also "The Will"

> **References:** *Choking Doberman*, 133; *Mexican Pet*, 127–128; *Too Good*, 88.

"The Unfortunate Gas Thief"

This story, popular among recreational vehicle owners, illustrates poetic justice (or "just deserts"); it is sometimes called "Gag Me with a Siphon." An RV owner has converted his second gas tank on the vehicle into a holding tank for his toilet and wastewater system. In some versions he fails to remove the decal reading "unleaded fuel only" from the filler tube. Late one night, while camped, he hears a commotion outside and comes out to check. In the beam of his flashlight he discovers that his holding tank has been opened, and a siphon hose is stuck into the filler tube. On the ground is evidence that someone who had been trying to steal gasoline had made himself very sick in the attempt.

"The Unfortunate Gas Thief" can be dated at least back to the late 1970s and has been spotted in the media as recently as 1992.

References: *Too Good*, 82–83; *Vanishing Hitchhiker*, 181–182.

"The Unlucky Contact Lenses"

Two people are sleeping in the same bed, or at least in the same room. One of them puts his or her contact lenses into a half-full glass of water for the night and leaves the glass on a bedside table. The other sleeper awakens in the middle of the night with a strong thirst; he or she fumbles for the water glass and drinks it dry—contact lenses and all.

This story is told on a variety of persons, including husbands and wives, lovers, prostitutes and their customers, and members of athletic teams on the road. A number of firsthand accounts of actual swallowed contacts have been reported, but the extended versions of the story involving celebrities, love affairs, prostitutes, and the like seem, as they say, "too good to be true." Some versions of the story describe a person swallowing his or her own contacts, but this seems even a more unlikely scenario than the others. Besides, how many contact wearers leave their lenses in a plain glass of water by the bedside overnight?

See also "The Welded Contacts"

References: *Mexican Pet*, 85–86; *Too Good*, 144–145.

"The Unlucky Driver's Examination"

This contemporary English legends describes a man taking a road test either on his motorcycle or automobile. The test may be either for the driver's competence or else to check the vehicle's brakes. The driver is told to stop as quickly as he can when the inspector either jumps out in front of the vehicle or sounds the horn of the police car in which he is following the examinee.

In the first version, the inspector jumps in front of the wrong vehicle and is badly injured. In the second story the driver being tested stops suddenly when he hears the signal, but it was another car blowing its horn, and the unaware inspector's vehicle crashes into the rear of the test car.

References: *Baby Train,* 214–215; Dale, *Tumour in the Whale,* 124–125; Smith, *Nasty Legends,* 77.

"The Unsolvable Math Problem"

One of the very rare urban legends that can be traced back to a specific source, "The Unsolvable Math Problem" is thoroughly discussed in the sources listed below, including variant texts.

In brief, the legend is that a college student arriving late for a mathematics examination manages to solve a problem written on the blackboard that was not intended to be part of the exam. Supposedly, the problem had stumped even Albert Einstein, but the student, unaware of its difficulty, finds a solution, thus proving the power of positive thinking.

The germ of this inspiring story was the actual experience of Stanford University mathematician George B. Dantzig in 1940, when he was a graduate student at the University of California–Berkeley. Dantzig solved not one but two previously unsolved problems, having mistaken them for homework in his statistics class. He related his experience years later to the Reverend Robert H. Schuller, host of a nationally popular TV religious program, and Schuller, after putting his own spin on the story, repeated it on the air and included it in one of his publications. By the time the story passed into legend via broadcasts, print, and oral tradition, Dantzig's name had disappeared, Einstein's had entered the story, and various other changes occurred to convert it into a standardized unaware-genius plot. A similar episode was included in the 1997 film *Good Will Hunting.*

References: *Curses!,* 278–283; *Too Good,* 452–456.

"The Unstealable Car"

A man secures his treasured automobile (vintage sports car, restored classic, immaculate limo, etc., or perhaps a valuable motorcycle) by chaining and locking it securely to thick metal hasps in his garage or between two large trees. Sometimes the car is also said to have been covered with a tarp. In other versions the car is parked tightly between two other large vehicles. In any case, when the owner next goes to unchain and use his car he finds it still locked up tightly, but it has been turned in the opposite direction from the way he had left it. Under a windshield wiper blade is a note: "If we want this car, we will take it" or, "When we want it, we'll be back to get it."

Although "The Unstealable Car" is widely told as the experience of a friend of a friend, nobody has, so far, produced any proof of its truth, neither a detailed news report nor even the note left behind. An Associated Press mention of the incident in an article about car thefts (distributed in September 1991) was merely an anecdotal report based on word of mouth. A variation on the theme describes someone's furniture rearranged while the homeowner is away; nothing is stolen, but a taunting note is left behind.

See also "The Dishonest Note"; "The Rattle in the Cadillac"; "Stripping the Car"

References: *Curses!*, 104–107; *Too Good*, 317–318.

Unwitting Thefts

See "The Accidental Stickup"; "The Stolen Wallet"

"The Unzipped Fly"

In an essay on stories of embarrassment, folklorist Roger D. Abrahams included this personal-experience story:

> When I was a kid, growing up in a small town outside of Philly, I was used to double-dating with my friend "Jelly-beans." He was a little fat, very klutzy, and a clown. One New Year's Eve we decided, since there were no parties, that we would be very grown-up and go into Philly to Bellevue-Stratford for dinner and dancing to impress our girlfriends. Well, we got there and were having a good time, eating and dancing, and at one point he went to the men's room. He came back and my girlfriend whispered to

me, "His fly's open." . . . I leaned over to him when he sat down and said to him, "Your barn door's open!" As unobtrusively as possible, he zipped up. Meanwhile the band had started up again, and I asked my girlfriend to dance. We had just gotten out to the floor when we heard this awful clatter and looked back and there was Jelly-beans with the tablecloth caught in his fly. We ran over to him, of course, and tried to help him get it out, but it was stuck. Well, we were all embarrassed, especially the girls, 'cause everybody, I mean *everybody,* was looking at us. Eventually we had to roll the damn thing up and walk over, across the dance floor, to the men's room. Of course, everyone clapped when we did this. We had to get a janitor up there with a pliers before we got it out, and even then I couldn't get Jelly-beans to go back into the dining room.

Later in his essay Abrahams admitted that the unzipped-fly incident "did not actually happen to me. . . . But it did happen to a couple of friends of mine exactly as recounted, or so it was reported to me." Probably Abrahams was either mistaken or (more likely) joking, since "The Unzipped Fly" is an urban legend well known both in the United States and abroad. Versions have been reported from Scandinavia, Belgium, and Ireland, but doubtless the story is told in many other countries as well. In her column for August 29, 1990, Ann Landers printed a version sent by a California reader in which a man's zipper catches a woman's fox-fur stole while both are riding on a bus. Landers presented the item as one of her favorite past columns, and she ran the story again on May 10, 1991. Other versions of the story involve a man in a theater whose zipper catches a bit of the hair or the dress of a woman seated in the row in front of him. In all of these double-zipped variations the unhappy couple must exit the scene while still firmly attached to each other, much to the amusement of onlookers.

In yet another variation on the theme, the young man whose zipper is open at a restaurant or a formal dinner party attempts to distract his tablemates so he can zip up. He directs their attention out the window where, to his embarrassment, two dogs happen to be copulating on the lawn.

Abrahams's explanation of such stories is that they "take a situation which, while it was happening, was out of control, and . . . impose on it a sense of order after the fact." He suggests that "the more you are able to retell the story, the more you feel able to put the event under control."

References: Roger D. Abrahams, "The Most Embarrassing Thing That Ever Happened: Conversational Stories in a Theory of Enactment," *Folklore Forum,* vol. 10, no. 3 (1977): 9–15; *Too Good,* 142–143; *Vanishing Hitchhiker,* 138–139.

"The Unzipped Plumber or Mechanic"

In both typical versions of this legend a wife, returning from shopping, sees a man whom she presumes to be her husband working under the sink ("Unzipped Plumber") or under his car ("Unzipped Mechanic"). Only his legs are sticking out, and she playfully unzips his fly and fondles him. Soon afterward the wife discovers her husband in the house reading the paper, and she learns that he had given up on the repair job he was doing and summoned a professional. They rush to the aid of the other man and find him knocked out cold from sitting up suddenly when his fly was unexpectedly unzipped.

In common with the previous legend (both of them popular as newspaper fillers and anecdotes), this one has been around the country and even the world for many years, possibly existing as long as zippers have been used on men's pants flies. Sometimes the unzipped legends are combined with other accident stories, and these may conclude with the laughing-paramedics motif.

References: *Too Good,* 140–141; *Vanishing Hitchhiker,* 147–148.

Urban Belief Tales

"Urban belief tales" is one of the terms used in the 1950s and early 1960s for what we now generally call "contemporary legends" or "urban legends." Richard M. Dorson, a pioneer in American modern-legend collection and study, employed this term (among others), but he seemed to prefer simply "legend" for the entire genre, defining it informally as "the story which never happened told for true." By 1968 Dorson had adopted (and had possibly coined) the now-familiar term "urban legend."

See also Belief Legend

References: Dorson, *American Folklore,* 249–254; *The Truth,* 14–15.

Urban Legend

The film *Urban Legend* (sometimes incorrectly cited as *Urban Legends*) was released in 1998 by TriStar Pictures and directed by Jamie Blanks. Starring in the film were Alicia Witt, Rebecca Gayheart, Jared Leto, Michael Rosenbaum, Joshua Jackson, and Tara Reid. Set on a fictional New England college campus, *Urban Legend* depicts members of a folklore class who suspect, after their study of contemporary legends, that a series of disappearances and murders have been following urban-legend plots. They research the topic, pursue various innocent suspects, and eventually discover the truth—that a student in their own class is the killer. Their folklore instructor, professor Wexler, is played by horror-film veteran Robert Englund; his character, once a suspect, becomes another of the killer's victims. (Some academics might say he deserved to die for his stereotyped portrayal of a folklorist whose major goal seems to be to browbeat and frighten his students.)

The horror legends selected for dramatic portrayal in *Urban Legend* were selected from folklorists' publications, as evidenced both by references in publicity material for the film and by the titles applied to legends in the script. If a particular legend does *not* usually contain a murder, the film's writers supplied one. The then nonexistent work *Encyclopedia of Urban Legends* appears in one scene, shelved in the college library next to actual urban-legend collections.

Urban Legend, although panned by most film reviewers, did reasonably well at the box office, earning at least as much as several other teenage slasher films of the past. Its concluding scenes, with the killer escaping and a new group of students discussing the legends and murders of the past, strongly hints at a sequel. One Hollywood producer who was pitching another film project involving urban legends characterized *Urban Legend*—with understandable, if exaggerated, disdain—as "a model of everything we don't want our films to be: writing, directing and acting were uniformly poor, and the final product was of no possible interest to anyone over the age of twenty."

The quasi-sequel to *Urban Legend* titled *Urban Legends: Final Cut* was released in 2000. One reviewer described it as "a dim-witted hodgepodge that puts the 'ick' in 'flick'." Although an urban-legend film is supposedly being produced as the main element in the plot of *Final Cut*, only one actual legend is depicted—a particularly nasty rendition of "The Kidney Heist."

See also Film and Urban Legends

Urban Myth

"Urban myth" is the favorite misnomer applied to urban legends by many journalists, broadcasters, and sometimes the general public. They are all using the term "myth" in the loose, popular sense of a false assumption or assertion, not in the folkloristically technical sense of an ancient or native cosmological story with religious significance. The term "folklore" itself has suffered from a similar kind of misunderstanding, as in the common expression "that's just folklore!" said about a variety of items with suspect veracity, whether or not they are really folklore. Serious students of these subjects will strive to keep their usage correct and consistent. There is no need whatever for the term "urban myth."

See also Definition of "Legend"; Myth

"Urban Pancake"

See "Car Stolen During Earthquake"

Urban Panthers

See Big Cats Running Wild

"Urine in Corona Beer"

In 1986 or 1987 a rumor began to circulate that Corona, an imported Mexican beer, was being contaminated with urine by brewery workers.

Encouraging the story is the fact that Corona is sold in clear bottles that reveal the bright-yellow color of the beverage. As Gary Alan Fine points out, the two themes of this rumor, "fear of contamination and fear of competition," both applied especially well to Mexico at the time of the story's emergence. Some American workers fear competition from south of the border, and legends like "The Mexican Pet" also dealt with supposedly less-than-sanitary conditions there. Furthermore, with Corona beer being the fastest-growing import at the time, the story also illustrates the "Goliath effect."

In a joking response to this ridiculous rumor, an American engineer calculated that to provide a level of 100 parts per million in a beer vat 20 feet in diameter and 20 feet high, some 75 full bladders would be required. This assumes (wrongly) that beer vats are open at the top and easily accessible to brewery workers. An article by P. J. Bednerski in the *Chicago Sun-Times* (August 23, 1987) about rumor expert Fredrick Koenig of Tulane University contained a photograph of professor Koenig with an open Corona bottle before him and holding a foaming glassful of its contents.

Although the Corona rumor has faded, the memory of it still compels some beer drinkers to declare, "I just can't forget that story, and I can't stand to drink that brand of beer!"

Another urine contamination rumor is that the open dishes of candy mints offered at many restaurant checkout counters when tested showed traces of urine coming from the fingers of men who used the restroom before leaving and failed to wash their hands thoroughly.

References: "Corona Beer Latest Target of Nightmare Rumors," *Denver Post* (August 15, 1987) [an article distributed by the *Los Angeles Times* and widely reprinted]; Fine, *Manufacturing Tales*, 169–171.

"The Vanishing Hitchhiker"

The most often collected and the most discussed contemporary legend of all, "The Vanishing Hitchhiker" is actually an exception to the rule that urban legends do not deal with the supernatural. In fact, it might be better to regard this internationally told story as being part of a continuing supernatural-legend tradition rather than as an "urban legend" in the usual sense of the term. However, popular writings have so firmly established "The Vanishing Hitchhiker" as belonging to the urban-legend canon that it would be difficult to detach it from that category now.

The essence of the legend's plot is contained more or less consistently in hundreds of collected variants; it involves a mysterious roadside figure who hitches a ride to a stated destination, then disappears from the moving vehicle (buggy, car, van, taxi, motorcycle, etc.). Sometimes the hitchhiker has first made some odd or prophetic comment, and frequently the ghostly nature of the rider is confirmed when the driver inquires at the address given and sees a photograph or other portrait of the rider. The picture is said to depict a long-dead relative of the home's inhabitants who was killed in an auto accident at the same spot on the road where the hitchhiker appeared. In a typical American version the hitchhiker is a young woman in a light party dress who borrows a coat or sweater from the driver, then vanishes, is identified by the portrait, and "returns" the garment by leaving it on her grave for the driver to find.

Other versions of the story identify the hitchhiker as an old woman, a Christian saint, a Mormon "Nephite," or even Jesus Christ Himself.

As English folklorist Gillian Bennett showed in her paper at the 1982 Perspectives on Contemporary Legend conference (see Smith, *Perspectives*, 1984, pp. 45–63), the story of the phantom hitchhiker is really neither modern, urban, nor legend. Bennett concluded that the story's "apparent consistency in detail breaks down on close examination, and there are many intermediate stories which lead back to older sets of tales which we commonly think of as distinct."

Numerous publications discussing "The Vanishing Hitchhiker" provide rich sources for evaluating or expanding this insight, and the huge scholarly literature devoted to this "classic automobile legend," as Brunvand dubbed it, renders any adequate summary of studies all but impossible. Consider that Brunvand in 1981 discussed material from about 40 sources dating from 1940 to 1979, that the Bennett and Smith *Bibliography* of 1993 lists 133 references to "The Vanishing Hitchhiker," and that Bennett (see below) in 1998 listed 82 references. Virtually every new collection of urban legends at least mentions the story and often contains yet another version.

Besides its undeniable status as a folk narrative (whether judged to be truly modern, urban, or even legend), "The Vanishing Hitchhiker" has inspired fictional writings, films, radio and TV dramas, artworks, advertising, tabloid-news exploitation, and popular songs. Although it might seem as if the folkloristic aspects of the story have been replaced by pop-culture manifestations, "The Vanishing Hitchhiker" continues to reappear in oral tradition, as when an eruption-predicting phantom hitchhiker was spoken of in the American Northwest shortly *after* the catastrophic eruption of Mount Saint Helens in 1980.

Interpretations of the various phantom, ghostly, and vanishing hitchhikers of legends—both old and recent—have tended to focus on the echoes of traditional ghost lore remaining in the modern narratives. Bennett, for example, sees the hitchhikers who go back to the cemetery as being "modern representatives of older traditions in which ghosts were forced to return to their graves before cock-crow." Because "death has selected these people at random," Bennett suggests that the hitchhiking ghosts' "endless journeys could be seen as attempts to retrieve what they have lost—a quest for life itself."

Bennett, however, also considered the possibility that the young female hitchhikers' flimsy garments in many stories might symbolize their innocence rather than (as others have suggested) a corpse's shroud, thus implying that "these sparkling creatures as having died between youthful virginity and adult sexuality." This is a theme that Alan Dundes developed via Freudian insights. In his essay on the bloody Mary ritual (See the entry "I Believe in Mary Worth"), Dundes outlined his own view of "The Vanishing Hitchhiker" as a "symbolic morality narrative":

> A girl who hitchhikes, that is, allows herself to be "picked up" by a perfect (male) stranger, runs the risk of losing her virtue (signaled by the wet blood spot in the car's backseat, a well-known locus of teen-age and even preteen necking and petting). The car to prepubescent girls and boys represents a potential mobile bedroom. Souped-up cars used to be called "hot rods," a bit of argot fraught with phallic overtones. Moreover, and this is critical, a girl who allows herself to be picked up in this way can never go home again. In more explicit terms, a girl who has once lost her chastity is punished for all eternity by trying desperately though to no avail to return to the sanctity of home with all its associations of family values.

See also "The Corpse in the Car"; "The Ghost in Search of Help"; Japan; Romania; South Africa; Supernaturalism in Urban Legends

References: Gillian Bennett, "The Vanishing Hitchhiker at Fifty-Five," *Western Folklore* 57 (1998): 1–17; *Choking Doberman*, 210–212; *Mexican Pet*, 49–55; *Too Good*, 231–234; *Vanishing Hitchhiker*, 24–46.

"The Vanishing Lady"

Citing a version published in *Colliers* magazine in January 1949, Ernest W. Baughman gave this story the motif number Z552*(a) and summarized it as the very last item in his gigantic *Type and Motif Index of the Folktales of England and North America* (1966), under the general heading "Horror Stories," as follows:

> A woman and her daughter take a room in a Paris hotel. The mother becomes ill. The physician sends the daughter to [a] remote part of the city for a special medicine. When she returns to the hotel, she is unable to find her mother. Moreover, she finds that the room which she thinks they have taken is unfamiliar, that it has obviously been redecorated and refurnished in her absence. The manager and staff profess never to have seen her before, and the names of her mother and herself are not on the register. In some variants she never does find the explanation for the situation; in others it is ex-

plained that the mother is discovered to have bubonic plague and that this means is used to prevent panic and also loss of business to the hotel.

In one of the earliest essays on any urban legend, the popular writer Alexander Woollcott discussed "The Vanishing Lady" in his 1934 book, beginning with a version "told me some years ago as a true copy of a leaf from the dread secret archives of the Paris police." In Woollcott's account, the two women—the widow and daughter of an English officer returning from India to their homeland—came through Paris during the time of the Paris Exposition. Woollcott's version was replete with details, and it concluded with the notion that the woman had died from "a case of the black plague smuggled in from India." Her death was kept secret so as to avoid panic during the time of the Exposition. Woollcott's attempts to verify the story led him back through several printed versions and eventually to a Detroit, Michigan, journalist who had published the story in 1898 but who could no longer remember whether or not he had heard it told or made it up. Woolcott concluded that "The Vanishing Lady" was "a fair specimen of folklore in the making."

Katharine Briggs and Ruth Tongue provided a version collected in 1915 in Yorkshire, England, in which the daughter simply goes to her mother's Paris hotel room the night after they have checked in and finds it empty and redecorated. She leaves Paris without an explanation, but later an English friend investigates and learns that the mother had died of cholera during the night and that the hotel staff had destroyed the evidence.

Although "The Vanishing Lady" no longer seems to circulate in oral tradition, it still occasionally appears in printed sources. Some Americans can remember reading about, or perhaps having seen on a TV mystery program, a version about a woman's death in a hotel during the New Orleans Mardi Gras or the Carnival in Rio.

References: Katharine M. Briggs and Ruth L. Tongue, eds., *Folktales of England* (University of Chicago Press, 1965), 98–99 ("The Foreign Hotel"); Curtis D. MacDougall, *Hoaxes* (New York: Dover, 1940; 1958 paperback), 289; Alexander Woollcott, *While Rome Burns* (New York: Viking, 1934), 87–94.

Variants and Versions

Collected texts of legends and other folk narratives (indeed, of any kind of verbal folklore) are sometimes referred to as "versions" or "variants" of that particular item. Although most folklorists nowadays do not distinguish between the terms "text," "version," and "variant," some past scholars have advocated using the terms "text" or "version" for any individual telling of a narrative and reserving the term "variant" for texts that differ significantly from the "norm" for that story type.

For most purposes, however, it is sufficient to speak in general of "a *text* of 'The Boyfriend's Death,'" or "a *version* of 'The Runaway Grandmother,'" or "a *variant* of 'The Dead Cat in the Package'" without implying a greater deviation from the standard story type in any of the phraseology. After all, variation is always implied in folklore as one of its defining characteristics. When collections of texts are grouped according to their contents, the terms "subtype" and "ecotype" (or "oikotype") also become useful. The important thing is to use such terms consistently within one piece of analysis and to explain clearly how one is employing the terminology.

See also Folklore; Tale Type

"The Veterans' Insurance Dividend"

Periodically since about the mid-1940s a bogus warning has circulated in printed, photocopied, and faxed form telling American veterans of World War II that following a recent act of Congress they qualify for a dividend on their GI insurance. The payoff is usually described as amounting to 65 cents per $10,000 of insurance for each month of active duty, or sometimes as 55 or 65 cents per $1,000. The warnings stress that no benefits will be paid unless the person applies in writing to the Veterans Administration (VA), and usually an application form is provided, complete with the address of a VA regional office in Philadelphia. Readers of the warning are urged to pass the information on to any veterans or veterans' groups they know.

During what it terms "active periods" the Philadelphia VA center alone has logged from 10,000 to 15,000 letters per week about the bogus insurance dividend, although Congress has never passed any such legislation, and there is no such program in progress. In a reply card sent to those who inquire, the VA calls the whole thing "a false and misleading rumor" and urges veterans to pass this debunking on to as many others as possible.

In the decades since the end of World War II "The Veterans' Insurance Dividend" has circulated less often and less widely than in the 1940s and 1950s, but as recently as 1992 some veterans were still receiving it, and some of these were still applying to the VA for their supposed benefits.

References: *Curses!,* 261–264; *Too Good,* 408–410.

"The Videotaped Theft"

Going back at least to 1982 is the legend about a father of the bride at a society wedding who discovers that the large amount of cash he had brought in his pocket to pay the band and the caterers at his daughter's wedding reception has disappeared. He borrows money or uses a check or credit card to pay the tab. Later, while viewing a videotape of the reception taken by a camcorder left running on a tripod, he spots the bridegroom (or groom's father) taking the money from the pocket of his jacket left hanging over a chair. The thief is confronted with the tape, confesses, returns the money, and the groom agrees to an annulment, thus illustrating poetic justice (or "just deserts").

Variations of "The Videotaped Theft" have been published in newspaper and magazine articles that variously describe the event as a Catholic, Jewish, Polish, Italian, or another group's wedding and that specify different amounts of money stolen and different ways that the incident was resolved. In a letter to the "Dear Abby" advice column published in 1991 an anonymous writer, who claimed to be a professional photographer, insisted that he himself had videotaped the incident; he asked Abby how to handle the situation. She advised him simply to call on the bride's father and show him the tape without offering any explanation whatever.

Significantly, although this legend was very popular through the 1980s and 1990s, nobody, not even some priests and ministers who tell the story, has yet produced a copy of the actual tape.

See also "The Bothered Bride"; "Indecent Exposure"

References: *Choking Doberman,* 140; *Too Good,* 84–85.

Violence in Urban Legends

Although many urban legends are humorous, whimsical, or merely bizarre, a significant number of them describe assaults, kidnappings, mutilations, rapes, and murders. Sometimes, it is true, these attempted attacks are thwarted, but still the theme—and at times the supposed actuality—of violence is a major part of the urban-legend tradition. Nobody denies that such crimes *do* occur, but such structured traditional stories with their repeated motifs and unverified details as "The Boyfriend's Death" and "The Attempted Abduction" and "The Kidney Heist" are clearly part of the world of urban legend, not the real world. A number of bogus warnings circulated via the Internet (e.g., needle attacks, "The Stuffed Baby," and "Lights Out!") describe supposed violent attacks upon innocent people. In legends like "The Hook," "The Severed Fingers," and "The Robber Who Was Hurt" the would-be attacker is prevented from acting by a violent counterattack. "The Hairdresser's Error" describes an innocent customer suffering a violent attack that resulted from someone jumping to the wrong conclusion.

Viper-Release Legends

A 1993 newspaper article from Johnson City, Tennessee, summed up a strange snake story that was circulating (see Kristen Hebestreet's 1993 work, cited below):

A friend of a friend heard the airplanes flying low over Spivey Mountain shortly before three copperheads slithered up and almost chewed his leg off.

Somebody's cousin's brother-in-law heard a Tennessee Wildlife Resources Agency wildlife officer or a Tennessee Valley Authority employee or a U.S. Forest Service ranger brag about stocking timber rattlers.

Every year, state and federal agencies categorically deny stocking snakes. Wildlife officers and foresters, all of whom deny stocking snakes, are inclined to blame snake handlers releasing the reptiles after church or marijuana growers discouraging people away from their illegal crop. . . . .

The fictions vary. Snakes may be dropped out of low-flying airplanes. Every year one hears a TWRA truck used to transport rainbow trout wrecked and that hissing knots of venomous vipers spilled out of the boxes instead of game fish.

The article went on to quote several officials who denied the stocking of snakes and were puzzled over why anyone would think snake-stocking could have any possible purpose in wildlife management. Nevertheless, one official mentioned that every year his office received 20 to 30 calls from citizens asking about the snake drops.

Similar stories were told in neighboring states, as revealed by a January 1997 item in the *Licking Valley Courier* of West Liberty, Kentucky, headlined "Agency Spokesman Says Snake Tale Not So." The article began:

> Rumors have circulated here for the past few weeks that the Kentucky Department of Fish and Wildlife had released a large number of rattlesnakes in this area. The reason, according to one version of the story: to keep the wild turkey population in check. Reportedly, a half a tractor trailer load of the reptiles were released. Another version of the story had it that the snakes were dropped into selected areas from a helicopter.

Again, spokespersons for the state's fish and wildlife department denied the snake-dropping stories, also mentioning that they were aware of similar rumors circulating in Ohio.

Viper-release legends, as such stories are called in Europe, have been well known for years, especially in France, Italy, and Switzerland. Jean-Noël Kapferer described the situation in France where the rumors began around 1976 and became a national concern throughout the early 1980s:

> During a radio program devoted to rumors, an announcer admitted his surprise on the air: "certain rumors are really far too improbable." . . .
>   The announcer's surprise concerned a rumor running rife in the Périgord, Lot, and Vaucluse regions in France. Proecology groups were said to

be dropping venomous snakes by plane into certain counties in order to preserve these virtually extinct species as well as (depending on which version one heard) to feed hawks and other birds of prey or destroy rats and field mice.

Kapferer suggested that such rumors actually seem not at all improbable to many French people because the stated motive for snake releases seemed "praiseworthy and plausible" and there existed some well-known programs of reintroducing endangered animal species into French mountain and forest regions. Furthermore, he wrote, most modern people in any country have only "an abstract knowledge of venomous snake physiology," and thus they might assume that snakes dropped from a plane or helicopter would fall very slowly or bounce harmlessly when they struck the earth.

Véronique Campion-Vincent, the French folklorist who has done the most detailed studies of viper-release stories, quoted numerous published and oral reports of supposed sightings of snakes being dropped from the sky in government- or scientific-sponsored programs. She traced some of the hysteria concerning the subject to "hostility in rural areas between ecologists and hunters," not an uncommon situation in other countries as well. Vipers, she suggested, in many people's minds, represent "the epitome of evil animals." Campion-Vincent felt that the snake-release stories—although entirely without any basis in fact—seemed to raise the question in people's minds whether the current ideas about protecting rare and endangered species might "lead the mighty to prefer animals, even the worst of animals, to men."

References: Véronique Campion-Vincent, "Viper-Release Stories: A Contemporary French Legend," in Bennett and Smith, *A Nest of Vipers* (1990), 11–40; Campion-Vincent, "Contemporary Legends about Animal-releases in Rural France," *Fabula* 31 (1990): 242–253; Kristen Hebestreet, "Agencies Rattled by Snake-Stocking Rumors," *Johnson City* [Tenn.] *Press* (April 11, 1993); Jean-Noël Kapferer, *Rumors: Uses, Interpretations, and Images* (New Brunswick, N.J.: Transaction Publishers, 1990; originally published in French in 1987), 70–71, 72–73, 147–149.

"Waiting for the Ice Man"

Similar to "The Nude Housewife," and perhaps its actual antecedent, is the story of a woman also caught in the nude, but this time the plot dates from the prerefrigerator era. Circulated until at least the late 1930s, this account described a housewife, who was just ready to step into her bath when she remembered that she needed to unlock the kitchen door to allow the ice deliveryman to reach her icebox. Stark naked, she opened the door, only to face the gas-meter reader. The flustered woman explained, "I was waiting for the ice man."

Rumors and stories about housewives' amorous affairs with ice deliverymen were common decades ago, as alluded to in Eugene O'Neill's 1939–1940 drama *The Iceman Cometh*. In a variation from England reported by Stephen Pile, a woman from Dartmoor in Devon rushed to her kitchen while undressed for her bath to remove some scones from her oven. Hearing a knock at the door, she assumed that it is the village baker coming to leave bread on her table. She "nipped into the broom cupboard," where she was quickly discovered by the gasman, to whom she commented, "I was expecting the baker"; to complete her bad day, the scones were burned as well.

References: *Curses!*, 193–194; Stephen Pile, *Cannibals in the Cafeteria and Other Fabulous Failures* (New York: Harper and Row, 1988), 184.

War in Urban Legends

See Military Legends

"The War Profiteer"

During World War II a pair of women were overheard talking on a bus or subway about how well their husbands were doing as manufacturers of arms or other war supplies. "I wish the war would go on forever," one of them commented. Another passenger came over and slapped the speaker, saying, "That's for my son who is fighting [or was killed] in the South Pacific [or Europe]. Sometimes there were two slaps, one for each of two military sons.

Although reported in *Time* magazine in 1942 and repeated during the war years with several variations, the incident was never verified by a witness or participant. Other similar stories described various rebukes to people who spoke in favor of the war or against America's fighting troops or who mocked a disabled young person, not realizing that he or she had been wounded or maimed by enemy action.

References: *Mexican Pet*, 71; *The Truth*, 149–150.

Warnings

See Bogus Warnings

"Watch the Margins"

See FBI Stories

Water-skiers

See "The Hapless Water-skier"

"Welcome to the (Wonderful) World of AIDS"

See "AIDS Mary"

"The Welded Contacts"

Bogus warnings have circulated in printed form since at least 1967 warning wearers of contact lenses that exposure to arc welding can cause the lens to bond so tightly to the cornea that when the lens is removed a circle of the cornea comes off with it. The warnings are quite specific, citing supposed instances of the accident occurring to welders working at Dusquesne Electric (a Pittsburgh company, sometimes misspelled in the warnings), the Union Pacific Railroad, and United Parcel Service. All named companies, several welding supply firms, and welding industry periodicals, as well as the American Academy of Ophthalmology, have thoroughly debunked these warnings. One line has become traditional in the denials: "Removing your cornea would be like pulling off your ear."

Despite the professional denials of cornea/welding accidents, the lack of any verification, and the rather obvious impossibility of the injury, copies of the "Welded Contacts" warning continue to circulate among workers in several industries, whether these companies actually have any welding going on or not. Typical of bogus warnings, the fliers often begin with a pseudo-personal "folksy" statement, like, "We would appreciate your calling the following hazard to the attention of all of your people immediately." The texts of the warnings are usually decorated with sentences of all-capital letters and such concluding lines as "DANGER!!!!!" and "—SHOULD BE POSTED EVERYWHERE—." These warnings are similar to others that refer to the allegedly extreme dangers of such devices as microwave ovens, butane lighters, and tanning beds.

See also "The Unlucky Contact Lenses"

References: *Choking Doberman,* 157–160; *Mexican Pet,* 165–166; *Too Good,* 402–404.

"The Welfare Letter"

Lists of language boners supposedly written by semiliterate applicants for (or recipients of) welfare checks have circulated since at least the 1930s in the offices of national, state, and local agencies that administer welfare and other social-service programs. The lists are sometimes head-lined "Examples of Unclear Writing" or "How Some People Murder the English Language." A dozen or so statements have recurred for decades in these lists, including these howlers:

> In accordance with your instructions, I have given birth to twins in the en-closed envelope.
>
> I want my money quick as I can get it. I have been in bed with the doc-tor for two weeks, and he doesn't do me any good.
>
> My husband got his project cut off two weeks ago, and I haven't had any relief yet.

"The Welfare Letter" seems to be the oldest such tradition, but simi-lar lists of language boners pertaining to other areas of life include "Ex cuses for Students from Parents," "That's What You Dictated, Doctor," "Lawyer's Questions from Actual Court Records," "From Actual Letters Written to Draft Boards," "Drivers Say the Darndest Things" (suppos-edly from insurance claims), "Signs Posted in Foreign Hotels," and "Ac-tual Excerpts from Student Exams." Although many amusing errors do indeed occur in these as well as other situations requiring written input from ordinary people, the lack of firsthand experience with such boners and the constant repetition of the same few error-ridden sentences strongly suggest that most such examples are apocryphal.

References: *Curses!*, 236–239; *Too Good*, 280–283.

"The Well to Hell"

An outlandish claim that was first rumored in 1990 among fundamen-talist Christian groups, then published in religious magazines and tracts, and finally trumpeted in tabloids was that scientists drilling a deep well somewhere in Siberia had broken through the roof of Hell and that the screams of the damned could be heard through the drill hole. Accounts frequently specified that the well had been drilled in the Kola Peninsula under the direction of a "Mr. [or Dr.] Azzacov." In fact, "The World's Deepest Well" was reported in the December 1984 issue of *Scientific American* in an article by the Soviet geologist Y. A. Kozlovsky, but he made no mention of any screams of the damned being heard.

Evidence was presented by investigator Rich Buhler in the July 16, 1990, issue of *Christianity Today* (vol. 34, no. 10: 28–29) that the story was circulated in Scandinavia as a prank by a Norwegian schoolteacher who had earlier heard it told during a visit to California. A Finnish religious newsletter gave the Norwegian's hoax further circulation, and some later versions of the story then claimed to be based on a "respected scientific journal" published in Finland. By the time the *Weekly World News* got hold of the story (April 7, 1992), it was published complete with a photograph of "Dr. Dmitri Azzacov," who was supposedly from "a university in Yugoslavia" and doing his drilling in Alaska.

References: *Baby Train*, 105–108; *Too Good*, 242–243.

"What Is Jazz?"

Usually attributed to pianist Thomas "Fats" Waller or to trumpeter Louis Armstrong (or occasionally to pianist "Jelly Roll" Morton) is the story about the jazz great's witty reply to a woman who asked him "What is jazz?" Supposedly, the jazzman replied something like, "If you don't know, don't mess with it" or, "If you got to ask, you ain't got it." Many histories of jazz, plus countless magazine and newspaper articles, have given their own versions of this incident, which has proven impossible to pin down to a specific time, place, and person.

Although this story is less a legend than an anecdote (i.e., a single episode, supposedly true, including a clever comeback believed to illustrate some facet of a person's life or personality), its longtime circulation in different variations applied to various performers makes it similar to such celebrity urban legends as "Bozo the Clown's Blooper," "The Elevator Incident," and "The Youngest Fan."

References: *Baby Train*, 220–222.

"Which Tire?"

This typical tricky-question story from academe illustrates how an instructor may foil students' attempts to pass an examination that they had failed to attend at the scheduled time. Two students from the same class party the night before the exam and sleep through the alarm clock. They offer the excuse that they were out of town and had a flat tire coming back to campus that prevented them from arriving on time. Their professor agrees to give them makeup exams but puts the students in separate rooms. The first question on the test is "Which tire?"

Several versions of this story name an actual professor at a specific university, and this individual may, indeed, have used the ploy, or at least claimed to have used it. But the story of the "Which tire?" exam is widespread and long-lived as well as resembling other tricky Q-and-A legends such as "Define 'Courage'" and "The One-Word Exam Question."

References: *Too Good*, 444–445.

White-Slavery Legends

International rumors and legends about the abduction of young women in order to trap them into a life of prostitution have circulated since the 1920s and 1930s when they were known as "white-slavery" stories. Often the women were said to have been approached in a department store, dress shop, beauty parlor, or theater, and frequently they were supposedly sedated using a hypodermic needle before being spirited away as slaves of the underground sex trade. In some countries—particularly France—these supposed crimes were associated with Jewish businessmen, but neither there nor anywhere else were any such actual crimes documented.

In recent years, after most white-slavery lore had faded, the theme emerged again in new wave of scare stories involving needle attacks against women in public places, often now said to be a supposed method of spreading AIDS or hepatitis to innocent people, presumably as a form of revenge coming from infected individuals.

See also "The Attempted Abduction"; France; Japan; Needle Attack Legends

References: *Baby Train*, 250–251; *Curses!*, 206–208; Mary deYoung, "Help, I'm Being Held Captive! The White Slave Fairy Tale of the Progressive Era," *Journal of American Culture* 6 (1983): 96–99; Kathleen Odean, "Slavers in Minnesota: A Psychological Reading of the Legend," *Midwestern Journal of Language and Folklore* 11 (1985): 20–30.

"Why I Fired My Secretary"

See "The Surpriser Surprised"

"The Wife Left Behind"

Numerous well-documented instances have been reported in the press of automobile passengers (often the wives of drivers) being forgotten at highway rest stops or other points on a trip and left behind when the driver, unaware of his passenger's departure, moved on. The abandoned passengers were later reunited with the driver, either with the aid of the state police or a helpful stranger. Many of these accounts have been "improved" in retellings and then have circulated further as both personal experience stories and as quasilegends. In the latter form, the real-life wife-left-behind stories may acquire motifs of—or merge with—the popular urban legend known as "The Nude in the RV," in which the husband is the one usually left behind after he falls asleep naked or in his underwear while riding in a trailer pulled by a car driven by his wife.

Confusing the distinction between actual incidents and urban legends on this theme is the fact that in England the variation of "The Nude in the RV" in which a wife is abandoned is usually called "The Wife Left at the Roadside." An Australian telling of the same story has been titled "Auntie in Her Panties."

See also Structural Approach

References: *Baby Train*, 231–232; *Curses!*, 126; *Too Good*, 111–112.

"The Wife on the Flight"

A big business—usually an airline company—begins a program allowing its traveling executives to bring their spouses along on business trips at the company's expense. After a considerable period of high usage of the benefit, the company polls several hundred wives of executives who had taken advantage of the offer, asking how they enjoyed the trip. Ninety percent of the wives reply, "What trip?"

This story has circulated among businesspeople, particularly in the airline industry, both in Canada and the United States, since at least the late 1960s, and one report links it to an airline promotion aimed at the wives of returned servicemen at the end of World War II. In variations on the theme, letters are sent to married people asking how they enjoyed a hotel stay or why they were missing a university's evening classes, both of which had merely been the spouses' covers for extramarital affairs.

References: *Baby Train*, 166–168; *Too Good*, 262–263.

"The Wildcat in the Suitcase"

Somebody—a farmer, a rancher, a group of students—captures a wild bobcat. The cat-captor manages to put the animal into a suitcase and sets off to deliver it to a zoo; on the way the car stalls (or is stopped for some other reason), and the suitcase is then stolen by a group of rowdies passing by in a van. The van proceeds just a few blocks up the street, then suddenly it stops. The doors fly open, and the occupants and the wildcat exit in several directions. The incident, widely known in the American South and Southwest, is sometimes told as having been a deliberate prank using an expensive-looking suitcase that is left by the roadside or at a train or bus station. The targets of the prank are often said to be members of a minority group, usually blacks or Hispanics.

"The Wildcat in the Suitcase" is similar to other urban legends in which an unaware thief steals some undesirable thing such as a dead cat, a grandmother's corpse, or a urine sample. Closest in its details to this legend is "Dog's Corpse Is Stolen," another story about an animal inside a suitcase that is stolen. Some American versions of "The Wildcat in the Suitcase" claim that the perpetrators were members of a country-and-western star's tour group. In the United States yet another version circulates in which a porcupine is the suitcased critter. In South Africa the local "Leopard in the Suitcase" version has variations in which a snake or a monkey is put into a piece of luggage, which is then stolen.

"The Will"

In early October 1996 the following item was circulated by the Associated Press and published in many newspapers worldwide with headlines like "Simple prayer brings riches," "Prayers make him millionaire," and "Businessman learns it pays to pray":

> HAMBURG, Germany (AP)—A Spanish businessman and devout Roman Catholic who stopped to pray at a church during a trip to Stockholm ended up a millionaire, the Bild newspaper said Wednesday.
>
> The church was empty except for a coffin containing the remains of a man, so Eduardo Sierra knelt down and prayed for the deceased for 20 minutes, the Hamburg-based daily said.
>
> Sierra, 35, signed a condolence book after he saw a note saying those who prayed for the dead man should enter their name and address. He noticed he was the first to sign. He would be the only.
>
> Several weeks later he got a call from the Swedish capital informing him he was a millionaire, Bild said.
>
> Jens Svenson, the man he had prayed for, was a 73-year-old real estate dealer with no close relatives. He had specified in his will that "whoever prays for me would get all my belongings," Bild said.

Despite the names and other specific details, the news item was bogus; this version of the unexpected-inheritance theme is an urban legend that has been known internationally since at least the mid-1980s and perhaps was told as much as 15 years earlier. Traditional versions are often equally specific as to the time, place, and even the participants in the incident, although one never hears a firsthand account from the actual inheritor of the fortune. American versions of "The Will" often set the story in New York City and describe the lucky heir not as a businessman but as a woman in need of a restroom who walks into a Manhattan funeral parlor to use their facilities and signs the visitors' book on her way out.

Time magazine's international edition of October 21, 1996, (reprinted in *Too Good to Be True*), thoroughly debunked the story of the Spanish businessman, giving details of their failed attempts to secure any verifiable facts from the *Bild* reporter who wrote the original article.

References: *Curses!*, 267–268; *Too Good*, 86–88.

"The Wispy Wire"

See "The Technology Contest"

"The Witch Who Was Hurt"

See "The Robber Who Was Hurt"

"The Witness's Note"

Told among American lawyers either as a joke or a true incident, and also known in England and Australia, is the story of the victim testifying in a rape trial who broke down in tears when asked to relate what the attacker had said to her: "He said, 'I want to . . . I want to . . .' Oh, judge, I just can't repeat those words!" The sympathetic judge said the woman could write the words on a piece of paper that would then be passed among the jury members.

One male juror was dozing, and when the woman next to him had read what was on the paper she nudged him and passed it along. The man started awake, read the note, smiled, and hastily stuffed it into his pocket. When the judge asked the man to pass the note along, he replied, "Your honor, this note is a private matter between this lady and myself."

One should not expect to find either the note itself or to meet anyone who was a witness or participant in this alleged incident. Despite its apocryphal nature, however, "The Witness's Note" became part of a 1988 episode of the TV series *L.A. Law*. In the Australian version published in Bill Scott's book *The Long and the Short and the Tall* (1985), the note records the woman's supposed provocative remark to the defendant, who "thus claimed that he had received encouragement." Down Under, again, the incident reappeared as part of a TV show.

References: *Choking Doberman*, 141; *Too Good*, 152–153.

"The Wordy Government Memo"

Claims have been made since the 1940s and 1950s that a U.S. government memo setting the price of cabbage (or referring to some other rather trivial regulation) required tens of thousands of words (often 26,911), while classics of clear writing like "The Lord's Prayer," "The Gettysburg Address," and "The Declaration of Independence" required only a fraction as many words. Variations of these claims have been stated and reprinted numerous times, citing different examples as well as including widely different figures, both for the alleged wordy memo itself and for the wordcounts of the counterexamples of concise expression. These latter items are usually of a patriotic or a religious nature. Although "The Declaration of Independence" is often said in these claims to contain but 300 words, in reality it includes far more than that.

European versions of "The Wordy Government Memo" sometimes refer to a British directive on "shell eggs" or to a French memo setting the price of duck eggs. A more recent European version claims that a memo issued by the European Economic Community (EEC) concerned the importing of caramel and caramel products. Predictably, the wordcount of the supposed EEC document was identical to that of many earlier American "cabbage" memos—26,911 words.

References: *Choking Doberman*, 194–196; Max Hall, "The Great Cabbage Hoax: A Case Study," *Journal of Personality and Social Psychology* 2 (1965), 563–569; *Too Good*, 283–284.

"Wormburgers"

See McDonald's Rumors

Worth, Mary

See "I Believe in Mary Worth"

Written or Printed Traditions

Although the term "folklore" is usually thought of, by definition, as referring primarily to the *oral* tradition, there are a number of traditional forms that have always circulated in written or printed form. These include autograph-book inscriptions, chain letters, epitaphs, graffiti, and broadside ballads. Furthermore, the printed circulation of such forms as folksongs, folktales, jokes, tall tales, proverbs, riddles, and the like has, over the centuries, helped to keep such materials alive as they passed back and forth between print and word of mouth.

Urban rumors and legends have always had a strong life as written, typed, and printed texts coexisting with their vigorous oral circulation. Some forms, including bogus warnings and hilarious reports, actually require some visual text component along with the oral tradition. And how would one transmit items like expensive-recipe stories without furnishing a copy of the recipe, or tell the Craig Shergold legend without giving a copy of Craig's address, or convey the style of "Grandma's Washday" without distributing the misspelled text itself?

Newspapers, particularly feature and advice columns, have long been an important medium for the transmission and discussion of urban legends. In recent years fax and e-mail have become major channels for the nonoral transmission of rumors and urban legends; such "faxlore" and "netlore" often draw from and feed back into the oral tradition. It must also be admitted that published collections of urban legends have had a strong influence on the public's awareness of the field, although the term "urban legend" (or "urban myth") is frequently misused by non-folklorists in conversations and in print.

See also Bogus Warnings; Computers; "The Good Old Days"; "Grandma's Washday"; Hilarious Reports; "The Missing Day in Time"; Popular Culture and Urban Legends; Xeroxlore

"The Wrong Car"

The above title gives away the plot of this recent legend, which might better be called "Sticking Up for One's Rights." The story that circulated on the Internet starting in 1998 was that an elderly woman was advised by her son to carry a small handgun in her purse for protection. She complied and soon had occasion to pull the weapon on someone, since she returned to her car in the mall's parking lot to find two men sitting in it, drinking beer, and eating. Brandishing the gun, the woman ordered the men from the car, and they quickly ran away. But her key did not fit the ignition, and the woman soon noticed her own look-alike car parked nearby.

Some versions of the story end with the woman going to the mall's security office to report that she tried to start the wrong car. Before she can fully explain, however, the security officer tells her that he doesn't have time for her report since there's a crazy woman running around the lot with a gun, ordering people out of their cars. Several versions of the story also included a racist element, with the woman being white and the men ordered from their car being black or Hispanic.

References: *Too Good*, 93–94.

"The Wrong Rattler"

A bit of traditional Southwestern rattlesnake folklore sometimes surfaces as a retold tale among urban folklore. In a folklorist's field report from north-central Texas the basic story is summarized thus:

A man kills a rattlesnake and throws it into the yard on his way into the house. A person in the house wants to see the rattles; so later, after dark, the man returns to the yard, finds the snake, and cuts a long string of rattles off. The next morning he finds the dead snake in the yard with rattles intact. The implication is that he has cut the rattles off a live rattlesnake, and only by luck has he escaped being bitten.

As told in an Austin, Texas, bar in 1990, a friend of a friend had killed a rattler near his woodpile using a hoe. After dark he went back out to collect the rattles for his grandson, and the next morning, finding the dead snake intact, he fainted when he realized his mistake. A listener to this performance commented, "Now just a minute; I heard that one in Louisiana!"

In some versions of the story the snake-killer's son or grandson goes out to collect the rattles in the dark. Many versions mention that the two snakes are mates, reflecting the folk notion that rattlesnakes always travel in pairs.

References: *Too Good,* 338–339.

"The Wrong Rest Stop"

An automobile legend known in Australia (and perhaps elsewhere) concerns the "escape lanes" (safety ramps) provided for heavy trucks on hilly major highways. The Australian versions are set in specific locations, such as the "Devil's Elbow" hairpin bends in the hills above Adelaide. On one such dangerous grade, a truck driver realizes that he has lost his brakes and struggles to keep the big rig upright as he roars around the tight turns of the steep road, praying he will be able to make it to the escape lane. Just as he rounds the last bend before the ramp—still holding the truck on the road—he sees to his horror a family halfway up the ramp having a picnic.

References: *Baby Train,* 232.

"The Wrong Teeth"

Documented in several European countries and in Australia is a legend about a person—man or woman—losing his or her false teeth while at

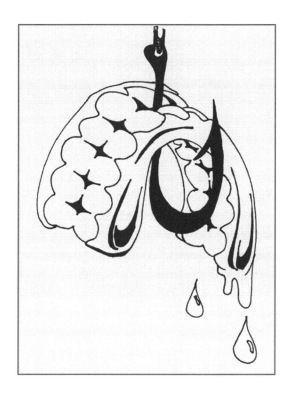

sea on a fishing, sightseeing, snorkeling, or surfing trip. Sometimes the victim has been seasick, and the teeth go overboard when he or she vomits. Seeking to comfort (or to tease) the victim, the spouse or another person removes his own false teeth and pretends to have caught them on a fishing line or to have found them on the beach. The victim inserts the false teeth, and, finding that they do not fit, throws them back into the sea in disgust, saying, "These aren't mine! Someone else must have lost them!"

See also Holland

References: *Mexican Pet,* 87–88; *Too Good,* 145; Eric Venbrux and Theo Meder, "'The False Teeth in the Cod': A Legend in Context," *Contemporary Legend* 5 (1995): 115–131.

Xenophobia in Urban Legends

Xenophobia—the fear and dislike of foreigners and other strangers—is displayed in a number of urban rumors and legends (as, indeed, it is also strongly expressed in many modern traditional jokes as well). Some would argue that such folk expressions serve as a safety valve for emotions, displacing acts of actual aggression against outsiders; others maintain that xenophobic expressions are deplorable and should be criticized and discouraged. However, it is very hard, if not impossible, to channel, control, or eliminate folklore of any kind.

Many items of modern xenophobic lore are based on stereotypes of foreign racial and ethnic groups, usually immigrants to a more developed country. In whatever country the rumors and stories occur, they tend to depict these outsiders as unclean, poorly educated, and unable to cope with modern technology. We hear similar charges made against, for example, Pakistanis in London, Southeast Asians in Canada and the United States, Turks in Germany and Sweden, Japanese in Turkey, Koreans in Saudi Arabia, Aborigines living in Australian cities, and gypsies in every place that they have roamed. In typical stories, these outsiders are said to have ruined the comfortable homes provided to them by a benevolent government, eaten their neighbors' pets, misused modern appliances, failed to learn the customs and language of their new land, and so forth.

489

Xeroxlore

Although Xerox is the company name of just one manufacturer of modern photocopiers, the name (derived from "xerographic reproduction") has become generic for all office copiers; therefore, American folklorists quickly adopted "Xeroxlore" as the term for all kinds of photocopied traditional material (formerly dubbed "typescript broadsides"). In Australia some collectors of Xeroxlore have called it "reprographic folklore." The phenomenon of producing, copying, displaying, and circulating traditional photocopied material is international and often overlaps into fax and e-mail formats as well. In general, most Xeroxlore serves to criticize and undermine the official office culture of what Alan Dundes calls "the paperwork empire." Examples of Xeroxlore are often posted or passed around in modern offices, and many workers keep a collection of unofficial photocopied material in a bottom drawer for sharing with fellow workers, usually out of sight of management. Besides office work and business culture in general, the typical subjects of Xeroxlore are sex, race, and antigovernment sentiments.

The range of genres found as Xeroxlore is huge and includes parodies of official notices, memos, letters, business cards, menus, curriculum lists, glossaries, tax forms, and application forms as well as jokes, cartoons, greeting cards, charts, graphs, games, dot-to-dots, and puzzles. In common with oral folklore, this material is usually anonymous and always exists in multiple variations. To those who suggest that Xeroxlore is too "modern" and trivial to constitute an appropriate research area, Paul Smith has responded, "Where would folksong and ballad scholarship be if researchers had ignored the existence of broadsides, chapbooks, and other forms of ephemeral literature?"

Only a small proportion of Xeroxlore directly pertains to urban rumors and legends. Some urban traditions described in this encyclopedia—such as "The Good Old Days," "Grandma's Washday," hilarious reports, and "The Welfare Letter"—require a typed, printed, or photocopied text in order to work. Other items that relate to this area are most bogus warnings and a handful of traditional narratives. Bogus warnings that are typically distributed in photocopies include "Blue Star Acid," "The Procter & Gamble Trademark," "The Welded Contacts," and "Lights Out!" Some urban legends that are usually circulated as Xeroxlore are "The Barrel of Bricks," expensive-recipe stories, "The Fart in the Dark," "The Halloween Party" (see "Sex in Disguise"), "The Missing Day in Time," "The Surpriser Surprised," and "The Wordy Government Memo."

See also Computers; Hilarious Reports; Written or Printed Traditions

References: Alan Dundes, "Office Folklore," in Richard M. Dorson, *Handbook of American Folklore* (Bloomington: Indiana University Press, 1983), 115–120; Michael J. Preston, "Xeroxlore" in Brunvand, *American Folklore: An Encyclopedia* (1996), 769–770; Graham Seal, *The Bare Fax* (Sydney: Angus and Robertson, 1996); Paul Smith, "Contemporary Legend and the Photocopy Revolution: An Exploration," in Bennett, Smith, and Widdowson, *Perspectives on Contemporary Legend II* (1987), 177–202.

"The Youngest Fan"

In his 1989 book *Dumbth*, a critique of modern American's education and intelligence, comedian and musician Steve Allen relates this story:

> Bill Herz, the magician, overheard two young teenagers talking on the street in New York City. One said to the other, "Did you know that Paul McCartney was in a band before Wings?"

In other versions of the anecdote the teens were supposedly overheard talking in a record store as they browsed through the rock albums filed under the letter *B*. Failing to know about the phenomenally successful group the Beatles, and associating McCartney only with the group he formed after the original quartet broke up, is just one example often cited for the supposed unawareness of today's young people. Other versions of the generation-gap legend describe someone failing to remember the name of the first man to set foot on the moon (actually Neil Armstrong), supposedly naming instead John Glenn, Jack Armstrong, or Neil Young.

References: *Baby Train*, 217–219.

Zipper Stories

In his definitive history of the zipper and its social and cultural significance, Robert Friedel writes, "The best evidence of the zipper's place

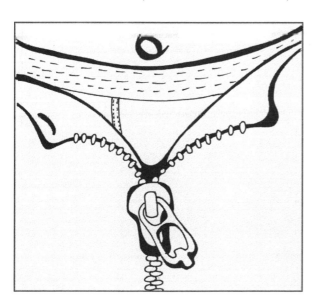

in the mechanical demonology of the twentieth century comes not from literature but from folklore" (p. 218). As examples, Friedel describes the two well-known urban legends treated in this encyclopedia under the headings "The Unzipped Fly" and "The Unzipped Plumber or Mechanic." Other zipper anecdotes, personal-experience stories, jokes, and legends tend to follow the same theme of an embarrassingly open fly and the comic results of a stuck zipper.

References: Robert Friedel, *Zipper: An Exploration in Novelty* (New York: Norton, 1994), *Too Good,* 138–139.

"The Zoo Section"

Known to at least one American college registrar, and possibly to others elsewhere, is the story of the prankster in the registrar's office who filled one section of freshman English with students whose surnames were all animal names. When the instructor read the list aloud the first day of class, the lineup sounded like roll call at the zoo: "Mr. Deere? Ms. Byrd? Mr. Bear? Ms. Fish?" and so forth.

References: *Baby Train,* 293.

SELECTED BIBLIOGRAPHY

Baker, Ronald L., ed. 1982. *Hoosier Folk Legends.* Bloomington: Indiana University Press.

Baughman, Ernest W. 1966. *Type and Motif Index of the Folktales of England and North America.* Indiana University Folklore Series, No. 20. The Hague: Mouton.

Bennett, Gillian, and Paul Smith, eds. 1988. *Monsters with Iron Teeth: Perspectives on Contemporary Legend III.* Sheffield, England: Sheffield Academic Press.

———. 1989. *The Questing Beast: Perspectives on Contemporary Legend IV.* Sheffield, England: Sheffield Academic Press.

———. 1990. *A Nest of Vipers: Perspectives on Contemporary Legend V.* Sheffield, England: Sheffield Academic Press.

———. 1993. *Contemporary Legend: A Folklore Bibliography.* New York: Garland.

———. 1996. *Contemporary Legend: A Reader.* New York: Garland.

Bennett, Gillian, Paul Smith, and J. D. A. Widdowson, eds. 1987. *Perspectives on Contemporary Legend II.* Sheffield, England: Sheffield Academic Press.

The Big Book of Urban Legends. 1994. Adapted from the Works of Jan Harold Brunvand by Robert Loren Fleming and Robert F. Boyd Jr. New York: Paradox Press, an imprint of DC Comics.

Blackmore, Susan. 1999. *The Meme Machine.* Oxford: Oxford University Press.

Bronner, Simon J. 1990. *Piled Higher and Deeper: The Folklore of Campus Life.* Little Rock: August House.

Brunvand, Jan Harold. 1981. *The Vanishing Hitchhiker: American Urban Legends and Their Meanings.* New York: Norton.

———. 1984. *The Choking Doberman and Other "New" Urban Legends.* New York: Norton.

———. 1986. *The Mexican Pet: More "New" Urban Legends and Some Old Favorites.* New York: Norton.

———. 1989. *Curses! Broiled Again! The Hottest Urban Legends Going.* New York: Norton.

———. 1993. *The Baby Train and Other Lusty Urban Legends.* New York: Norton.

———., ed. 1996. *American Folklore: An Encyclopedia.* New York, Garland.

———. 1998. *The Study of American Folklore: An Introduction.* 4th ed. New York: Norton.

———. 1999a. *Too Good to Be True: The Colossal Book of Urban Legends.* New York: Norton.

———. 1999b. "Urban Legends." In Margaret Read MacDonald, ed. *Traditional Storytelling Today: An International Sourcebook.* Chicago: Fitzroy Dearborn. Pp. 572–576.

———. 2000. *The Truth Never Stands in the Way of a Good Story.* Champaign: University of Illinois Press.

Buchan, David. 1981. "The Modern Legend." In A. E. Green and J. D. A. Widdowson, eds. *Language, Culture, and Tradition.* University of Leeds and University of Sheffield. Pp. 1–15 [paper presented at a 1978 conference].

Craughwell, Thomas J. 1999. *Alligators in the Sewer and 222 Other Urban Legends.* New York: Black Dog and Leventhal.

———. 2000. *The Baby on the Car Roof and 222 More Urban Legends.* New York: Black Dog and Leventhal.

Dale, Rodney. 1978. *The Tumour in the Whale: A Collection of Modern Myths.* London: Duckworth.

———. 1984. *It's True. . . It Happened to a Friend: A Collection of Urban Legends.* London: Duckworth.

Dawkins, Richard. 1976. *The Selfish Gene.* Oxford: Oxford University Press.

Dickson, Paul, and Joseph C. Goulden. 1983. *There Are Alligators in Our Sewers and Other American Credos.* New York: Delacorte Press.

Dorson, Richard M. 1959. *American Folklore.* University of Chicago Press.

Fine, Gary Alan. 1992. *Manufacturing Tales: Sex and Money in Contemporary Legends.* Knoxville: University of Tennessee Press.

Genge N. E. 2000. *Urban Legends: The As-Complete-as-One-Could-Be Guide to Modern Myths.* New York: Three Rivers Press.

Gilovich, Thomas. 1991. *How We Know What Isn't So: The Fallibility of Human Reason in Everyday Life.* New York: Free Press.

Green, Thomas A., ed. 1997. *Folklore: An Encyclopedia of Beliefs, Customs, Tales, Music, and Art.* 2 vols. Santa Barbara, Calif.: ABC-CLIO.

Hand, Wayland D., ed. 1971. *American Folk Legend: A Symposium.* Los Angeles: University of California Press.

Holt, David, and Bill Mooney. 1999. *Spiders in the Hairdo: Modern Urban Legends.* Little Rock, Ark.: August House [with accompanying audiocassette].

Koenig, Fredrick. 1985. *Rumor in the Marketplace: The Social Psychology of Commercial Hearsay.* Dover, Mass.: Auburn House.

Langlois, Janet. 1987. "Urban Legends and the Faces of Detroit." In Kurt C. Dewhurst and Yvonne R. Lockwood, eds. *Michigan Folklife Reader.* East Lansing: Michigan State University Press. Pp. 107–120.

Lynch, Aaron. 1996. *Thought Contagion: How Belief Spreads Through Society.* New York: Basic Books.

Morgan, Hal, and Kerry Tucker. 1984. *Rumor!* New York: Penguin.

———. 1987. *More Rumor!* New York: Penguin.

Pratkanis, Anthony R., and Elliot Aronson. 1992. *Age of Propaganda: The Everyday Use and Abuse of Persuasion.* New York: W. H. Freeman [see esp. "The Psychology of Factoids"].

Roeper, Richard. 1999. *Urban Legends: The Truth Behind All Those Deliciously Entertaining Myths That Are Absolutely, Positively, 100% Not True!* Franklin Lakes, N.J.: Career Press.

Sanderson, Stewart F. 1982. "The Modern Urban Legend." The Katharine Briggs Lecture, No. 1, delivered November 3, 1981. London: The Folklore Society. 15 pp.

Smith, Paul, ed. 1983. *The Book of Nasty Legends.* London: Routledge and Kegan Paul.

———. 1984. *Perspectives on Contemporary Legend.* University of Sheffield, England: Centre for English Cultural Tradition and Language.

———. 1986. *The Book of Nastier Legends.* London: Routledge and Kegan Paul.

Thompson, Stith. 1955–1958. *The Motif-Index of Folk-Literature.* Rev. ed. 6 vols. Bloomington: Indiana University Press.

Toelken, Barre. 1996. *The Dynamics of Folklore.* Rev. and expanded ed. Logan: Utah State University Press.

Turner, Patricia A. 1993. *I Heard It Through the Grapevine: Rumor in African-American Culture.* Berkeley: University of California Press.

INDEX

Note: boldface numbers indicate main encyclopedia entries.

ABOUT THE AUTHOR

Jan Harold Brunvand, professor emeritus of English at the University of Utah, is the world's foremost authority on urban legends. He is the author of (among other works) *Too Good to Be True* (1999), *The Study of American Folklore* (4th Edition, 1998), and *The Vanishing Hitchhiker* (1981).